DEPRESSION

Comparative Studies of Normal, Neurotic, and Psychotic Conditions

DEPRESSION

Comparative Studies of Normal, Neurotic, and Psychotic Conditions

EDITH JACOBSON, M.D.

INTERNATIONAL UNIVERSITIES PRESS, INC.
New York

Library of Congress Catalogue Card Number: 74-162056

ISBN: 0-8236-1195-7

Manufactured in the United States of America

Contents

Preface

The theoretical and clinical problems discussed in this book played an essential role in my work with borderline cases and with ambulatory patients belonging to the manic-depressive or schizophrenic group of psychoses. My interest in this type of patient had been aroused in the late 1920s, primarily because their pathology raised questions pertaining to superego development. Some of my earliest psychoanalytic contributions dealt with these issues (1930, 1937). At that time the psychology of the ego and its defenses was in the center of attention. During this period, moreover, I was treating a female patient who suffered from recurring severe states of depression. Since she was accessible to psychoanalysis, she lent herself to a study of ego and superego pathology in such states. The surprisingly good therapeutic result in her case encouraged me to treat and observe similar patients.

But the psychological exploration of the affective disorders inevitably must extend into broader areas. Examining the mood disorders, we find depressive and elated or excited hypomanic or manic states not only in all psychoses but also in all types of psychoneuroses (Lewin, 1950). Even healthy persons show, within certain limits, remarkable vacillations between high and low mood levels. These observations induced me to extend the study of cyclothymic depressions to related affective states and mood vacillations in schizophrenia. I tried to explore and compare the emotional and ideational pathology and the underlying conflicts in different types of psychoses, and to delineate the differences between psychotic mood conditions and those found in neurotics and normal persons.

The comparative study of normal and pathological psychic manifestations is a legitimate research procedure. The pioneering work of Freud and Abraham certainly encouraged such comparisons. Even some clinical psychiatrists who were not interested in the purely psychological exploration of mental diseases have expressed their belief that cyclothymia might be a pathological exaggeration of normal—biologically caused—vacillations of mood activity. Such comparative studies, especially those including psychotic disorders, presuppose and rest upon the clarification of many fundamental clinical and theoretical psychoanalytic questions, particularly in the area of ego and superego pathology. Freud laid the ground for a psychoanalytic investigation of psychoses in "Mourning and Melancholia" (1917) and, above all, in his analysis of the Schreber case (1911). But further progress in this area was not possible until Freud had developed his new structural concepts and focused on the role of aggression in human development.

It is noteworthy that during this phase in the history of psychoanalysis Freud wrote his papers on "Neurosis and Psychosis" (1924a) and on "The Loss of Reality in Neurosis and Psychosis" (1924c) and again returned to the problem of the affects. The result was a new theory of anxiety centered on the assumption that all affects originate in the ego (1926). These illuminating papers by Freud, the brilliant papers on problems of ego psychology by Hartmann, Kris, and Loewenstein, Mahler's work on infantile psychoses, and some outstanding contributions by Helene Deutsch have established a basis from which further clinical and theoretical explorations can proceed.

When we observe psychotic cases from the viewpoint of current ego psychology and try to arrive at theoretical conclusions, however, we frequently find that our terms and concepts are not yet clearly defined and often even confusing. For this reason, I felt compelled to advance along several lines of investigation.

In my paper and book on the self and the object world (1954, 1964), I discussed the establishment of self and object representations in the child and their role in the building up of object relations, identifications, and identity formation. These issues are of the greatest significance for the understanding of psychoses. So are the problems concerning affects and moods. As Rapaport (1953) correctly emphasized in his paper, "On a Psychoanalytic Theory of Affects," we have not yet developed a satisfactory general theory of affects.

For this reason I start this book with a chapter devoted to a discussion of the basic problems and unsolved issues in the psychoanalytic theory of affects.

All other chapters are essentially clinically oriented. Most of them present extensive case studies, some of severely ill patients who, it should be emphasized, were all treated by regular analysis. The chapters in Part I present material gained primarily from the treatment of neurotic patients, while Part II presents material gained from the psychoanalytic treatment of borderline and psychotic patients who suffered from depressions. I have approached my basic topic—depression—in various ways. Some studies deal with developmental problems, others with specific characteristic defenses or the nature of identifications and object relations. In comparing normal, neurotic, and psychotic phenomena, I also discuss problems of differential diagnosis and treatment. In an Appendix I present my impressions gained from follow-up studies of patients whom I treated as children and from a number of adult patients whom I was able to follow up for many years, in some instances as many as thirty-five years.

Some of the chapters in this book are based on previously published papers, others are here published for the first time. All of them have been thoroughly revised, rewritten, shortened or expanded. They complement and are closely related to my book on *The Self and the Object World* (1964) and my Freud Anniversary Lecture, *Psychotic Conflict and Reality* (1967).

This preface is intended to facilitate the reading of this volume, by indicating the common frame of reference for the individual chapters which appear to deal with such varied issues. I should be happy if this book, and the two monographs to which I have referred, might add to the clinical understanding of psychotic patients and especially of those narcissistic and borderline cases which nowadays abound in psychoanalytic practice. In addition, I hope that they may contribute to the further development of our psychoanalytic ego psychology and of a future psychoanalytic theory of psychosis.

Acknowledgments

I should like to thank Miss Paula Gross for her devoted secretarial work and support in preparing this book. I also want to express my profound gratitude to Mrs. Lottie M. Newman for editing this volume and for her helpful suggestions concerning its organization. Nor can I let this opportunity pass without remembering the late Ernst Kris, who greatly encouraged and stimulated my work by discussing with me the earlier papers on which this book is based.

PART I

1

On the Psychoanalytic Theory of Affects

Freud's first theory of neurosis, which was, as it were, an affect theory, has never lost practical significance. Such authors as Ferenczi and W. Reich, who strove for improvements of our technique, emphasized time and again that interpretations were ineffective as long as they failed to evoke intensive emotional responses in the patient. Even though we now know that the production of affective storms is often a therapeutically undesirable side effect, the handling of the emotional attitudes and reactions of our patients is still one of the central problems in our clinical work.

The pathology of affective phenomena is especially prevalent in psychotic states, but when we set out to study such pathological affective states as neurotic and psychotic depressive conditions from the clinical and metapsychological points of view, we become aware of the need for a consistent affect theory. This, psychoanalysis has so far failed to develop. In fact, the development of the psychoanalytic drive theory appears to have halted our efforts to form equally clear theoretical concepts of the affects and their relations to the psychic drives.

It was Freud himself who emphasized our meager knowledge of the affects (1920, 1926) and who turned the spotlight back onto this

---

This chapter is based on "The Affects and Their Pleasure-Unpleasure Qualities in Relation to the Psychic Discharge Processes," first published in *Drives, Affects, Behavior,* Volume 1, edited by R. M. Loewenstein. New York: International Universities Press, 1953, pp. 38-66. It has been extensively modified and expanded.

puzzling problem. In *Inhibitions, Symptoms and Anxiety*, he laid the foundation for clearer and more modern concepts. When we search for further analytic papers on this subject, however, we are amazed to find how few analysts have dared to tackle this challenging but intricate problem and to carry further Freud's work in this area. Thus it appears worthwhile to discuss a series of unresolved problems, controversial issues, and contradictory opinions.

DEFINITIONS OF AFFECT, EMOTION, FEELING

Surveying the major contributions to the literature on affects, one is immediately struck by our terminological confusion. The lack of precise definitions of emotion was deplored by both Rapaport (1942) and Reid (1950) as harmful, but this condition still obtains today. At the same time we must realize that precise definitions, though a prerequisite for clear theoretical thinking, frequently develop only as the result of theoretical and clinical research.

I shall begin with Freud's definition of affects, emotions, and feelings. During the first stage of analytic theory, Freud equated the affects with the energetic forces. Later (1915a) Freud defined affect as a subjective, conscious experience. Discussing the ideational representations of the instinctual drives, he said:

> For this other element of the psychical representative [apart from the ideas] the term *quota of affect* has been generally adopted. It corresponds to the instinct in so far as the latter has become detached from the idea and finds expression, proportionate to its quantity, in processes which are sensed as affects [p. 152].

In these remarks Freud regarded the affect not as identical with the instinctual drive, but as a consciously perceived expression of the underlying instinctual process. Affect is one part of the drive representation which must be distinguished from the other part, the ideational drive representation.

In "The Unconscious" (1915b) Freud distinguished between affects and feelings. The term "affects" referred to the whole set of psychophysiological discharge phenomena, which are physiological insofar as they express themselves in body changes and psychological insofar as they are perceived as feelings.

When we compare Freud's definitions with those of Rapaport or

Reid or Cobb (1950),[1] the very titles of these authors' books point to one rather conspicuous terminological difference: American psychology favors the term "emotions" for both the physiological and psychological manifestations. But Rapaport (1942) states that this term "is used so broadly that it is difficult to ascertain its precise meaning."

> . . . the word "emotion" is sometimes used to designate a *phenomenon,* and sometimes to designate the *dynamics* underlying a phenomenon or group of phenomena. For instance, in the description of any single "emotion" such as fear or rage, the expression "emotion" refers to a phenomenon; but in a psychosomatic disease the expression "emotion" refers to the dynamics and etiology of the disorder. Furthermore, when used to denote phenomena the expression "emotion" denotes sometimes physiological and motor phenomena, such as facial expressions, and sometimes phenomena of conscious experiencing, such as "feelings." Similarly, when used to denote the dynamics underlying phenomena the expression "emotion" sometimes denotes physiological dynamics [p. 11].

Nevertheless, Rapaport does not favor the establishment of a new, purified, and unequivocal terminology. He prefers to deal with emotions in psychosomatic terms: as a process with physiological and psychological manifestations. The emotional process may find direct and momentary expression on either the physiological or psychological level, but, if prevented from immediate discharge, may "issue in a chronic alteration of the physiological processes, as seen in psychosomatic disorders, or of the psychological processes, as seen in neuroses, psychoses, and character disorders" (p. 11f.).

Reid delved even more deeply, in some respects, into the difficulties of finding correct definitions. On the one hand he supported the restriction of the term "emotion" to "the private, consciously felt affect," in accordance with a definition by Hinsie and Shatzky (1940). On the other hand he felt that the term must be amplified

[1] The books of both Rapaport and Cobb give evidence of our growing endeavor to correlate the current physiological and psychological theories of emotions, and to explain the somatic and the psychic emotional manifestations as different expressions of the same underlying dynamic processes. While Rapaport's concepts are based on Freud's drive theory and on an understanding of the unconscious, we miss these in Cobb's theoretical and even in his clinical presentations. Thus the physiological part of Cobb's book is more interesting and informative to the analyst, who has so little time for physiological studies.

to include the "relevant" causal context, by which he means the external and internal, genetically determined factors that stimulate the emotion. He concluded: "an emotion is at once physiological, psychological, and social—since other persons are usually the most highly emotogenic stimuli in our civilized environment" (p. 30f.).

Reid evidently conceives of emotions as being at least a manifestation of energetic forces. His final formulations, however, clearly indicate his reluctance to integrate the psychoanalytic drive theory with his concept, let alone to make it the basis of his definitions.

Looking back from Reid's lengthy formulations to Freud's simple but pointed definitions and to Rapaport's clear statements, we can conclude that there is no reason why psychoanalysis should not adopt or more readily use the term "emotion." Moreover, the recent advances of physiological and psychological research make it appropriate to broaden Freud's original definitions. The terms "emotions" and "affects" might be used synonymously to designate the whole complex set of psychological and physiological manifestations. Such a definition would include the affective motor phenomena and behavior patterns as well as the phenomena for which the term "affect equivalents" has been customarily employed, and—supplementing Freud's short reference to the circulatory and secretory manifestations—all the neurophysiological and endocrinological aspects that several decades of research have gradually discovered. The term "feelings" might be limited to the subjectively felt experiences.

Reid's limitation of the term "emotion" to the "more violent stirred-up state of the organism" would be acceptable only if we could find another term to cover the "mild" affective phenomena, on both the psychological and the somatic levels. As long as we lack such a term, we cannot very well ignore the existence of all the mild, enduring, and composite feelings and feeling states which are in the field of our daily psychoanalytic observation. The definitions of Hinsie and Shatzky and Reid are convenient for the experimental psychologist and the neurophysiologist, who study only single "violent" affects rather than the whole range of human feelings. But these definitions fail to take into account that life proceeds in continuous dynamic processes which find expression in a constant shifting between calm or excited psychological and physiological emotional states. Such definitions might easily tempt us to regard emotions as altogether pathological or exceptional phenomena, and to forget that even in the most "detached" ego states and ego functions we are never without emotions and feelings.[2] The broader implications of these statements are discussed throughout this volume.

I share Brierley's opinion that "we should avoid a good deal of confusion if we used different words for different grades of affectivity" (1937). We might apply the term "affects" to the more violent states, such as rage or fear, and the term "feelings" to the milder and more enduring inner experiences, such as sympathy and pity, happiness, love, and resentment. But a distinction on the grounds of intensity is not a fundamental one and cannot possibly be sharp. Brierley's own terminology, for instance, is based not on quantitative but on qualitative and genetic considerations. I may point out here that for practical reasons I shall not always adhere strictly to the proposed terminological distinction between emotions, affects, and feelings.

THE RELATIONSHIP OF AFFECTS TO THE PSYCHIC SYSTEMS AND THE INSTINCTUAL DRIVES

When Freud wrote his papers on metapsychology, he still used a topographic model of the psychic apparatus. He dealt with two essential and closely connected issues: where in the psychic systems (*Cs.–Ucs.*) did affects and feelings originate, and what was their relationship to the instinctual drives? With regard to the first issue, Freud said:

> . . . the system *Cs.* normally controls affectivity as well as access to motility; . . . Conversely, too, we may say that as long as the system *Cs.* controls affectivity and motility, the mental condition of the person in question is spoken of as normal. . . . Whereas the control by the *Cs.* over voluntary motility is firmly rooted, regularly withstands the onslaught of neurosis and only breaks down in psychosis, control by the *Cs.* over the development of affects is less secure [115b, p. 179].

These remarks concerning the limited control of the system Conscious over the affects might easily be understood to mean that Freud

[2] Although Kurt Goldstein (1951) uses a different approach, he expresses similar opinions.

regarded the unconscious as the site where affective development originates. But in the same paper Freud explicitly stated that all affects develop in the system Conscious—or, as we should now prefer to say, in the ego—with the exception of anxiety. He made this one exception on the grounds of his original theory that repression transforms libido into anxiety. It may be noted that in this theory, contrary to Freud's own definitions, the relations between instinctual energy proper and the affects are not strictly defined. However, as both Brierley and Rapaport have emphasized correctly, it is important to distinguish between the affect, an expression of psychic drives, and the drive itself, and to study their relations.

Concerning the relationship between emotions, memories, and instinctual drives, Rapaport concluded that "memory organization and emotional experience would be two among many possible expressions of these basic factors, which may be called psychic energies, strivings, or drives" (1942, p. 271). But in the Preface to the second edition of his book, Rapaport himself pointed out that his clarifying statements did not yet take into consideration Freud's later anxiety theory and the development of psychoanalytic ego psychology during the last decades.

In *Inhibitions, Symptoms and Anxiety* (1926), Freud again took up the problem of affects and, in particular, of the anxiety affect. The main points of Freud's new theory can be summarized as follows: (1) Anxiety is not the result, but the motor of repression. (2) It arises in the ego, according to a pattern that is probably phylogenetically preformed, but is, in the individual, physiologically established by the trauma of birth and psychologically reproduced by the ego as a signal in situations of danger.

> Anxiety [Freud (1926) remarked] is an affective state and as such can, of course, only be felt by the ego. The id cannot have anxiety. . . . On the other hand it very often happens that processes take place or begin to take place in the id which cause the ego to produce anxiety [p. 140].

Freud's new theory of anxiety disregarded the economic point of view. Since the ego was now seen as a system endowed with energy of its own, the question of the resources from which the ego draws energy for the development of activity had lost significance.

Freud made only a few remarks on the origin and nature of

affects other than anxiety. Equating the affects with inherited hysterical attacks, he regarded all affects as, so to speak, inherited, once purposeful and adaptive reactions to traumata imposed by reality. Anxiety thus represents a special case insofar as it is, as Nunberg (1932) pointed out, a "fixated affect."

Freud's remarks on the historical origin of affects are of course in keeping with his revised drive theories; i.e., his conception of a repetition compulsion, his hypothetical assumption of life and death instincts which strive to re-establish former states that had been disturbed by the traumatic influence of reality. In all these propositions, we note, Freud returned to his old idea of the historical significance of "trauma."

Freud's new theory of anxiety has in many ways had a profound effect upon our theoretical and clinical thinking. It opened new vistas to our understanding of normal and neurotic development. His discussion of the physiological factor in the development of the anxiety pattern has stimulated research along psychophysiological lines, particularly in the psychosomatic field. His emphasis on the causal role of reality events in the formation of mental life as such has once again focused attention on the role played by reality in emotional reaction patterns.

CLASSIFICATION OF AFFECTS

By focusing on the origin and the unique function of anxiety as the specific unpleasurable affect that induces repression, our present anxiety theory is much more consistent with the pleasure-unpleasure principle than Freud's purely economic hypothesis. The earlier assumptions, according to which pleasure was transformed into unpleasure by the reality principle, and repression served to avoid unpleasure, had ignored the important signal function of certain unpleasurable affects and their directive influence on the psychic processes.

As Freud remarked, the confusing problem of transformation was resolved by his new theory of anxiety. Obviously, he no longer conceived of anxiety, or of reactively formed affects such as shame and disgust, as derivatives or transformations of the original instinctual drives. Rather, he regarded them as manifestations of direct ego responses to such drives. This suggests, first of all, that it is certainly better to define affects in general very broadly as representative of underlying energetic, and not merely instinctual, processes. But if there are affects that correspond to instinctual discharge processes and other affects that represent ego responses, the new conception compels us to distinguish between different types of affects, to define their nature, and to search for suitable classifications.

The need for classification arises not only from our current insight into the nature of anxiety and related affects, but also from the fact that during the last decades ego psychology has opened the way to an understanding of such affects and affective states as grief, guilt feelings, depression, boredom, apathy, laughter, elation.

A good psychoanalytic classification of affects must be based on the following essential considerations: (1) it should aim at relating the affective phenomena to the corresponding psychoeconomic processes and cathectic conditions; and (2) it should take cognizance of our present theoretical position. Classifications should integrate the new anxiety theory and the division of psychic forces into libidinal, aggressive, and neutral (desexualized, de-aggressivized) energy. They should consider genetic aspects, the modern structural distinctions, and the current state of ego psychology.

A set of classifications might establish a firm basis for systematic studies of affective development and affective vicissitudes. As will be seen, however, the search for useful classifications of affects highlights many confusing and unresolved problems concerning the nature and qualities of affects. In view of our insufficient understanding of the affects and the meaning of their qualities, it is not surprising that most attempts at psychoanalytic classifications of affects have proved to be of limited value.

A comparison between Landauer's (1938) and Glover's (1948) conceptions, distinctions, and classifications of affects discloses puzzling contradictions. These arise from attempts either to regard all affects—in adherence to Freud's early definitions—as instinctual representations, or to separate the affects from the instinctual drives and align them exclusively with the ego. This latter trend characterizes Landauer's (1938) interesting, but confusing and speculative ideas which oppose rather than relate the affects to the instinctual drives.

A glance at Glover's (1948), on the other hand, reveals the complications and contradictions which arise when we adhere to obsolete definitions and conceptions. Glover distinguishes between simple and compound, primary and secondary, tension and discharge affects. His differentiation between simple affects, or affect components, and compound affects, or affect fusions, constructively relates the affects to the underlying drives and establishes a firm basis for the study of specific affects.

Brierley (1937) sketched out the lines that such studies should follow. They must center around the gradual fusion of early affect components and their development into complex, adult emotional attitudes and experiences, and must consider the correlations between instinctual and affective development. Brierley's idea of classifying affects and employing different terms according to the different stages of development is most constructive. Her special terminology, however, is impractical in view of the generally established use of the term "emotions" in the sense defined above.

Glover's second suggestion—to distinguish between primary and secondary affects—immediately leads him into difficulties, which in part he recognizes. Anxiety, he admits, though reactive, is undoubtedly a primary affect. But because he insists on defining the simple affect as "a specific emotional response to any given vicissitude of a particular instinct" (p. 45), he is forced to resort to the "instinct of self-preservation." Thus both his distinctions and definitions of primary and secondary reactive affects appear unacceptable.

We might consider replacing this classification with one that employs our current structural concepts. Certain affects have always been characterized in this way; guilt feelings, for instance, are commonly defined as arising from a tension between ego and superego. Even though all affects are ego experiences and develop in the ego, one of their qualitative determinants must be the site of the underlying energetic tension by which they have been induced and which may arise at any point within the psychic organization.

Such a classification of the affects not only introduces structural thinking into the theory of affects; it would also reinstate psychoeconomic considerations which Freud's last discussion of the anxiety affect might tempt us to disregard. In fact, it might help us to combine both formulations with the current conception of anxiety and similar affects. I would suggest the following classification:

(1) simple and compound affects arising from intrasystemic tensions:
  (a) affects (such as sexual excitement, or rage) which arise directly from instinctual (sexual or aggressive) tensions, i.e., from tensions in the id;
  (b) affects that develop directly from tensions in the ego (e.g., fear of reality and physical pain, as well as components of the more enduring feelings and feeling attitudes, such as object love and hate or thing interests);

(2) simple and compound affects induced by intersystemic tensions:
  (a) affects induced by tensions between the ego and the id (e.g., fear of the id, components of disgust, shame, and pity);
  (b) affects induced by tensions between ego and superego (e.g., guilt feelings, components of depression).

As will be noticed, the use of the term "tension" circumvents the problem of conflict. In view of the psychoanalytic "conflict" theory of neurosis, I must at least point out that tension is not to be equated with conflict.

Whereas affects which develop from intersystemic tensions (such as guilt feelings) are certainly always expressive of intrapsychic conflicts, affects arising from intrasystemic tensions may, but need not, be indicative of "conflict." I may add that in my classification I have not included tensions, i.e., "conflicts," between ego and reality. To a greater or lesser extent, every affect involves an emotional response to reality. But the underlying psychic tension, although induced by external stimuli, can arise only within the psychic organization, and not between the latter and the outside world.

These remarks indicate that the value of the classification suggested above is likely to prove limited. It will certainly lend itself to oversimplifications unless we keep in mind the compound nature of most feelings, especially of the enduring feelings, feeling states, and moods (which will be discussed in detail in Chapter 3).

The feelings and the emotional attitudes to which I refer are, e.g., kindness and heartlessness, sympathy and cruelty, love and hostility, sadness, grief, and happiness, depression and elation, and all the highly individualized affects and affective states that correspond to our various ego functions; i.e., our personal object and thing interests. All such phenomena are highly complex fusions of affect components, which belong to both groups in the classification suggested above.

Even when we analyze the broad unconscious background of an apparently simple affect, we find that it may be evoked concomitantly by an external stimulus and by intersystemic or intrasystemic tensions. Thus, an outburst of rage—in terms of my classification in (1a)—may be induced by an external provocation. At the same time, it may express a sudden breaking through of aggression that had long been inhibited by a struggle between ego and id, a defense of the ego against some other instinctual drive (such as a sexual impulse), or a defense of the ego against some demand of the superego.

In other words, while the basic theoretical value of this classification is that it approximately defines the affective type from the dynamic and structural points of view, it cannot divulge the meaning even of a specific and apparently simple affect. In fact, the final affective expression, in the mature, highly differentiated psychic organization, may develop from a series of intersystemic and intrasystemic psychic tensions. These may be interrelated, condition one another, and arise simultaneously or sequentially at various sites in the psychic apparatus. Hence affects can be understood only from the simultaneous study of the associated perceptive experiences and the conscious and unconscious ideational processes.

In his discussion of affects at the Annual Meeting of the American Psychoanalytic Association in 1952, and in his later paper "On the Psycho-Analytic Theory of Affects" (1953), Rapaport likewise pointed to the simplification inherent in my classification. Moreover, he maintained that it "succeeds in restating the 'conflict theory' of affects in structural terms" (p. 192). I do not believe that this argument is valid. As I emphasized above, tension is not identical with conflict unless we unduly broaden the concept of conflict. I also stated that affects *may*, but *need not*, be an expression of conflict. We certainly cannot deny the existence of affects and affective states that are expressive of conflict. However, both in this chapter and in Chapter 3 of the present volume as well as in other publications (1954b, 1964), I have placed special emphasis on the point that affects and feelings as such are normal psychic manifestations.

Rapaport (1953) also wondered whether my theory "in its classificatory simplicity . . . may not preclude a theoretical accounting of the many shades and varieties of affects arising in the taming process, as well as those varieties of continuous 'affective states' . . . which appear to be quasi-stable formations integrating complex id, ego, and super-ego contributions and their shifting balances into something like a sub-structure" (p. 193).

This I had stated myself in the published paper which Rapaport subsequently discussed. However, Rapaport made another point which I regard as significant. He mentioned that "the structural point of view does not seem to stop at the analysis of ego, id, super-ego factors; it enters upon the study of structuralization within each of these, as well as upon the study of structuralization of functions uniting components from all" (p. 193).

This leads to a problem which I may not have sufficiently considered in my original paper on which this chapter is based: that of the affective "defences (counter-cathectic energy-distributions), which may be regarded as alterations of discharge-thresholds." Rapaport stated, "The damming up of drives by defences makes for more intensive and more varied use of the affect-discharge channels and of the corresponding 'affect-charges'" (p. 194). I quite agree with these comments, and likewise with his statements regarding "the development of the ascending hierarchy of motivations." But most of what is stated here I have expressed, although in different terms, in my paper (1954b) and my book on *The Self and the Object World* (pp. 84-86).

THE TENSION-VERSUS-DISCHARGE CONCEPTS

Glover's (1948) further qualitative distinction between tension and discharge affects brings up some fundamental and debatable issues in the psychoanalytic theory of affects. It poses the question whether affects are either tension or discharge phenomena or both, a problem closely related to the mystery of the pleasure-unpleasure qualities of feelings. Our insufficient understanding of the affects and feelings is reflected in the divergent opinions of the various authors on these issues.

As Brierley (1937) points out, the discharge idea is still present in *Inhibitions, Symptoms and Anxiety*. True, but it must be noted that when Freud spoke of the unpleasure qualities of tension, he must at least have related unpleasurable affects to rising tension.

While I agree with Brierley that at first sight our modern concept of the role of the anxiety affect in normal and in neurotic development appears to contradict the discharge idea, I hope to demonstrate that the tension concept does not really contradict the discharge concept.

From Brierley's statements I have the impression that her tension concept is based on general conclusions drawn from the particular quality and unique signal function of the anxiety affect. The quality of anxiety certainly suggests the description of this affect as a tension phenomenon.

Before presenting my own viewpoint, I shall cite Rapaport's (1942) opinion on this issue. He refers to MacCurdy's (1925) theory, which seems to suggest that emotions, though discharge phenomena, are vicarious modes of discharge which occur only when psychic forces are prevented from immediate and adequate motor discharge. This theory leads in the direction of Rapaport's views at the time when he wrote his book (1942); he then adhered to the discharge idea, but apparently came to the conclusion that all affects develop from libido dammed up by repression. Subsequently, however, Rapaport revised his ideas, which suggest a "conflict" theory of affects, i.e., precisely what he believed to be implied in my classification.

In fact, I believe that despite their differences, MacCurdy's views, Rapaport's previous conceptions, and Brierley's ideas and interpretations of her clinical examples have some questionable implications. All of them come very close to assuming that affects in general are pathological phenomena due to a damming up of psychic energy that cannot be properly discharged. They recall Reid's definition of emotion as "a violent, stirred-up state of the organism" and the popular conception of neurotics as "emotional people."

If Brierley is correct in assuming that our modern conceptions of anxiety and its function support her views, then the influence of Freud's second anxiety theory becomes evident. We certainly cannot dispute the fact that anxiety and related unpleasurable affects appear to have "tension" qualities. However, contrary to Brierley's belief that her tension idea harmonizes with the pleasure principle, her conception is actually not in keeping with it. Insofar as pleasure and unpleasure are supposed to control psychic life, they must function as "indicators"—the term used by Hartmann (1927)—or as signals serving the regulation of the psychic economy. But Freud's formulation that the psychic organization aims at *avoiding* pain and at *gaining* pleasure permits us to regard pleasure at least as an ultimate goal.

Brierley's ideas and similar views that consider affects in general to be tension phenomena or regard them as caused by a damming up of psychic energy seem to ignore the pleasurable affects which, according to Freud's original opinion, are attached to relief of tension. Despite Freud's revision of this assumption, it would be absurd to regard feelings of relief, for instance, as tension phenomena. We must not forget that pleasurable affects are attached, as it were, not only to all normal ego functions, but particularly to direct instinctual discharges, i.e., to primary process experiences. Affects such as those expressive of sexual or oral gratification do not support the view that all affects arise as a consequence of inhibited motor discharge, even though it is correct that frustration, inhibition, and repression change the intensity and quality of affects.[3] In the course of ego and superego development the affects are indeed increasingly modified, and this permits us to characterize a great number of the adult affects and affective states as tension affects.

The clue to Brierley's—as I believe, erroneous—tension idea appears to be her reference to consciousness as a sensory organ and to the affects as arising from the stimulation of the inner surface. Certainly, our sensations and feelings are phenomena of inner perception. Freud's (1900) diagram of the psychic apparatus, in Chapter VII of *The Interpretation of Dreams,* and his description of the psychic processes as proceeding from the system of perception to the motor system, might tempt us to place the feelings at the beginning of the stimulus-reaction arc. On the other hand, Freud's concepts of the "identity of perception" and of dreams representing wish fulfillments preclude the equation of stimulus and perception. In fact, Freud's diagram of a psychic process according to the model of the reflex does not correspond to the psychoeconomic concept of a psychic discharge process. Viewed from the psychoeconomic standpoint, an external or internal stimulus leads to rises of tension, which result in a psychic release and discharge; this process finds expres-

[3] Incidentally, I consider it incorrect to characterize all neurotics as hyperaffective; they may be hyper- or hypoaffective, or may manifest other quantitative or qualitative signs of affective disturbances.

sion in motor phenomena as well as in sensations and feelings perceived by the outer and inner surface of consciousness. We therefore commonly and correctly speak of sensations and emotions as "responses" or "reactions" to the stimulus.

In other words, whereas a neurophysiologically oriented diagram may represent a psychic process as proceeding from stimulus perception to motor reaction, according to dynamic and psychoeconomic conceptions such a process should rather be described in terms of rise of intrapsychic tension caused by external or internal stimulation—discharge of tension—sensory, affective, and motor reaction.[4] But my preliminary arguments against the tension concept of affects are not yet sufficient to settle this issue. Obviously, we cannot take a definite position before making an inroad into the still unresolved problem of the pleasure-unpleasure qualities of feelings and their relations to the psychic economy.

THE PLEASURE-UNPLEASURE QUALITIES OF AFFECTS

In the *Three Essays on the Theory of Sexuality* (1905a) Freud writes:

> In spite of all the differences of opinion that reign on the subject among psychologists, I must insist that a feeling of tension necessarily involves unpleasure. What seems to me decisive is the fact that a feeling of this kind is accompanied by an impulsion to make a change in the psychological situation, that it operates in an urgent way which is wholly alien to the nature of the feeling of pleasure. If, however, the tension of sexual excitement is counted as an unpleasurable feeling, we are at once brought up against the fact that it is also undoubtedly felt as pleasurable [p. 209].

In the further course of this discussion Freud analyzes carefully the pleasure experience of sexual excitement and of its discharge, and introduces the distinction between forepleasure and end pleasure. But his explanation of the mechanism of forepleasure, which enabled

[4] In this context I refer to Fenichel's (1945) remarks: "Stimulus intake and stimulus discharge, perception and motor reaction stand extraordinarily close together; they are inseparably interwoven" (p. 36). Fenichel points to Freud's (1925) pertinent paper, "A Note upon the 'Mystic Writing-Pad,'" which demonstrates the original connection between perception and motor reaction.

Freud to gain insight into the psychology of wit, does not exactly clarify our issue.

That Freud himself did not regard the problem as resolved is evident in the repeated discussions of this subject in his later theoretical papers. In *Beyond the Pleasure Principle* (1920), Freud said:

> We have decided to relate pleasure and unpleasure to the quantity of excitation that is present in the mind but is not in any way 'bound'; and to relate them in such a manner that unpleasure corresponds to an *increase* in the quantity of excitation and pleasure to a *diminution.* What we are implying by this is not a simple relation between the strength of the feelings of pleasure and unpleasure and the corresponding modifications in the quantity of excitation; least of all—in view of all we have been taught by psycho-physiology—are we suggesting any directly proportional ratio: the factor that determines the feeling is probably the amount of increase or diminution in the quantity of excitation *in a given period of time* [p. 7f.].

As we shall see, the idea expressed in this last sentence was again taken up in "The Economic Problem of Masochism" (1924b). In *The Ego and the Id* (1923) we observe once more Freud's striking insistence on considering unpleasurable any tension or excitation, and pleasurable only the diminution of excitement or elimination of tension. Even before he conceived of a death instinct (in accord with Schopenhauer's view that the goal of life is death), his opinions on pleasure-unpleasure remind one of this philosopher who defined pleasure as the absence of pain. Thus it was a logical development that in his proposition of the death instinct Freud first identified the pleasure principle with the Nirvana principle. He regarded the former as in the service of the latter, but his remarks were at times confusing (see, e.g., 1920, p. 55f.). He considered the life instinct and the death instinct as opposing drives, and the latter as being "beyond the pleasure principle."

How are we to reconcile this thesis with the assumption that the ultimate goal of both instincts is elimination of tension to which, in the case of the life instinct only, a pleasure premium is attached. We are not surprised that these confusing ideas led Freud (1924b) to correct himself:

> But we have unhesitatingly identified the pleasure-unpleasure principle with this Nirvana principle. Every unpleasure ought

> thus to coincide with a heightening, and every pleasure with a lowering, of mental tension due to stimulus; the Nirvana principle (and the pleasure principle which is supposedly identical with it) would be entirely in the service of the death instincts, . . . and it would have the function of giving warnings against the demands of the life instincts—the libido—which try to disturb the intended course of life. But such a view cannot be correct. It seems that in the series of feelings of tension we have a direct sense of the increase and decrease of amounts of stimulus, and it cannot be doubted that there are pleasurable tensions and unpleasurable relaxations of tension. The state of sexual excitation is the most striking example of a pleasurable increase of stimulus of this sort, but it is certainly not the only one.
>
> Pleasure and unpleasure, therefore, cannot be referred to an increase or decrease of a quantity (which we describe as 'tension due to stimulus'), although they obviously have a great deal to do with that factor. It appears that they depend, not on this quantitative factor, but on some characteristic of it which we can only describe as a qualitative one. If we were able to say what this qualitative characteristic is, we should be much further advanced in psychology [p. 159f.].

And now Freud once again hinted at the significance of the time factor for the quality of feelings:

> Perhaps it is the rhythm, the temporal sequence of changes, rises and falls in the quantity of stimulus. We do not know [p. 160].

Freud concluded that we are still justified in regarding the pleasure principle as "the watchman over our life" (p. 161).

We realize that of the three principles mentioned, only the first—the Nirvana principle—is an economic law, its goal being elimination of tension. The second—the pleasure-unpleasure principle—refers to feeling qualities; and the third—the reality principle—refers to the factors that modify it. Regarding the life instincts, Freud did not mention an economic law—such as the constancy principle—that might somehow relate to the pleasure principle. Nor does Freud discuss the relations between affect qualities and the death instinct, except to observe that the latter is beyond the pleasure principle.

Perhaps Freud deliberately omitted these issues out of caution. If pleasure and unpleasure both can be related to either rises or falls of psychic tension, and if the death instinct is beyond the pleasure principle, then the relations between pleasure-unpleasure qualities and the psychic economy become very obscure indeed. We see that Freud's new suggestions reach very far and in doing so open many new problems. In any case, they imply that the pleasure-unpleasure principles cannot be considered economical principles.

RELATIONS BETWEEN PLEASURE-UNPLEASURE AND PSYCHIC ECONOMY

I believe that the study of a complex affective experience involving all structural systems would not inform us clearly enough about the original relations of pleasure-unpleasure to tension and relief. Hence, a rediscussion of the sexual pleasure experience—group (1a) according to my classification—appears to be the best approach to this problem. (I may add that by choosing the sexual pleasure experience as a suitable example for what I want to demonstrate, I do not imply that I regard all affects as consciously felt experiences.) Let us go back to Freud's early opinions on this issue.

Freud's relating unpleasure to increase and pleasure to decrease of tension was the logical outcome of his physiological orientation: he considered the reflex as the model of the psychic apparatus. Regarding the pleasurable experience in the sexual act, only the explanation of forepleasure seemed to present major theoretical difficulties. But both the forepleasure and the end pleasure attached to the orgastic discharge of sexual energy represent compound affective experiences. What gives orgasm its peculiar oscillating quality is that it involves rhythmic waves of feelings of climactic excitement, switching to feelings of relief and, finally, satisfaction. Thus the orgastic discharge experience is not simply pleasure in relief, but fuses—or rather, vacillates between—two opposite pleasure qualities: a high excitement pleasure expressive of tension mounting to a climax, and a relief pleasure indicating the final decline of tension. And we must conclude from the quality of the orgastic end pleasure itself that the discharge process encompasses both mounting and falling tension; and that both can induce pleasure, though of changing quality. This consideration is apt to resolve the seeming contradictions between Freud's discharge concept of the affects and Brierley's assumption that all affects are tension phenomena. Evidently the affects, even though corresponding to discharge processes, can be expressive of either rising or falling tension. What appears incorrect and misleading is to place "tension" and "discharge" in direct juxtaposition, an inaccuracy that is reflected in our terminology.

The terms "tension," "excitation," and "excitement," or the terms "discharge" and "relief," are frequently used synonymously. "Excitement," I should think, describes only a feeling quality that corresponds to mounting psychic-energetic tension. The terms "tension" and "relief" may be used either for the feeling qualities or for the corresponding levels of energetic tension. Whereas these are terms of static description, "discharge" designates something dynamic. It can refer only to the flux of psychic forces, i.e., to the energetic process itself, which finally results in a drop of tension. It is significant that Freud never characterized the affects as "discharge" in contrast to "tension" phenomena, but defined them as "corresponding to processes of discharge."

When we relate tension to discharge, we must realize that, in the sexual as in any other psychic release process which develops from the depth to the surface of the psychic apparatus, the strength of the stimulus may cause the tension to mount even while discharge has already begun to operate; until the point is reached where the energy, having come to the surface, can be fully dispersed and the level of tension decline. To get a clear notion of these conditions we may visualize a receptacle, such as a bathtub, where water is simultaneously flowing in and draining out. As long as the influx is stronger than the outflow, the water level will rise; as the volume of the influx decreases, the level will begin to fall; and after the influx has ceased, the water will finally be drained out.

I am aware that this comparison in terms of "quantities" represents a useful, but questionable, simplification. Obviously, the relations of the rises and falls of tension to the discharge processes are very complex.

The complexity of the correlations between psychic tension and discharge may be visualized when we remember that the psychic apparatus is a wide area, at one point of which the level of energetic tension may rise while it drops at others. Rapaport (1953) correctly pointed out that the discharge processes are only one among many psychic processes. Mobile energy is constantly being distributed and bound at one place, while it is mobilized, released, and discharged somewhere else. Cathectic and countercathectic processes occur simultaneously at different sites of the psychic organization. There may be changes in cathexis with either libidinal or aggressive or neutral psychic forces, changes regarding the countercathectic conditions and, furthermore, cathectic shifts from one site of the psychic field to the other. But as was already emphasized above, our affects and especially our conscious feeling experiences—complex, subtle, and highly differentiated though they are—divulge very little of these complicated conditions in the depth of the psychic apparatus. They cannot reveal anything about the manifold changes of the level of tension below a certain threshold, because they are the expression not of "bound" psychic energy but of the energetic flux,[5] and of this flux only after it has overstepped a certain threshold of tension.

The preceding discussion of the relations of mounting and falling tension to the discharge processes facilitates the clarification of our two confusing problems; namely, the tension-versus-discharge issue; and the relation of pleasure-unpleasure to tension and relief.

With regard to the first, I can only repeat that the mode of posing the question was obviously wrong. The problem is not whether affects are either tension or discharge phenomena. We can certainly adhere to Freud's original definition that the affects correspond to discharge processes; but we may supplement this definition by the statement that affects appear to be expressive of the rises as well as of the falls of tension in the course of a discharge process, and that they develop during the initial period of continued increase of tension. If the affects are expressive not of tension—in contrast to discharge—but of the flow of mobile psychic energy released and the changes in the level of tension—or in the amount of excitation in the course of a discharge process—then Brierley's tension concept becomes more meaningful, but her argument against the discharge idea loses its meaning. In the light of the conception I have presented, Glover's distinction of tension and discharge affects does not appear to be well chosen either. It would be preferable to distinguish either affects, expressive of discharge at the stage of mounting and falling tension, or, in the case of conscious affective experiences, simply and descriptively, feelings of emotional tension, excitement, and relief.

[5] Significantly, Freud (1920) related pleasure and unpleasure, as was already noted, "to the quantity of excitation that is present in the mind but is not in any way 'bound.' "

THE URGE FOR A CHANGE OF THE PSYCHIC SITUATION

The study of the orgastic pleasure experience confirmed Freud's final opinion by disclosing that even in a primary process experience, such as sexual excitement and orgasm, pleasure, though of a "different quality," may be attached to both the increase and the decrease of tension.

Rapaport (1953) questioned whether I did not equate the affects with the subjectively felt experiences or even with their pleasure-unpleasure qualities. Whereas I had previously underscored these distinctions, I did use the example of orgasm, i.e., of a subjectively felt experience, for the study of the relationship between the affects and their pleasure-unpleasure qualities and the discharge processes. But it is true that my conclusions, which are in harmony with Freud's last statement on the relations of pleasure-unpleasure to tension and relief, preclude using "pleasure-unpleasure" as mere referents to the economic situation, as Rapaport and likewise Gill and Schur do.

At this point I want to make some comments on Schur's interesting book, *The Id and the Regulatory Principles of Mental Functioning* (1966). His discussion of the pleasure and unpleasure principles, his emphatic distinction between these regulatory principles, and his use of the terms "pleasure" and "unpleasure" in this special context certainly present us with challenging problems.

Schur defines the unpleasure principle as regulating "the *necessity* to withdraw [meaning both physical withdrawal and the withdrawal of special cathexes] from excessive stimulation impinging upon the mental apparatus from the outside, 'outside' implying both outside the organism and outside the mental apparatus" (p. 137). He underscores that in contrast to the pleasure principle, which involves an "approach" response, there "is no motivational force to *seek* an object in order to withdraw from it" (p. 151). This is certainly correct. But in this connection Schur does not discuss the alternative devices of either flight (withdrawal) or fight as responses to external and internal danger.

In his brief chapter on "The Id and Aggression," Schur states: "From our clinical experience we have reason to assume that the aggressive drive is also subject to regulation by the unpleasure and pleasure principles." While he emphasizes that aggressive discharge "is mostly combined with a discharge of the libidinal drive" (p.

121), he does not mention the fight response to danger. The fight response is very important, however, from the evolutional point of view (struggle for survival), and for the understanding of inner conflicts and defenses. As Hartmann (1950) pointed out, the countercathectic formations use more or less neutralized aggressive forces.

Schur defines the pleasure principle as regulating "the need to re-create by action or by fantasy any situation which has created the experience of satisfaction through the elimination of drive tension" (p. 145). In his terms the "fight" response would also be regulated by the pleasure principle, since it involves an "approach" response and may lead to pleasurable aggressive excitement and final satisfaction by elimination of drive tension.

We would thus have to conclude that the "flight" (withdrawal) response to danger is regulated by the unpleasure principle, whereas the "fight" response is regulated by the pleasure principle. This points to the difficulties arising from Schur's sharp distinction between a pleasure principle and an unpleasure principle. This distinction then compels him to make further distinctions: whereas sexual stimulation aims at pleasurable discharge, and hence is regulated by the pleasure principle, "the experience of pain (excessive stimulation, later danger) stimulates withdrawal and is regulated by the unpleasure principle" (p. 150).

On the experiential level Schur then points to the differences between feelings of relief following the disappearance of tension (pain, danger, etc.) and feelings of pleasure following instinctual satisfaction. No doubt these differences in the affective qualities exist. On the other hand, any excessive stimulation—including sexual stimulations—may result in unpleasure to the point of pain, and any pleasurable instinctual gratification (sexual or aggressive) also induces feelings of relief. Moreover, even unpleasurable discharge processes, such as crying, bring about feelings of relief. These considerations lead to the problem of the relationship between the pleasure-unpleasure principles and the affective experience of pleasure and unpleasure.

Since Freud came so close to the confusing equation of the pleasure and unpleasure principles with the Nirvana and constancy principles, Schur drops the latter altogether. He regards both pleasure and unpleasure principles as "basically economic regulatory principles dealing with the accumulation and avoidance of tension and also with the seeking of stimuli and objects for discharge of tension" (p. 157).[6] Thus, with regard to these regulatory principles Schur employs the terms pleasure and unpleasure only as referents to the economic situation, i.e., to (excessive) increase or decrease of tension.

For this reason Schur criticizes Freud and other authors, including myself, for not clearly distinguishing between the principles and the affective experiences. In contrast to Schur, I tend, for clinical and theoretical reasons, to adhere to the idea of a constancy principle. Furthermore, in accordance with Freud, I believe that the terms pleasure and unpleasure are and must remain referents to (conscious) feeling qualities. Schur's ideas about this issue are in accord with his opinion that affects are not expressive of drive discharge processes, but represent complex ego responses to instinctual (energetic) processes. Consequently, he disconnects the affects and their pleasure-unpleasure qualities from the instinctual processes, from the economic conditions, and hence from the regulatory pleasure-unpleasure *principles*. In my view, this would require the choice of new terms for the regulatory principles.

It is interesting that in his extensive quotations from "The Economic Problem of Masochism" Schur does not include Freud's significant statements (p. 159f.), which I cited above, on pleasurable excitement and unpleasurable feelings of tension.

In ending my discussion of Schur's ideas, I want to emphasize that I found his definition of the pleasure principle very useful. It implies a considerable widening of the concept, which to some extent takes care of the problem to which I here have given such special attention: namely, pleasurable and unpleasurable tension, and pleasurable and unpleasurable discharge.

This brings me back to the pleasure-unpleasure qualities of the affects. Freud's major reason for maintaining that tension cannot be pleasurable had been that in the case of forepleasure there is an urge to change the psychic situation. He did not again attempt to tackle this puzzling problem.

[6] I may add that in Schur's opinion, "These formulations are not meant to detract from the importance of economic formulations, which are meaningful and heuristically valid concepts, but are meant only to discourage the assumption that an economic formulation can be sufficiently meaningful per se without a consideration of the other metapsychological points of view" (p. 201). This is certainly correct.

In Chapter VII of *The Interpretation of Dreams* (1900), Freud defined the wish as a psychic striving developing from unpleasure and aiming at pleasure.[7] This definition could hardly be maintained if we were to assume that an "urge for a change" could also develop from pleasure. If there is any wish attached to pleasure, it is for the pleasure to last. But this wish refers to our fear of loss of pleasure. That pleasure should involve wishes or urges for a change of the psychic situation sounds so contradictory that we easily understand Freud's dilemma.

We might resolve the dilemma by the formulation that while we want to avoid pain (unpleasure) and gain pleasure, we need not necessarily wish indefinitely to maintain a specific pleasure. After all, there is an enormous variety of pleasure experiences. The urge for a change arising in a pleasurable situation might refer to a wish either for more intense pleasure or for a different quality of pleasure. I again use the example of sexual pleasure: the urge for a change during the forepleasure phase would appear to express not the wish for relief, but the wish for a climax; the expectation of the final relief pleasure is embedded even in the orgastic excitement. Furthermore, in a situation of relief, after a period of enjoyable relaxation, we can observe an increasing need for stimuli inducing a different type of pleasure, an excitement pleasure; or, to put it more cautiously, a need for a different type of discharge process involving more intense excitement.

If this is valid, we must conclude that tension pleasure may induce the urge for more intense excitement; climactic pleasure, the urge for relief; and relief pleasure, the longing for again experiencing pleasurable tension. This schematization reflects the dynamic course of life, which represents not only inevitable changes between pleasure and unpleasure—stemming from the demands of reality—but, insofar as it is pleasurable, alternates continuously between excitement and relief pleasures, which correspond to discharge processes involving rises and falls of psychic excitation from a certain median level.

In this case, we should have to interpret the meaning of "wishing" more broadly. Wishing would always be wishing for pleasure, but it would represent a striving for cycles of pleasure having dif-

[7] Schur (1966) devotes two chapters to a discussion of the development of the wish from the phylogenetic and ontogenetic aspects.

ferent qualities, alternating between excitement and relief; cycles corresponding to our biological existence and rooted in our instinctual life. In view of the great variety of pleasurable experiences, however, I mentioned above that we may also feel the urge for a change with regard to the special type of pleasure.

When Goethe states that "nothing is harder to bear than a series of good days,"[8] he evidently means that in a prolonged specific pleasure experience we become gradually aware of unpleasure feelings indicating the "urge for a change" of the situation. The wish to supplant one kind of pleasurable experience with another certainly affects the pleasure qualities of the original experience by adding unpleasure components, which will be fused with the original pleasure components and more or less disguised by them. To be sure, in general we very rarely gain sheer, unmixed pleasure from one special experience for a prolonged period of time.[9]

This leads to the problem of moods, which will be discussed in Chapter 3. Here I wish to mention only that because of a change of mood, we may feel that tonight we want to "do something different" from what we did last night. This may have something to do with a general change of the discharge patterns.

Even if our problem has not really been resolved, its discussion may at least bring us closer to an understanding of the relations between the pleasure-unpleasure principles and the psychic economy.

CONCLUDING FORMULATIONS REGARDING THE RELATIONS BETWEEN THE PLEASURE-UNPLEASURE PRINCIPLES OF PSYCHIC ECONOMY

As stated above, Freud in his final discussion of this issue did not again mention an economic law, corresponding to the Nirvana principle, which would regulate the life instincts. He mentioned only the pleasure and reality principles. Practically, however, we all work on the premise of a principle of constancy that must be consistent with the pleasure-unpleasure principles.

In *Beyond the Pleasure Principle* (1920), Freud described this

[8] "Nichts ist schwerer zu ertragen als eine Reihe von guten Tagen."

[9] In a discussion of this study, Ernst Kris called attention to opinions expressed by H. Deutsch (1927). Her ideas have much in common with the ones presented here, except that her emphasis rests on the driving force of the eternal dissatisfaction of human beings, whereas I stress the longing for a change that can rise even from pleasure.

law as a tendency of the psychic organization to keep the level of tension constant or as low as possible. We can eliminate the latter alternative, which led to the erroneous equation of the pleasure-unpleasure and Nirvana principles. But how can the pleasure-unpleasure principle be identical with a constancy law, if both tension and relief can induce either pleasure or unpleasure? The problem grows in view of the facts gained from our previous investigation of orgasm. The evidence that even direct sexual discharge induces a pleasure experience involving tension pleasure, climactic excitement pleasure, and relief pleasure led me to the assumption that the psychic organization may show a striving for cycles of pleasure alternating between excitement and relief, which correspond to swings of tension around a median tension level. Should this hypothesis be valid, the pleasure principle would not have the function to bring about a relief of tension. The pleasure principle and later on its modification, the reality principle, would only direct the course of the swings around a middle axis of tension, i.e., the modes of the discharge processes.[10] Pleasure qualities would be attached to the swings of the tension pendulum to either side, as long as the corresponding psychophysiological discharge processes can select certain preferred pathways and the changes of tension can take a definite course—depending, so it seems, on certain still unknown proportions between the amounts of excitation and the speed and rhythm of discharge.

If we were to regard this as the function of the pleasure principle, it would appear to be in direct contradiction to a constancy law. But the assumption that the pleasure-unpleasure principles work independently of, or even contrary to, the psychoeconomic laws is not tenable.[11] Thus we must conclude that the constancy law may have to be redefined so as to be in harmony with the pleasure principle.

This is also suggested by the consideration of the various functions of the psychic organization, functions that must be consistent with psychoeconomic laws. The essential laws that govern psychic

[10] This assumption would be in accordance with Schur's widened concept of the pleasure principle, had he not equated the experience of satisfaction with the elimination of drive tension, and besides evaded a discussion of pleasurable excitement (such as in laughter) and of unpleasurable discharge (such as by crying). These affective responses will be discussed in Chapters 2 and 3.

[11] Although reinforcing Freud's idea that the life instincts are the "disturbing elements," such an assumption would lead us to an equation of the constancy and Nirvana principles, as opposed to the pleasure principle.

life serve the control and gratification of the psychic drives, the function of adaptation, and the function of self-preservation. A failure of any of these functions corresponds to disturbances in the psychic economy.

An economic law aiming at the maintenance of a constant level of tension would, however, not be equal to such complex functions. We must therefore look for a different and broader characterization of the psychoeconomic laws. We recognize a law of constancy in the sense of a tendency to maintain an equilibrium and an even distribution of the energetic forces within the psychic organization. As Rapaport (1953) stressed, however, "tension" as such is inherent in the idea of a "psychic organization." The function of this law would be not to reduce tension, but to establish and maintain a constant axis of tension and a certain margin for the vacillations around it; furthermore, to enforce the return of the tension pendulum to this median line and to control the course of the swings of tension.

The pleasure and unpleasure principles would thus be subordinate to the superior, general constancy principle. It is not the deviations from the middle axis as such that would represent disturbances of the psychic equilibrium. Deviations from the preferred and biologically preconditioned pleasurable course of the tension pendulum, or a failure to maintain the tension axis constant, or its rise or fall above or below a certain level, or a widening or narrowing of the margin for the swings of tension—any of these factors would bring about an upset of the psychic economy.

MODIFICATION OF THE AFFECTS UNDER THE INFLUENCE OF THE REALITY PRINCIPLE AND OF STRUCTURAL DIFFERENTATION

The foregoing conclusions about the affects and their pleasure-unpleasure qualities were derived from the study of sexual excitement and orgasm, i.e., of a libidinal, primary process pleasure experience—group (1a) of my classification. We have not yet explored the nature and qualities of the affects that develop in the course of structural differentiation and secondary process formation under the influence of the reality principle.

I do not intend to discuss at length the modifications of emotions, their "taming," and the affect defenses established during ego and superego formation,[12] but I must focus at least on some essential aspects of affective development—in particular, on the changes of the affect qualities arising with the integration of the so-called "tension" affects into the psychic organization.

As a brief introduction, I shall continue my discussion of the affective qualities attached to aggressive discharge and the psychic laws controlling the latter. With regard to the psychic laws, I have so far disregarded Freud's proposition of the death instinct and of the Nirvana principle. But we cannot evade the question whether the aggressive drives are "beyond the pleasure principle" and controlled by a "Nirvana principle," or whether they obey the same laws as the libidinal drives.

A glance at the psychoanalytic literature discloses that most analysts, although they accept the existence of two inherently different kinds of drives, refuse to work with the death instinct theory. The main reason for this rejection may be that Freud's proposition of life and death instincts is founded on rather speculative assumptions foreign to his earlier conceptions and definitions of the drives. In any event, valid arguments can be raised in objection to the death instinct theory. (I refer again to Schur's discussions of this issue.)

Not only are aggression and its derivatives in the service of all pleasurable libidinal and ego functions; as Hartmann, Kris, and Loewenstein (1949) pointed out, pure aggressive release can undoubtedly also induce pleasure. The primary goal of aggression is evidently not the gain of pleasure. But I mentioned above that in situations of danger, sheer aggressive forces are normally mobilized and needed in the service of self-preservation. These normal functions and the vicissitudes of aggression can hardly be explained as the expression of a struggle between the death instincts and the life instincts, the latter turning the former to the outside and keeping them in check until the time of final victory of the death instincts, which is death. Even though the two kinds of drives are opposed to one another or may be in conflict with each other, and although either one of the drives can be used for the purpose of warding off the other, they normally appear to have complementary functions in the service of life, and to be equally ruled by the constancy prin-

[12] I have dealt with these issues at some length in my book on *The Self and the Object World* (1964).

ciple and the pleasure-unpleasure principles. The dangerous effect of sheer, uncontrolled aggression on the outside world does not contradict this assumption.[13] Difficulties in our understanding arise in view of those masochistic phenomena which reinforced Freud's conception of the death instinct. Self-destructive tendencies, such as appear in the depressive states, do not seem to aim at the maintenance or reinstatement of a constant level of tension, but rather aim at its elimination. And how can the pleasure principle be effective in persons who manifest uncontrollable wishes for self-destruction?

A discussion of the reality principle and its influence on the discharge processes may facilitate our understanding of masochism from the viewpoint of the constancy and pleasure-unpleasure principles, without our having to resort to the assumption of a Nirvana principle.

In "The Ego and the Affects" (1941) and *The Psychoanalytic Theory of Neurosis* (1945), Fenichel beautifully described how with the development of the ego, with the organization of ideational and thought processes, and with increasing neutralization of the drives, the psychic organization gains an ever-increasing subtle power over the distribution and release of energetic forces and, consequently, over the affective manifestations. As Freud remarked early (1900), the binding of psychic energy in lasting object cathexes by the ego probably leads, first of all, to a general rise of the level of tension (the "tension axis"). Considering the threshold idea, we may surmise that this corresponds to a rise of the thresholds above which affective and motor discharge becomes imperative.

The effects of ego formation on the discharge processes and affective development must be described from different angles.

We usually regard the transition from affective to functional motor activity, insofar as it leads to a general taming of the affects for the purpose of adequate ego function, as the ego's greatest accomplishment with respect to the affects. The subduing and taming of affects are achieved by the ego's increasing ability to inhibit,

[13] From the standpoint of self-preservation, the mastery of the aggressive forces and their emotional expression appears to be of even greater significance than the management of the libidinal drives because, in contrast to libido, uncontrolled aggression may lead to realistic harm and result in self-destruction. This is why a reduction of the libidinal forces, which are needed for the control of aggression, is bound to have such fatal consequences.

control, and curtail the discharge, with the support of countercathexes, and to postpone action by the interpolation of thought processes.

Although Fenichel (1941) focused on the taming of affects and the affective defenses established by the ego, he also mentioned that this process does not normally reduce the affects to mere signals or to safety valves for discharge, effective only in case adequate motor function cannot take place. In fact, affects may, but need not, function as signals or safety valves. The development of reasonable action does not imply the elimination of emotional responses, an idea that is reinforced by too strict an opposition of affective responses to adequate drive action or reasonable ego function. I stress once more that even in the infant's first instinctual and functional activity, in sucking, an intense affectomotor reaction is attached to adequate functioning. But the child's biological dependency, the slow maturation of his ego, and the inhibition of infantile sexuality and aggression, all of which either preclude or limit drive action and ego function, make the affects' safety-valve function indispensable, and this function remains of special significance throughout childhood. The affects are also responsible for the fact that in human beings the emotional life maintains an independent existence, not only alongside of but also apart from reasonable thought and action. What turns us into human beings is, indeed, the organization not only of our thought processes, but also of a wide range of feelings, of complex emotional attitudes and affective states unknown to the animal.

Although the organization and differentiation of adult emotional life are partly dependent upon the taming process, the latter represents only one aspect of affective development. The other aspect is the opening up, by the maturation and development of both the instinctual and the ego organizations, of innumerable new channels for affective and motor discharge. Thus the development of self and object representations and object relations, of ego functions and sublimations, and of adult sexual behavior leads to the development of affect components with new qualities, which are then integrated with earlier infantile affect components into new units. These developments contribute at least as much as the taming power of the ego and superego to the constructive remodeling of the affects and affective qualities, to the molding of complex affect patterns, emotional dispositions and attitudes, and enduring feeling states; in short, to the enrichment as well as to the hierarchic and structural organization of emotional life.

With these different influences in mind, I shall now focus on one of the characteristic changes brought about by these developmental processes: the generation of affects manifesting conspicuous tension qualities, such as suggested to Brierley (1937) that all affects are tension phenomena. This holds not only for unpleasurable affects, such as signal anxiety, disgust, shame, and guilt feelings, but also for many pleasurable component affects of the adult. As is well known, the small child is unable to bear tension, but gradually learns not only to tolerate but even to enjoy tension.

The study of tension tolerance and of the adult tension affects presupposes, first of all, a clarification of what is meant by infantile tension intolerance. I have proposed that direct instinctual pleasure experiences also entail pleasurable rises of tension. Observations of small children seem to confirm that certain types of discharge involving excitement, i.e., tension pleasure, already play a part in the infantile psychic organization. In this context I refer to Lewin's (1950) distinction between the first active (excitement) phase and the ensuing passive phase in the situation of being nursed. Tension pleasure as such cannot be regarded as an achievement of the ego. But in the course of ego and superego formation the child normally learns to tolerate or even to enjoy such rises of tension as were formerly unbearable.

Our next question pertains to the nature of the pleasurable and unpleasurable "tension affects" that originate with the development of the psychic systems. Are they, too, expressive of discharge processes, as are the affects attached to primary process experience and function? Although Fenichel adheres to the discharge concept of affects, his discussion of tension affects bypasses this point. I do not believe that we can find any facts contradictory to the assumption that these tension affects, too, are expressive of discharge processes, although of discharge inhibited, slowed up, possibly incomplete, and in any event modified by the ego under the influence of the reality principle. This interpolated system, insofar as it is opposed to and interferes with direct discharge, prolongs and modifies especially the course of the initial rises of tension during the discharge process and thereby produces the characteristic tension qualities attached to this type of affects.[14]

With regard to anxiety, for example, there is no doubt about its tension quality. Whenever it is sufficiently developed, however, its signs and symptoms clearly indicate that it is also expressive of discharge—a discharge originally enforced by the psycho-organismic distress of the newborn and serving the adjustment to his new existence, but later on fixated and reduced to a signal effective in situations of external and internal danger. This discharge concept makes intelligible why anxiety can be so easily libidinized, i.e., used directly as a concomitant outlet for sexual energy, or in complex fusions with other affect components can play such an important role in many types of adult pleasure experiences, especially in those we call "thrilling."

The molding, integration, and internalization of the signal-anxiety pattern, and the significant economic function which this affect acquires, are a characteristic expression of the influence of the reality principle and of ego formation upon affective development in general.

The meaning of the reality principle for affective development can best be understood by a reconsideration of the relations between the pleasure-unpleasure principles and the law of constancy. Wheras the latter aims in general to maintain the psychic equilibrium, according to the conception presented above, the pleasure principle seeks to direct the course of the vacillations around the median level according to preferred discharge patterns. It thus appears likely that in certain situations the pleasure principle can make itself independent and that these two laws can then be in opposition to each other. The pleasure principle might yield to economic necessities, or it might assert itself at the expense of the general psychic equilibrium.

The first case can be found whenever reality interferes with our wish for pleasure. Unpleasurable or painful experiences will occur as soon as the constancy law tries to enforce the re-establishment of the psychic equilibrium by discharge processes that cannot pro-

[14] My remark on the incompleteness of discharge refers, in particular, to chronic or lasting states of unpleasurable, anxious, or painful tension that may represent a psychoeconomic condition characterized by repetitious, attenuated, and insufficient unpleasurable discharges of small amounts of psychic energy.

ceed according to the preferred, pleasurable patterns. But the constitution of the reality principle in the psychic organization means more than that. It represents a partial submission of the pleasure principle to other functions of the constancy law, as reflected in the effort of the ego to accept, firmly integrate, and even internalize certain attenuated unpleasurable discharges in the psychic organization for psychoeconomic reasons.

The anxiety signal, this special mode of attenuated unpleasurable discharge that the ego induces in situations of danger, is only one outstanding example of such temporary suspension of the pleasure principle for superior economic purposes. In general the growing dominance of the constancy principle over its sublaws, the pleasure-unpleasure principles, accomplishes, by molding and integrating not only signal anxiety, but many other unpleasurable tension affects with signal function, the increasing tolerance for tension and promotes, furthermore, the development of compound pleasurable tension affects.

But the problem of adult tension tolerance and tension pleasure leads us back once more to the other aspect of affective development, upon which I wish to lay special emphasis. I refer to the fact that the primitive psychic apparatus still has only a limited number of psychophysiological pathways and hence of modes for pleasurable affective discharge at its disposal. For this reason the infantile intolerance of tension is also an expression of the child's inability to discharge through the channels of mature ego functions and sublimations as well as of adult instinctual activity. The child cannot bear tension because his psychic organization is not yet equipped for its adequate affective and motor discharge.

During the pregenital stage, for example, the instinctual organization is not yet prepared to bring about a fully pleasurable genital discharge; and in some children this state can persist until puberty. The pleasurable genital discharge pattern has not yet been molded. Sexual overstimulation, and in particular premature genital stimulation of the child, will thus arouse anxiety—independent of concomitant sexual prohibition—and may lead to what Greenacre (1952, 1971) has frequently discussed in her papers: to an overflow from the stimulated area to other erotogenic zones, resulting in diffuse discharge processes with corresponding affective experiences that blend pleasurable and directly painful sensual and feeling qualities.

The premature encouragement or enforcement of ego functions and sublimations in a child will have a similar effect.

To summarize: the success or failure of affective development, particularly of the development of normal tension tolerance and of discharge patterns bringing about pleasurable tension affects, depends on the optimal collaboration of three major influences: (1) of the reality principle (represented mainly by the parental prohibitions and demands); by curbing direct instinctual discharge, postponing action, and introducing attenuated unpleasurable affects with signal function, the reality principle leads to a taming of the affects and a certain reduction of pleasure for economic purposes; (2) of the instinctual maturation that shapes new modes of direct pleasurable drive discharge; and (3) of the maturation of the ego; insofar as this leads to the development of the thought processes, of judgment, and of the autonomous ego functions and sublimations, it partly eliminates the need for anxiety signals and also creates innumerable new channels for pleasurable functional motor and affective discharge.

Since the opening up of new pathways for pleasurable discharge promotes the successful fusion of attenuated unpleasurable tension components with pleasurable components into compound pleasurable affects, the maturation process works in many ways in favor of the pleasure principle and gains back for the latter much of the territory lost to the influence of the reality principle. Whereas the achievement of tension tolerance and the introduction and internalization of tension affects of the anxiety type point to the victory of the reality principle over the pleasure principle, the development of sound judgment and of a multitude of compound tension-pleasure experiences emphasizes the tendency of the pleasure principle to reassert itself.

The acceptance and integration of unpleasurable modes of affective discharge to the extent that they acquire pleasure qualities is probably connected with the factor of pleasurable "anticipation." The expectation of future gratification appears to induce pleasure affect components, which we are entitled to call signal affects, too, although of the pleasurable variety.

The discussion of the three major influences on affective development, and especially on the development of tension tolerance and tension pleasure from the viewpoint of the psychic principles, brings us close to the problem of masochistic phenomena and neurotic and psychotic emotional behavior in general. Repeated experiences of premature sexual overstimulation, along with sexual prohibitions and premature enforcements of sublimations, will tend to fixate and internalize anxious and painful affective discharge, and to fuse it with pleasurable modes of affective discharge. This will result in the development of pathological emotional behavior patterns of the masochistic variety.

In neurotic suffering the pleasure principle has lost most of its power, even though its efforts to reassert itself must not be underrated. But the outstanding examples of internalization of unpleasurable modes of discharge for psychoeconomical reasons are masochistic states. Whereas masochistic perversions (in my experience, especially those found in schizophrenics) represent an extreme pathological example of fusions between unpleasurable and pleasurable affect components, in conditions of moral masochism, and particularly in depressive affective states, the pleasure principle may become a complete victim of economic necessities. This is why these conditions appear to be "beyond the pleasure principle." In the case of grief and depression, the constancy principle attempts to reestablish a kind of psychic equilibrium, first, by an unpleasurable slowing down and inhibition of all the psychic discharge processes, and then by discharge in ways and modes which are painful and which in depression may also become dangerous from the viewpoint of self-preservation. In the light of this conception, self-destructive behavior and suicide would not indicate that the aggressive drives are beyond the pleasure principle and *aim* at the total elimination of tension. The explanation would be that, first, the pleasure principle is sacrificed in the effort to restitute the psychic equilibrium; in trying to enforce a lowering of the high tension level at any cost, the constancy principle eventually also fails in the function of self-preservation and can accomplish a total elimination only by self-destruction. In this context I refer to Schur's (1966) constructive discussion of the repetition compulsion. He assumes that "compulsive repetitiveness" with regard to traumatic experiences is an attempt to "undo the traumatic situation."

But there also are pathological conditions that show how the pleasure principle can achieve a triumph over the economic principles. This may occur whenever pleasurable discharges are pursued regardless of the general psychic economy and the functions of adaptation and self-preservation. This can be observed in the perverse and delinquent behavior of persons who have not accepted the reality principle. The most conspicuous examples, however, are manic states in which bound energy, mainly aggressive, is continuously mobilized and speedily discharged on the outside. Such processes may induce a spurious, enduring, pleasurable affective condition; but they occur at the expense of the psychic economy, which then breaks down completely and induces a general energetic impoverishment of the psychic apparatus. The manic excitement thus can result in a state of psychophysiological exhaustion which is no less dangerous than suicidal impulses and actions, as a consequence of and despite the fact that the pleasure principle is dominant and that aggression is discharged not in the self but on the outside.

THE ROLE OF THE SPEED FACTORS IN AFFECTIVE EXPERIENCES

In my rather extensive discussion of the pleasure-unpleasure qualities of affects and their relations to the increase and decrease of tension, I have not yet touched upon the laws that determine under which circumstances rises and falls of psychic tension induce pleasure or unpleasure. As mentioned above, Freud realized eventually that these affect qualities did not appear to be in direct proportion to the absolute height of tension; rather, they seemed to depend on the changes in the rise or fall of tension and on the relations of the latter to the rate of speed of the psychic processes. Although we are aware of the eminent role that this speed element plays in psychic release, we know very little about it. Yet the consideration of its influence on the affective qualities has already proved to be helpful in the study of specific affective phenomena.

Relevant examples are the studies of the musical process and the musical experience by Sterba (1946) and Kohut and Lavarie (1950); and Kris's (1939) contribution to the psychoanalysis of laughter, an affective experience that occurs when high tension is built up and then suddenly and speedily relieved. Kris emphasized the importance of the suddenness and the "surprise" element in this affective experience.

The analysis of laughter demonstrates that, for a psychic experience to evoke pleasure, the maintenance of a certain constant proportion between the given amount of excitation and the speed of its discharge is not required. What does matter for the specific pleasure or unpleasure qualities are the changes in the rate of speed, the changes of tension, and the changing proportions between the two.

At first glance it would seem that high speed and pleasurable feelings, and low speed and unpleasurable feelings, would be in direct proportions, depending, of course, on the amounts of excitation to be discharged. Instinctual excitation discharged directly and speedily appears to induce pleasure; but the same amount of excitation, if inhibited and hence more slowly discharged, seems to induce unpleasure. But this statement cannot be correct, especially if we remind ourselves how many affective explosions have a painful quality and how frequently sexual discharge occurs too speedily. We must therefore conclude that high-speed processes can induce unpleasurable feelings and that many low-speed psychic release processes are pleasurable, such as those that occur in enduring pleasurable feeling states. On the other hand, we cannot, in these cases, specify the exact proportions between the amount of excitation and the speed with which it is discharged. As pointed out above, our lack of quantitative measures for psychic forces and for the speed conditions imprisons us in the realm of vague surmises.

This much is certain: when we talk, for example, of unpleasurable feelings of high tension, we do not refer to the absolute level of tension. The amount of sexual excitation may be very large when the energetic flux reaches the highly pleasurable orgastic climax, whereas comparatively lower levels of tension may be perceived as unpleasurable excitement if the speed of the psychic process, particularly during the period of rising tension, is slowed down and the rate of speed—the acceleration—is changed by barriers blocking the discharge.

Certainly we find in the adult psychic organization a much greater variety of pleasure experiences that are not evoked by high-speed processes than in the primitive psychic organization. This is related to the development of the ego and the acceptance of the reality principle, i.e., to the gradual modifications of the affect patterns which I mentioned above. With regard to the speed element, adult tension tolerance and tension pleasure mean that the ego has succeeded in developing new, pleasurable, low-speed process patterns which, as the neurotic hyperaffectivity manifests, a weak ego may be unable to achieve. On the other hand, due to the severity of repression, the neurotic ego, more than the normal ego, may try to prevent acceleration, to slow down or modify the ways of release and discharge in certain undesirable psychic processes.

I would like to express at least some conjectures about the relationship that might exist between speed and rhythm and the different kinds of instinctual energy, i.e., libido, aggression, and the neutralized drives. What first catches the eye is the significant role of rhythm in libidinal processes, in contrast to the release of aggressive forces. In pregenital and genital libidinal release, this is apparently related to the peculiar interplay between sensory and motor excitations which induce and enhance each other. The differences in the psychophysiological pathways employed by the two kinds of drives for their discharge may also account for the climactic phenomena and the corresponding speed curves that genital discharge as well as many aim-inhibited libidinal processes manifest. Considering the explosiveness of aggressive phenomena, on the other hand, we can conclude that direct aggressive release seems to occur with higher speed than direct libidinal release. This would imply that the pleasure-unpleasure qualities of the two kinds of drives depend on different speed laws. We may also surmise from the observation of excited affective states such as rage, laughter, or orgasm—all of which may lead to convulsive motor phenomena—that there is some special connection between excitation of the motor apparatus and the high speed of energetic flux. This points to the influence of the psychophysiological channels employed by the drives on the speed of discharge and hence on the resulting affect qualities.

The psychoanalytic study of the instinctual vicissitudes has taught us that the libidinal drives have a particular plasticity and flexibility. This quality of the libidinal drives is probably related to the multitudinous pathways through which libido can be released. At the same time, the libidinal processes manifest a greater variability in the speed and acceleration of their release.

Whereas aggression is always linked with "activity" and "explosiveness," we commonly distinguish passive and active types of libidinal pleasure—notwithstanding the fact that all drives are of course "active." The striking differences between genital activity and pregenital passive pleasure—such as that gained by sucking, or by rhythmical stroking or rocking—certainly correspond to differences in speed and acceleration. In the latter type of pleasure it appears that sensory or proprioceptive stimulation mobilizes small amounts of energetic forces which can easily and pleasurably be discharged at low speed, whereas in genital discharge the speed curve takes a "dramatic" course.

A study of these different types of erotic pleasure makes us aware of the important role that outside stimuli play in the speed conditions of the psychic processes. The ideational and self and object representations in the ego represent central areas where psychic energy is accumulated, bound in lasting cathexes, and thus prevented from direct discharge. On the other hand, it appears that the outside stimuli have the function not only of helping to mobilize bound psychic energy, but also of cathecting and forming a sort of gathering pole at the stimulated area, which attracts and directs the energetic flux toward the site of final discharge. The speed of the discharge processes and the affective qualities thus depend greatly upon the quality and intensity of the external stimuli. The regulating and selective influence of the various types of external stimuli on the mode and speed of psychic release is of great importance for the special study of affective phenomena.

I conclude with a remark about the speed conditions in processes representing sublimated and autonomous ego functions, where mainly neutralized energy is released and discharged. Evidently it is this increasing neutralization, in the course of ego formation with its change of the qualities of the drives, that permits not only the binding of mobile energy, but also the acceptance and development of complex pleasurable affective experiences showing those intricate variations between high and low speed which characterize so many of the sublime pleasure experiences.

2

On the Child's Laughter and the Function of the Comic

In this chapter I shall call attention to one particular emotional manifestation: laughter and the development of humor in children. The clinical material which will be presented in support of my thesis does not stem from the analysis of children, but was derived from two adult cases. This has certain advantages. In the analysis of adults we frequently can trace adult personality traits back to their roots in specific childhood experiences; in this process the mechanisms underlying such early reactions are often more completely clarified than is possible in the analysis of children.

I

The psychological literature on laughter and related phenomena such as wit, humor, the comic, is so extensive that instead of giving a full bibliography, I refer to two tables found in "A Study of Laughter in the Nursery School Child" by Blatz, Allin, and Millichamp (1936). One table lists authors who have developed theories on laughter; the other is a review of observational and experimental work on laughter and smiling in children of different ages.

The psychoanalytic literature contains some fundamental contributions to the understanding of the comic. Freud initiated the discussion of this subject in *Jokes and Their Relation to the Uncon-*

First published in *The Psychoanalytic Study of the Child,* 2:39-60, 1946.

scious (1905b), which considers mainly economic and topographical perspectives. Freud showed that laughter provoked by wit results from a saving of psychic expenditure due to a momentary lifting of inhibiting forces which permits a return to infantile pleasures. Later Freud and others called attention to the role of ego and superego in comical productions and in humor. Reik (1929) investigated the role of introjection and projection in Jewish jokes by comparing them with manic-depressive mechanisms. Freud (1927b) interpreted humor as a spiteful triumph of narcissism and the pleasure principle over the miseries of life, effected by a momentary change of cathexis from the ego to the superego which, looking down from a bird's view, comforts the frightened ego as a father comforts a child in harmless trouble. Kris (1938) supplemented Freud's economic theory on laughter and wit by pointing to the importance of "the speed at which tension is relieved," to the "element of suddenness in this economic process [which] is responsible for the nature of comic pleasure." He suggested that "most comic phenomena seem to be bound up with past conflicts of the ego, that they help it to repeat its victory and in doing so once more to overcome half assimilated fear" (p. 89). It should be possible to confirm this and other analytic theories by clinical investigations, in particular of laughter and the comic in children.

Some special psychological studies on smiling and laughter in infants, preschool, and school children have been published by Brackett (1933), Blatz, Allin, and Millichamp (1936), Dearborn (1900), Justin (1922), Enders (1927), Kenderdine (1931), Washburn (1929). Bühler (1930), Gesell (1925), and many others have also touched upon the subject. Most of these authors have merely collected useful data about smile- and laughter-producing stimuli, from the observation of physical, social, and ideational experiences. No contributions to this problem have thus far been made by child analysts.

In studying the material referring to children up to three years we can clearly group the various stimuli according to common elements; this is worthwhile because it suggests hypotheses on the infantile origins of smile and laughter reactions.

The table given by Blatz, Allin, and Millichamp shows in the first place that especially smiling, but also laughter, occurs in infants and babies as a general reaction to or in anticipation of intense gratification of any kind. The table reveals, furthermore, that smiling—and much more conspicuously, laughter—are at a slightly higher age level (two years, two months) bound up with a great number of experiences, all of which are connected with the motor system.

Studies by Spitz and Wolf (1946), which were based on the research work of Kaila (1935), show that smiling is elicited from infants as a social response to an approaching person—specifically by the horizontal-vertical configuration of the face combined with the rhythmical nodding of the head toward the face of the child. This itself points to the significance of movement as a laughter-producing stimulus.

If we omit the purely emotional and ideational stimuli listed by Blatz et al., we see that laughter is elicited from children of two months up to two years by three groups of stimuli:

(1) by short, especially rhythmical, exteroceptive stimuli: tactile (tickling), visual (bright color, artificial light), auditory (loud noises);

(2) by proprioceptive stimuli: induced or voluntary fast motor activity of the whole body or parts of the body, at first particularly by rhythmical movements (e.g., first, shaking of hands and arms, swinging or tossing to the arms of another; later, active play, physical and verbal movement);

(3) by observation of sudden or fast movements of persons or objects (e.g., first, gestures, rhythmical hand-clapping or knee-dropping, peekaboo, quick movements of toys or bright objects; later, conspicuous or absurd mimic expressions, such as grimaces, laughing, funny talk).

Stimulation by sound, light, or color is usually described in combination with observation of fast movement: shaking of a rattle or bright toy, rhythmical hand-clapping, droll sounds, prattle, laughter, funny talk—all of which go along with conspicuous gestures or expressive movements of the face. Hence noise and light stimuli may be listed under groups (1) and (3).

It may be assumed that the observation of expressive movement, as in (3), has an "infectious" stimulating effect on the motor system, as, for instance, in the yawning, crying, and laughing of adults. This means that the child who observes fast movements does not actually participate in the experience; he does so only emotionally, finding release in laughter instead. Since the stimuli of group (3) are mentioned among those responded to earliest and most frequently, between the third and twelfth month, it may not be too daring to assume that this very inability of the baby to respond to the exciting perceptual stimuli with corresponding motor activity may help bring about a restriction of motor release; instead the child finds release in laughter, which involves only a specific muscle group —that which is exercised early and is therefore ready to function. In this connection we recall Kris's (1939) statement: just as in the development of mankind gesture language is replaced by verbal language, so in laughter archaic motor pleasure is revived and socially permitted.

Before investigating the three groups of stimuli further, we must ask whether there is a link between the smile as response to or in anticipation of intense gratification and laughter provoked by stimulation of the motor system. As all infantile cravings seek relief through the motor system, it is not difficult to understand that any intense gratification may elicit smiling, the mild twin of laughter, while the latter as a much stronger reaction becomes more specifically linked with experiences in the realm of the motor system itself.

Since stimulation of the motor system as such does not produce laughter, we have to search for the specific elements that are responsible for this effect. What appears to be of greatest importance is speed—the suddenness of the stimuli and the fastness of the movements, the factor stressed by Kris. There are, in addition, certain affective prerequisites for the production of laughter.

The observational material suggests that even in very early, simple laughter experiences—such as "tossing or swinging a child to arms of another" or "sudden reappearance of examiner from under a table"—a sequence of affects develops in two phases, coordinated to the stimulation and to the final discharge, which may alternate rhythmically and bring about waves of laughter.

There is first the initial phase of "thrill," i.e., of anxious tension mixed with quickly increasing pleasure which dissolves the fears. The fear elements stem apparently from the speed, the suddenness of the stimulating movements, i.e., the intensity of the motor experience. The pleasure is partly direct motor pleasure; partly it seems to be purely emotional enjoyment derived from an awareness of the harmlessness of the procedure and from anticipation of a most pleasurable end. The sources of these significant emotional prerequisites for the production of laughter are either memories or previous similar laughter experiences or social factors: the gay, joyful, promising attitude of the person who handles or is observed by the child. In the earliest smiling reaction, as studied by Spitz and Wolf (1946), the element of anticipation is represented by the visual impression gained from the configuration of the approaching face.

The second phase, the final discharge, often comes as a surprising climax, evidently brought about by the sudden slowing down or stopping of the movement; there is a sudden relief, with intense pleasurable convulsive motor discharge in laughter.

These two phases, and the affective and emotional components involved, may be exemplified in a typical laughter game which can be performed with children under one year:

A person lets his hand move up along the body of the child, who is in a prone position. This movement up toward the face is made with increasing speed, and is accompanied at first with slightly threatening sounds and facial expressions; then it is ended suddenly by tickling the child's neck and laughing. The child, after an initial stage of thrill, bursts out laughing.

In this and other similar laughter experiences the surprise factor plays an important part and is effective in provoking a sudden outburst of laughter. Incidentally, the example given is hardly different from laughter experiences in amusement parks, e.g., in the roller coaster. The speedy sliding down representing the first phase of thrill is followed by a second phase of slowing down, during which laughter occurs; this is followed again by another quick "risky" ride down, provoking a new wave of laughter.

Summarizing the elements common to the three groups of early laughter experiences as distinguished above, we come to the following formulation:

When intense, especially rhythmical, stimulation of the whole or a part of the motor system produces a sudden or surprising, fast, enjoyable experience which, though first suggesting danger, arouses pleasant anticipation of relief, laughter comes about as a final intensely pleasurable motor release. The original close relationship between laughter and motor experience paves the way for later stages in the development of laughter from a reaction to complex experiences of body mastery to, finally, a victory of the ego over the outer realistic and the inner instinctual worlds.

From their observations on laughter in nursery school children, Blatz et al. offer an interpretation that comes rather close to psychoanalytic theory: "Laughter and probably smiling may be considered as socially acceptable tics or compensatory motor mechanisms accompanying the resolution of conflicts that have, for a shorter or longer period, kept the individual on the horns of a dilemma" (p. 27). The experimental situations described in their paper clearly show that the nature of these conflicts hinges upon physical control or other ego achievements. Some examples of physical activities are: the child laughs after having reached the bottom of a slide, after having jumped into a pool, after a toy thrown by the child has landed in the water. In all of these examples, both intense fast motor activities and purposeful actions, physical achievements, are involved. In other words: laughter, produced in the previously described group by sudden or quick rhythmical movements or intense playful purposeless activity, is brought on here by successful motor functioning in the service of the ego. And as another series of experiments by Blatz et al. shows, it may finally be tied up with ego achievements that are no longer associated with physical activity.

Blatz et al. call these "completion of events," and conclude that in most cases of laughter it may be assumed that "the child foresaw the conclusion of the event. . . . He has learned by experience to expect this result. [But also] he has learned by experience that there are elements of danger in such a procedure" (p. 26). These observations and conclusions correspond well with the hypothesis offered by Kris (1938) and the formulation I stated above.

The decisive difference between complicated and simpler types of laughter-producing stimuli lies in the shift—caused by the ego's participation in the experience—to narcissistic pleasure components. They gain in importance as the experience is increasingly bound up with ego achievements in physical functions and with the mastery of instinctual conflicts, rather than only with expressive motor activity. As the ego becomes more involved in the experience, the fears provoked by the speed of movement stimuli are replaced by fears of the ego failing to master outer realistic or inner instinctual dangers. In both cases laughter comes about only if the fears are quickly dissolved by the anticipation of pleasure, which in the later complex experiences means the expectation of a victory by the ego, founded on the awareness of having learned how to master such a dangerous situation.

In complex comic phenomena, especially in comic art presentations, the categorical factor, i.e., the awareness of comic phenomena, such as the expectation of a joke that is going to be told, of a picture meant to be funny, of the happy end of a comic performance, contributes largely to the "anticipation of amusement" which counteracts the fears.

The laughter occurs in all cases apparently "after completion of the event." In the case of stimulation by fast movement it comes about when the movement stops; in complex laughter experiences, when the achievement is secured at the moment of success. It seems that one must here consider the role of the superego, which permits the laughter as a well-deserved reward; the successful ego can now afford to let down the defenses, regress to uncontrolled infantile pleasure, and find relief through the harmless channel of laughter.

With regard to wit it might be said that wit seduces the ego to spite the superego, and out of the awareness of its strength to permit regressive infantile gratification through laughter. With regard to humor it might be said that the experience starts with a feeling of real failure—or identification with it—which is overcome by part of the ego detaching itself, climbing up to the height of the superego, and undoing the failure by setting its strength against it, as if saying: the "real" core of myself is invulnerable, whatever happens elsewhere.

Another significant point must be stressed: the simpler and more primitive the laughter-producing stimulus is, the more does the laughter express "pure uncontrolled motor pleasure." The more complex the stimuli, the broader becomes the margin for the variety of affects and emotions that can be discharged through laughter, and the richer become the shades of laughter, e.g., from subtle tender amusement, to bright and joyful, to mildly ironical, to grim sardonic or triumphant laughter. While increasingly complex stimuli develop, simple primitive types of stimuli remain partly effective, and adult laughter experiences may come from sources that combine all kinds of stimuli.

A special role in the stimulation of laughter in the adult is played by observations which, as mentioned above, are also most effective and most frequent in stimulating the laughter of the child. It is highly interesting to compare the early, simple laughter experiences of this type, such as laughing at observing quick movements, with later ones, such as laughing at another person's physical or moral failure, and with most complex ones, such as laughing at jokes, cartoons, comic art performances.

I start with a comparison between laughter at observing quick movements and laughter at observing physical failure, e.g., when a person stumbles and falls on the street. In the first case the child apparently laughs as he participates in the movements. In the second case he laughs in reaction to the other person's "ridiculous" failure in regard to body control. In view of what has been said above, we may interpret the emotional process which arouses the laughter as follows: the observer feels at first tempted to participate in the observed uncontrolled movement, but in doing so experiences fright. (Children often laughingly mimic the gait of drunkards or similar "failures.") The observer's fears are quickly overcome by the realization of his own body mastery. Having thus established his feeling of superiority, he may now relax and again permit himself to participate in the experience through a similarly uncontrolled but socially accepted and harmless release, the outburst of laughter, which represents both pleasure and narcissistic triumph, and is in addition an outlet for aggressive impulses *(Schadenfreude)*.

II

The part played by instinctual conflicts in the production of laughter in children has not received any consideration. Except for Annie Reich's (1949) paper on "The Structure of the Grotesque-Comic Sublimation," no clinical papers have been published that might verify the correctness of analytic theories on this subject. As indicated in the introductory remarks above, the clinical material to be presented here has been gained not from the analysis of children but from adult patients. It refers, nevertheless, to laughter provoked in children by observations that mobilized instinctual conflicts.

Before presenting this material I shall insert a report on direct observations made in a nursery school. A psychoanalytically trained observer describes preschool children giggling and laughing in response to situations of instinctual danger:

Two-, three-, and four-year-old children of both sexes respond with a great deal of giggling to anxiety situations. At the age of two and three they often giggle in situations that concern awareness of sex differences. They do not giggle while actually observing the anatomical differences—they react rather with intentness, surprise, puzzlement, and other expressions. At the same time, however, they giggle about "absurd" displacements. For example, they use the words that have to do with genitals or with toilet functions, apply them to other objects, and laugh uproariously; or they change the word somewhat and use it out of context; for example, a child who refers to his stool as "po-po" may call some other child's penis "po-po-pony," and make a great joke of it. Similarly, they laugh inordinately at all absurd (i.e., displaced) situations: one child puts on a rubber without a shoe, and an epidemic of giggling goes through the nursery group. A child puts on another one's hat or shoes, and this provokes giggling, whether it was done originally as a clowning trick or by mistake. It is at three and four that the children giggle while they observe sex differences.

At first glance these observations seem to contradict the thesis of Kris that "comic pleasure . . . refers to a past achievement of the ego which has required long practice to bring it about" (p. 85). Children of two to four years have hardly achieved complete mastery over their toilet functions and are just beginning to cope with the dangerous problem of sex differences. This apparent contradiction can be resolved, however, by considering that the above-reported reactions were observed in a group situation. It may be assumed that in a group children draw sufficient mutual ego support from each other to feel momentarily masters of situations which would certainly produce anxiety if each of them were alone. The report indicates, moreover, that over a long period (age two to three) the children need defensive measures such as displacement, word distortion, symbolism, in order to bring about the giggling reactions, before they can directly laugh in response to anxiety situations (age three to four).

We are therefore justified in assuming that the observations do not contradict but rather confirm the thesis of Kris. The fact that group reactions are more complex and differ from individual reactions gives special importance to the analytic investigation of individual cases.

The two childhood memories reported below were recalled by adult patients at a time when the analytic work focused on their striking sense of humor, which they had used as an effective defense in the treatment.

III

The first patient, Mrs. A., was a fifty-year-old college teacher. After a few years of disappointing married life she had divorced her first husband and married another divorcé who had made her rather unhappy again. In her climacterium she developed severe depressions, precipitated by the lung infection of her only child, a son by the first husband. I shall focus here not on her depression, but on a personality trait that came to the fore when she was in a normal or slightly hypomanic state.

As soon as the patient emerged from her depression, she turned into a different person: a charming and brilliant woman who impressed people by her excellent sense of humor. Having a great capacity for perception—particularly of human weaknesses—Mrs. A. would make strikingly good, dry remarks about other persons as well as about herself, which would precisely "hit the mark." Her characterizations of people were astoundingly subtle and witty, varying between "tender ridicule" and sharp attack, according to her state of mind. One might say that she was a born caricaturist, her medium of expression being words. She herself was not much of a laugher, even when well; in fact, she rarely laughed aloud.

In normal states, her humor was good-natured and served, for instance, to help her students over painful situations of exposure. With the onset of a depression her humor would turn grim and gradually get lost in bitter criticism and complaints. Her smile and her laughing, losing their spontaneous quality, at first became strained, and later on, compulsive. During such periods her unnatural, embarrassed, or aggressive-apologetic laughing obviously pointed to the defensive function of her humor; such laughing occurred whenever unconscious anxieties were touched.

In her analysis Mrs. A. recalled a childhood memory which shed light on the unconscious origins of her sense of humor. When she was about four years old, she watched a little boy urinating and reacted with a "profound feeling of inner amusement." Thinking back on this incident, Mrs. A. felt sure that her amusement had expressed a feeling that this was "a pretty funny way for an inferior little boy to function." She did not remember feelings of envy. It was characteristic of her that as far as she could recall there had never been any definite overt desire to be a boy or a man, such as is frequently associated with a purer type of penis envy. Mrs. A. thought, though, that she was "inwardly tickled" by the performance and that "the tickled reaction was the shadow of envy." In her experience the threat to the ego was fused with some erotic stimulation, and the inner laughing substituted even then for the outer demonstration of her feelings.

The boy she observed belonged to a family in which there were many sons. They were next-door neighbors, members of a minority group, and of a much lower social class. Vaguely she connected these boys with dirty and sexual activities. In her family there were only girls. She had three older sisters and a younger one. Her father was at that time the only man in the family. (A brother was born when she was seven years old.)

The father came from a socially lower and less cultivated background than her mother. Moreover, he as well as two of Mrs. A.'s older sisters—one of whom was a "tomboy," the other known to have "masculine brains"—were afflicted with hernias, i.e., physical deformities. Accordingly, Mrs. A. had identified being a boy or being like a boy with moral and physical as well as social, national, and racial inferiority. Later on, her choice of husbands and professional friends corresponded to this concept. Her first partner, especially, had in many ways behaved like an inferior little boy rather than like a man.

Her disparaging attitude toward boys seemed at first to include her father. Material that appeared during the first period of analysis indicated that her oedipal attachment and her admiration of men had revolved around the figure of her grandfather. Her feelings toward her father, a queer paranoid personality of doubtful character, who had rejected and ignored her, had been a mixture of resentment, hurt, and contempt from childhood on.

Only in the last stage of analysis did we uncover very early sexual experiences with the father which had left deep traces in her emotional life. They were touched upon for the first time in association to two dreams. One was a dream about being on trial for having killed a child—a crime of which she felt innocent. In the other dream a baby fell off a table while she was preoccupied with professional work; again her feeling was that this was not her fault.

Both dreams reflected the recurrent and slightly paranoid complaints of Mrs. A. about being exploited, misjudged, or blamed for wrongs committed by others. The first dream was linked up with a recent experience. One of her husband's professional friends, a school principal, was on trial for having seduced and ruined a minor, who was his pupil. Mrs. A. had openly expressed her condemnation of his deed. When he was exonerated, she felt stupefied—as if she were condemned instead of him. The second dream specifically referred to her first husband. His behavior had been so irresponsible that it fully justified her contempt of his moral weakness. He had expected her to be the head of the family, had wanted her forever to be the giver, and had never permitted her to be the receiver. At the same time, he had always blamed and wronged her, projecting, as it were, his own faults onto her. Mrs. A. correctly suspected him of being jealous of her higher intellectual achievements. Whereas she actually shied away from any competition with both men and women, he had treated her as a masculine competitive woman, which in fact she was not.

Their conflicts had come to a peak when Mrs. A. had had her baby. Her husband had accused her repeatedly of being a career woman rather than a mother. Actually, her difficulties at that time had been caused not by her unwillingness to accept motherhood, but by her husband's complete failure to take over the part of a father and to support his family. She was forced to go back to work soon after delivery. She blamed him bitterly for having deprived her of the happiness of motherhood, which otherwise she would have enjoyed tremendously. He had, in reality, behaved almost as if getting a child was a crime for which she had to pay.

The neurotic attitude of her husband made Mrs. A. feel unjustly accused of aggressive masculine as well as of overpossessive feminine desires, whereas the role of a man and of an ever-giving mother had actually been imposed on her as a penalty for faults that were not hers but his.

The material showed that Mrs. A. had unconsciously fused the figure of the unethical school principal with that of her husband, and that both men represented her father. She had always blamed her father, who was a judge, for having only legal instead of true ethical codes. Since early childhood she had been aware that he, a representative of the law, had maintained a secret love relationship with a girl who was a regular guest in their home. As a little girl, Mrs. A. had shifted her curiosity about the sex activities of adults from her parents to her father and his mistress. Her suspicions were covered by a screen memory from the age of four or five: she was going with her sister to call on this young woman. She carried a package containing a toothbrush, which the latter had left on a visit to their house. When the young woman playfully asked what was in the package, the child replied, "Your toothbrush." The young woman then made a laughing wisecrack about such a great big package containing only a toothbrush. The child had felt ridiculed and very much hurt. Further associations showed that Mrs. A. had unconsciously identified with this woman in relation to her father, who later on abandoned his mistress with an illegitimate child.

The patient had recurring dreams of abdominal tumors. During the analysis she fell ill with attacks of colitis and in this context brought fantasies of an "unborn second child" and of oral impregnation causing malignant stomach diseases. All these fantasies, which at first seemed to relate to observations of her father and his mistress, turned out to have originated in even earlier childhood experiences.

Mrs. A. had been a sick, weak baby with feeding problems. Her mother, a conscientious but overstrict and cold woman, had never given her love, but had taken good care of her mainly to spite the father, who regarded the child as unfit to live. The little girl whose development was delayed was much ridiculed by her family as a little dumbbell until she went to school, where she turned out to be a brilliant student. The second sister, her father's favorite, stood out in her memory as the one who had teased her relentlessly by first flattering her and then ridiculing her for having been taken in by the flattery. Between three and four years of age, prior to the incident of "inner amusement," the patient had severe pneumonia. Once when she was very sick in bed she had overheard her father saying that it might be better if she died. The child recovered, and never forgot this "death sentence."

The last period of analysis brought evidence that during her first years of life, when the girls were not yet at school, the children had indulged in sexual activities: in mutual exhibition and probably also in genital play. This phase reached its climax during a long visit of a little girl cousin and her brother. In many of the patient's dreams these group activities were represented as "mass parties," in which Mrs. A. usually played the role of a neglected outsider. There were sufficient indications for assuming that the patient had experienced pregenital and genital overstimulation and some form of vaginal masturbation before the age of three. Moreover, during this period she must have been intensely envious of her older sisters' superior sexual organs and functions. She had believed that she possessed "no clitoris—well, hardly any" and for this reason could not masturbate manually the way her sisters did.

It is noteworthy that in this case where older sisters were the first objects of observation, the "clitoris envy" preceded the "penis envy" and was later on fused with it. During the early childhood years the "clitoris girls" were the superior children whom she later identified with the "little penis boys," as opposed to big men. This also accounts for the profound difficulties which Mrs. A. had to overcome later in life when she had to compete with both men and women.

This stage of uninhibited sex experiences ended, earlier than is common, with her severe illnesses between three and four. It was followed by a period of complete suppression of sex and aggression, accomplished by building up very strong and overstrict reaction formations.

Further associations about girls being impregnated against their will, or in a state of unconsciousness, revived vague memories of having been seduced to sexual activities by her older sisters and her boy cousin when she was still a baby, "too dumb to know what she did." As the analysis progressed, the material pointed more and more to very early sexual incidents. She had probably observed a sexual scene between her father and a German housemaid—possibly also an abortion performed on the same girl—all of this before the age of four.

A dream of lying in a crib and seeing a big penis in a beam of light focused on it was linked up with the memory of her father clamping his big hand on her mouth as she lay crying in bed. The associations suggested that Mrs. A., as a little girl of about two or three, might have watched her father's genital. She herself felt, with great inner conviction, that she had actually been seduced by him to touch his penis. According to further material connected with her father, it seemed likely that once as a baby, when she was in bed with him, her face must have come close to his genital, whereupon she had a bowel movement, for which her father beat her. In these memories her father's penis appeared to be fused with her mother's breast; they may therefore have referred to her mother rather than to her father. However far her experiences with her father had gone, they had evidently thrown her into panicky sexual excitations. Their specific nature was clarified by associations to the above-mentioned screen memory of his clamping his hand on her mouth. These excitations brought to the fore defensive wishes to bite off his fingers; these wishes covered deeper oral aggressions against his genital and, deepest of all, impulses to bite the breasts of her aggressive mother. It appeared that watching and touching her father's penis, and probably observing a fellatio performance—all of this happening at the preoedipal stage, as it were—had aroused overwhelming visual and oral impulses that were fused with panicky vaginal excitations.

Consequently, the kernel of her fantasies of oral impregnation and the "unborn second child" turned out to be the illusion of an incorporated intra-anal or intravaginal baby-phallus. Her illusory concept of a penis hidden inside of her body was supported, as is often the case, by the early arousal of anal as well as vaginal sensations.

It became clear that the little girl had considered the rejection and ridicule of her family, as well as the pneumonia, to be consequences of her early sexual fantasies and experiences. She regarded them, as later in life she regarded her bad marital and professional experiences and her child's illness, as punishments unjustly imposed on her by her father, the cruel judge, who condemned her to death while being the real culprit himself. This was the unconscious core of her complaints of always being blamed or punished for "crimes without guilt," crimes which the accuser himself had committed. It is understandable that these complaints revolved around feelings of being accused of castrative masculine and feminine strivings, of aggressively craving a penis or a baby.

We now turn our attention back to the childhood memory, her observation of the little boy's urinating. The uncovering of earlier sexual experiences with her father sheds light on the unconscious background of the little girl's reaction of "inner amusement." The sight of the little boy, the ensuing comparison between their genitals, was bound to have a traumatic effect. It would stir up envy and fear of the penis, oral and genital castrative wishes, urinary impulses, and anxieties about herself being castrated. Her way of overcoming the emotional upheaval was a revival of earlier scenes which conjured up the far more impressive picture of her father's genital and led to a comparison between previous and present experience. To put it in the words of the patient: "Compared with what I had seen before, this was nothing."

The comparison between past and present situations suggests various implications. The superficial realistic ones refer to her own different position and the difference between her partners in the two experiences: in the past she had been a helpless baby, dumb enough to be seduced and overpowered by her father's big genital; since then she had grown up and changed; there was no reason to get excited at nothing but a little boy's small penis. On a deeper, irrational level, however, her own unconscious fantasies led the comparison far beyond reality: "Compared with the big penis I took in, not only with my eyes, but in fantasy through mouth and genital, the little boy's penis is inferior. His performance is a 'ridiculous show.'" Her conclusion led to a reversal of the frightening present—and underneath, the past—situation: "It is not I who lack the penis, who am castrated and ridiculous. He is, whereas I possess a powerful genital inside of my body."

Since the patient's narcissistic inflation and the projection of her own deficiency onto the boy were based on objectionable fantasies, she needed further justification which she achieved by also projecting her guilt onto her partner. Again resorting to past experiences, in particular her secret knowledge of her father's and sisters' forbidden sexual activities, her train of ideas ended like this: ". . . and it serves him right to be laughed at, because I did nothing wrong. He—and my father and sisters—are the real culprits." Thus exonerated, the little girl could in righteous amusement permit herself to indulge in watching and inwardly laughing. With the same emotional act she rid herself of sexual and aggressive tensions and, for the moment, successfully overcame the castration trauma. That she reacted with "inner amusement," rather than with overt laughter, expressed the superiority of her "inner penis" and of "inner experiences" over the little boy's external genital and his "showy" demonstration. This attitude Mrs. A. maintained throughout her life.

Her "inward laughter" represented both an emotional discharge and a triumph of the ego which felt free of guilt and fear, at the expense of the little boy and, on a deeper level, of the father. The little girl could be all the more amused since the sight of the boy simultaneously proved to her that he was not really castrated: he did have a little penis, after all.

Mrs. A.'s childhood experience with the little boy shaped the pattern of her future sense of humor. It may be mentioned that the projection mechanism, which in humorous moods would lead to much pleasure and narcissistic gain, was partly sustained during depressive periods; having a different economic function, it was then sustained only as a defense which manifested itself in her paranoid complaints and criticisms. These would sometimes be accompanied by unnatural and strained laughing. Yet during periods of depression the patient would frequently identify, in dreams and associations, with the very persons who would otherwise be targets of her ridicule.

IV

Another patient reported a similar infantile memory of laughing in which the underlying mechanisms resemble in some ways those of the first case.

Mr. B., a forty-year-old bachelor, had a talent for charmingly telling good jokes and funny anecdotes. His humor had less pleasant aspects, however, and occasionally was rather grim or sardonic. I shall cite one especially interesting example. Mr. B. was extremely musical without being really creative, which he resented very much. His main hobby was to select the most imperfect work of a great composer and transcribe it for two pianos. He would do this masterfully, but in such a way that it would produce an overwhelmingly funny effect on his listeners.

Mr. B. was in treatment for phobic fears and difficulties in his love life. A typical Don Juan, he had had innumerable escapades with promiscuous girls, but also maintained long-lasting secret relationships with very respectable married women. He was constantly harassed by fears that his mistresses' husbands, with whom he always kept up cordial personal and even business relations, might discover his love affairs and retaliate by ruining him financially and socially.

The way in which Mr. B. selected his women friends and set up his triangle affairs clearly pointed to his infantile sexual fixations. One of his favorite sexual fantasies, which he eventually acted out while he was in analysis, was to have another man perform intercourse with his mistress while he watched, focusing his sexual interest on observing the woman having an orgasm. The analysis of his perversion took a long time because of the complicated vicissitudes of his instinctual drives. He had an interesting childhood memory of a watching experience which appeared to be a forerunner of his later perversion as well as of his sense of humor.

As a boy of seven he had spent his vacation with his mother at a fashionable summer resort. Lacking suitable company, he had felt lonesome. The other children around him belonged to a socially higher milieu. They were better dressed and better behaved than he. Their parents were respectable and distinguished, unlike his mother who was a divorcée. Gradually, he was accepted by this group, however, and then took part in their activities. Once the boys and girls arranged a game which ended in a general kissing scene. He did not participate. At first he was surprised and stupefied that these "nice" children would do such things; then, suddenly, he got into an elated state. Laughing and clapping his hands, he excitedly goaded them to continue and go further in their sexual amusements.

Associations to this screen memory revolved around his masturbation conflict. Throughout this summer the boy had been preoccupied with sexual fantasies involving the "nice and innocent" little girls around him. His thoughts had made him feel very guilty, as if he "polluted" or "raped" the girls in his mind. He was sure that the other "fine" boys of "good American stock" never masturbated and never had fantasies such as his. Full of admiration for their social and moral superiority, he had tried hard to maintain a façade of being a well-bred boy, who was, at least as far as moral integrity was concerned, their equal.

The kissing episode broke down his illusion. His discovery that these boys and girls behaved worse than he did revived earlier childhood memories, in particular of situations where he had been caught in sexual activities.

The leading memory went back to an incident that had happened at the age of five. He was caught in sexual activities, and at the same time had heard rumors about the bad morals of his parents. His father, though originally engaged to the patient's aunt, had seduced her sister; when the latter became pregnant, he had to marry her, although the child was born before the marriage. She divorced him after two years. When this aunt discovered the boy in sexual play with her little daughter, she made a violent scene with him and his mother, hinting at the bad morals of his parents as the reason for his naughtiness.

The boy had never gone through a true latency period because his belief in the moral standards of his parents had broken down too early. Feeling doomed to be as bad as they were supposed to be, he had built up reactive ideals, which he would pin on such superior, immaculate families as those he encountered in the summer resort. But being unable really to identify with them, he instead made an effort to imitate them. This caused a growing split in his personality, which reflected his parents' hypocrisy. He developed an outer façade of being a good, innocent baby, but led a secret, well-concealed inner life, absorbed by aggressive, sexual fantasies. His "secret" made him shy and timid at home and with other children, and constantly fearful of being "found out." When he entered school, he was ridiculed as a "sissy" by the other children who saw him as an overprotected, overgood child. His reaction to the ridicule was shown by the recollection of a scene in which he had urinated in the presence of his parents. His mother had pointed to his genitals and laughingly said to his stepfather, "Look how cute!" The boy had felt very ashamed, as though he had been caught masturbating.

When he saw the boys and girls in the resort kissing each other, he re-experienced his previous disillusionment in his parents, but now only in relation to the children and not to their parents. Although these children had such wonderful, superior parents, they were unmasked as being not better but worse than he, the son of bad parents. When they acted out what since the seduction of his little cousin he had done only in masturbation fantasies, it was they who deserved to be laughed at. His amazing discovery, depressing at first, quickly brought about a tremendous relief from guilt feeling and inflated his ego. His elation indicates that he had suddenly scored a moral triumph over the others—in the deepest layer, over his parents. Remaining a harmless passive onlooker, he now could secretly gratify his own sexual desires by watching and discharge his affects by applauding and laughing.

V

A summary comparison between the childhood memories of these two patients shows that they have much in common on the surface as well as in the unconscious core. The analyses revealed that prior to the specific incidents, both patients had frequently been ridiculed, supposedly because of sexual sins. In their early childhood both had made shocking discoveries about the sexual life of their parents or parent substitutes. In both cases the memories concerned the witnessing of a sexual performance of other children which, coming as a surprise to them, suddenly aroused instinctual impulses, in particular envy and the desire to participate in the performance, but also great anxieties. In the first case more distinctly than in the second case, the central conflict was the castration conflict. Both children warded it off by a successful projection mechanism which led to their laughing at the other parties. For this purpose they utilized memories of earlier childhood experiences: these involved, on the one hand, knowledge of their parents' sexual sins and, on the other, sexual incidents, similar to the present ones, in which they themselves had actively been engaged.

The comparison of past and present situations enabled both children to deny their own sinfulness, to project it onto their partners, and to retaliate for having been exposed and ridiculed by reversing roles. In this way they gained superiority over their seducers and over the present temptation as well as over their guilty past. In their roles of being merely passive observers, both children felt free to participate in the sexual performance through watching and laughing at the others the way they themselves had been watched and laughed at. In both cases the laughter or amusement response expressed a triumph of the ego and the pleasure principle, which relieved them of objectionable aggressive and libidinal tensions.

The present situation, fusing with and utilizing earlier events, evidently gave these children an opportunity to master the present as well as the past experiences. The successful outcome appeared to be due to the advances in ego development which had occurred since their earlier experiences. Looking back, the children felt strong enough to do what they had been unable to do then: to exert sufficient control over their instinctual impulses. With the growth of this capacity they were able to unmask, condemn, and laugh at their seductive partners and parents. Moreover, the incidents which provoked their laughing reactions occurred with persons who were neither their parents nor adults. The sinners whom they unmasked and laughed at were children, equals in age, though admired or envied as superiors. In the case of the boy I emphasized that he depreciated the other children as bad offspring of respectable parents. He thus maintained an idealization of the latter, while he unmasked the sins of the former.

It is also of interest that the laughter reaction of the boy, like the "inner amusement" of the girl, was supported by the awareness that "nothing really bad or serious" had happened to the other party, after all. The girl realized that the little boy she observed did have a penis; the boy knew that what he had seen was only a game approved of by a group of children who nevertheless remained what they had previously been: "immaculate little girls" and "fine American boys."

When later on Mr. B. re-enacted the triangle scene, he was disgusted with his girlfriend for "taking it seriously" instead of regarding it as "only an amusing little game."

In both cases analysis uncovered the change of narcissistic cathexis, the elation of the ego, the victory of the pleasure principle, and "the saving of psychic expenditure" at the moment of laughter, all of which had been posited by Freud in his explanations of humor. The amusement of the two children, however, was not yet a truly humorous reaction; rather, it was a forerunner of the sense of humor which both developed later in life as characteristic personality traits. Being an infantile reaction, it lacked the precious wisdom and mild superiority of humor. The laughing of the children meant a narcissistic victory at the expense of their partners, a triumphant retaliation, achieved by projection mechanisms which were induced by comparisons between past and present experiences.

VI

The childhood memories presented here have another distinctive characteristic in common: both children behaved like an audience at a comical (funny) performance. This circumstance induced me to end this chapter with a short excursion into the field of comic art.

The type of comic art I have in mind here is the American comic film in which the hero goes through an endless series of calamities, disasters, and persecutions which provoke roaring laughter in the audience. The comical effect resembles that achieved by the clown, who does everything wrong and is constantly beaten up, or by the funny dwarf of past centuries, whose misshapen figure, in grotesque caprices, amused his master.

Kris (1934) speaks of the clown as a figure related to caricature. He explains the art of caricature by tracing its origins back to primitive magic charms and to the belief that the picture is identical with the object depicted. Although caricature is related to ancient customs of punishing distorted pictures of adversaries in effigy, it is really supposed to affect not the enemy but the onlooker. Magical thinking, the primary process, does not control the artist; he masters and uses it for his artistic goals.

What distinguishes the clown and his modern counterpart, the helpless and hapless film hero, from caricature is that he is a living, gesturing, speaking, and acting figure. For this reason the effect of caricature is short-lived, that of the clown or comic film hero prolonged. On the other hand, as is the case in caricature, the clown and the comic film hero are endowed with certain exaggerated characteristics which "unmask" their inferior personality and make them ridiculous.

This is precisely what the two patients did in fantasy to the children whom they were watching. What they accomplished by a complicated emotional process, the transformation of a potentially threatening scene into a performance which from their subjective view was only funny, the artist achieves by the comic art presentation. Apparently he stimulates in the audience psychic mechanisms similar to those that made the two children laugh.

Let us call to mind the comic film hero who in pursuit of some ridiculous goal meets with catastrophes, falls and hurts himself, is persecuted or beaten up. Whereas the spectacle of such suffering and calamity would normally invite unpleasant identifications and arouse anxiety, aggression, disgust, sympathy, and pity, the audience roars with laughter. Yet on closer observation one discovers that the waves of laughter are interrupted by brief periods of tension, which is discharged again in new outbursts of gaiety. These interpolated tensions indicate what I have previously said about the laughter reaction to seeing a person stumble and fall: identification with the hero, participation in his actions, does not completely obviate the comical effect; on the contrary, it induces it (Kris, 1939).

The audience, tempted to identify with the unfortunate hero, immediately escapes from such painful sympathy by having a good look at him. Seeing this caricature of a hero, his grotesque gestures and actions, the onlooker can say to himself: "This cannot happen to me. I am a different person; in fact, a wonderful person compared with such a misfit."

In other words, the comic film permits the onlooker, having made a tentative identification, quickly to detach himself again from the suffering hero by unloading onto him—as did the two patients—all the inferiority he dreads having himself, the sins and weakness of the past which he has long since mastered. As he succeeds in warding off the danger of painful sympathies, he withdraws them from the victim and switches to the pursuer. Like the two children, he feels: being punished serves this impossible fellow right; and he discharges his affects and his own mobilized infantile impulses in laughter and *Schadenfreude*—pleasure in the hero's being hurt. He can do so all the more freely because he is certain of the "happy ending." Nothing serious is going to happen, anyway. "Laughing means: enjoying the misfortunes of others, but with a good conscience" (Nietzsche).

Those who know the German humorist Wilhelm Busch, painter and poet, may recall the last rhymes of "Pious Helen," one of his best creations. It depicts Uncle Nolte, who represents the reader and onlooker, after learning about the tragicomic death of his sinful niece Helen: at first mourning, then moralizing, and at last looking up to heaven hypocritically, with a broad grin. I append my translation of the verses:

When Uncle Nolte heard the news
He was distressed and had the blues.

But having mourned enough and cried,
He said, "I told you so, all right!
Good deeds—this principle is true—
Are bad ones that you fail to do.
Well, well!—I'm really glad, my friend,
Because, thank God, I'm different!"

[Als Onkel Nolte dies vernommen,
War ihm sein Herze sehr beklommen.
Doch als er nun genug geklagt:
"O!" sprach er, "ich hab's gleich gesagt!
Das Gute, dieser Satz steht fest,—
Ist stets das Böse was man lässt.
Ei ja!—Da bin ich wirklich froh!
Denn, Gott sei Dank! ich bin nicht so!"]

3

Normal and Pathological Moods: Their Nature and Functions

THE GENERAL NATURE AND CHARACTERISTICS OF MOODS

As a point of departure for the study of moods I resort to a practical, commonplace example which shows mood vacillations within a normal range in a young man, named John.

John had fallen in love with a girl, Anne. His emotional situation resulted in experiences which evoked conspicuous moods. John had spent a very pleasurable evening with Anne, who had shown most favorable responses to his courtship. Having left her in a very happy mood, he had fallen asleep with marvelous daydreams and woken up in high spirits. He devoted himself eagerly to his daily work, looking forward to the next evening which he again would spend with his sweetheart. His happy, elated mood lasted all day.

But in the late afternoon he called her up to confirm their date and was shocked to learn that she had decided not to see him for the next three days. She gave no reasons. The level of his mood dropped sharply. During the next days he tried in vain to persuade

---

This chapter is based on "On Normal and Pathological Moods: Their Nature and Functions." *The Psychoanalytic Study of the Child,* 12:73-113, 1957.

The present version has been modified in the light of my own formulations presented in *The Self and the Object World* (1964) and those suggested by E. M. Weinshel in his paper on "Some Psychoanalytic Considerations on Moods" read on December 16, 1967, New York, and published in 1970. In this contribution to the panel on "The Theory of Affects" Weinshel corrected some of my errors and called attention to a series of very significant points which I had neglected.

her over the phone to change her mind or to give him at least a plausible explanation for her behavior. Her responses alternated between kind, even loving, and cool, detached, or even hostile ones. She appeared to be in a conflict whose causes were unknown to the unfortunate lover.

Dependent on her attitudes, John vacillated during these days between periods of rather good, expectant moods and angry, irritable, sad, hopeless, dejected, and depressed moods. When he was in a good mood, he anticipated gratification from all the world around him; he slept well and got up early; he disregarded the rainy weather, the disagreeable attitude of his boss, the negligence of his typist. Insofar as his attention was not diverted by thoughts about Anne, he could think and act more quickly and imaginatively than he usually did, and cope easily with the manifold difficulties in his job and everyday life. When his mood was bad and angry, he reacted with irritation to his superior, with temper outbursts toward his secretary, and got into a row with another car driver. When sadness overcame him, he was flooded by memories of sad events in the past and present and felt like weeping. When he was discouraged and depressed, he felt inert and indecisive; he was, indeed, not in a mood to work or to be active at all.

His moods affected even his characterological peculiarities, e.g., his reaction formations. In general John was a kindly man, given to intensive reactions of pity when confronted with suffering. In a happy and elated mood, however, the successful lover tended to ignore the gloomy aspects of life around him altogether; and while his mood alternated between hopeless, dejected, and furious, the sight of suffering made him feel either sorry for himself or angry and disgusted with the world around him. John's rapid and intensive emotional vacillations also disclosed his (constitutional or acquired) propensity to react with strong, though not pathological, mood fluctuations to both pleasurable and painful experiences.

From the description of the various familiar mental phenomena which John displayed, we may draw some basic inferences with regard to the nature of moods in contrast to affective states of a different order. John's being in love, for instance, is an enduring feeling state, but it is certainly not a mood. With the changing fortune in his love, he underwent a variety of pleasure and unpleasure experiences that alternatingly expressed specific libidinal and aggressive discharge patterns. They reflected either John's sexual and emotional neediness, his expectation of relief, his gratification, or his frustration, his disappointment, his dissatisfaction. Even these different emotional reactions do not represent moods, but they induced a series of mood conditions.

These changing moods found expression in particular qualities of his feelings as well as of his thought processes and his performances during the whole day, no matter what their object had been. They affected his emotional responses, his attitudes, and behavior with regard not only to his girlfriend, but also to his work and to the whole surrounding object world, and influenced the choice and the course of all his activities.

In this context Weinshel's remarks (1970) are pertinent. He speaks of the ambiguous, shadowy, or even "slippery" quality of moods. He emphasizes their complex, highly refined nature, and points to both differences and close relations between moods and specific character traits.

Moods seem to represent, as it were, a cross-section through the entire state of the ego, lending a particular, uniform coloring to all its manifestations for a longer or shorter period of time. Since they do not relate to a specific content or object, but find expression in specific qualities attached to all feelings, thoughts, and actions, they may indeed be called a barometer of the ego state.

The ubiquity and uniform coloring of a mood, its distinct and pervasive nature, and the obvious connections between its various manifestations are responsible for its conspicuousness. Without knowing the whole complex gamut of a person's feelings and thoughts at a particular time, we can indeed guess his mood from his facial expression and behavior, even if he is not fully aware of it. Since mood manifestations actually represent a unit, the separate investigation of the feeling aspects of a particular mood, even if it be in the foreground, is of course inadequate without concomitant scrutiny of the associated phenomena in the realm of thoughts, attitudes, and actions.

My statements are in keeping with Webster's brief definition of mood, which expressly designates mood not as an affective state but as "a particular state of mind, especially as affected by emotion, as to be in a mood to work." This definition also refers to the fact that moods, as in my example, are induced by significant emotional experiences expressive of one or more focal discharge processes. Such an experience may be stimulated from within (through physiological or purely psychological processes) or from without, and need not come to full awareness. It may be significant either in terms of the current reality or because it is associated with significant conscious or unconscious memories. But whatever the part of past or current events in the provocative experience, the ensuing mood manifests the spreading influence of the focal discharge process, of which this experience is expressive, on all other discharge patterns. Hence, the moods must reflect common qualities and characteristic deviations in the speed course and rhythm of the sum total of drive discharge processes that develop over a certain limited span of time. They may be designated as a temporary fixation of generalized discharge modifications. Once a mood has established itself, it affects all patterns of responses to stimuli or objects of the most diverse kind, including, as in my example, typical, individually acquired emotional responses to specific stimuli; e.g., reaction formations, such as shame or pity, individual preferences or dislikes.

This brushing off of particular qualities and modifications of focal and affective discharge patterns on all others distinguishes the nature of moods sharply from that of affective states, such as love or hate and their manifold derivatives, which develop from specific, though possibly complex, tensions and relate to definite ideational representations. The nature of such states is determined not only by the specific drive quality and by the stability and intensity of the cathexes, but—in contrast to the moods—by the specific objects in which the feelings are vested.

It is noteworthy that these object-directed emotional states as such are not even characterized by pleasure-unpleasure qualities. Feelings of pleasure or unpleasure arise only with gratification or frustration of the underlying strivings, under the influence of ego and superego which help to mold the various discharge patterns. Moreover, such feeling states and the discharge reactions which develop with their varying vicissitudes may become moods as they spread out and dominate the whole field of the ego for a certain span of time. Thus, anger at somebody or something may turn into an angry mood, love or hate into a kind of hostile mood, anxiety into an anxious mood, as soon as they have ceased to relate only to special, selected objects or ideas.

When scanning our common vocabulary for moods, we detect that they cover a very broad field of mental states. The mood attributes refer by no means only to pleasure-unpleasure qualities, or to a high or low level of mood. They are not even restricted to feeling qualities, but may point to ideational and such functional and behavioral aspects as are predominant in the mood manifestations. For example, we may be either in a dull, an uninspired, in an alert, a creative, or in a contemplative, thoughtful, philosophical mood.

In addition, as mentioned by Webster, we speak of being or not being in the mood to do this or that, such as this morning feeling or not feeling in the proper mood to work, in the evening to turn to our preferred hobby, and at night to have fun or rest.

Although a particular mood asserts itself indiscriminately in relation to all kinds of objects, it may also stimulate a special type of pursuit. In this case we describe the mood quality according to a different category than in the case of a good or bad, a sweet or angry mood. We refer to an awareness or an impulse indicating that our discharge patterns are at that time especially well suited for certain aims, pursuits, or objects. In a state of gaiety, for instance, a person will be in a mood to joke or listen to jokes. Such moods may originate in an initial experience of a special quality, the repetition or avoidance of which appears desirable. Gratifying work may keep us in a mood to work, or even encourage continued absorption in the same subject; being fed up with a special kind of activity may, by evoking unconscious or conscious wishful fantasies, result in a mood to do the opposite, such as to seek pleasure instead of work.

It is almost impossible to classify moods, except according to categories which either are on different levels or overlap with each other. Moods may, e.g., be popularly classified as good or bad moods, a distinction that refers primarily to pleasure-unpleasure qualities but hints at a general prevalence of libidinal over aggressive drive discharge: both the angry and the depressed mood must be considered "bad" moods. But someone might be in a triumphant mood which is felt to be good and pleasurable, though based mainly on aggressive discharge. On the other hand, sadness, which must be regarded as a "bad" mood, appears to involve special libidinal discharge patterns. Moods may also be distinguished from the perspective of the speed of discharge, according to high or low mood levels, which do not quite correspond to good or bad mood qualities. One may be keyed up or excited in a pleasurable or unpleasurable way, with a prevalence of either libidinal or aggressive discharge phenomena. Or a person may be in a quiet, either happy or gloomy mood. Moreover, moods might be distinguished according to the conspicuous prevalence of mood phenomena in the area of feelings, thoughts, or actions, such as a happy or an unhappy mood, a thoughtful or dull mood, an enterprising or lazy mood, an apathetic or enthusiastic mood (Greenson, 1953, 1962).

This only goes to show that attempts at mood classifications are neither very promising nor very constructive. But the attempt to classify them according to qualities, in whatever category, makes us aware that we commonly conceive of moods in a dualistic way; i.e., in terms of good or bad, happy or unhappy, high or low, active or passive, kind or angry, etc. This reflects, of course, the unmistakable dualism in all psychobiological happenings: the drive dualism, the vacillations between tension and relief, and the inevitable changes between pleasure and unpleasure enforced by reality.

So far moods have been defined as a temporary fixation of generalized discharge modifications, induced by a significant experience whose discharge pattern lends its qualities to all discharge patterns. But precisely how can characteristics of a focal discharge process impose themselves on all discharge processes?

To produce a mood, the provocative experience must be of a particular intensity and cause unusually high energetic tensions which cannot be immediately and sufficiently relieved by a focal discharge process only. In this case the memories of the provocative experience will remain strongly hypercathected; thus they may attain the power to influence the energetic and cathectic conditions in the whole realm of the ego.

In John's case, for example, his happy experience with Anne not only had left an intensely vested memory of his initial success and gratification. Its stimulating effect had been such that it replenished him for a certain period with libidinal surplus energy sufficient to raise the narcissistic and object cathexes in all areas of his ego by virtue of general cathectic displacements. Thus during that delightful day the libidinal resources at John's disposal were richer, while the aggressive forces had been reduced. Consequently his self-esteem rose not only as a lover, but also with regard to his abilities in other areas. He likewise showed increased libidinal investments not only in Anne, but in the whole world around him. At this point the significant factor of anticipation had been called into play. Drawing general inferences from his initial success, John from now on anticipated happy and gratifying experiences modeled after the first one; not only with Anne, but with all other objects around him.

This inner situation can be described in a different manner. The replenishment and the redistribution of the libidinal forces through generalized cathectic shifts had evidently resulted in temporary, qualitative modifications of the concepts of the self *in toto* and of the entire object world. These concepts had assumed a special coloring whose optimistic quality differed from the usual one. Generalized complementary notions had been fixated in John: he thought of himself as an active, successful, happy-go-lucky fellow, and accordingly of the world around him as a gratifying, benevolent, pleasurable place. With regard to the object world, these notions represented a generalized transference of certain hypercathected, pleasurable attributes from Anne to all objects; with regard to himself, the generalization and temporary fixation of a momentary, hypercathected, correspondingly pleasurable aspect of the self. The hypercathexis of such special notions can apparently be sustained only through hypocathexis of all contradictory inferences derived from past experiences, i.e., by way of a temporary denial of unsuitable memories. (I shall discuss the tendency to generalization in Chapter 4.) By calling the respective notions "complementary," I wish to convey that they always reflect a definite aspect of the interrelationship between the representations of the self and the object world. In a particular mood we might indeed consciously feel: today I am a different person and have a different relation to the world; and the world, in turn, looks different in relation to me.

In John's case, his pleasantly modified optimistic notions then became the carrier of correspondingly hopeful fantasies that induced further pleasurable reactions and successful, gratifying actions. Had John had a striking success in a competitive business transaction, he would also have felt elated. But in this case his experience might have favored a triumphant mood expressive of increased aggressive investments in all kinds of objects and pursuits; this would have given impetus to further aggressive reactions and actions. This only goes to show the extent to which the proportion between libido and aggression, and their distribution in the cathexes of the self and the object representations, influences the mood qualities and the whole ego state. Since our moods affect our attitudes and behavior patterns, the responses we get as a result of our actions will commonly tend to confirm and promote the notions on which our mood is based, until reality interferes sufficiently to bring about changes of these concepts and consequently of our mood. John's good mood, for instance, lasted as long as the hypercathexis of his happy memories and of the concepts based on them could be maintained in the face of reality. The influence of reality on moods will be discussed in greater detail below.

To repeat: it appears that an experience causes a change of mood only if it can bring about qualitative changes in the representations of the self and of the object world. It stands to reason that the temporary fixation of such drastic qualitative modifications can then, in its turn, exercise a generalized influence on the qualities of all discharge patterns.

This description is of clinical value inasmuch as it directly pertains to familiar phenomena observed in pathological mood conditions. We know that in depressed and elated states the whole self is felt to be "different," either bad and inferior or good and superior, and the entire object world correspondingly appears unpleasantly or pleasantly transformed. But we must realize that not only in pathological but in any type of mood variations, our self and object representations undergo such qualitative modifications. Certain shades within the normal range of moods, which have little reference to special pleasure-unpleasure qualities, arise from very subtle modifications of the object and self representations. These are moods whose attributes point not to emotional or functional characteristics, but to ideational trends, e.g., the contemplative, thoughtful, philosophical moods previously referred to.

At this point I want to refer again to Weinshel's paper. He suspects that he may have overemphasized the "structural" aspects of moods, but I did not really consider the moods as "psychic structures," or at least avoided using the term as broadly as Rapaport suggested. Apart from that, however, I am in full agreement with Weinshel's "most crucial statement":

> [Moods] are psychological structures, of varying complexity and stability, reflecting a certain degree of synthesis and organiza-

> tion, and depending on contributions from all three psychic systems. . . . In the mood, we can observe a mixture of affects as well as the products of varying defensive activities directed against the affects. It is likely that the overall mood structure helps play a part in the binding of affects; and the bound affects, in turn, contribute to the overall mood structure. At times, the affective discharges associated with moods appear to be massive and relatively archaic; at other times, the affects involved reflect the development of highly differentiated affect discharge structures; and often both extremes coexist [p. 315].

All these statements are most significant, and especially so with regard to the nature and function of moods.

THE ECONOMIC FUNCTION OF MOODS; EARLY MOOD PREDISPOSITIONS AND THEIR DEVELOPMENT

We are indebted to Freud (1917) for his remarks on the constructive economic function of the mourning process which accomplishes the gradual return of libido to current, realistic aims and gratifications. Freud concluded that pathological depressive processes seemed to have the same economic effect. Our previous scrutiny of the processes underlying mood conditions in general, however, permits us to extend Freud's economic considerations even further.

If it is characteristic of all moods that they allow a repetitive affective discharge on a great number and variety of objects, such a prolonged discharge in small quantities, combined with reality testing, must liberate psychic energy from fixated positions and reopen the gate to new investments. This gradual discharge process certainly tends to protect the ego from the dangers of too explosive, overwhelming discharge, even though moods do not preclude and may induce repeated, sudden, dramatic discharge reactions, such as outbursts of sobbing or laughter or anger. Thus, moods in general appear to serve a definitely useful, though primitive, economic function. The ultimate economic success will, however, depend largely on the extent to which this prolonged discharge process permits true reality testing. In this respect we find decisive differences between normal and anomalous mood conditions, which will be discussed below in the comparative study of normal and pathological moods.

In view of the primitive nature and function of moods, it is not surprising that we find a propensity to moodiness, inappropriate moods, and conspicuous or prolonged swings of mood in persons who are characterized by a particular inability to tolerate tensions, to accept loss as a frustration; persons whose ego operates predominantly on a primary process level with high quantities of deneutralized psychic energy which threaten to be discharged suddenly.

We must assume that such persons call on this primitive type of economic regulation so continuously and conspicuously because they are in need of it. Their ego evidently lacks the capacity for subtle, "secondary process" modes of economic functioning and affective defense; it does not have a sufficient number or variety of discharge channels and differentiated discharge patterns at its disposal. Since this is indicative of either an arrested or a regressively archaic ego and superego structure, we are not surprised to find that the mood pathology is so prominent in psychotic disorders. Even though psychotics and to some extent also neurotics display an economic need and hence a propensity for conspicuous mood deviations and pathological mood qualities, we must emphasize that the normal ego, too, preserves the use of this primitive modality.

For very good reasons Weinshel does not agree with the emphasis which I originally laid on the primitive nature and function of moods. In fact, I believe that at that time my ideas on moods, in general, had been unduly influenced by clinical observations of pathological moods.

Weinshel underscores correctly that

> . . . there are so many different moods, which tend to vary considerably in their structure and organization, the quality of their composition and components, and their overall relationship to the ego and its functioning. Therefore it may be preferable to speak about archaic elements within the mood rather than labelling them, in a blanket-fashion, as archaic. . . . in addition to the more archaic discharge patterns that can be detected in moods, we can also observe the operation of higher level, more organized discharge patterns of secondary process as well as primary process activity, of tension maintenance as well as peremptory discharge. . . . The quality and the nature of the processes involved is not necessarily archaic. On the contrary, the latter are not infrequently neutralized and relatively highly differentiated and developed . . . without the 'quasi-stability' provided

by the mood structure, the more disorderly affect discharge would interfere with many of these functions. . . .

Consideration should be given, then, not only to the complexity and the stability of these mood structures but to the 'elegance' with which the ego is often able to combine diverse psychic elements, emanating from varied sources and reflecting multiple levels of development, into some semblance of unity and harmony. I would also stress . . . that this is not distinctive of all moods and that the degree of this elegance, harmony, and stability shows a marked variation in different moods and in the same mood at different times [p. 317f.].

These statements are quoted because I feel that they contribute greatly to our understanding of the nature and function of moods.

In John, for instance, I described a sequence of rather normal mood phenomena that developed his experiences with Anne. To be sure, John showed a definite proclivity to strong and rapid mood vacillations. Evidently his ability to keep his narcissistic and object-libidinal cathexes on an even keel, notwithstanding outside influences, was not too well developed. Although his mood qualities remained within the common affective range, we might regard his mood instability as marginal or, at least, as expressive of a particular mood predisposition.

In persons with definite mood predispositions we find a conspicuously frequent recurrence of special, temporarily fixated modifications of the concepts of the self and the world, based on generalized inferences and transferences from the past. In people with chronic mood deviations, such as chronic pessimists or chronic optimists, these concepts and the resulting discharge patterns become enduringly fixated.[1]

Within the frame of general affective predispositions we can, in fact, observe individual predispositions to certain prevailing or recurring mood conditions already in earliest childhood; e.g., to even or uneven, to good or bad moods, or to definite mood vacillations. Of course, little children display noisier and more intense affective

[1] The special meaning of "fixation" in this frame of reference, versus fixation in the common analytic usage of the term, is self-evident. By (infantile) fixation we mean either the tendency to respond to certain stimuli with preferred discharge patterns modeled at earlier developmental stages, or else the enduring hypercathexis of a special conscious or unconscious object representation. In this connection I may express the suspicion that the lasting infantile fixation to a love object always goes along with the fixation of corresponding infantile features of the self representations.

manifestations in general because of the still insufficient ego-superego control. Their moods are usually of brief duration and change rapidly. Their inability to sustain moods, especially painful moods, for a long time is due to the relative instability of object cathexes, their tension and pain intolerance, their readiness to accept substitute objects and gratifications. The affective scale of children is more limited owing to the developmental lack of ego differentiation. As a result of constitutional and environmental influences, of instinctual maturation, of ego and superego formation, early infantile affective and mood predispositions will thus naturally undergo many changes. But at any developmental stage they constitute an outstanding characteristic of the total personality.

An individual's general affective predisposition reveals his inherent preference for special affectomotor reactions. The mood predisposition, on the other hand, reflects his greater or lesser tendency to fixate, for longer or briefer periods, special concepts of the self and the world, and, consequently, special affectomotor discharge patterns, with but scant regard to the varying external stimuli.

Regarding the early infantile influences on the development of pathological mood predispositions, we can easily visualize the impact of repetitive or prolonged exposure to the same type of experiences, such as overgratification or deprivation. Their influence on the mood development is especially harmful at a stage when the need-gratifying object is still the main representative of the object world and when the child, as yet unable to discriminate between different objects, has a natural tendency to easy cathectic displacements from one to all objects. In such a child the primitive tendency to generalize his experience will be maintained and become the carrier of a definite, anomalous mood predisposition.

From the psychoanalytic study of manic-depressive states, which show a severe pathology of the superego functions, we know that superego formation has a singular influence on the development of affect and mood control and thus of mood predisposition. I touched upon this problem in my paper (1954) and book on *The Self and the Object World* (1964) where I discussed the complex control system arising with the constitution of the superego. Suffice it to repeat that superego formation has a modulating effect on emotional expression in general; that the rises and falls of self-esteem become specialized indicators and regulators of the self- and object-directed cathexes in the total ego, and of the resulting discharge processes.

We must realize, however, that the main function of the superego in normal adults is a selective one. In fact, only as long as guilt feelings remain localized and refer to specific—conscious or unconscious—forbidden strivings can they serve as an effective warning and directive signal. Then they do not induce a mood, but set the defensive activity of the ego in motion. But the presence or absence of generalized superego pressure tends to inhibit or stimulate ego activity in general by slowing up or hastening the speed of object-directed discharge, irrespective of special aims and objects, in a uniform manner. In this case superego approval or disapproval will no longer relate to special, unacceptable instinctual strivings; it will refer to opposite notions of the total self in terms of black and white, of "being good, expecting reward" or "being bad, expecting punishment." Such generalized notions may also develop in normal persons and cause mood vacillations within a limited range. The ego will then make temporary use of a more primitive economic modality, at the expense of superego function at a higher level. But defective superego structure or superego regression may lead to a permanent loss of the signal function of the superego, which is then replaced by a tendency either to conspicuous rapid or extreme pathological mood swings, or to a more or less fixated lowering or rising of the mood level.

No doubt the role of the superego and of superego formation in the establishment of general affect and mood control is most significant. Yet it must be repeated that long before superego formation, some children may show an impressive mood stability, whereas others may very early suffer from unusual moodiness or even from infantile types of mood pathology.

The conspicuousness of such early infantile affective and mood predispositions shows the extent to which they are determined by such factors as the child's inherent drive intensity, the depth and intensity of his object cathexes, his inherent tendency to respond to frustration, hurt or deprivation with lesser or greater, rapidly passing or more enduring ambivalence. Thus we must not overrate the influence of the superego and of superego formation on the moods and the level of mood. Moreover, with complete maturation during the period of adolescence, the superego's rigid, controlling grip becomes relaxed, permitting the ego greater freedom and flexibility. Its influence then extends mainly to the regulation of the mood level and to the toning down and modulation of moods and affects in general. But the manifold and rich affective colors reflect the ego's structure and the freedom of its responses.

The contributions made by the superego to keep the moods and the affects on a comparatively even level do not justify the inference that normal persons manifest less variety of mood phenomena. Quite the contrary: comparing normal and pathological mood manifestations, we are impressed by the fact that people with pathological and conspicuous mood qualities or mood swings appear to lack all the subtle shades and nuances that we find in normal persons. This may be caused by ego defects as well as by an archaic or defective superego structure. Consequently, qualities and vacillations of mood are good indicators not only of a person's current conflictual or conflict-free situation, but also of the pathology of ego and superego. They assume particular symptomatic and diagnostic significance in psychotic disorders. The loss of differentiated mood shades manifests itself especially clearly in cases where the mood remains fixated at a high or low level for a prolonged period of time. The dark shades of low and the sharp lights of high spirits appear to absorb and outdo the delicate mood shadings. The monotony of their mood is one reason why not only chronically depressed but also chronically hypomanic people get on our nerves.

These considerations concerning mood are equally valid with regard to affective phenomena in general.

Weinshel tends to regard all tamed or controlled affects as signal affects only. I would counter that the more subtle, delicate tamed affects as well as very intense feelings, such as in experiences of love or enjoyment of art or nature, can be "controlled" affects; either type of affect may, but need not—or not only—have signal functions. The severer the affective and mood pathology, the more restricted and less varied are the affective scale and the emotional tones. At first sight this statement does not seem to be true with respect to the hysterics, whose affects and moods frequently show such sparkling luster. Although their affects are overintense and dramatic, they are not really modulated. Their range of emotional colorings is limited due to the lack of subtle, subdued emotional and mood shadings. The affective iridescence of schizophrenics is even more deceptive in this respect. Their affects and moods are sometimes fascinating because of their unfamiliar, strange, uncanny nature; but they are not rich, warm, and vibrant: they have a cold and brittle quality. The pathology of affects manifests itself not only in hyper- or hypointensity of affects and moods, in anomalous mood vacillations and the pathological reduction of finer emotional shadings in favor of cruder or strange affects and moods, but also in the striking differences between warm and cold affect qualities which I have previously discussed (1954, 1964).

To summarize the essential points I have tried to bring out so far: moods are ego states characterized by generalized discharge modifications which temporarily influence the qualities of all feelings, thoughts, and actions. They are evoked by intense experiences which cause high energetic tensions leading to an overflow and spreading of energy throughout the ego by virtue of energetic shifts. These processes go along with generalized transference phenomena, a point that emphasizes the differences between moods and object-directed feeling states. The latter are characterized by libidinal or aggressive investments in specific objects. But the moods transfer the qualities of the provocative experience to all objects and experiences; thus they impart a special coloring to the whole world and hence also to the self. Since they permit gradual, repetitive discharge on many objects and are subject to reality testing, they must be regarded as a special economic modality of the ego.

TWO NORMAL TYPES OF MOOD VARIATIONS: THE NATURE OF SADNESS AND GRIEF, OF GAIETY AND CHEERFUL ELATION

States of sadness and grief, of gaiety and cheerful elation, lend themselves especially well to illustration and further elaboration of these points. I have therefore selected these two opposite types of normal moods for a more extended study and re-examination.

In "Mourning and Melancholia" Freud (1917) pointed out that grieving persons tend to dwell on their memories of the happy past. But this seems to contradict my contention that the overinvestment of the provocative experience—which in grief would be the tragic event of loss—is what induces the mood.

Since the term "grief" singles out a particular prolonged and profound state of sadness caused by the loss of a love object, I prefer not to restrict my study to the state of grief but to extend it to sadness in general. Let us first examine the nature of sadness and the types of experiences that induce this affective condition.

To be sure, sadness is an emotional response of the ego to suffering. The suffering may arise from realistic external or from inner, conscious or unconscious, sources; it may develop from identification with the suffering of others. The suffering that promotes sadness always seems to be caused by experiences—or fantasies—of loss or deprivation, such as by loss of gratification either previously gained or expected, by loss of love, by separation, or, in the case of mourning, by loss of a love object. But it may also have physical sources, although sadness does not seem to be directly evoked by physical hurt or pain. During sickness, especially prolonged illness, sadness may develop from the concomitant emotional suffering caused by the loss of instinctual and emotional gratifications. Even though sadness develops from experiences of loss and deprivation, which tend to provoke aggression, its qualities hint at the involvement of predominantly libidinal cathexes. Angry and sad moods, for example, commonly exclude each other, although it frequently happens that aggression is used as a defense against a painful experience of sadness.

In other words, unlike depression, sadness as such does not involve an aggressive conflict, either with external reality or endopsychically. It certainly does not arise from inner tension between ego and ego ideal, but seems to be induced by tensions within the ego. Practically, of course, states of sadness frequently show depressive features, and in depressed states feelings of sadness may prevail. But clinical observations suggest that sadness predominates in depression only as long as the libidinal investment in the object world can be maintained by the veering away of aggression to the self.

During treatment severely depressive patients who have withdrawn their libido from the object world may indeed display an intense longing for sadness. They may even consciously realize that could they only be sad and weep, they would "feel for the world" again. And actually a relieving "sweet sadness" may break through at the moment when they are achieving a libidinal recathexis of their lost love objects and of pleasant memories relating to them.

Quite in contrast to depressive states of this type, we find in grief and in normal sadness of any kind a preoccupation with the happy experiences of the past—or the expected gratification which could not be attained—combined with painful desires to gain or regain them. I have pointed to the seeming discrepancy between this undeniable overinvestment of grieving persons in their happy past, and the supposed hypercathexis of the sad events which induced the grief.

The example of a recently widowed woman in deep mourning helps to clarify this point. In an interview with this woman I could easily observe how she would talk, for some time, about her past happy life with her husband; then, turning to the painful period of his illness and death, she burst into tears; only to go back to her wonderful memories, and return to the tragic events and her painful current situation with another eruption of grief.

This vacillating attitude seems to be characteristic of the processes underlying states of sadness and grief. Apparently, the painful experience of loss leads to an inner dichotomy. On the one hand, the emotional pain—like physical pain—seems to regenerate and mobilize libidinal forces which, flooding back to memories of the happy past, stir up those highly charged longings to regain the lost gratifications. On the other hand, the highly vested memory of the tragic event has become the carrier of sad anticipations. Both wishful fantasies and painful anticipations spread out and tend to be attached to all objects to which the deprived person tries to relate. Especially those associated with the lost objects or pleasure seem to invite this nostalgic search for happiness lost. Confronting the deprived person with what he cannot attain or regain, reality in its turn confirms the sad anticipations and fixates a tragically altered picture of the self and the world. While reactivating and recharging the sad memories, however, the repetition of loss on many objects lends itself to innumerable painful but relieving discharge processes. At the same time, these very repetitions revive the happy memories and wishful fantasies again. Thus, reality promotes a circular process which continues, with corresponding affective discharge manifestations in ever-diminishing quantities, as long as the mood lasts. Eventually, prolonged reality testing achieves a gradual renunciation of the wishful fantasies and liberates libido for new pursuits.

Hence, states of sadness or grief appear to develop as a contrast effect induced by the discrepancy and vacillation between equally overinvested, opposing memories and fantasies. Highlighting the contrast to the happy past, and painting the inviting and then depriving reality in dark colors, the frustrated search for happiness lost makes the world depriving and empty, the self deprived and poor.

Yet, is it true that sadness and grief lead to the impoverishment not only of the world, but also of the self (ego)? In his comparison of grief and depression, Freud (1917) stressed the lowering of the ego feeling, the ego impoverishment in melancholia, in contrast to the grieving person. "In mourning it is the world which has become poor and empty; in melancholia it is the ego itself" (p. 246).

But any commonplace example will confirm that sadness, too, affects the self, though in a significantly different manner than depression. This is the decisive point. Freud's remarks refer to the waning of self-esteem in depression, the criticism regarding the world and the self, which is not characteristic of states of sadness and grief. Inasmuch as the sad person cherishes his past, he will feel deprived but not bad and worthless or empty. In other words, the libidinal cathexis of his self in its current situation is reduced, but not in favor of aggression; the libidinal object cathexes are likewise maintained, though they may also be reduced. An increase of aggression in the cathexes of the self and the world, which would lead to either angry or depressed mood, is prevented by the precious memories of a happy past and of a previously rich self. I shall return to this point and, in particular, to the different attitudes toward the past in the discussion of depression.

Inasmuch as the stability of his self-esteem and his object relations is essentially unshaken, a grieving person may be able to sustain his normal relationships, interests, and activities. But the gratifications which they may otherwise grant, though consumed, cannot be properly enjoyed, since any pleasure, if permitted to develop at all, is tinged with pain because of what is searched for and missed. We can observe, for instance, that a sad person listening to a beautiful concert may be profoundly moved by it and even enjoy it, but at the same time respond with painful waves of sadness and with an outburst of tears. In profound mourning, of course, we frequently see that persons restrict their object relations because of their absorption in the memories of lost happiness and their hopelessness regarding the future. Some refuse to have experiences which cannot be associated with the love object; others shrink back from anything that points too painfully to their loss. But even though the object world of grieving persons is temporarily narrowed and all experiences bear the touch of sadness, the object relations, insofar as they are maintained, are not changed with regard to their libidinal quality. Inasmuch as they are, sadness is mingled with hostility or depression.

Since full satisfaction of the self cannot be gained as long as sadness prevails, object relations and ego activities acquire a subdued quality. They lack the audible pulse of cheerful activity, those noticeable, recurring waves of increasing narcissistic and object cathexes which result from full gratifications and prepare renewed pleasurable experiences and actions. The oppressive nature of "silent sadness" has evidently much to do with a general restriction of free affectomotor discharge caused by reduced transference on reality, a transference which is either too painful to bear or in hopeless grief not even needed. But the affective inhibition of grief manifestations may also point to an underlying ambivalence problem; in this case the sadness will have depressive features. At any rate, the more strongly and persistently the longing is attached to and confronted with reality, the more intense and uninhibited will be the discharge by weeping, crying, sobbing. This may turn sadness into a relieving and even a rich experience. Though painful, these repetitive dramatic discharge eruptions will lead to an all the more drastic relief, the more they involve not only secretory (quiet weeping) but full affectomotor discharge (sobbing). For this reason we may feel even greater sympathy for the unrelieved, "quietly sad" person.

I may here refer to the assumptions expressed by Bibring (1953) in his paper on depression. First of all, I am doubtful whether a mood condition, i.e., an ego state, can be regarded as a primary ego response comparable to anxiety. While I would not object to describing sad or even depressive reactions as such primary responses, I believe and have tried to show that the development of a depressed state involves a more complex cathectic process. Moreover, the situation of helplessness and hopelessness resulting from an inability to change the situation is certainly also present in states of grief without depressive features. My clinical material does not confirm this hypothesis, but the problem deserves further investigation.

Sadness is often intermingled with self-pity, which induces a special, gratifying, narcissistic element into sadness by hypercathecting not so much the gratification lost as the "poor, deprived self that needs love and sympathy." The unpleasant effect on the observer has to do with his justified suspicion that this poor self has gained much more importance than the lost object.

States of gaiety or normal, cheerful elation are the pleasurable counterpart of sadness. Like sadness they are founded on libidinal processes, which in their case, however, lead to pleasurable discharges. When opposing the state of sadness and grief to joyful, happy mood conditions, we encounter an interesting question. Are such pleasurable moods also evoked by an inner "contrast" situation? Or do they simply develop whenever happy anticipation aroused by an uncommonly pleasurable wish fulfillment imposes itself on all other experiences? To be sure, in order to induce a cheerful, happy, gay mood the provocative experience must have a certain momentum, something that makes it unusual or extraordinary. This suggests at least a certain "contrast" to the uneventful past. Practically, moreover, joyfulness develops very frequently from a happy event following a previous state of worry or sadness; e.g., when a person expects or experiences the return of a love object whose absence had previously saddened him. In this case the present wish fulfillment, as opposed to the painful past, provokes abundant cheerful anticipations which paint the world and the self in glamorous "contrast" colors.

Analogous to sadness, joyfulness also arises from a discrepancy, though from an opposite one: between a world unpleasant as it was and might continue to be, and pleasant as it turned out and is now expected to be. We recall that in "Mourning and Melancholia" Freud mentioned this contrast as the motivating experience for normal elation. But gay, joyful, elated moods do not by any means develop regularly subsequent to conditions of strain or worry or sadness. They certainly cannot be regarded only as expressions of relief from trouble. Nor can we agree that pathological states of elation, as has been suggested, are mere reactions of relief from a previous depression. Nevertheless, we must remember that the gain of pleasure is always a "regaining" which must inevitably conjure up memories of previous loss or deprivation or suffering in general; all the more so, the more intense and the more unexpected the wish fulfillment.

In this connection we may recall what we know about the psychology of laughter, the most dramatic expression of gaiety, comparable to the weeping in sadness. A most significant factor in this affective reaction is the suspense effect evoked by the building up of high tension followed by sudden, unexpected, drastic pleasurable relief. Here, too, we find the idea of a "contrast." The building up of tension would be unpleasant and provoke disagreeable anticipations, but for the gay emotional atmosphere which creates "opposite" expectations of cheerful relief. It is the suddenness of this relief that sets off the eruption of laughter (see Chapter 2).

In view of this we may well suspect that the "contrast effect," as achieved by the factor of "unexpectedness," plays a significant role in all states of cheerfulness, gaiety, and pleasurable elation. To be cautious, we may assume that cheerful moods are evoked by pleasure experiences of unexpected intensity which are in sharp contrast to a previous indifferent or unpleasant situation. In either case, the embellishment of the world must originate in the fact that reality, by contradicting or surpassing anticipations derived from the past, grants unexpectedly high pleasure. When in a cheerful mood, we can indeed frequently observe a strange undertone of surprise or wonder that life can really be as enjoyable as this. We can assume that the factor of unexpectedness in the provocative experience is also operative in the development of sad moods. The occurrence of very good or very bad events seems to be forever "unexpected." For this reason we observe in cases of prolonged fatal illness that the relatives during the period of preparation for the worst have worked through their grief and are no longer mourning, or even are relieved, when death actually comes.

Some remarks may be added concerning the undeniable closeness between sadness and joy, between weeping and laughter. I am not referring to the fact that explosive laughter can also lead to secretory discharge, i.e., evoke tears. What I mean is the strangely scintillating state "between laughter and tears," the "tragicomical" category. We can easily understand such midway or mixed conditions and the rapid transition from the one to the opposite state if we remember that these opposite moods both arise from a contrast between happy and unhappy, good and bad notions. In normal moods it is reality that confirms either the one or the other notion, that swings the mood to the good or bad side of the scale. Tragicomical situations may well concomitantly or alternately point to the darker or brighter aspects of life, thus inducing a mixed or vacillating, iridescent, sad-humorous mood condition.

A COMPARATIVE STUDY OF NORMAL, NEUROTIC, AND PSYCHOTIC MOOD DEVIATIONS

Our understanding of affective states depends, to a great extent, on the total symptomatic and psychodynamic picture in whose frame they commonly appear. At first sight we would frequently be at a loss to distinguish, from the phenomenological point of view alone, between normal mood deviations and those which arise from pathological desires or from neurotic conflicts. In this case, not the mood itself is pathological in nature but its motivations. And in cases where the symptom formation exhausts itself in the development of a mood condition, such as a depressed state, we find ourselves occasionally in serious differential-diagnostic doubts regarding the neurotic or psychotic nature of the condition.

The reason for these difficulties is that moods, with either normal or pathological qualities or motivations, are in any case an economic modality of the ego, which partly reinstates a primary process type of mental functioning.

Inasmuch as moods involve transference phenomena of a generalized nature, they may lead to a temporary impairment of critical judgment and discrimination with regard to one's own self and the object world. They may produce a primitive, "subjective," prejudicial or even illusional type of feeling, thinking, and behavior, which tends to resist reality testing. To the extent to which this reality testing can assert itself, the mood condition will subside. Insofar as moods, normal or anomalous, color or a least overstate one aspect of reality and understate or blot out differing or opposing aspects, they involve, to some extent, mechanisms of denial and distortion of reality. But the nature of this denial is quite different in normal and in pathologically motivated mood conditions, and provides us with significant differential-diagnostic criteria.

Mostly, in normal moods the denial does not extend to the provocative external event or to its immediate emotional impact which evokes the mood. If a person mourns the death of his wife or is jubilant on the return of his son, the reasons for such moods are realistic and mostly conscious. But, as Weinshel pointed out, even in normal moods, people often are unaware of what provoked their mood. Moreover, Freud correctly stated that in grief the whole world has become empty, at least from the subjective standpoint of the grieving person. The gloomy color which the world assumes for him is the result of what we may call a normal denial: the denial of potential substitute gratifications which life might grant if he could only accept them. In this case, as in any other normal mood condition, the mood certainly has a realistic basis. A person often has a distinct, sometimes painful awareness that his mood is "subjective" in nature: that the world and the self as such have not changed; that they only "appear" different because "he is in such and such a mood." The blotting out of notions contradicting the mood is not complete, and the qualitative modifications remain within normal bounds.

Thus moods are within the normal range and appropriate in quality as long as they are compatible with the momentary external and internal reality and can be recognized as temporary ego states due to conscious reactions to realistic events. They will yield to reality testing and consequently be controllable and of limited duration. The less conscious a person is of the sources from which his moods arise, the less easily can the psychic situation be mastered and the more inappropriate are the mood qualities. The duration of a mood also depends, of course, on the impact of the provocative experience. In grief, for instance, it may be so severe that the economic process requires a long time to achieve its purpose. Grief certainly demonstrates particularly well that the duration of a mood as such is not a criterion for its normal or pathological character. The rapid passing of grief or other moods may well be an expression of defective or shallow object relations. It may be caused by special affective or other types of defenses. And a very prolonged mourning period may be caused either by the severity of the loss, or by an inability to resolve unconscious conflicts involving the lost object.

From the fact that even psychotic depressive states tend to pass spontaneously, as it were, Freud concluded that the economic process in such states must be essentially the same as in grief. But this cannot be wholly correct. In fact, as soon as unconscious conflicts participate in the development of the mood, they preclude an ultimate economic success. I have already referred to the limited economic function of pathologically motivated moods. The economic failure rests on the fact that infantile fixations prevent a reality testing sufficient to guarantee a true liberation of psychic energy from its original fixated position. What happens is essentially the same as in the case of a repressed infantile traumatic experience which a person unconsciously tries to overcome by repetitions of the trauma. Each time, this will result in relieving, affective discharge reactions. However, since repression precludes reality testing that would lead to mastery of the traumatic situation, the repetitions will continue unless the repressed experience is brought to consciousness.

Similarly, moods arising from unconscious sources permit only a sort of spurious reality testing, causing repetitive discharge reactions which are economically useful inasmuch as they finally lead to a temporary subsiding of the mood. But the hypercathexis of the pathogenic, repressed memories survives the mood and tends to turn reality into a constant source of renewed provocations, thus re-establishing the disturbed (anxious or hostile or depressed) affective state. If the mood deviation arises from a pathological narcissistic conflict, reality testing becomes even less effective or, in psychotic mood conditions, impossible.

Moods induced by narcissistic conflicts permit in general less reality testing than moods evoked by conflicts with the external world. Although the latter affect the self too (as was pointed out in the case of grief), they require predominantly a testing of external reality.

In the case of narcissistic conflicts the mood disturbance arises from the discrepancy between the self representations and the ego ideal (superego) or the wishful image of the self. Hence it requires predominantly a testing of inner reality. External reality can be used only as a medium on which the self can assert its value. Unfortunately, the self-critical agents, which test our inner reality, are deeply rooted in the unconscious and therefore highly arbitrary. Moreover, our self representations are in general even less realistic than our object representations; consequently self-awareness is not too well developed even in normal persons. Thus, our chances for correct self-evaluation are, at best, limited. Indeed, those introspective capacities which are a prerequisite for constructive reality testing appear to be a rather exceptional gift.

The difficulties of reality testing manifest themselves even in moods evoked by a narcissistic conflict that has a realistic basis. Let us consider the simple case of a man who is depressed because he is doing badly in his job. His depression arises from the discrepancy between his own narcissistic expectations and his realistic failure, which makes him temporarily feel that he is altogether an inadequate person. The disapproval of his superiors will, of course, influence and probably confirm this picture of himself. But the more reasonable his expectations, and the more his self-evaluation is founded on correct, rational judgment, the more likely is his self-esteem to be restored by increasing self-assertion in his job. Yet, even though he tests his ego functions on the medium of external reality, i.e., on his work, it is the critical part of his ego—or, in moral conflicts, the superego—that has the last word and determines the good or bad quality of his self and consequently his mood.

With regard to such moods I must modify my previous statement that moods involve a generalized, temporary transference from one object to the whole object world. In moods caused by narcissistic conflicts, not longings for objects but narcissistic desires are attached to the world or are expected to be satisfied through the medium of the world. The higher and more illusory the narcissistic expectations and the less realistic the object and self representations are to begin with, the more pathological will be the conflict and thus the resulting mood.

A woman who unconsciously believes herself to be castrated and has a phallic image of herself is bound to find evidence for her inferiority in any little failure and to react to it with depression.

The infantile origin and the power of the superego make moods evoked by unconscious superego conflicts especially resistant to reality testing. The latter becomes impossible when the superego has replaced the object world and, independent of its standards and judgment, condemns and punishes the self or, the opposite, renounces its critical functions.[2]

I shall use some concrete examples to examine the different kinds of denial and distortion in neurotic and psychotic states. If a person

[2] It is noteworthy that in true depressives, the longings for love and approval are not rooted in happy memories of the past, as is the case in grief. They are reactive in nature and, even if attached to the world, are removed from past and current reality. For example, a woman who had responded to the loss of her husband with a severe paranoid-depressive state, in which she complained about her disillusionment with the world and the senselessness of her life, said, when reminded of other widows in worse situations, "They have at least happy memories in which to live."

were to get into a bad (irritable or angry or depressed) mood because his breakfast was ten minutes late, we should certainly suspect him of being neurotic. His mood exaggerates the importance of the provocative external event; it definitely distorts his own situation in the world and is, if not inappropriate, at least irrationally motivated. But if a public speaker were to develop a profound depression after a successful speech, he would be seriously ill. In this case his reaction to success and the resulting mood would be inappropriate, i.e., paradoxical. The drop of his self-esteem and of the mood level, which might be isolated from a full, conscious, intellectual awareness of his success, would deny its meaning as a result of unconscious conflicts of a masochistic type. And, finally, if a devoted husband who just lost his wife were to respond with an elated mood manifesting itself in hectic pleasure-seeking, the state would be severely pathological. If such a mood were induced by a denial of the factual events, it would be definitely psychotic: his fantasies would not distort, but completely replace reality. If he were denying only the tragic impact of reality (Lewin, 1950), the denial would be less severe and not necessarily psychotic. In such a case we commonly speak of a denial of the underlying sadness, but this is not quite correct. The denial of a mood condition looks different. Persons whose facial expressions, attitude, and behavior betray their bad mood, often remain unaware of their condition or even pretend to be in good spirits. Many patients with objective signs of a depression consult the physician for physical reasons and cannot accept the correct diagnosis of their conditions. In these cases the mood awareness[3] is affected and an existing mood denied.

These examples prove that we must make a distinction not only between many types, but also between varying degrees of denial and distortion which can be involved in mood development. In general, denial affects both the self and the object world; but it may lead to more conspicuous distortions of one or the other. It may be directed against the provocative event itself, against its impact, or its meaning. Moreover, the denial may operate directly against external reality, or affect primarily the inner imagery and only secondarily—by way of projection—external objects and facts. And finally, there

[3] Mood awareness, which is mainly feeling awareness, develops as part of the self representations and hence is a narcissistic phenomenon, whereas the affects and the moods as such are ego experiences involving both the objects and the self.

may be a secondary, defensive denial of an existing—appropriate or inappropriate—mood condition, i.e., a disturbance of mood awareness.

The foregoing considerations regarding the different types of denial[4] and normal and anomalous moods, and the limitations of reality testing in the latter, can be applied to a comparison of some special mood conditions and their pathological counterparts.

In certain respects the traditional comparison between grief and depression (Freud, 1917) has been misleading. It suggested, by implication at least, that depressive states are always pathological, as opposed to the normal nature of grief. Moreover, in one way or another, the pioneering papers of Freud (1917), Abraham (1911, 1924), Rado (1928), Melanie Klein's work (1948), and Lewin's illuminating studies on depression and related states (1950) have laid great emphasis on the role of early infantile response patterns in the modeling of such conditions. Hence, we tend to link them with introjective and projective mechanisms and severe ambivalence conflicts causing regression to narcissistic, oral and anal positions. Thus, we easily lose sight of the fact that both depressed and elated states may well develop within the range of normal mood conditions.[5]

This was shown in the example of John, who reacted to his varying experiences with Anne with alternating states of happy elation, sadness, anger, and depression. All these responses had sufficiently realistic roots to lead to appropriate mood conditions, which remained quantitatively and qualitatively within normal limits. Further evidence of their normal nature was the successful effect of reality testing. Not only did his mood easily yield to changes in Anne's attitudes; when Anne, after some weeks of a troubled relationship, broke up with him, he went through an emotionally stormy period. But then he succeeded in re-establishing his affective and mood equilibrium, and some months later formed a satisfactory attachment to another girl.

This example certainly shows that the different qualities of sadness and depression as such are not expressive of the normal nature of sadness and of the pathological nature of depression. Inasmuch as these differences arise from a prevalence of libidinal or aggressive

[4] Other aspects concerning denial are discussed further in Chapter 4.
[5] In "Mourning and Melancholia" Freud discussed states of normal elation.

forces in the whole realm of the ego, they point to the dangers inherent in depressed as well as in hostile mood conditions. Whereas the libidinal nature of sadness and grief (without depressive features) is indicative of an absence of conflict, hostile and depressed states always develop from aggressive tensions and hence are the expression of a conflict situation—either neurotic or psychotic, or one with reality. In other words, such conditions have a pathological potential that gains momentum to the extent to which the unconscious enters the conflict or—even worse—to which regressive processes are set in motion.

Moreover, the narcissistic disturbance, the affection of the self to which I already referred in discussing sadness, is more ominous even in normal depression than in mere sadness and more consequential with respect to the ego functions.

The aggressive, critical element is what lends value properties of quite a different order to the world or the self in hostile or depressive moods than in sadness. The values whose loss or gain evokes sadness or happy elation are those of pleasure, of gratifications gained from the world. We may call them id values. But in depressed moods or states of hostility, of aggressive excitement, the world and the self appear inadequate, faulty, bad, or injurious. They are derogated, criticized with regard to their strength, ability, superiority, or moral perfection, i.e., in terms of ego or superego values. Thus the core of the narcissistic disturbance in depression is always an experience of failure, though not necessarily of moral failure. The more the superego contributes to the conflict, the more will the self be conceived of as morally bad, expecting punishment from without or within. Frequently, though, the conscious feelings and ideas of inadequacy fend off hidden guilt conflicts.

Such qualitative changes in the relationship between the world and the self can be found even in the range of normal hostile and depressed mood conditions. But the particular modification or disturbance of this relationship depends on the individual—either realistic or neurotic or psychotic—nature of the underlying conflict, and consequently on the vicissitudes of the instinctual forces in its development. We know that hostile and depressed moods can gain intensity through the calling away of aggression from the self or vice versa. Thus, angry moods need not be primarily caused by hurt or disappointment. They may develop from narcissistic conflicts, e.g., from guilt conflicts or experiences of failure or faults when the self-directed aggression is secondarily turned toward the object world. They may then protect the person from a depressed condition. This tendency to blame the world rather than oneself is all too familiar even in normal persons.

Reversely, depressive states may be induced by a shift of aggression from the objects to the self. Since this vicissitude prevents a devaluation of the object world, it serves as an effective defense against ambivalence conflicts, especially when the latter involve the danger of loss of a significant love object. It may be stressed that these vicissitudes per se do not necessarily involve introjective and projective mechanisms. Depending on the degree to which such mechanisms are used, people either criticize themselves for the world's inadequacies or blame the world for their own faults. In the latter case the hostile state assumes paranoid qualities. I shall return to the problem of paranoid mood conditions.

At this point I wish to focus on the modifications of the self and the world arising from these vicissitudes. As stated above, in mood conditions the self and the world assume "complementary" qualities. But if the veering away of aggression to the self in depression is accompanied by a reactive libidinal hypercathexis of the world, they may acquire an opposite coloring. The world may then be inflated and appear glorified, idealized or even aggrandized at the expense of the bad, deflated self. Reversely, in hostile states the world may appear to be bad, inadequate, or worthless, in favor of a good, superior, inflated self.

In persons who relate to the object world only by way of narcissistic identifications, all conflicts, even those involving the object world, are narcissistic in nature. Since in this case the boundaries between self and object representations are indistinct, any deflation of the world is cast back upon the self.[6] Should this happen, the self and the world may be felt to have assumed identical qualities. This may be observed in pleasurably hypomanic moods in which both world and self appear to be rich, wonderful, ideal, or again in those pessimistic, depressive conditions in which the world and the self are represented as equally bad, unpleasant, empty, or worthless.

The point of departure for these last considerations was the

[6] This will be discussed more extensively in Chapters 9 and 10, which deal with problems of psychotic identifications in cyclothymic and schizophrenic patients.

shifts of aggression between the self and the world to be observed in hostile and in depressed conditions. It seems necessary to underline, however, that depressive states do not always develop from attempts to resolve ambivalence conflicts by a turning away of aggression from the love object (the object world) to the self. They may well be directly evoked by a primary, narcissistic conflict. Freud (1917) stressed this point in reference to melancholic depression and in this connection hinted at the possibility of a primary, endogenous ego improverishment. But narcissistic conflicts which evoke depressed states are by no means always indicative of narcissistic regression leading to drive defusion. Such states may be intensified or influenced by infantile narcissistic conflicts, but they may also be caused directly by realistic experiences of failure, inadequacy, or moral transgression.

I again resort to the example of a person doing badly in his job. Even if he is not neurotic, he may well react to his failure with a depressed state and general feelings of inadequacy. If he is normal, these will subside to the extent to which his work improves and he is able to assert himself. Should he feel tempted to commit or actually have committed a morally wrong or questionable act, we would not be surprised if he were to respond with remorse and depression.

In order to study the specific influences which different realistic or neurotic motivations or conflict situations exert on the qualities of the resulting moods and, due to differences in reality testing, on their course and vicissitudes, I shall present a few brief examples of sad, distressed, and hostile mood conditions.

The first example concerns Miss C., an attractive, flirtatious, hysterical girl who was unconsciously in search of an incestuous love object and tended to develop striking and erratic mood variations. She suffered alternately from dramatic depressed and rather uncontrolled hostile states. According to the mood of the moment, she complained that either lack of opportunity or her own lack of charms prevented her from getting a husband. Her bad moods passed temporarily whenever she met a man who showed some interest in her and looked like a suitable partner. But they returned when nothing further developed from such encounters. At last, she succeeded in forming a promising attachment to a nice young man who resembled her brother. But since her object choice was determined by her incestuous desire, guilt feelings compelled her to relinquish this man. She managed to irritate him so much by her erratic behavior that finally he lost patience and gave her up. This rejection threw her into a serious, anxious depression with continuous outbursts of uncontrolled, copious weeping and sobbing. After recovery from this depression, the girl would probably have continued her frustrating search (and recurring reactive depressions and hostile states) had she not decided to undergo psychoanalytic treatment.

The second example illustrates normal grief with depressive features. Mrs. D., a middle-aged widow in a state of profound mourning after the loss of her husband, came to me to discuss certain family problems. Although she was not an analytic patient, these interviews gave a revealing picture of her emotional state. A woman with a very intense emotional life and vivid affective expression, she showed rather stormy mourning manifestations. Although controlled in the presence of other people, she wept copiously when alone, dwelling on her memories of the beloved partner. She felt the need again and again to visit the same places in the mountains whose beauty they had enjoyed together. In her mourning state, the scenery would move her even more than before; but a beautiful view, a sunrise or sunset now evoked outbursts of weeping in association with her memories of the delight she had shared with her husband. Despite her dramatic reactions, however, she conscientiously stuck to her work, albeit with a lack of enthusiasm. She even found comfort and enjoyment in it, but these were mingled with her all-pervasive sadness. Although she reduced her social activities, she felt a definite need for the company of those old friends who had also been close to her husband and would talk with her about him.

Mrs. D. reported that in the beginning of her grieving period, she had felt very depressed and remorseful for having failed her husband in so many ways. She particularly regretted that she had so often let him provoke her to angry outbursts. Since she wept while talking about this, her guilt reactions likewise seemed to be vivid, painful experiences accompanied by tears.

Mrs. D.'s grief reactions were strikingly different from those of her friend, Mrs. E., whom she sent to me some months later because she was worried about her condition. Mrs. E. also was a widow, and one and a half years ago had lost her sister to whom she had been uncommonly attached. Since that time she had been in a chronic depressed state from which she could not recover.

In contrast to Mrs. D., Mrs. E. was an emotionally overrestrained, somewhat detached, obsessive-compulsive personality. For her, the beauties of nature had ceased to exist; she could not respond to them with any feeling. Her emotional life seemed to have become empty. She could take no serious interest in anything, not even in her work. At the same time she felt very restless. She avoided the company of her friends and preferred to spend her free time at parties or on visits with casual acquaintances. It turned out that these attitudes were in keeping with her basic defenses. By refusing to relate deeply to the outside world unless she was certain of being granted pleasure, she had always avoided being confronted with painful realities. Both her detachment and her hunt for superficial pleasure saved her from the onslaught of those very painful emotions to which Mrs. D. submitted. The compulsive type of her affective defenses suggested the presence of much more intense ambivalence conflicts than in the case of Mrs. D. Mrs. E. spoke much of her guilt feelings about everyone and everything—except her late sister. Evidently, she had to deny and displace them because she could not bear to face the intensity of her conflict with the sister and the hostility from which it arose.

Comparing the mood conditions in these three cases, we find that in Miss C. the central conflicts, causing hostile and anxious-depressed states, were definitely not problems of ambivalence but oedipal conflicts. Miss C. was not a girl who suffered from an inability to love. Her hostile behavior with men was only a defense against her incestuous impulses. Her anger at the world, which "did not offer her sufficient opportunities," was unconsciously directed at her oedipal rival, her mother. And her depressive complaints about her lack of charms referred likewise to her inability to compete with her mother. They covered up her unconscious need for punishment, caused by her incestuous guilt conflict. Her rationalizations concerning her mood disturbances resulted in a rapid passing of her hostile mood whenever she met a promising man, and her depression vanished as soon as she was able to gain his attention. This is what I meant by speaking of a spurious or pseudo reality testing. She could test reality only within the bounds of those motivations for her moods of which she was aware. Thus she was grieving about the loss of her lover, yet without knowing why she lost him and why she could not find or accept any man. Her unconscious oedipal conflicts were the reason for an acting out that led inevitably to a continuous recurrence of her mood disturbances.

In the case of Mrs. D., we can observe a rather normal mourning process that in many ways confirms and exemplifies my previous statements on sadness and grief. What lent a depressive coloring to her sadness was a conflict caused by hostility feelings toward her late husband, feelings of which she apparently had been and was fully aware. This awareness permitted the development of an introspective process. The testing of her inner reality was sufficient to help her fairly soon to overcome her remorse and the depression induced by it.

Quite in contrast to Mrs. D., Mrs. E. responded to the loss of her sister with grief turning into a chronic state of depression, which to my knowledge even now, after two years, has not essentially changed. A series of pathogenic features combined to produce this unduly prolonged disturbance. The central problem in her case was an ambivalence conflict of infantile origin. It had led to frank manifestations of hostility toward the sister, which after the latter's death Mrs. E. endeavored to forget and to deny. But even though she had also loved her sister very dearly, her grief could not find frank expression because she could not face the depth of her loss. She tried to evade the experience of sadness by running after superficial pleasures which left her empty. In other words, Mrs. E. escaped from a testing of both the external and her inner reality. The unfortunate fact that she denied the impact of her loss, the nature of her past relationship with the sister, and the true reasons for her guilt feelings precluded reality testing that might have resolved her conflict. It did not even permit relieving discharge reactions that might have gradually re-established a normal mood level.

When we compare the depressed states in these three persons with regard to their influence on ego functions, we are again impressed by a significant difference. To be sure, in Miss C. the mood disturbances affected her activities, inasmuch as her constant preoccupations and her acting out with men, and the resulting emotional vacillations, undermined her ability to concentrate on her work and other pursuits. But there were no signs of a general depressive inhibition of thoughts and actions.

In Mrs. D.'s case, the grieving resulted in a preference for certain activities and relationships with concomitant limitation or exclusion of others. Mrs. E., however, suffered from depressive inhibitions of her thought processes and her work, inhibitions that were covered up by her restless pseudo activities.

This comparison suggests that the degree to which depressed states cause generalized inhibitions depends on the intensity and the nature of the underlying ambivalence conflicts, and the extent to which the depression aims to ward off hostility toward the world (the love object).

The inhibition of ego functions in depressed states leads to a further ego problem: the different identifications in grief and depression. In the case of Mrs. D. a conspicuous feature came to my notice. This woman talked about a grieving reaction which she had also experienced in the past after other object losses. It pertains to the identification with the love object which quite normally follows the loss of a beloved person. I had mentioned above that sadness may arise from identification with the suffering of others; this element also plays a role in grief. Mr. D.'s last illness had been brief but painful. His wife had shared his suffering with him, and after his death continued to feel and behave as though sharing with him the painful loss of life, in the same way as they had previously shared its manifold pleasures. Thus her fantasies encompassed not only the loss of her own gratifications, gained from and with the husband, but also the happiness he had enjoyed and of which he was deprived by his death. Although I have not found any references in the literature to this reaction, it is certainly a common mourning phenomenon given frequent expression in painful outbursts, such as "If only he—or she—were still alive and could have seen or experienced this or that happy event!" It is characteristic that Mrs. E. did not seem to react in this manner.

In the case described above, this magic fantasy of identification with the love object's loss of life's joys seemed to be the point of departure for certain superego and ego identifications which gradually developed in the course of the mourning period and led to lasting structural changes in the ego. In fact, I could observe that these especially painful thoughts had turned into an increased, constructive preoccupation with those interests and activities which her husband had particularly enjoyed or had liked her to pursue. Mrs.

D. behaved as if by doubling her own efforts in these areas she could make up for what he had lost. When her mourning was over, she remained, for instance, more attached to those beautiful mountains than she had previously been; and, in general, she pursued more intensely those interests which her husband had shared with her. Besides, she developed ambitions particularly in those areas of her own work in which he had shown special interest and ambition for her (superego identifications). Years later she would respond to achievements in these areas with painful feelings of sadness at the idea how her husband would have enjoyed her success. Viewed in terms of her initial identification with the husband's fate, her future realistic identifications replaced not only the lost husband and the gratifications he once had granted, but also his lost life and the gratifications he had gained from her and with her. This double aspect shows that identifications in grief also serve to preserve in memory the inner relationship to the object now lost.

Here we observe that in grief the identifications develop as a constructive outcome of the grieving process. They may start—and possibly always start—at a magic fantasy level; but they gradually progress to the ego level and eventually bring about solid, selective ego alterations. Evidently, the libido liberated in the mourning process cannot be immediately used for new personal object relationships which would replace the one lost. Instead, it is absorbed by the identifications and used for investments in new sublimations and ego functions. In fact, we frequently see that grieving persons, after the first stormy mourning period is over, begin to double their efforts in work or start new, absorbing activities founded on identifications with the lost object.

We know the extent to which ambivalence conflicts may interfere with the building up of such identifications during the mourning period. Mrs. E., for instance, escaped from her grief precisely into those superficial pleasures which her rather severe and sick sister had not been willing and able to share with her, which indeed she had frankly rejected and criticized. Thus, Mrs. E.'s activities seemed to originate in her rebellion against the older sister—a mother figure. On the other hand, we may suspect that her guilt feelings not only prevented her enjoyment, but were responsible for depressive reactions to those very pursuits.

In some patients who belonged to the obsessive-compulsive type

I observed another kind of mourning reaction. They did develop identifications with the ambivalently loved lost object, but they responded with depression when catching themselves in the very attitudes or character traits which they had rejected in their love object. In other words, because they had loved the lost object, such patients identified with it. But inasmuch as they had hated it, they punished themselves for their hostility by first assuming the object's bad characteristics along with the good ones (masochistic identifications) and then hating themselves for this.

Thus the identification processes in grief may have many different vicissitudes; they may have constructive results or, under the influence of neurotic ambivalence conflicts, secondarily provoke depressive conditions and other pathological manifestations. But they bring about structural changes in the ego and develop gradually as an outcome of the grieving process, whereas in psychotic conditions narcissistic identifications introduce and mark the onset of a depressive period. Since these latter processes are founded on archaic incorporation fantasies, they cannot succeed in exerting a constructive influence on the ego but may lead to the development of delusional ideas.

This brings me to the psychotic hostile or depressive mood conditions, which I shall discuss rather briefly. I stated above that we do not always have sufficient criteria to distinguish at first sight between neurotic and psychotic mood conditions. If we can observe them clinically over a prolonged period and also have the opportunity to study them psychodynamically, we find characteristic differences in the nature and structure of neurotic and psychotic emotional states even when the latter do not lead to delusional symptom formation. What are the factors that determine their different qualities and their different course?

Psychotic disorders are characterized by severely regressive processes involving all systems, and these processes go along with drive deneutralization and drive defusion. Consequently there is a tremendous surplus of deneutralized aggression which may invade all systems. Eradicating the superego functions, these aggressive forces may flood the ego and provoke it to destructive actions; or they may accumulate in the superego, thus smothering all ego functions, and possibly lead to self-destruction. As a result of the drive defusion and of ego and superego regression, the conflicts inducing mood conditions occur at a very primitive, narcissistic as well as sadomasochistic level; the mechanisms used for the purposes of defense and restitution are archaic in nature.

This state of affairs has of course a paramount influence on the distortions of the self and the object world, and thus accounts for the ineffectiveness of reality testing in psychotic moods. Especially when delusions develop, the delusional ideas and the corresponding affective mood manifestations are, as we know, rigidly fixated and more or less inaccessible to external influences and events. They indicate a withdrawal from the object world, which has removed the mood from reality and reality testing.

I shall not discuss the special varieties of pathological modifications and delusional distortions which the self and object representations may undergo in the course of psychotic hostile or depressive mood development. We are sufficiently familiar with their clinical manifestations and with the specific mechanisms which bring them about. But I shall briefly consider the specific nature of those mechanisms of introjection and projection which may result in psychotic forms of identification.

I have previously stressed that shifts of aggression between the self and object representations need not always go along with introjective and projective processes. The latter are by no means always identical with the introjection of object images into the self images (or superego, respectively), or with the projection of self images onto object images. It is only these latter processes which are characteristic of psychotic conditions. They bring about different types of pathological identifications in different groups of psychoses, which will lend their particular psychotic qualities to the distortions of the self and the world.

I shall deal with the problem of psychotic identifications in the second half of this book, but one essential point belongs in the present context. In melancholic depression, the patient's self representations appear to have assumed those very qualities which he unconsciously ascribes to his love object. Inasmuch as such a type of identification leads to a fixated, possibly delusional, but only qualitative modification of his total self representation, it must evoke and be part of a mood condition.

Yet in schizophrenic delusional identifications the patient may be convinced that he has "become" a different person. In this case his self representation does not appear to be qualitatively changed as a result of the identification. He may replace his own with the new, delusional identity. Such a process does not involve a mood development, although his new identity will of course influence his whole ego state. If a person believes he is Napoleon, he will certainly manifest grandiose attitudes and corresponding behavior; but he may vacillate between a benevolent-friendly, a tyrannical-aggressive, and a paranoid-hostile state, all of which may be in harmony with his paranoid delusion.

What I said is, of course, equally valid with regard to the delusional changes of the object world. As long as they are qualitative, the world may appear to be rejecting, accusing, intentionally slighting. Spread-out paranoid delusional ideas may arise as part of a paranoid-hostile or a paranoid-depressive mood or a mixed condition. But truly paranoid delusions, where a new identity may be attached to previously well-known persons, do not appear in the frame of a mood. This is why patients with fixated and systematized delusions of persecution may appear quiet and inconspicuous on the surface, until they pick up a gun and shoot Mr. X because they know he is not their old lawyer or physician but a secret agent instigating a Communist plot against them.

This difference between the two types of psychotic identification—between the one causing qualitative delusional changes of the self and the world, which evoke mood conditions, and the one that creates new identities—has clinical significance. It makes comprehensible why paranoid ideas of the latter type lend themselves to systematization. Since they do not involve generalized transference phenomena but remain localized and centered about definite single objects, they may leave whole areas of the ego unaffected. Within the area of the ego where the paranoid system develops they may of course spread out, may jump from one object to another, or may gradually extend to a number of persons who become associated with and part of the plot.

This restriction to a particular ego area, which may remain isolated, is especially characteristic of true paranoia. As we know, such patients may appear perfectly sane and emotionally undisturbed until something is touched upon that relates to the paranoid area; only then does their illness become manifest. It is this localization which permits a gradual systematization of the delusion, a development that does not occur in paranoid moods.

In paranoid schizophrenics we can observe both: paranoid notions in the frame of paranoid mood conditions, and true paranoid delusions with or without systematization. In paranoid mood conditions, especially those having a cyclic course, we may have great difficulties deciding whether they are the expression of a schizophrenic process or of a manic-depressive psychosis; only long-term observation enables us to make the correct differential diagnosis.

The problem just discussed immediately leads to another question. Why and under what circumstances does this pathological process sometimes exhaust itself in the production of a psychotic mood condition without further symptom formation, as is the case in manic-depressive disorders; of a condition which may develop to a peak, then gradually and spontaneously subside, and leave the person practically restored until another episode sets in? While I cannot answer this question, I may venture some tentative hypotheses.

Infantile environmental factors certainly may have a paramount pathogenic or predisposing influence on the development of psychoses, and disturbing current experiences may provoke the final psychotic break. But few psychiatrists doubt that psychoses are based on endogenous, as yet unknown, physiological processes. The more suddenly the pathological, psychophysiological psychotic process sets in, the more rapid will be the processes of regression and drive defusion. In this case the sudden surplus amount of destructive energy can attack and overrun the whole ego. To put it differently: the ego, suddenly taken unawares, is unable to do more than to call immediately on mood development as a safety valve for discharge. Since moods are states involving the whole ego, however, they are apt to interfere with special defensive operations of the kind that can be used for the solution of localized conflicts. This precludes the formation of symptoms other than those expressive and part of the mood condition. But we must not forget that psychotic mood conditions encompass a much wider range of symptoms than do neurotic mood conditions. We remember not only the physiological symptoms, such as insomnia and loss of weight and appetite, but also the variety of hypochondriacal manifestations. The objection may be raised that schizophrenic episodes as well as periods of psychotic depression usually have a forestage announcing the imminent onset of the acute illness, and that depressive or hypomanic periods often seem to develop gradually.

The onset of the acute episode is, however, in most cases sudden. Manic-depressive patients whose depression worsens gradually may nevertheless remember precisely the day when their depression began and often also the day when it was over, when they "woke up" and suddenly "felt different, healthy again." My suspicion that the sudden acute onset of the illness is the reason for an involvement of the whole ego, causing immediate mood development, appears to be further confirmed by the comparison of the prognostically more favorable type of schizophrenia that is characterized by recurring episodes and symptomatology created by a slowly developing schizophrenic process. The latter may affect first one, then the other area, or else slowly expand, invade the whole personality, and eventually lead to a general mental disintegration. Such patients may of course show a particular moodiness. They may tend to react with sudden, inappropriate affective outbursts and mood swings. They may impress us by the flat, cold qualities of their affects and the loss of feeling capacities. But in the course of such chronic or progressively developing disorders there is hardly a stage where characteristic, prolonged mood conditions become predominant in the total clinical picture.

The question of the different influences of suddenly or slowly developing physiological changes on the symptomatology leads us back once more to the economic problem with which I shall terminate this study.

I concluded that psychotic mood conditions which led to delusional development offer little chance for reality testing. But I noted that the repetitive, prolonged discharge as such might be economically effective enough to cause the mood eventually to subside, for some time at least. In these ominously quiet, paralyzing types of depression in manic-depressive patients, however, and in states of catatonic-depressive stupor, there is hardly an opportunity left for affective discharge to the outside. The discharge is, as it were, mute; it is centripetal. Thus in some way patients with melancholic forms of depression who noisily attack themselves may be better off, inasmuch as they can at least discharge their self-directed aggression by way of self-accusations.

How is it possible, under these circumstances, that depressive conditions in which the tensions cannot be relieved by discharge to the outside ever come to an end? And yet we observe that patients who have spent months or even years in a catatonic stupor may get up one day, begin to move and eat and talk, and within a brief period may return to life.

Such observations make us suspect that psychotic depressive or manic conditions are terminated, not by the economic process involved in the mood, but by physiological changes which may set in suddenly or slowly. These processes may also change the proportion between aggressive and libidinal forces in favor of the latter, and thus enable the patient again to vest libido in the external world. From my clinical observation I gained the impression that only at the moment when patients begin to reinvest psychic energy in the world and to discharge onto the outside world, the mood reacquires a useful economic function whose value increases as the patients become accessible to treatment and capable of reality testing. This is why psychotherapy in a psychotic-depressive period is most profitable during the final phase.

4

Denial and Repression

In the last chapter I mentioned the important part that the mechanism of denial plays in normal and especially in pathological mood conditions. Both this chapter and the next one deal with the problem of denial and with the states of depersonalization in which denial plays such a significant role. In both chapters case material of the same patient will be presented because it lends itself to an exploration of the phenomena to be discussed.

I

Among the manifold defenses employed by the ego we find certain mechanisms, such as isolation, denial, introjection, projection, which appear to play a far more prominent role in borderline or psychotic patients than in neurotics. Apparently, such patients call upon this type of defense because of a deficient repressive ability of the ego. But this statement does not cover the much more complicated facts.

To be sure, these patients do not present an even, firm barrier of repressions with solid countercathectic ego formations which permit only certain id strivings and id derivatives to pass or intrude into the ego. Latent psychotics may have very rigid reaction formations, mostly of a compulsive type, but the latter are very fragile. During treatment we observe that such patients obstinately cling to them in frightened awareness that their potential breakdown might

First published in the *Journal of the American Psychoanalytic Association,* 5:61-92, 1957.

usher in an overt psychosis. As to the nature of their repressions, we are surprised to find that the same patients who are at any moment ready to produce undisguised id material, such as conscious incestuous and homosexual fantasies, may present amnesias covering the most significant and traumatic childhood periods like an iron curtain that cannot be lifted. Their oedipal and preoedipal past is—or may become—alive in terms of the present, but quite disconnected from their infantile history, which cannot be unearthed.

For instance, a schizophrenic boy of nineteen would at times develop abundant pregenital and genital incestuous and homosexual fantasies. This boy remembered a series of injurious childhood experiences with his parents and nurses, which he repetitively recounted in support of his paranoid defenses. But he was unable to produce any pertinent infantile memory material that could be linked up with his current fantasies and used for a reconstructive understanding of the past. On further observation I could see in this patient, as in other psychotics, that these undisguised, constantly varying fantasies and impulses appeared at the surface concomitantly with the collapse of his reaction formations; they were actually only disconnected id fragments, such as could be currently used for the purpose of denying and screening other more threatening fantasies. During such periods this boy developed overt incestuous fantasies whenever he felt sexually stirred up by a young girl. The incestuous fantasy screened his wish to free himself of his mother by killing her. At other times, impulses to rape, knife or strangle women in the street appeared in situations of overwhelming passive, masochistic, homosexual temptations.

Hence we might say that such patients summon up parts of the id, not only because of the breakdown of the repressive barrier, but as a poor, temporary substitute for more normal ego defenses. To the extent to which structural differentiation and drive neutralization get lost, structural conflicts are thus replaced by conflicts between opposing instinctual strivings which have invaded the ego and may be alternately used to deny and screen each other. Since the defensive fantasies are apt to arouse panic again, erratic fantasy variations may develop, indicative of the patients' frantic flight from one instinctual position to the other.

Sometimes the infantile and recent memories and memory defects of these patients appear to be organized and to function in a similar fashion. There may be amnesias covering significant childhood periods, yet suspiciously clear memory material referring to other infantile phases. But these infantile memories have a different quality than those of neurotics. They may be strangely undistorted —e.g., sexual scenes or other events remembered in precise details— and may be either emotionally isolated and decathected or, in other cases or other stages, affectively overinvested and recounted as if happening today.[1] Again we gain the impression that these overly lucid memory islands, though lacking the structure of screen memories, have a defensive function and safeguard the complete amnesia of particularly frightening or disappointing childhood events. Though not at all confused, such patients may be quite unable, for instance, to recall how they spent the last day, while frantically focusing attention on a side issue, on an infantile fantasy or the like. It is significant that these queer amnesias do not selectively blot out single painful experiences but are, so to speak, a wholesale business.

Their nature certainly makes us suspect that they involve mechanisms of massive denial of external and internal reality.[2] This suspicion finds confirmation through the study of certain neurotics who occasionally show a similar type of infantile amnesia and forgetfulness with regard to current events. But in contrast to psychotics, they usually are able to recover these experiences. I may add that the closer latent psychotics get to an overt psychotic state, the more they tend to ignore the current reality and to overcathect the past or what they believe to be the past. Comparable to hysterics who present memories of infantile seduction which turn out to be only fantasies, they may then present what they believe to be recollections or make emotionally hypercathected, fantastic reconstructions of their recent and their infantile past. Such material turns out to be a delusional distortion of the past, i.e., a reprojection of current, delusional fantasy material onto the past. Unlike hysterics, such

[1] Mahler and Elkisch (1953) point to the "fabulous memory" of psychotic children as evidence of the ego's inability to execute repression. In general, their findings in infantile psychoses are most relevant for this chapter and dovetail with the observations and opinions presented below.

[2] Here I refer to Eissler's paper, "An Unusual Function of an Amnesia" (1955). His patient's amnesia "had the function not only of denying that she had suffered a trauma, but also of experiencing the world as one in which no trauma can occur. . . . [He wonders] how often it may happen that what appears on the clinical level like a childhood amnesia is in reality a screen memory with a negative content" (p. 77f.). His example beautifully demonstrates my point.

patients tend, of course, to maintain a delusional conviction regarding the truth of their supposed recollections.

I shall at this point break off my remarks on psychotics. What I wish to stress is that in view of such puzzling observations we cannot simply speak of a lack or deficiency of repression in such patients. They display complex anomalies in their defensive system which present a challenge to the analytic investigator. But this is beyond the scope of this discussion. When I wrote this paper in 1957, I felt that any new observation on the nature of denial, its way of operation in contrast to repression, and its collaboration and interaction with the latter and with other defense mechanisms would be of value. At that time I stressed the preliminary nature of my study and the need for further research. In the meantime my paper seems to have stimulated analytic observations along these lines (Geleerd, 1965; Modell, 1961; Moore and Rubinfine, 1969; Siegman, 1967, 1970).

Of course, the use of denial is by no means a prerogative of psychotics. As pointed out by Kris and others, denial can serve a valuable function even in normal life. Many neurotic patients, though predominantly narcissistic personality types, employ denial as an auxiliary defense. Patients who are accessible to analysis certainly lend themselves better to the study of this mechanism than psychotics.

II

Some of my analytic cases with conspicuous similarities in their defensive operations appeared to highlight rather sharply some characteristic features of denial. I have selected one of these patients for a brief presentation of pertinent case material.

Mr. F. was a highly intelligent, cultured, refined young man in his early thirties, who had come from the West Coast and had recently married. Clinically he combined a compulsive-depressive personality structure with tendencies to act out and to develop sporadic psychosomatic and hysterical conversion symptoms. Despite his feelings of inadequacy the patient was competent in his work, though at times blocked by his compulsive-depressive inhibitions. In general, he suffered from a lack of initiative and of genuine pleasure in all activities, including sex. His main complaint was that his emotional life was so dull and subdued. He was a detached "onlooker," walking, as it were, always in the shade, craving for the sun. Despite these affective disturbances, to which I shall return, the patient was able to maintain an affectionate relationship with his wife, a warm, impulsive woman who had attracted him by the very intensity of her emotional and instinctual strivings.

In the transference he developed an equally touching, mild, affectionate attachment which for years strictly excluded sexual desires or overt hostility. His feelings toward the analyst and toward his wife were clearly associated with two significant childhood figures. One of these was the orphaned daughter of friends, ten years his senior, a warm, rather seductive girl who lived in their home for many years. The other was the patient's only brother, who was born when the patient was six and died of polio at the age of three. The child had shared the room with him. The patient had the most vivid, affectionate memories of the little brother, and of his tragic illness and death to which he had reacted with profound grief and depression, wishing that he himself had died rather than this charming, beloved child. It took years to uncover his resentment at the little intruder, which had caused him habitually to run away to friends after school because there was "no place for him at home."

The patient's relationship to his father had also been very close until his adolescence, which ushered in a period of increasing ambivalence, rebellion, and estrangement. The father died of a septic condition when the patient was eighteen. Learning that his father had passed away, he had a severe shock reaction and an attack of "shaking all over the body," almost to the point of convulsions. The attack imitated the chills which the father had had during the last days of his life. After the father's death, the family discovered that during the last years he had spent all his savings on a mistress. But the patient did not remember ever having consciously blamed the father for his wrongdoing. Quite the opposite: he had developed a sort of gleeful admiration for the father's "courage," based on his feeling that the latter had been "justified" in starting this expensive extramarital love affair as an antidote to the unpleasant mother. Quite unconcerned with the salvage of the financial situation, which was handled by his father's closest friend, Mr. F. immediately left his mother with a tremendous feeling of liberation and went to another city.

The patient's conviction that he had never been jealous of his darling brother was surpassed only by his firm belief that he had never loved his mother. He described her as a very beautiful but cold, depressive, and unintelligent woman, who constantly nagged him and habitually had an expression of hurt and reproach written on her face. All he had ever felt toward her was cold resentment, irritation, and the wish to get rid of her. During an earthquake in his hometown he hoped and wished, consciously and coldly, that she would be killed. When friends remarked that he was a rather bad son, his spiteful response was that she had been a much worse mother. He felt he would be ashamed of loving such a worthless person. But the patient had a suspiciously complete amnesia covering the first four years. In the course of the analysis we found that his stubborn assertion of never having loved his mother screened and denied his profound preoedipal attachment to her, which had been traumatically disrupted at the age of three and a half.

His relationship to his mistress had developed several years after his father's death, following a disappointing love experience with a beautiful girl who resembled his mother. At that time the patient had been very depressed and physically ill. In contrast to his mother and to his first sweetheart, this girl was very brilliant, like his father, and she had generously offered to take care of him during his illness. He had turned to her, as in his early childhood he had turned to his father when he had felt deserted by his mother. It is also important that she had a disability of her leg, which reminded him of his brother's polio. Although he had never been in love with her, he admired her, needed her support, and felt deeply obligated to her. But after learning that she had secretly had an abortion, he felt hopelessly committed to her. Their personal and sexual relationship deteriorated; yet he continued to live with her for six years, unwilling to marry but unable to leave her who reminded him more and more of the sick, nagging, reproachful mother. He became increasingly passive, depressed, and finally as coldly resentful toward her as toward his mother. In these relationships to mother and mistress the patient emulated and simultaneously rebelled against his father who had felt compelled to marry the mother after having seduced her, but who behaved to her in a hostile, derogatory way, without ever deserting her as the little boy had spitefully suggested.

When the patient felt that he could not stand the situation any longer, the idea occurred to him that since he could not desert his mistress, he might kill her—by poison, for instance, to which he might gain access. These murderous temptations did not have a true paranoid quality. At this stage the patient did not even blame his mistress as he had blamed his mother; he simply felt that, worthy as she was, he did not love her, that he was chained to her and wanted to get rid of her. The idea to kill her did not arouse any conscious guilt feelings. He was convinced that he would not suffer remorse after the crime, as long as he was safe, i.e., sure of not being caught.

Of course, the patient did not carry out his plan. Instead he consulted a friend, a lawyer, much older in years, who knew and highly appreciated his mistress, and who urged him to stay and marry her. Thereupon the patient managed to catch his friend in a grave error of professional judgment. At this point he left him with feelings of great relief and now felt able to separate from his mistress, to fall in love with another girl, and eventually to marry her.

We need not go into the transparent homosexual conflict with the father, which he revived with his friend. Suffice it to say that his acting out repeated the events after his father's death. The discovery that the hypocritical father, who had preached and formally adhered to morality, had himself secretly sinned, absolved the patient of his own guilt toward his mother. After exposing his friend, however, he again managed to exonerate him by throwing the blame back on the woman, in this case his mistress. Both he and his friend had been fooled by her pretense of love and kindness. Freed of his bondage, he now could identify with the glorified, wishful image of a father who, instead of secretly sinning, would have ruthlessly exposed and deserted the mother and looked for marital happiness with another woman.

His acting out epitomizes his superego pathology. Although the patient was at times severely depressed and self-critical, he readily professed that he did not own a real conscience, i.e., a set of guiding ethical principles. He lived mainly according to certain formal rules of what he regarded as "proper or improper behavior." He saw no reason for himself or others to feel guilty about bad thoughts, so long as they did not turn into actions. Moreover, in glaring contrast to his practical inhibitions, he would loudly speak up for "freedom from hypocritical morality" and defend any actions which he personally regarded as "justified." Thus, cold death wishes and even murderous temptations could develop without any signs of anxiety or guilt in a man who was otherwise unable to feel or express the slightest anger and who behaved like an exceedingly decent person.

A childhood memory from the age of five to six opened the way to a deeper understanding of his anomalous superego functions. The patient had spent the summer in the country with his pregnant mother. He recalled that one day during that summer he had taken a stick and pierced a little toad in the garden. The toad, with its big belly, became associated with the pregnant mother. The patient remembered that he could not stand the sight of this injured toad because it "looked at him reproachfully." He just wanted to get rid of it, "to make it disappear." He killed the toad. It then became clear that whatever he had done to placate and please his mother, and later on, his mistress, they had forever "looked at him hurt and reproachfully" like the injured toad.[3] This intolerable, reproachful look, however, kept him captive to these women to the point where he wished to "make them disappear" like the toad. Since to desert them would have involved open fight and hurt, this could be accomplished only by a painless elimination of these loathsome objects.

The gradual appearance of conscious guilt feelings in the patient, especially toward his mother, ushered in the analysis of his oedipal and preoedipal conflicts. In the beginning the patient had disclaimed not only having a superego but, even more so, having an oedipus complex. In fact, he could not really believe in an unconscious, either in himself or in others. His disbelief in the existence of a superego and an id was clearly reflected in his emotional attitudes. Whenever he had yielded to his superego, it had been without conscious conviction; when he had given in to his id, it had been without passion or pleasure. His craving for any kind of emotional experience, even though it might be profoundly upsetting, proved to be a longing for a "frank" conflict between violent emotional and instinctual strivings on the one hand, and an audible, strong, convincing inner voice of conscience on the other.

It was a turning point in the patient's analysis when he dreamed of an airplane crash involving himself, his mother, and his brother Billy, who was, however, not the real but "a second" Billy. The child

[3] The patient's investment in women's facial expression and its link with the mother's depressive condition remind one of the case described by Kris in "The Recovery of Childhood Memories in Psychoanalysis" (1956).

was killed. He and his mother survived, but she became insane. Visiting her in a sanitarium, he felt deep pity and love for her, such as he had never felt in real life.

This dream impressed the patient so profoundly that I suggested it might refer to a real childhood event. At that moment it suddenly occurred to him that his mother must have had a miscarriage when he was three and a half. "If this should be true," he said excitedly, "I can believe in the unconscious." The dream came, indeed, very close to the truth. The miscarriage had occurred at that time, caused by a trolley accident; it had taken place at home, in his father's absence, and his mother had been physically ill and depressed for many weeks thereafter. This was the trauma which had broken up the relationship to his mother. The complete amnesia covering his relationship to her during the first childhood years had safeguarded the denial of his early attachment and of the severe conflicts aroused by her pregnancy and miscarriage.

Moreover, the disastrous impact of the traumatic incident was denied and screened by very lucid memories of sexual games, at the age of four, with a little girl who had invited him to masturbate her. His vivid recollection of her "pretty" organ and of her intense genital pleasure had been convincing evidence that the female genital was a potent organ—indeed, much more beautiful and powerful than the penis. This firm belief served his denial of the genital injury inflicted upon his mother, and of the resulting profound castration and guilty fears.

Obviously, the child had witnessed and guessed much of what was happening.[4] Left in the hands of a maid, he had felt lost and confused, unable to blame his bleeding, sick mother or to accuse his father on whom he now depended so badly. Subsequent material showed that in his fantasy this accident was a crime which, as he believed, his parents—ultimately the mother—had committed, but for which his sick, depressive, reproachful mother appeared to blame him forever. Six years later the death of little Billy repeated the earlier trauma. From then on the patient carried the heavy load

[4] The following incident made us suspect that the patient had actually witnessed the miscarriage. In his twenties, he saw a moving picture of a forceps delivery. When the forceps was applied, Mr. F., who had not found a seat and was standing as he watched, fell to the floor in a dead faint. He hurt his head so severely that he needed immediate surgical care.

of guilt feelings, unacceptable and unbearable because in his mind the parents were the "real criminals."

We now understand his pathological reactions to his mistress. Her secret abortion, which was also followed by a prolonged period of sickness, enhanced both his guilt conflicts and his rebellion to an intolerable degree. His murderous ideas represented an ultimate, magic, defensive device supposed to free him from an undeserved punishment. At the same time they aimed at a revengeful, punitive elimination of the "true criminal."

The analysis of this material shed light on his (allergic) psychosomatic and hysterical symptoms which represented masochistic identifications with the injured or dying members of his family.

To the degree in which he ceased to deny, intense guilt feelings, then pity, and finally waves of affection toward his mother were permitted to appear and to replace his symptoms. Eventually his own "guilt" came to the surface, i.e., his severe preoedipal and oedipal rivalry conflicts and, in particular, the intense envy and hate hidden in his homosexual attachment to his father and in his maternal involvement with his little brother.

What can we learn from this case report for the study of denial?

III

The patient's nuclear problems developed during his mother's pregnancies and were centered about wishful fantasies of a sadistic attack on her womb. Normally a child masters his fear, envy, and hate of a future rival through repression of the forbidden impulses, safeguarded by his affection for mother and baby and by additional reaction formations. In this patient, fate precluded such a normal solution. Unfortunately, his sadistic wishes found fulfillment: first in the mother's miscarriage, her illness, depression, and desertion; then in the death of Billy, whom all his desperate love could not save. Thus the magic wish fulfillment turned into a punishment which became the germ of his sadomasochistic personality development. Throughout his life the patient vacillated between meek submission to the punitive power and hostile rebellion against the injustice of his penalty. His need for his mother's affection had been throttled so early and so traumatically that she became and remained the main target of his hostility, and thus of his pathological introjections and projections. Being what she was, she was bound to absorb most of the fear and aggression veered away from father and brother, and lent herself easily to the roles of the victim, the murderer and the judge, the seducer (the id) and the retaliator (the superego).

After the loss of Billy, the patient began to show all the signs of a chronic depression. But he was not aware of this state or other masochistic manifestations, since his goal had been to ward off the "undeserved" guilt conflict with which life had burdened him. For this purpose he established a powerful, though ineffectual superstructure of magic defenses supposed to protect him from both: from his guilty fears and the guilt itself; from his insidious masochistic, self-punitive trends and from his deeper, sadistic tendencies. Let us scrutinize the nature of these defenses in which denial played the predominant part. We may begin with the patient's struggle against his unconscious guilt feelings.

As Freud (1916) pointed out, hysterical patients suffer from an unconscious need for punishment. But their repressions and affective inhibitions are in general selective and remain restricted to specific forbidden impulses and the corresponding guilt feelings, both of which find meaningful expression in the hysterical symptoms. Otherwise impulsive and hyperaffective rather than inhibited, hysterics commonly suffer from anxieties and know the pangs of a bad conscience except in the area of repression. Mr. F.'s defenses, however, operated in a far more radical manner. He managed to ward off not only specific guilt feelings but all guilt feelings and anxieties, and not only the forbidden impulses but all genuine impulses. His defenses, indeed, were drastic enough to kill two birds with one stone: they dealt simultaneously with the superego and the id, so thoroughly that he could deny the existence of both. How did he achieve this goal?

My previous statement that the patient suffered from general inhibitions of feelings, thinking, and acting must be specified. The case material showed that he not only isolated ideas from the associated affects, as compulsives will do, but quite generally disconnected actions, thoughts, and feelings and treated them differently. Emotionally pale, evil thoughts were permissible if they did not become bad actions, since they could not do any harm. But finally even his murderous ideas and the actual desertion of his mistress could be sufficiently rationalized and justified to appear acceptable. His main objective was certainly a general stifling of his emotions, so complete that he could escape the truly affective experience of any unacceptable instinctual drive, either sexual or aggressive, and consequently of any anxiety or guilt—in short, of all undesirable and unpleasurable feelings. With the help of this device he could allow even the most forbidden strivings to emerge into consciousness.

But for this escape he paid dearly with the loss of real pleasure in his life, which was extremely dull and blank. When undesirable feelings and impulses arose nevertheless, he managed to deny their true nature. He sometimes appeared to be downcast, showing all the signs of anxiety or guilt on his face, but did not admit to feeling depressed, anxious, or guilty. Since his death wishes were cold and passionless, he had no difficulty in denying their hostile nature and in using them as a magic defense. His sexual activities were so compulsive that he could experience them as "a job that had to be done." He had the same attitude toward his work, from which he failed to derive any genuine pleasure. Occasionally he hurt his wife by rather cruel remarks, but was quite unaware of his behavior. When told what he had done, he would be unable first to remember the incident, then to understand why such a remark could have hurt her. At last, feeling quite miserable, he would deny that he suffered from remorse. The way his defenses operated calls to mind the joke about the man who, accused of having borrowed, damaged, and failed to return his neighbor's pot, claims (1) that he returned it intact; (2) that it was broken to begin with; and (3) that he never borrowed it in the first place.

As in the joke, the defenses which I described so far were not effective enough. The patient's denial needed further support from mechanisms of projection, which likewise dealt radically with both the id and the superego. His superego fears were thus externalized and retransformed into fears of injured women who would hurt him by their reproachful look. However, not only the punitive superego was pinned on parental figures, essentially on women, but also the guilt itself: the id strivings. We remember his exposure of the hypocritical authorities, which pretended to be good (the ego ideal), but were actually sinners (the id), blaming him for their sins (the superego). His projective defense was further enhanced by his glorification of immorality, which truly made him a hypocrite, since it meant a return of the repressed under the disguise of an ideal.

The collaboration and interaction of his defenses, of massive repressions and generalized inhibitions assisted by isolation, denial, introjection, and projection mechanisms, fortified his defensive structure to such an extent that he was ultimately able to disclaim the existence of his id and his superego or, as I would prefer to say, to disown them. His disclaiming, disowning, and projection of these psychic structures onto the outside established a different basis for dealing with his problems. He could then handle intrapsychic conflicts as though they were conflicts with reality. He could avoid crime and punishment either by self-effacing appeasement or, if necessary, by flight from or elimination of dangerous objects.

This accounts for his acting-out tendencies, which we regularly find in patients with his type of defenses. Noteworthy in this connection is the enormous hypercathexis of perception in his acting out. Looking and being looked at played a dominant role in his emotional and sexual life. His sexual fantasies and activities were tuned to one main motif: the denial of his sadistic and castrative wishes, the unmasking of such strivings in the female partners, and the denial or undoing of their castration. In his fantasies aggressive women would, for instance, seduce him by displaying their irresistible desire for his penis which he would passively offer for their use. The fantasy of surprising women in sexual activities would induce not only sexual excitement but feelings of gleeful triumph.

With his wife he could maintain a rather satisfactory relationship by consistent endeavors to please her and to gratify her sexually, with simultaneous renunciation of his own psychosexual demands and his own genital pleasure. Since with her he succeeded in "making the reproachful look disappear" (undoing her castration) by producing and watching "the expression of sexual delight on her face," he felt amply rewarded and could repay her with feelings of grateful affection. Failing to achieve this goal, as with his mother and his mistress, he became sexually and emotionally inactive, cold, and detached, sometimes to the point of depersonalization, pretending that he himself or she did not exist. In despair about this state, he eventually felt that she must be eliminated lest he should die.

IV

My description of the patient's defensive operations was intended to focus attention on those features of denial which differentiate the particular way it works from repression. For the further scrutiny of this problem we must keep in mind that the term "repression," as defined by Freud (1915b), refers essentially to the defense directed against the drives or rather their ideational representations (with simultaneous inhibition of the corresponding affects). Traditionally the term has been applied more broadly, even by Freud himself.[5] By the "repression of memories" we mean, for instance, not only the defense directed against the instinctual drives, but also the forgetting of the external events. Since denial operates originally and basically against external reality, this is a point which will gain significance in the course of this discussion.

As long as the defense mechanism of denial was not studied in its own right, there was little need for terminological precision. That it was scarcely studied until recently is remarkable because as early as 1900, Freud stated: "It is a familiar fact that much of this avoidance of what is distressing—this ostrich policy—is still to be seen in the normal mental life of adults" (p. 600). And on p. 618, we find what we would now regard as two nice examples of denial. But at that time Freud presented them merely as evidence of the censorship between the preconscious and the conscious. This is pertinent with regard to the topographical difference between repression and denial, to which I shall return later.

The most careful and subtle study of denial and the way it operates was done by Lewin (1950). His book includes a review of the previous literature on denial, giving credit to the remarks by Abraham and to publications by H. Deutsch, A. Angel, Anna Freud, and, of course, Freud.

Lewin quotes Freud who, contrasting repression with denial, hinted at least indirectly at the interaction of these defenses, which he believed to arise and to be effective during the same infantile period. Clinical observations leave no doubt, however, that denial is a more archaic, more primitive, and historically earlier mechanism

[5] In *Inhibitions, Symptoms and Anxiety* (1926) Freud described as the "repressive process" in phobias the whole defense process which in addition to repression involves auxiliary mechanisms, such as regression, displacement, and projection.

than repression—in fact, its forerunner; a defense which originates in the child's efforts to get rid of unpleasant perceptions of the outside world. As Lewin says, in summarizing Freud's last remarks (1940a): "Denial disclaims the external world . . . as repression disclaims the instincts" (p. 52f.). Thus, denial is fundamentally always denial of perceptions, which can be achieved by the withdrawal of cathexis from the undesirable perception. Insofar as denial "may assist or replace repression," it can also be used as a defense against " 'internal' reality." In contrast to repression and the defenses that "operate directly against instinct, . . . denial is called upon mainly to avoid anxiety" (p. 53f.). This is a significant statement which is certainly validated by the case material I have presented. I emphasized that the main objective of my patient was to avoid anxiety and, more generally, all feelings of unpleasure.

As the optimist and the hypomanic so convincingly demonstrate, the goal of denial is the avoidance of unpleasure. But what about the denial of pleasure, for instance, in the pessimist and the depressive who undoubtedly disclaim and deny any pleasurable aspect either in the external world or in themselves? Suffice it here to consider the simpler case of the pessimist. His chronic anticipation of the worst is certainly also intended to protect him from future pain and hurt. A very masochistic patient, who was terrified of physical hurt, developed fantasies in which he returned from the war crippled or blinded. He felt that this might help him to tolerate what might actually happen. Thus even the denial of pleasurable reality still appears to aim at the avoidance of anxiety and pain, even though it may fail in its purpose.

Ultimately all defenses serve the avoidance of anxiety, but in repression signal anxiety mobilizes a defensive struggle against the sources of danger, i.e., the instinctual drives. With regard to denial, Lewin states correctly that "when the instinct representations have become conscious and make a claim on the ego to be accepted as reality (which would be called here 'internal' reality, but which can be treated by the ego as if external), denial may make its appearance" (p. 53).

In fact, it seems characteristic of denial that to begin with the ego reacts to the danger signal by an immediate attempt to ignore this very signal itself. I am inclined to believe that this immediate, initial denial of the danger signal is what prevents the ego from embarking on a true defensive struggle. Instead of expelling the inimical drives from its realm, all the ego can do is to deny their presence or the dangerous, painful impact of the drive invasion.

These considerations are pertinent with respect to the difference between repression and denial. Contrary to repression, which makes the ideas unconscious and inhibits the corresponding affects, denial apparently can at best achieve no more than prevent ideas which have reached the preconscious from becoming conscious.[6]

As in Freud's aforementioned examples, denial thus appears to establish a censorship or rather a protective screen between the preconscious and the conscious. It is a defense which seems to work within the realm of the ego. This is in harmony with Freud's remarks on denial in his paper on "Fetishism" (1927a) and in "An Outline of Psycho-Analysis" (1940a), where he spoke of a split in the ego caused by denial. Comparing repression and denial, he stated that in each of them we find two contradictory ideas or attitudes. Whereas in the case of repression the one exists in the ego and the opposing one in the id, in the case of denial both remain in the ego, thus causing a split in the ego. And Freud concluded that the difference between them is essentially a topographical or structural one.

But Freud's ideas on denial and the split of the ego in denial leave certain questions unanswered. He himself remarked that he used the case of the fetishist only as a particularly impressive example of such a split in the ego caused by two opposing ideas. Except for the special mode of conflict solution, the basic defense in fetishism indeed does not appear to be different from that of all those patients, male or female, who attach to women an "illusory penis" in order to avoid the frightening idea of female castration.

This outstanding example of denial, the denial of female castration, illuminates the distortion of reality which is regularly involved in this defense. Actually, each one of the two opposing ideas distorts realistic facts: even though women do lack a penis, they are certainly not castrated. The child's common misinterpretation of the female genital perceived reveals the direct influence of the id on the initial perception—a phenomenon studied by Fisher (1954, 1956). The immediate, painful distortion of reality is in this case the concrete, external reflection and confirmation of the child's own castration

[6] In this connection see Kris's paper "On Preconscious Mental Processes" (1950).

fears and wishes. What is important for our comparison between denial and repression is that in denial the opposing idea employed by the ego as a defense against the frightening notion is again an id fantasy, this time a wishful, pleasurable one. This pleasurable idea may likewise use certain perceptions which lend themselves as confirmation.

In summary: the opposing ideas are both cathected in the ego and, under the influence of instinctual conflicts, distort the perception of reality; the pleasurable, wishful idea then serves the denial of the painful, frightening notion.

This appears to be characteristic of the primitive way in which denial works in general. Lewin (1950) states, referring to a patient, that denial was "a function of the pleasure ego, and . . . indicated this early type of ego organization" (p. 58). Comparing denial and repression, we see that in repression countercathectic ego formations safeguard the repression of unacceptable drive representations. In the case of denial, a wishful id fantasy that tends to distort reality is used as a defense against an opposite, frightening idea which likewise distorts reality.

This comparison calls back to mind my initial remarks on psychotics who use manifest id strivings as a defense against opposing, more frightening id impulses. Thus it appears that whenever denial is used, structural conflict—at least in a limited area—may be replaced by instinctual conflict, within the realm of the ego. This implies that denial tends to affect the thought processes, to interfere with logical thinking, with recognition of the "truth," and with reality testing to an incomparably greater extent than repression.

It is a clinical fact, however, that in neurotic patients these opposing ideas usually are truly and deeply repressed, i.e., cathected in the id, even though the defensive, wishful fantasy of the phallic woman is closer to the surface and finds manifest expression in the patients' ego attitudes, in their social or sexual behavior. But Freud's unfinished paper "Splitting of the Ego in the Process of Defence" (1940b) suggests that Freud actually referred to the original, infantile situation when these ideas first arise. Such ideas, representing an original distortion and denial of realistic perceptions which cause a split in the ego, may in the further course of development undergo a process of true repression. We realize that the term denial need not always refer to denial as a current defense; we may quite correctly speak of a repressed idea which denies an opposite, undesirable, equally repressed notion. Clinically we frequently find, when such repressed ideas re-enter consciousness, that patients may still refuse to accept reality, and resort once more to denial and distortion as an ultimate means of defense. This consideration will prove relevant in my subsequent discussion of the interaction between denial and repression in the development of infantile amnesia. The fact that ideas denying and distorting reality may be repressed in no way contradicts the assumption that denial as a defense can only make or keep an idea preconscious.

Carrying the comparison with repression further, Lewin (1950) shows that "denial may operate like repression in a dual capacity. It may oppose the intellectual recognition of an external fact, say a death. . . . Or it may oppose the affective impact of the external fact" (p. 53f.). Thus, we can now add that denial may not even prevent unacceptable ideas from reaching full consciousness. But in this case denial may still avoid anxiety and unpleasure either by disguising the true nature of such undesirable ideas or, as an ultimate device, by preventing awareness of the unpleasant nature of the corresponding affects. Mr. F.'s case material furnished ample evidence of all these methods employed by denial.

Lewin stressed that not only external but also internal reality can be denied, which is then treated "as if external." The problem is how denial can manage to handle internal reality in the same way as external reality.

The first clue to the answer can be found in my earlier discussion of the child's denial of female castration. I indicated that the contradictory images of the castrated and the phallic woman, which distort reality, are a concrete or quasi-concrete expression of the child's instinctual conflicts and fears. Thus, the denial in this case utilizes external reality for the purpose of an indirect operation against internal reality.

In Mr. F., too, the denial of female castration played a dominant role in his defense against castration and guilty fears and the underlying forbidden impulses. But his fortress of defenses was erected on much broader grounds. He employed denial as a defense not only against unpleasant ideas and affects provoked by the perception of external reality. In collaboration with repression he also used denial directly against instinctual fantasies, wishes, and impulses. Evidently this is the much more intricate problem which I shall presently try to tackle: even though denial cannot effectively ward off the instincts, to what extent and in what way can this defense operate directly against internal reality, in the sense of the drives themselves?

We recall that originally the child cannot distinguish between external and internal reality, i.e., between his sensory perceptions of the frustrating or gratifying objects, and his inner unpleasurable or pleasurable experiences. If denial handles psychic manifestations as though they were external reality, the prerequisite for denial of the inner world must be a partial regression—not to this earliest but to a "concretistic" infantile stage where the child, though already aware of the difference between internal and external world, between himself and the objects, still treats both in the same manner.

I do not think it would be correct to speak at this stage of an "externalization" of internal reality, at least not in the sense of a confusion or equation of inner and outer reality. For instance, if little Johnny after a temper tantrum assures his mother that now bad Johnny is gone and good Johnny is here again, he is fully aware that it is he who was angry and who now feels loving again. But he still experiences and expresses the change of his thoughts and feelings, of his own state and behavior, in concretistic, personifying, and generalizing terms of a disappearance of bad and a reappearance of good Johnny. This example of little Johnny certainly brings the case of Mr. F. to mind. And it is also very significant for the problem of depersonalization, which will be discussed in Chapter 5.

I reported that my patient was unable to experience, qualify, and discriminate specific acceptable or unacceptable feelings or ideas, fantasies, or impulses. Even though he commonly did not use slogans, he conceived of such psychic manifestations in general terms of "aggression," or "sex," or "love," or "conscience," or "passions," as if they were concrete parts of the self which appeared or disappeared, which he lacked or had lost, and which he would like to discover, recover, and own. This epitomizes what I wish to propose: that denial presupposes an infantile concretization of psychic reality, which permits persons who employ this defense to treat their psychic strivings as if they were concrete objects perceived.

Moreover, such persons also treat the psychic manifestations perceived in other persons in the same manner. My patient, for instance, did not genuinely respond to a woman's angry and hurt, or loving and pleasurable feelings, but simply watched her face, trying either to evade her "reproachful and hurt look" or to make it disappear by producing "an expression of delight on her face." In other words, lacking an empathic understanding of other people's feelings and thoughts, reactions and actions, these patients "watch," or "close their eyes to," the concrete, "visible" expression of their state. Often their insensitiveness to less visible, indirect, subtle forms of emotional expression in others reveals itself in a striking tactlessness. This tendency—to treat psychic phenomena in others as well as in themselves as if they were concrete—explains the ease with which the denial of external and the denial of internal reality collaborate in the area of interpersonal relationships.

Consequently we find in such patients not only a general shift of cathexis to the area of perception and apperception, but also a primitive type of perceiving and apperceiving psychic phenomena in terms of looking at them as if they were concrete parts of the objects or of the self. Withdrawal of cathexis from painful perceptions as well as apperceptions, with simultaneous hypercathexis and intensified observation of desirable ones, can thus remove unpleasurable experiences from vision and replace them by pleasurable ones.

Examining this concretization of psychic reality more carefully, we realize that it must make abundant use of processes of isolation and disconnection. It must involve on the one hand a cutting apart of psychic units; on the other, a merging and categorical regrouping of the separated components that tends to turn them from abstract-functional into new, quasi-concrete composites. Mr. F. disconnected fantasies and thoughts not only from the associated feelings, but even from the corresponding actions. He then dealt with each of these psychic categories independently and radically, as if with separate, concrete, imagistic parts of the self. Disregarding the different frame of reference, he would also tend to isolate, to fuse into units, and to deny *en bloc* all those psychic elements which happened, for instance, to come close to consciousness simultaneously with an unacceptable psychic content.

This mode of operation explains why denial works not in a selective, specialized manner, as does repression, but in a massive, global way which easily induces an indiscriminate, collective generalization of defensive processes, with displacements and transference manifestations expanding to all objects, areas, and activities.[7] I emphasized that Mr. F. suffered not from specific but from generalized inhibitions and would respond not with specific affective reactions, but with generalized mood conditions; consequently, he complained about the absence of a conscience or of passions or of ideas, of sexual needs, of aggression, or of pleasure, *in toto.* Lewin's description of hypomanic screen affect illustrates the same point.

In the introduction I indicated that the massive effect of denial can be observed especially well in the peculiar quality of the amnesias, the forgetting of patients who employ this defense abundantly. This point brings the question of the collaboration between denial and repression back into focus. Mr. F. lent himself to a study of this type of forgetting. His infantile amnesia covering the early childhood years was so complete that for several years the analytic material did not give the slightest hint of the traumatic events at three and a half. His forgetting of this unhappy period was all the more amazing since we discovered that his mother had repeatedly talked about the incident. The patient had either "not listened" or "listened, but not asked questions" or "immediately forgotten again." This also was characteristic of his attitude to current conflicts. Whenever he had an experience that mobilized undesirable feelings, he would simply "not attend" and manage quickly to forget everything that had happened during this period of time.

In other words, instead of coping with the specific current conflicts which aroused painful feelings, he simultaneously withdrew attention from the external stimuli and from his inner responses, and then immediately and indiscriminately erased the memory of all the internal and external experiences surrounding the specific, disturbing conflict. In the analysis, the patient's difficulties in listening and recalling upsetting sessions left no doubt about the close collaboration of repression with denial of internal and external reality as auxiliary defense in such a type of amnesia. The question arises how far denial may even normally prepare and assist what we call the repression of memories.

[7] Here I may refer again to the above-cited paper by Mahler and Elkisch (1953) who describe the failure in selective repression, the irreversible connection of the perception and the affect, "baby and crying," and the "syncretic engram conglomeration" in a psychotic child.

I previously remarked that infantile amnesias involve not only the defense directed against the instinctual drive representations, but extend far beyond this process to the area of perception. In connection with Freud's paper on "Fetishism" I had pointed out, furthermore, that ideas originating in a denial and distortion of reality, such as the concepts of the castrated or the phallic woman, may become truly and deeply repressed. For a re-examination of the defenses collaborating in the forgetting of an infantile memory, let me resort to a typical sexual childhood experience apt to be forgotten (repressed).

A little boy at the phallic stage suddenly sees the genital of his father who is urinating. What are the various memory components of such an experience and their possible vicissitudes? The memory would first of all encompass elements pertaining to the perception of the event, such as the sight of the penis, the father in the process of urinating, the whole associated setting of the scene, and the father's emotional expression and behavior during the event. But the significant part of the memory, from the standpoint of the defense, would be the little boy's inner experience, i.e., his various emotional and instinctual responses to these stimuli.

At this point I refer back to my remarks concerning the immediate distortions which perceptions suffer under the impact of instinctual wishes and fears. As the child's concept of the castrated or phallic woman shows, the infantile images of the objects and of the self are always forged from perceptions of external reality and from fantasies arising from within under the influence of the instinctual impulses and conflicts. Consequently, the boy's various instinctual responses, his homosexual and hostile impulses, would find a concrete expression not only in the memory of the specific scene perceived, but also in the lasting imprint left on the father image as well as on the image of his own self. Insofar as they are painful, these concrete and imagistic elements would lend themselves to denial as a first, primitive form of defense, which as such could achieve a forgetting of the memory.

But the castration fear engendered by the experience, at this stage of development, would certainly necessitate much more drastic measures. Subsequently a true defensive process would set in. It would operate directly and specifically against the forbidden libidinal and hostile wishful fantasies and the associated affects aroused by the event. This repressive process would eventually pull down into the unconscious even those elements of the memory which were originally warded off by denial.

In summary: we must surmise that the defensive process resulting in infantile amnesias normally utilizes denial in a preparatory and supportive function. This denial eliminates from consciousness preferably those painful elements of the external events and internal imagery in which unacceptable instinctual drives and fears have found a concretistic expression. A pathological prevalence of denial in the defensive processes would be reflected in the above-described quality of the infantile amnesias and of the available infantile memory material. We should find unusual and radical distortions of external and internal reality, past and present, along very definite lines, such as repression would be unable to achieve.

We shall now leave the problem of neurotic denial and its interaction with repression. But before approaching the next subject, psychotic denial, I must point to the intimate link between denial and the other two archaic defense mechanisms which were an integral part of Mr. F.'s defensive operations. If psychic manifestations reassume the character of concretistic images of parts of objects and of the self, they naturally lend themselves to primitive processes of introjection and projection. Here we are on familiar ground. The distinction between the collective mode of operation in denial and the more selective one in repression immediately calls to mind analogous differences between earlier infantile, primitive forms of identification and the more advanced identifications in the ego and the superego on a higher maturational level. Like denial, the first are based on concretistic fantasies of total or partial incorporation of good or bad objects into the self, or their expulsion from the self. The identifications arising at a more advanced stage also involve mechanisms of introjection and projection; but, like repression, they represent selective processes, inasmuch as they result in the development of certain standards, attitudes, and character traits taken over from the love objects.

Mr. F.'s case material lent itself to a study of the interplay between denial and such primitive processes as introjection and projection. I discussed the patient's denial, disowning, and projection of the bad or frightening parts of his self onto the outside, and briefly touched upon the underlying sadomasochistic identifications arising from primitive fantasies of incorporation of the bad, sadistic, injured, reproachful, and punitive mother.

We know that early infantile experiences of severe disappointment and desertion by the mother, such as this patient had undergone, may result in a proclivity to archaic mechanisms of identification. Such cases as that reported by Rosen (1955) warrant the question how far the traumatic exposure to frightening perceptions, particularly during the preoedipal phase, may create a special propensity for an abundant use of denial. In some other cases featuring denial as prominent mechanism of defense I found traumatic, terrifying events suddenly perceived during early childhood. In one instance it was the sudden sight of the dying mother who had committed suicide; in another, of the mother who had been robbed and murdered; in a third, a sudden miscarriage of the mother in front of the child; in yet another case, continuous, stormy primal scene experiences up to the age of nine.

In the case of Mr. F., I am convinced that the mother's miscarriage, followed by her illness and depression, and the revival of these experiences by the painful illness and death of his brother account for the prominent role of denial coupled with primitive introjection and projection mechanisms in his defensive operations. Evidently, the patient at the age of three and a half was not enough advanced in his ego development to cope successfully with the tremendous ambivalence conflicts which were suddenly unleashed by the traumatic events.

In fact, what appears to be common to these three primitive modes of defense is that from the energic and economic points of view they all work with large amounts of deneutralized drive energy. One of my reasons for selecting the case I have presented was that the original killing fantasies underlying the mechanism of denial had found manifest expression in his murderous ideas. This brings us close to the problem of psychosis and psychotic versus neurotic defenses. I believe that the regressive deneutralization and defusion of the drives and the prevalence of vast amounts of aggressive forces in psychotics are responsible for the breakdown of ego and superego functions, for the replacement of more advanced modes of defense by archaic ones (see Chapter 9)[8] and for the psychotic qualities and functions of the latter.

Comparing, from this perspective, repression, reaction formations, and the advanced forms of identification with denial and primitive introjection and projection mechanisms, we may assume the following. The use of small amounts of neutralized aggression directed by the superego against the ego or by the ego against the id appears to enable the ego to ward off specific, selected, unacceptable drive components with the support of equally specific countercathectic ego formations of a neutralized nature. In contrast, denial and archaic processes of introjection and projection operate with large quantities of deneutralized aggression (and opposing sexual forces) directed against dangerous self and object images or external objects.

Applying these considerations to psychosis, it follows that the psychotic conflict induces radical cathectic shifts of sexual and aggressive drive energy from one object or object image to another, or from the objects to the self or vice versa. We observe indeed that psychotics retransform not only functional psychic units but whole functional systems, such as the (ego-)id or the superego(-ego), into omnipotent object or self images which, insofar as they are dangerous or frightening, are attacked and eradicated, as I have shown in my book on *Psychotic Conflict and Reality* (1967).

The mechanisms underlying manic and depressive states will be discussed in Part II of this volume. Here I wish to point only to the massive assault by the personified, sadistic superego on the bad self, which results in a generalized inhibition of ego functions during depressive periods, or to the overthrowing of the superego during manic phases, which permits the ego to join forces with the id.

Schizophrenics often express their hate of the id or superego in unmistakable terms. The schizophrenic boy mentioned above, for instance, would at times mercilessly throttle all instinctual strivings, aggressive or sexual, on all levels. Working day and night, he deliberately ceased all sexual activities, went on a fasting diet, stopped smoking and drinking, at the same time avoiding any dangerous,

[8] In this connection Hartmann (1953), who shares my opinion, also refers to such mechanisms as the directing of aggression to the self or the outside, and the turning into the opposite, which Freud long ago had mentioned as the earliest modes of defense.

seductive contacts with women or with men. Ultimately, he expressed his wish to get rid of his badness by cutting off his penis. In such frantic, generalized defensive efforts, it is difficult to decide how far repression still participates or whether archaic defenses alone are at work. At any rate, sexual and aggressive drive manifestations would disappear completely at such times. Visualizing the enormous effort required for such a generalized defense, we are not surprised that it must fail. In this boy I could observe how his overstrained ego gradually bogged down and a state of empty, catatonic depression developed during which he was completely unable to work and had feelings of deadness and of loss of the self. Then suddenly a break would occur; the patient would rebel and express his hate of all prohibitions or of the authorities representing them. From one day to the next, the id reappeared and established its unmitigated power. An agitated, paranoid psychotic state would develop with pathological eating spells, uninterrupted masturbation, and with constantly varying, heterosexual and homosexual, polymorphous-perverse fantasies and homicidal impulses of the kind which I described in my introduction.

In psychotics, repression and other more normal defense mechanisms fail and are replaced by archaic defense processes. But denial, introjection, and projection are not a prerogative of psychotics; in neurotics we find such primitive defenses collaborating and interacting with repression. What, then, is the difference between psychotic and neurotic denial, introjection, and projection?

Here we must ask, first: what exactly are our criteria for designating certain mechanisms as psychotic? Katan (1950a, 1950b, 1954), who called attention to the nonpsychotic part in the personality of psychotics, regards as truly psychotic only those mechanisms of restitution that lead to delusional symptoms. But it is an oversimplification and in some respects even misleading to distinguish so strictly between the psychotic and the nonpsychotic (prepsychotic) part of the personality, and between psychotic (restitutive) mechanisms and nonpsychotic (neurotic and prepsychotic) defenses.

To begin with, in speaking of the nonpsychotic part in the personality of psychotics we must consider the conspicuous, basic differences between the personality structure and defense system of neurotics and of latent psychotics even preceding the prepsychotic stage. I am referring to their defective structural differentiation, the fragility and deficiency of their ego and superego functions, their insufficient repressive ability, and the prevalence of archaic defense mechanisms, features to which I have already pointed in my introductory remarks. I may here add an essential point which I discussed in my book (1967): the tendency of latent or ambulatory psychotics to externalize their conflicts, to act out, and to employ external objects and reality as an aid for their failing defenses. Observations on two schizophrenic adults and two latency children, whose future psychotic breakdown I predicted correctly, convinced me that these predisposing defects can be noticeably present as early as at the beginning of the latency period.

It is indeed these very same mechanisms—isolation, denial, introjection, projection—which are apt to assume psychotic qualities and functions when a manifest psychosis develops. Instead of being used for the purpose of instinctual defense they will then, in part, be employed in the service of psychotic "loss and restitution" processes. In contrast to repression, their archaic nature lends itself to such aims. During the manifest psychotic stage we may thus, at times, simultaneously find "nonpsychotic" and "psychotic" denial, introjection, and projection.

Moreover, it appears altogether questionable whether we should regard only mechanisms of restitution as truly psychotic. For instance, when a patient hates and tries to kill and eradicate either his id or his superego *in toto,* this is, in my opinion, a characteristically psychotic type of defense. And not only the mechanisms of restitution but also those eventuating in the preceding object loss are indicative of a defensive effort which is psychotic in nature.

In any case, the functional transformations in the ego's defenses, which lend them psychotic qualities, appear to depend on the above-discussed regressive changes of drive quantities and qualities occurring in the psychotic process. As regards the difference between neurotic and psychotic denial, introjection, and projection, the decisive factor thus is the depth of regression in psychotics.

To repeat: the neurotic ego that uses such defenses has only partly regressed to a stage where internal psychic reality, though clearly distinguished from external reality, is still treated in the same concretistic manner. Although neurotic denial may involve processes of disconnection, isolation, and collective joining of psychic elements, which turn them into quasi-concrete, imagelike units, the latter do not lose the quality of being psychic in nature. The line of demarcation between internal and external reality is maintained, even in view of such introjections and projections as I observed in Mr. F.

In psychotics, however, the pathological process leads to a real fragmentation, a splitting, a concretization, and externalization of psychic manifestations, to the point of lending them truly concrete qualities. Consequently we find an equation between what is abstract and psychic and what is concrete and physical in nature; as in the schizophrenic boy, who equated instinctual strivings first with badness, then with the bad penis or with bad objects, and consequently wished to get rid of the id by cutting off his genital or killing bad people.

We are familiar with the psychotic concretization of the abstract, which Hartmann (1953) rediscussed in his paper on schizophrenia. It involves continuous, archaic processes of introjection and projection, leading to a confusion between internal and external reality; between objects and their inner images; between perceptions of objects and object stimuli, and the inner responses to them; and consequently, between objects and the self. The result may be delusional fusions between split-off elements or parts of the self and the object representations, i.e., psychotic identifications of the type discussed in Chapter 10.

In connection with the psychotic concretization, Hartmann also discussed Freud's idea that psychotics disconnect words from their meaning and, shifting the cathexis from abstract thoughts to their formal word symbols which can be concretely perceived, turn the latter into object substitutes. Expanding Freud's thesis, I am inclined to believe that psychotics may convert into object substitutes not only words but any split-off, formal, psychic elements, e.g., components of affective expression, such as weeping, laughter, gestures, or even actions. I am indebted to Dr. Isidor Silbermann for apprising me of an observation which would confirm such an idea. Upon asking a schizophrenic boy who had inappropriate fits of laughter why he was laughing, he received the answer: "That is Johnny." An affective expression, laughter per se, had become an object, Johnny. We can assume that schizophrenic mannerisms may have the same meaning and function.

Let me turn back, from the general problem of psychotic defenses and psychotic concretization of psychic reality, to the specific topic of denial. We know that denial and distortion of reality play a complex role in the development of psychosis. Here I want to restrict myself to one special question: How far is the psychotic withdrawal of cathexis from objects and from the self induced by processes of massive denial of external and internal reality? We recall Mr. F.'s denial and disowning of his conscience and his instinctual drives, which led to feelings of inner emptiness and deadness, though never to the point of fear of loss of the self; furthermore, his cold detachment from his mother, resulting from wishes to hurt her and to make her reproachful look disappear.

The relation between denial and psychotic loss of object and self cathexis certainly requires thorough clinical and theoretical scrutiny. But we can observe that schizophrenics tend to relate themselves to objects by sensory instead of emotional contact, and also the opposite: that they may decathect objects by flight and avoidance of sexual contact, of touching, smelling, seeing, or listening to the object. In the schizophrenic boy, the retreat from the object world regularly announced itself by attempts to avoid the sight of dangerous men or women. When meeting such persons, he decathected them by literally closing his eyes and ears, and by spitting them out; whereas good people would be cathected by watching, imitating, and inhaling them.

Another patient refused to see his parents because keeping them at a distance made him feel toward them as to distant relatives. When he re-established his relationship to his parents, he saw the image of his father, who had been "locked up and hidden" in his self, visually emerge from his body "till down to the knees"; he became so frightened of the picture that he quickly tried to make it disappear by "locking it up again." The same patient revived his feelings for his mother by carrying around her picture and watching it intently throughout the day. In all these examples, we note, the loss and revival of feelings are accomplished by visual disappearance and resurrection of the object image which is equated with the external picture.

In concluding this chapter, I return to my point of departure: the discrepancy, in certain psychotics, between the ease with which id contents become manifest and the impervious character of the infantile amnesia. Actually, there is no discrepancy between these phenomena; they are quite consistent. The memories and the massive memory defects are built on the same broad basis of denial and distortion of reality on which the current pathology rests. The amnesias are not the result of true drive repression; this is the reason for both the invasion of the id into the ego and the difficulties in lifting the veil from the infantile history. The analytic recovery and reconstruction of the past presuppose a reality testing, a historical dating, a grouping, a fitting and integration of current drive manifestations into an organized context of external and internal historical reality. The psychotic is all the less capable of this the more he denies and loses contact with reality. Sometimes we observe that to the extent to which the psychotic recovers his capacity to test reality and use more normal defenses, he may develop the ability to work on his past.

In principle, we find the same difficulties in neurotics whose acting out constitutes a resistance against "remembering" and reconstruction of the past. I remarked above that, in general, patients who deny show a propensity for acting out. To put it reversely: acting out appears to be regularly linked up with a bent for denial. From the therapeutic standpoint we should be aware that our endeavors to make patients relinquish their acting out, in favor of recovery and reconstruction of the past, must be directed essentially against their denial and distortion of reality.

5

Depersonalization

Even though depersonalization involves a disturbance of object relations, it is an experience pertaining to the representation of the physical and mental self. In the first case, the person will complain that his body, or rather certain parts of the body, do not feel like his own, as belonging to him. He may describe them as being estranged from himself or as being dead. This experience may go along with subjective sensations of numbness and of changes in size and volume of the estranged body parts. The person may try to touch and feel them in order to convince himself that they are really "his."

There are states of depersonalization pertaining to the genitals and to the sexual act, which at first sight may impress us as cases of impotence or frigidity. When carefully questioned, such patients will report that they experience their genital as dead, as estranged, as not being their own. Male patients of this type may suffer from psychic impotence, but they may have erective potency, be able to perform the sexual act, have an ejaculation, and even some kind of orgastic experience. But in this case they perceive themselves as going through the act without being "present"; their penis performs as if it were not their own.

Whenever the depersonalization extends to the mental self, there is a feeling of unreality of the self and of being "outside of the self." The depersonalized patient will think, react, act; but his exper-

---

First published in the *Journal of the American Psychoanalytic Association,* 7:581-610, 1959.

ience is that of a detached spectator who is observing another person's performance. Not only his actions but his own thought processes appear to him unfamiliar and strange. As Schilder (1928) mentioned, acute experiences of psychic depersonalization frequently start with an attack of dizziness. Patients often complain about their inability to imagine familiar persons and things visually (Hartmann, 1922). While some patients have alternating or combined experiences of bodily and mental depersonalization, others may suffer only from either bodily or mental self-estrangement.

It is striking and characteristic that depersonalization is an experience which very often does not find any objective expression. Sometimes patients report that they are just going into a depersonalized state, or that they were "outside" and are now "back again," without giving evidence of any change in their affectomotor expression, their thought processes, and their behavior.

I

A perusal of psychoanalytic literature shows that the term depersonalization is broadly applied to phenomena which, though closely related, are somewhat different in nature. Some authors, such as Nunberg (1932) and Schilder (1928), include in it the feelings of estrangement and unreality with regard to the object world which often, but by no means always, accompany it. Others restrict the term to the type of experience which I have described above. That depersonalization arises from a disturbance in a person's relation with his own self has been emphasized, for example, by Federn, most clearly in his paper "The Ego as Subject and Object in Narcissism" (1929). Hinsie and Shatzky (1940) stress the same point, but define depersonalization as "The process of being dissolved, of losing the identity, personality, the I. A mental phenomenon, characterized by loss of the sense of reality of oneself. It often carries with it the loss of the sense of the reality of others and of the environment" (p. 155). This definition equates depersonalization with experiences of loss of identity. Both manifestations can frequently be observed in schizophrenics.

Persons suffering from sporadic, transitory, or even prolonged states of depersonalization, however, do not always show fears or feelings of loss of identity. And many borderline or schizophrenic patients who are constantly concerned with the question of their identity, of "who am I, what am I really?" do not complain about feelings of depersonalization. In fact, the experience of depersonalization, though indicative of a narcissistic disturbance, is not limited to psychotics. We can observe it even in normal persons, after trauma, and in neurotics, especially those who have a narcissistic personality structure.

Such patients need not suffer from inhibition or lack of affects. But pathological processes causing severe emotional inhibition or blocking or affective emptiness may find expressions in states of emotional detachment to the point of depersonalization. Evidently, the vividness of the "I"-experience is linked up with and dependent upon the degree of emotional aliveness, and gets lost to the extent to which the affects are held down or are "dying." But such cases of emotional death as may gradually develop in severely depressive and in schizophrenic persons have a different quality than experiences of depersonalization that set in acutely. They lack, especially, the frightening experience of becoming suddenly the outside observer of the performing part of the self. In psychotics, true experiences of depersonalization frequently appear at the initial stage of the psychosis. It is my impression that they develop as a kind of midway phenomenon in processes which eventually lead to generalized states of inner death, of self-extinction with loss of identity.

Before presenting clinical material, I shall survey briefly some psychoanalytic studies on depersonalization.

That this phenomenon involves a split in the ego has been particularly emphasized by Nunberg (1932). According to him, depersonalization is always a response to the loss, especially the sudden loss, of love or of the love object:

> The perception of the loss of a love object or the lowering of libido quantities is accompanied by the feeling that the reality of the perceptions and sensations of the ego has been lost. That destructive instincts are released is indicated by the painful complaints of patients in this state. . . . Since the complaints of the patients may be interpreted as castration complaints . . . the conclusion is therefore justified that identification of the ego with the genitals occurs. . . . the feelings of estrangement are the direct result of the *sudden* transposition of the libido from the object to the ego [p. 134].

Schilder (1935) characterizes depersonalization as a "picture which occurs when the individual does not dare to place his libido either in the outside world or in his own body" (p. 140). Significantly, he regards sadomasochism (besides voyeurism) as a most important component. Bergler and Eidelberg (1935) regard depersonalization as a defense against anal exhibitionism which is transformed into voyeurism and accepted by the ego in the form of self-observation. They point to the role of denial in depersonalization.

Oberndorf, in his paper "The Rôle of Anxiety in Depersonalization" (1950), goes back to Freud's analysis of *déjà vu,* in which estrangement and depersonalization are viewed as defense mechanisms tending to hide something from the ego. Oberndorf stresses especially the erotization of thought and the formation of a superego inharmonious with the body ego (feminine superego in a man and masculine superego in a woman), and that this disharmony leads to a repression of the alien element, which in turn causes the feeling of estrangement. The cases he describes are supposed to show depersonalization as a specific defense against anxiety, a phenomenon of simulation of death closely related to the "playing dead" defense used by animals when in great danger.

Blank (1954), describing and comparing the mechanisms underlying states of depression, hypomania, and depersonalization in a young female patient, found depersonalization to be "an emergency defense against the threatened eruption into consciousness of a massive complex of feelings of deprivation, rage, and anxiety. . . . depersonalization was called into play when the hypomanic defense failed to keep dangerous affects in repression" (p. 36).

As a metapsychological description of the state, the formulations by Fenichel (1945) are the clearest. But Fenichel omits consideration of the role of aggression, which had been correctly stressed by Nunberg.

> In stages of estrangement, an increased narcissistic cathexis of the body is countered by defensive reactions; in depersonalization, an increased narcissistic cathexis of mental processes is handled in the same way. In depersonalization, overcharged feelings or conceptions are repressed. . . . The experiences of estrangement and depersonalization are due to a special type of defense, namely, to a countercathexis against one's own feelings which had been altered and intensified by a preceding increase

in narcissism. The results of this increase are perceived as unpleasant by the ego which therefore undertakes defensive measures against them. These defensive measures may sometimes consist in a reactive withdrawal of libido; as a rule, however, they are built up by a countercathexis. [Fenichel then quotes Schilder's (1928) statements that in depersonalization we have two conflicting directions, namely, the directions toward and against feelings of body sensations, and furthermore that] "The organ which carries the narcissistic cathexis is the one more subjected to depersonalization" [p. 119f.].

Before presenting my own ideas on depersonalization, I must emphasize that the clinical material on which they are based does not stem from psychotics, but from normal and neurotic persons who lend themselves better to psychoanalytic exploration. Comparative observations of psychotic cases suggest, however, that the nature of the processes leading to depersonalization is essentially the same in normal, neurotic, and psychotic persons.[1]

II

I believe it is fruitful first to examine the psychological roots and the nature of this phenomenon in a comparatively normal group of persons.

Many years ago I had the opportunity to observe a group of political female prisoners in Nazi Germany, whose reactions I described in my paper "Observations on the Psychological Effect of Imprisonment on Female Political Prisoners" (1949). To my surprise I found that during the first weeks or months of arrest, many of these rather normal individuals developed states of depersonalization, evidently in response to their traumatic experiences.

Until then I had not encountered this phenomenon in any of my analytic patients. Thus, all I noticed and mentioned in my paper was the transparent connection of such states with the universal reaction of prisoners to the narcissistic blow inflicted by their arrest: the feeling that "this could not possibly have happened to *me*." Since then the psychoanalytic study of depersonalization in some of my patients has permitted me to form more concise ideas about this condition.

[1] See the recent papers by Arlow (1959), Bird (1958), Levitan (1969, 1970).

First, I shall repeat and elaborate upon some pertinent observations reported in the above-mentioned article. The prisoners reacted to their sudden, unexpected arrest with a transitory state of shock, general stupefaction, and considerable confusion, accompanied by feelings of unreality about themselves and their environment. During this period many of them developed symptoms and behavior indicative of sudden, general, severe regression to a more or less infantile position. But after a few days, this state usually subsided; the prisoners recovered their sense of reality; they attempted to face, accept, adjust to their unfortunate situation, and to regain their previous adult level. After some weeks most of them were again in a sufficiently good emotional balance to sleep and eat normally, to take up manual and intellectual work, to enjoy reading and the companionship of their cellmates. On the whole, it was remarkable how well the ego and the object relations of this rather stable group withstood the impact of all the hardships.

During the harassing period pending trial, however, the prisoners would suffer from anxieties and from continuous vacillations between sad-depressed and hopeful-optimistic moods and attitudes. And, especially during the first months, many complained about recurring experiences of depersonalization, from which they had never suffered in the past. These states developed particularly after terrifying cross-examinations and similar upsetting incidents which were usually followed by brief periods of emotional upheaval and distress.

When called to such interrogations, many prisoners suddenly became intensely activated in anticipation of a battle of wits with the prosecutors. Those who succeeded in being well composed, highly alert, and shrewd in their answers reported that they had managed to overcome their fears by deliberately trying to get into a cold state of detachment which certainly came rather close to depersonalization. In fact, this detachment often led to experiences of having no body, no sensations, no feelings, of having indeed nothing left but a coldly fighting brain. The defensive function of the emotional detachment was clearly evident and very successful in such situations, inasmuch as anxiety and other undesirable emotions had disappeared, and a high level of ego functioning could be maintained with control and direction of aggression into the proper channels of organized thinking and behavior.

But in the wake of such interrogations and other injurious events with which prison life abounded, highly unpleasurable and unwanted experiences of depersonalization sporadically recurred. The prisoners woke up at night, feeling that their limbs or their face did not belong to them. They would anxiously touch the estranged body parts, trying to recover the feeling of intactness of their body self. During the day they were suddenly overcome by frightening experiences of psychic self-estrangement; with feelings of being outside their self and of watching themselves think, talk or act, as though they were another person, and the like.

From the prisoners' reactions to the cross-examinations we can infer that these true states of depersonalization were posttraumatic manifestations and originated in a continued defensive struggle aiming at the mastery of the traumatic situations. In order to study the processes which brought on this particular pathology, we must gain clearer insight into the nature of the traumata to which the prisoners were subjected and of the conflicts aroused by their experiences.

The sudden arrest and imprisonment imposed on these persons a drastic and highly painful change in their entire life situation. To understand the traumatic impact of this change, we must remember that our feeling of "familiarity" with regard to the social and emotional climate in which we live originates not only in the libidinal ties to our environment but in a great variety of identifications with it. They include ego-superego identifications as well as all kinds of subtle identifications on a more primitive narcissistic level, partly of the "appersonation" type. We may tend to underrate the extent to which the consistency and homogeneity, and hence the stability, of our self-image depends on the compatibility, harmonious interplay, and collaboration of those innumerable identifications with all the familiar personal and impersonal, concrete and abstract objects of our past and present life and environment. They involve not only our family, our home and place of residence, our work and work situation, our property and personal belongings, but also the social, vocational, national, racial, religious and ideological group to which we "belong."

We know that abrupt changes from the familiar to a new, strange, and unfamiliar scene or environment, even in cases where the change is most pleasurable, can bring about mild, fleeting experiences of depersonalization. But these prisoners, forcefully expelled from the world in which they had formerly lived, deprived of partners, relatives and friends, of their work, interests and pleasures, of decent food, personal belongings and even of their clothing, had suddenly been thrown into a most repulsive new role and existence. Locked up in a cell, they were treated as severe criminals without regard to their past social and individual position. Exposed to the silent or noisy, humiliating or brutal assaults by the living conditions in prison and to the ordeal of a harassing trial with merciless cross-examinations, they found themselves not only in a most unfamiliar, but in a very frightening, degrading, helpless, and hopeless situation, facing the prospect of some years, at best, in a penitentiary. The sudden impact of the arrest, the forcefulness and repetitiveness of subsequent traumatic experiences, and the helplessness of their entire condition were bound to shake the foundation on which their life and their self heretofore had rested. These events threatened to undermine and break the array of all those identifications on which the image of their old, independent self was founded. The prisoners tended to replace this self-image with a new, intolerable one based upon identifications with the degraded, criminal world in which they now lived.

There were many evidences that the defense struggles of these prisoners were essentially directed against this danger. In my 1949 paper I described how the political prisoners eventually managed to protect themselves by very sound, effective safeguards, to which I shall refer later. But in the beginning their weakened ego was unable to cope adequately with the dangerous influences of their new environment, and unfortunately the conditions in prison and the ever-recurring traumatic events stirred up inner conflicts which propelled them toward acceptance of the role of criminals.

To be sure, legally these political prisoners were criminals, inasmuch as they had committed one of the worst crimes: high treason. Whereas prior to arrest practically none of them had ever consciously doubted her moral right to rebel against the current regime, the arrest and imprisonment, which meant defeat and—unconsciously—punishment, tended to affect her moral position. Indeed, the prisoners invariably suffered from doubts and guilt feelings. Only some among them had serious doubts of an ideological nature; later on, they confessed that they had temporarily felt confused and tempted to condemn their former beliefs and to accept the Nazi ideology. But in most of them the guilt conflicts were consciously centered about self-reproaches for having involved their family and friends in their calamity. The intensity and the content of these guilt conflicts, which paved the road to depressive and moral-masochistic reactions, were indicative of a revival of infantile conflicts with parental authorities even in those whose actions had not been primarily thus motivated. Of course, the helpless situation of imprisonment as such tended to smother the tremendous hostility it provoked and to veer it toward the self.

But the prisoners' political and moral convictions might have lent them greater support in their inner struggles, had they not been exposed to the instinctual dangers arising from the world in which they now lived. This prison world was pervaded by an offensive and infectious atmosphere—an atmosphere created by the criminal inmates as much as by the sadistic-seductive parental attitudes of guards, prison officials, and cross-examiners. The vicious influence of this pregenital, sadomasochistic atmosphere, which invited regressive instinctual trends and infantile identifications and relations with the delinquent environment, was probably the most pathogenic factor in the instinctual and guilt conflicts of these prisoners.

This influence asserted itself most dangerously in situations of cross-examination, although it was by no means limited to them. We are familiar with the psychological tricks of cross-examiners in countries under dictatorship. They try to obtain confessions not only by using a brutal, sadistic approach, but also by suave, seductive, emotional, and ideological appeals. This is the gravest danger, inasmuch as it tempts the lonesome prisoner to enter into a highly erotized, sadomasochistic, and infantile-dependent relationship to his torturers. Reports from persons who yielded to such an appeal and confessed leave no doubt that this was the inner danger the prisoners attempted to ward off by an emotional detachment which made them "invulnerable."

Indeed during the interrogation, which offered an opportunity for counterattack, the ego had a good opportunity to fight successfully against the dangers from without and within. The realistic battle with the enemy required an overinvestment of the thought processes, which permitted a withdrawal of cathexis from the feelings, to the point of complete detachment from the brutal and seductive adversary as well as from the vulnerable self that was tempted to respond to the seduction. This hypercathexis of the thought processes made them a reasonable vehicle for aggressive discharge to the outside, and concomitantly served as a countercathexis against the inner dangers of either masochistic submission or sadistic explosion. In this situation the defensive process could still maintain the level of a forceful repression and inhibition of threatening id impulses.

But when brought back to their cells the overexcited prisoners, deprived of a realistic object and outlet for their hostility, would suddenly feel utterly deflated and disturbed. Their transitory feeling of triumphant elation would yield to the depressing insight that, however strong the defense, final defeat had to be expected. Then the danger of a renewed, sudden, pathological process, which might overpower the ego, became acute. In fact, after such cross-examinations the prisoners found it very hard to return to reasonable activities. For many days they could not resist the temptation to go on, at least in fantasy, with furious, frustrating, and exhausting fights against their persecutors. In these imaginary battles, wild sadomasochistic fantasies often broke through to the surface. Besides, during such periods they tended to infringe the prison rules and got into serious trouble with the guards and authorities.

It is noteworthy that the experiences of depersonalization usually developed when the prisoners were disturbed rather than depressed; when they vacillated between relapses into excited pregenital fantasy life and actions and periods of normal behavior and quiet work. They were indicative of a failure of the ego and superego to prevent temporary regression and instinctual defusion, and to gain mastery over the tremendous hostility provoked by the traumatic experiences. Unable to ward off temporary invasions of unacceptable infantile id impulses by means of normal defenses, the prisoners thus vacillated between two contradictory states. Relinquishing normal ethical standards and behavior, the weakened ego would for some time permit indulgence in pregenital, sadomasochistic "delinquency." Then the past standards were re-established, and the ego returned to a normal level of behavior and functioning.

In this situation of failing repression, the ego, trying to regain its lost position, called on an ultimate, infinitely more primitive defensive device. Reflecting the schism between the alternating ego states, a split between two opposing self representations occurred. The ego attempted to reaffirm and restore its intactness by detaching, disavowing, and denying the existence of the regressed, "criminal" self, or rather by pretending its nonexistence.

It is of interest in this connection that as far as I could observe, the body parts tending to become estranged and dead were commonly the face, especially the area of the mouth, and the arms and hands, i.e., those body parts which were unconsciously or even consciously involved in fantasies of attacking and being attacked.

Depersonalization thus appears to be the pathological result of a conflict within the ego, between the part that has accepted and the part that attempts to undo identification with a degraded object image; in this case, with the image of the infantile, pregenital, sadomasochistic, castrated criminal. (It is significant that in those few prisoners who felt tempted to turn Nazi, this identification established itself under the guise of a new ideal contradictory to their previous one.) The nature of the primitive identification processes preceding and leading to depersonalization will be exemplified more clearly in the clinical cases.

I said in the beginning that at first sight depersonalization seemed to be a response to the severe narcissistic blow inflicted by the arrest, and to reflect the prisoners' feeling that "this could not possibly have happened to me." This interpretation is still valid, so long as we do not neglect the complexity of the ego's responses to the traumatizing external events. What could not and should not have happened is, evidently, less the narcissistic injury from without than the narcissistic blow inflicted from within upon an ego that experienced weakness vis-à-vis the threat of sudden regression, instinctual defusion, and destructive drive invasion.

It was indeed interesting to observe how the states of depersonalization subsided to the extent to which the prisoners were able to recover their past ego and superego strength, to return to regular, consistent manual and intellectual work, and to renounce indulgence either in masochistic brooding over their misfortune or in sadistic—real or fantasied—attacks on their persecutors.

I mentioned above the effective safeguards against the dangerous influences of their environment which these prisoners gradually established. Their defensive devices were clearly, and partly consciously, designed to draw a line of demarcation between political and criminal inmates, and to emphasize the difference in the level of their personalities. Thus the political prisoners consolidated into a strictly separate group that rejected and prohibited intimacy of any kind with the criminals as well as with the Nazi prison authorities. They introduced a firm, ethical code of behavior, and especially encouraged reading, intellectual work, and all types of sublimation. Among their many rules, the most prominent were those that promoted bodily cleanliness and neatness, curbed oral greed, insisted on the sharing of food and other privileges, developed kind mutual relations, and prevented open rebellion as well as weak submission to the guards and other prison authorities by the adoption of coldly polite, dignified attitudes. Quite obviously these group regulations were meant to offer special protection from pregenital and sadomasochistic trends and seductions.

The validity of these assumptions will be tested by examining experiences of depersonalization in some clinical cases.

III

Mrs. G., a young mother suffering from an anxiety hysteria, had a charming little daughter of five to whom she was attached by very close narcissistic ties. She had transferred to the child fantasies originating in her relationship to her powerful mother. In fact, her imagination had equipped the little girl with an illusory penis and even transformed her into a penis belonging to herself. These fantasies offered her a constant narcissistic supply without the fears and hostility aroused by her dominating mother.

One morning the young woman had to take over the care of her daughter's little boyfriend of the same age. Led to the bathroom, both children took down their pants and exposed their genitals. The mother looked and could not avoid perceiving the difference. At this moment her sight became blurred, she felt dizzy, detached, and anxiety arose. After a short while she experienced a previously unknown, sudden, transitory feeling of depersonalization: a feeling of being unreal, of being no longer herself.

What had happened? The perception of the little girl's genital in comparison with that of the boy had destroyed the patient's phallic illusions and inflicted a severe castration shock upon her. She reacted with a sudden libidinal withdrawal and an immediate denial of the frightening perception, which found expression in her feeling of detachment and her visual disturbance.

The analytic material left no doubt that her initial defense and symptom formation helped her to ward off her sudden hostile, sadistic reactions to the "castrated" as well as to the "phallic" child. Instead of responding to the disillusioning perception with an outburst of open hostility, she put them both temporarily "out of existence" by means of a primitive denial mechanism which brought about a visual disturbance. This defense and symptom formation, however, failed to protect her from repercussions of the frightening perception on her own self.

Her narcissistic relationship to the little girl predisposed her to respond to her withdrawal from the child with a temporary narcissistic regression causing an immediate shift of libido and aggression to herself. This transformed her conflict with the love object into a narcissistic conflict: a conflict between two opposing identifications, leading to a split in her self representation. Inasmuch as the mother had loved the child, she felt certainly tempted to accept what had now turned into a masochistic identification with the "castrated" little daughter. But insofar as she had hated and retreated from the deflated object, she tried to undo this identification. By replacing and restoring the lost phallic object with a reactively hypercathected phallic self image, she now could detach, decathect, and disavow the "castrated" self. Thus she eliminated it magically in the same way as she had initially eliminated the external love object.

We see the analogy between this patient and the prisoners. In her case, too, the state of depersonalization arises from an experience which, because of the patient's neurosis, has a traumatic effect. Again the shock seems to provoke a brief regressive process with sudden drive defusion, stirring up an amount of anxiety and hostility that cannot be mastered by repression but requires a more primitive and drastic defensive device.

What makes this example instructive is that we can observe two phases in the symptom formation. The first, which brings on blurred vision, relates to her conflict with the object. The second, which leads to depersonalization, reflects a conflict within the ego and pertains to her self image. The case reveals a significant fact regarding the predisposition to depersonalization. It certainly shows the validity of Nunberg's statements inasmuch as depersonalization may develop as a response to sudden loss of love or of a love object. But the prerequisite for this particular symptom formation was the narcissistic nature of this patient's object relationship to her child, which caused her to respond to the shocking sight of the latter's genital with an immediate withdrawal and narcissistic regression.

The next patient, Mr. H., was a highly gifted professional man in his thirties; he, too, had a hysterical personality, although with obsessional features.[2] Since his childhood he had suffered from anxieties, depressed states, and recurring brief, frightening experiences of depersonalization. He described them beautifully as feelings of being "insubstantial, without a shadow, so to speak—except for the persistent observer of the whole process." Otherwise the patient had a very intense emotional life and showed warm feeling qualities. He was happily married, worked hard, and had very rich sublimations.

His states of depersonalization had started when he was five, after the death of his mother who died during childbirth. The little boy had been prepared for the arrival of a baby. During her pregnancy his mother had tried to place him in a kindergarten, but there he had cried for her so bitterly and consistently that he had to be sent home. One day, suddenly, she had left for the hospital. She never returned. He vividly remembered the grownups weeping and whispering in the room next door, and his grandmother saying: "As long as there is life, there is hope;" this referred to the newborn, who some hours later also died. The next day the child found himself in the grieving grandmother's apartment, removed from his home, his room, his toys; deserted by his mother and his old nurse; and, for a brief period, also separated from his father. No explanations of what had happened were given to him then or for years thereafter.

Left to his own surmises and fantastic interpretations, he went into a disoriented, depersonalized state, unable to believe that he could be the same boy as before the tragic events. He had become a different, in fact, a bad boy. To be sure, these events had been most traumatic. The analysis showed, however, that their impact on the child was so very grave because of his overclose and overdependent pregenital relationship to his mother, and the overpermissiveness of

[2] I shall discuss this case from a different point of view in Chapter 7.

his nurse who had weakly submitted to all his tyrannical demands. The mother's attempt to place him in a kindergarten during her pregnancy had provoked an unusually passionate rivalry conflict which found expression in his severe separation anxieties. Consequently, her sudden, unexpected, and unexplained death, followed by the loss of his nurse and the temporary separation from his father, left him feeling utterly frightened and abandoned. The analysis revealed that the circumstances of his mother's death had mobilized wild primal scene fantasies in which he visualized the mother as a victim of the father's passion, and the father as the sexual murderer of the mother. The violence of his fantasies became apparent in his vivid memory of a picture ornamenting the parental bedroom: a poorly dressed couple, closely embraced, was shown running away through thunder and lightning, in wild mountain scenery; the young man held a big horn in his hand.

Actually, the father was a kind man; he stayed with the boy, in the home of relatives, and gave him constant love and affection. But even though he glorified the mother and spoke of her as an angel, after her death he kept a succession of mistresses, sometimes in a separate apartment, frankly defending his hedonistic attitude toward life.

The result was that the patient developed most contradictory feelings toward his father. He was deeply attached to him; but he severely condemned him and detached himself not only from the father's "immoral" attitudes, but also from his own preoedipal past with mother and nurse. When the latter visited him in his beginning latency, he found her "disgusting" and felt completely estranged. Subsequently he developed a family romance fantasy, which he maintained throughout his adolescence, of being the son of an aristocratic British family. Eventually he turned into a puritan, by forming a reactive ego ideal founded on the myth of his angelic mother and on his family romance notions. His puritanism found reinforcement in the restrictive attitudes of his severe grandmother. In general he adhered to his very stern moral code and convictions. But he tended to develop highly erotized, latent homosexual, masochistic relations to older men, especially superiors, which involved considerable acting out.

Characteristically, the patient married a woman who came from a higher social class than he did. But although he was happily married, his home life was frequently disturbed by stormy family scenes between himself, his temperamental wife, and his impulsive children. One special field of sublimations, kept strictly isolated from his professional work, permitted him secret indulgence in very regressive, sadomasochistic, pregenital fantasies (including fantasies of mutual devouring) under the beautiful but rather thin disguise of a highly idealized, aesthetic pursuit. His states of depersonalization evidently developed when his ego was invaded by unacceptable, regressive pregenital, sadomasochistic "primal scene" elements that also formed the basis for his identifications with his parents.

What connects this patient with the next two cases are certain features in his ego and superego structure. I pointed to his father's rather shaky superego which had caused the patient to build up a reactive ego ideal and an overstrict superego. In general his superego was perfectly effective, and his ego well developed and on a high level. Nevertheless, under the cloak of an "ideal" pursuit and of an "ideal" marriage with a socially "high-class" girl, his identifications with the immoral-sadistic father and with a correspondingly masochistic pregenital mother image had gained entrance into his superego which, thus deceived, permitted relapses by the ego into an acting out of his regressive fantasies, in limited areas.

In his case, the states of depersonalization certainly originated in the severely traumatic childhood events. The predisposing pathogenic factors—the pregenital seductions by mother and nurse, the harmful seductive influence of a father with a defective superego and ego, and the resulting contradictions in his own personality—must not be underrated; they probably were responsible for the continuous recurrence of depersonalized states throughout his childhood and adult life. It is significant that in the pathogenesis of the next two patients, the factors mentioned here played an even more striking part.

IV

In contrast to the preceding cases of acute, transitory experiences of depersonalization arising in emotionally uninhibited, hysterical personality types, the depersonalized states in my third patient, Mr.

F., developed on the basis of severe, generalized affective inhibitions. Mr. F. (whom I discussd in Chapter 4) was essentially a compulsive-depressive young man, whose main complaint was a chronic emotional detachment that sometimes led to experiences of depersonalization. He belonged to the group I mentioned in the beginning: persons who either suffer from psychic impotence or, at other times, go through the sexual act without enjoyment and true orgastic experience, in a mildly depersonalized state, watching themselves perform.

In Chapter 4 I discussed the elaborate defense structure built up by this patient essentially for the purpose of warding off severely sadomasochistic, pregenital impulses. Moreover, I showed that his denial and projection mechanisms, which resulted in a state of painful emotional detachment, were simultaneously directed against the superego and the id, and were designed to rid him of his early preoedipal, sadomasochistic identifications with his parents, essentially his mother. I described that a break with the mother had occurred at the age of three and a half, when she had a near-fatal miscarriage at home—which he probably witnessed—followed by physical illness and a depressed state of several weeks' duration. From then on the patient felt open, cold hostility toward his mother, denying that he might ever have loved her. This denial was directed not only against his preoedipal attachment to her, but in particular against his identification with both mother and child. I suggested that this traumatic early childhood event, which was revived at the age of seven by the tragic death of his younger brother, might account for the preponderance of denial in this patient's defenses.

From his transference reactions I am inclined to infer that he had responded to the first trauma with a transitory depressed-depersonalized state which repeated itself after the death of his brother. Later analytic material shed more light on the infantile origins of the identification—or "disidentification"—processes underlying his depersonalization.

When the patient's pregenital strivings began to break through to the surface, he developed recurring gastrointestinal symptoms: nausea, colon spasms, and diarrhea. As in the past, he tried to ward off their meaning and his fear (of cancer) by denial and detachment. He ignored and neglected his illness by continuing to eat as he pleased, though with the usual lack of real enjoyment. It turned out that he felt estranged from his sick intestines and "refused to regard them as his own." He was "angry" at his guts and wanted to scold them, like this: "You behave like a naughty child, but you will have to accept and get used to what I eat!" In this situation the "angry he" played the role of the rejecting, scolding mother who ignored the baby's illness and forced the "bad child" (who ate forbidden food and lost bowel control) to submit, eat ordinary meals, and accept pain and punishment. His "sick intestines" were here equated with his sick baby brother. But in his refusal to go on a "baby diet" he was also identified with the rebellious, bad child who wanted to eat what he pleased, and, besides, with the seductive mother who offered dangerous oral freedom. This is why the patient not only felt estranged from his illness, but was equally detached from the "greedy" self and unable to enjoy his unreasonable oral excesses.

This example is so very interesting because it shows collaborating processes of bodily and mental self-estrangement directed against multiple identifications with different, degraded, early infantile object images.

Eventually the patient found what he felt to be a perfect solution of his dilemma: the best remedy would be a bottle of good red wine; that would certainly stop his diarrhea. This slick problem solution meant to reconcile and unite mother and child: himself with his estranged, sick guts and with his indulgent, greedy self. The loving mother will give the child the bottle that he really wants and that cures him at the same time.

This incident also illuminates the patient's need for multiple projections in support of his denial. In Chapter 4 I reported that unconsciously he felt unjustly accused by the mother of crimes which he had not committed: the murder of the children and the poisoning, i.e., the pregnancy, the miscarriage, and illness of his mother. His projections pointed to his family—essentially the mother—as the "true criminals." His estrangement from his "sick intestines" as well as from the indulging self shows basically the same tendency to deny that "he" could be the criminal. But instead of projection onto other objects, he tries in the states of self-estrangement and depersonalization to get rid of these undesirable identifications by splitting off the unacceptable parts of his self image from the acceptable ones and disowning the first in this manner.

The contradictions in this patient's behavior, the seemingly strict and punitive attitude toward his sick body, with which he disguises his negligence and unwillingness to accept temporary restrictions, are characteristic of his ego and superego structure.

The superego pathology accounting for the many contradictory features in the patient's character was described at some length in Chapter 4. Compulsive traits, such as neatness, aestheticism, decency, kindness, existed side by side with isolated, cold, overt death wishes toward his mother and mistress. While under the pressure of a cruel, restrictive superego, he consciously brandished the torch of an ideal favoring utter instinctual (pregenital) freedom without guilt feelings. Although frankly desirous of being able to drink, whore, steal, throw away money as he pleased, he would complain about his temperate, too reasonable attitudes and his inhibitions—quite unaware that at other times he actually did drink and spend money quite excessively, and indulged in pregenital sexual fantasies and behavior. He did not notice and admit his behavior because his indulgences were certainly devoid of the vivid feeling tone and the pleasure he craved and left him in a depressed mood.

This patient's makeup can best be characterized by saying that he had tried, without achieving real success, to build up a consistent, compulsive personality structure. This is what one can frequently observe in obsessional-compulsive patients, but not to the same extent. He showed contradictions in his superego and ego, which became conspicuous during adolescence as he began to suspect and frankly rebel against his restrictive and seemingly compulsive father, who in fact had similar contradictory character traits. Thus the patient had developed an alternately too restrictive and too lax, though punitive, superego, and hence oscillated between manifestations of an inhibited and impulsive ego. His auxiliary defenses (isolation, denial, detachment, projection) served to protect his ego from continuous invasions of pregenital, sadomasochistic drives. These drive invasions were based on early identifications with his parents and his baby brother.

In Mr. F., as in Mr. H., the id had found its way into the superego under the guise of a conscious ideal. In Mr. H.'s case, it was an ideal, aesthetic pursuit; in Mr. F.'s, a frankly "delinquent" ideal of "freedom"[3] which greatly influenced his behavior. In some cases of borderline or psychotic depression where experiences of depersonalization stood out in the symptomatology, I observed that (similar to Mr. F.'s case) the patients' self-reproaches had a more realistic core than is commonly the case in melancholic depression. These patients had either gone through periods of impulsive or delinquent behavior, or at least once had planned or actually committed something "immoral" or "unforgivable."

Mr. F.'s efforts to prove that the parents—not he—were the true criminals certainly resemble the emotional situation of the prisoners. The difference lies in the realistic nature of the latters' circumstances. They actually lived among criminals and had good reason to feel that they were unjustly treated and that their cross-examiners and prosecutors—rather than they themselves—were the "true" criminals.

Among the truly criminal inmates of the penitentiary I found one particularly interesting example of severe depression with depersonalization, which sharply highlighted this kind of conflict situation. This was a girl serving an eight-year term for complicity in robbery and murder. She had been a secretary. Her social behavior had been normal until she fell passionately in love with a criminal psychopath who enticed her to assist him in the murder and robbery of an old woman. He escaped and left her behind, holding the bag. The girl as I just mentioned, was severely depressed; she was a model prisoner who accepted the penalty as due her, and while in the penitentiary contracted tuberculosis. She aroused my interest because she had pretended to be a political prisoner until she was found out. Then she was eager to tell me her story and confessed that she—the idealistic, rather sophisticated girl she had always believed herself to be—felt completely estranged and unreal about her criminal self, and at times could not believe that she had committed such a crime. This state of depersonalization had started even before she was apprehended. During the whole period of her enslavement to her criminal lover she had felt as though in a trance: like not being the

[3] The idealization of sadomasochistic notions, in a grotesque or even delusional form, can be observed in certain paranoid schizophrenics. An example is a severely paranoid schizophrenic boy of twenty who idolized Hitler and identified with him. When he worked he imagined he was either "Hitler bombing and invading a city" or "Hitler the martyr, dying for his nation and his cause."

same person, like being compelled to act as she did, etc. Her pretense of being not a criminal but a political prisoner was in line with her self-estrangement and the split in herself.

In her case we see a complete breakdown of the superego under the influence of a passionate enslavement, which permitted her identification with the adored criminal love object to assert itself completely in her ego. The fact that the girl experienced her passion as being under the "hypnotic" influence of her lover brings this example close to what happens in real hypnotic states and in fugue states.[4] In hypnosis a sudden regressive process, which allows a revival of former superego-ego states, is artificially induced through the medium of the hypnotist. As to fugues, Fisher and Joseph (1949) found that they set in when murderous impulses threaten to break, or actually have broken, through to consciousness.

I must forego the wish to examine the transparent relation between hypnotic and fugue states and the state of depersonalization more thoroughly. Instead I shall report a final case example which is most illuminating with regard to the infantile origins of depersonalization. It shows the development of states of self-estrangement in childhood as a result of seductive experiences, and points again to the predisposing influence of early parental seduction and a contradictory parental superego.

V

Mrs. J., a young divorcee in her twenties, came for treatment because of depressive reactions and masochistic attitudes which had interfered with her love life. In spite of her symptoms the patient had unusual ego strength which manifested itself in her heroic struggle against severe illness. Since infancy she had suffered from recurring attacks of cystitis and pyelitis. The almost chronic illness had imposed considerable physical and general ego restraint on the child, and necessitated constant medical care including very painful irrigations of the bladder. Besides, her condition had for many years prevented her from gaining urinary control. For this failure, as for her illness in general, the little girl had been incessantly and un-

[4] When I presented the first draft of this paper at the Austen Riggs Center, Dr. Brenman and Dr. Rapaport called my attention to the relation of depersonalization to experiences in hypnotic and fugue states.

justly blamed by her unreasonable parents, who did their best to deny the child's real physical damage and to relieve their guilt feelings by projections and by exhibition of their own suffering. They had indeed good reason to feel guilty, inasmuch as the little girl had been subjected to continuous seductions by the therapeutic procedures which involved examinations and rather careless manipulations of the genital area. These treatments were carried out not only by the physician, but partly also by the parents, including the father. Thus, from the first years of life through the latency period, the child had been exposed to sadistic genital, urethral, and anal overstimulations that fused sexual excitement and pain.

Most traumatic were the irrigations of the bladder, for which the little girl would prepare herself in anxious anticipation. Soon she learned to accept them with the support of a clever device. Before the procedure began, she would silently address her bladder and would scold and punish it as follows: "Shame on you, bad bladder, go away and stay over there in the corner." By this magical removal of the bad and sick organ from her body she made herself physically numb, or at least sufficiently toned down the unbearable tension and pain to lie quietly and tolerate the procedure without anxiety and rebellion. When it was terminated she would gaily release the bladder: "Now you are good again and may come back to me."

The touching simplicity of the little girl's effective device, which at least reduced her pain, did not betray its deeper meaning and the underlying instinctual conflicts which it failed to resolve.

The fact was that the therapeutic-sexual situations had a seductive effect on the father as well as on the child. He was overattached to her physically rather than emotionally and, as a memory showed, had transferred his own incestuous desires from his mother to this daughter. During the patient's adolescence he continued to behave in a seductive manner. The patient responded to her father's behavior with shock, disgust, hostility, and eventually with detachment from him, as formerly from the mother. She escaped from the unhealthy home situation first by attaching herself closely to the warm and interesting family of a girlfriend. Under their beneficial, stimulating influence she started to bloom emotionally as well as intellectually. She began to study and to develop many interests and sublimations. But when she lost these friends through external circumstances, she accepted the first serious proposal she received, married, and moved away from her hometown at the age of eighteen.

Not surprisingly, the patient had chosen a psychopathic husband who forced her into a severely masochistic position which was a replica of her childhood situation. For seven years she stubbornly denied her unhappiness and failure, maintaining the façade of an undisturbed marital relationship. During these years the highly intelligent and gifted girl abandoned all her own ambitions, interests, and abilities for the sake of her talented but irresponsible and parasitic husband. Accepting subordinate jobs at which she worked hard from morning till night, she lived, as it were, on a regressive and restricted ego level, in an emotionally numb, chronically depressed-depersonalized condition reminiscent of her worst childhood period.

But her analysis revealed that throughout these years she had maintained a secret fantasy life that was constantly nourished by the seductive influence of the pregenital atmosphere which her partner created. This private world of hers included sexual fantasies that were almost undisguised derivatives of the tormenting childhood experiences.

The analysis of her fantasies and of her infantile memory material shed light on the deeper structure and meaning of her infantile defensive device. The "sending away" of her "bad" bladder was supposed to protect her not only from pain and hurt, but even more from the danger of violent sadistic motor, anal, and urinary outbursts and, the reverse, masochistic enjoyment of being "raped" by the father. Indeed, the little girl, wishing to retaliate and reverse the situation, had never forgotten her gleeful feelings when, at least once, she had rebelled and urinated right in the face of the attending physician.

Her talk with her bladder betrays that the treatments meant punitive measures and concomitantly sexual gratifications to her. Certainly the "bad" bladder was she herself, the bad little girl who wanted to and did indulge in incestuous pleasure, who deserved and received punishment. By ejecting the organ from her body self she could disown both crime and punishment, and displace them onto the personified bad bladder. But at the same time the "bad" bladder, which she scolded and punished, represented her "bad" parents from whom she wished to detach herself; parents who seduced and simultaneously punished her, and who—even worse—exhibited their own suffering and blamed her for it.

It is significant that the patient suffered from obsessional doubts whether she or her parents should be blamed for her misfortunes, and tried to find evidence for their guilt. Thus, like Mr. F., she felt that not she but the parents were the truly guilty ones.

It is characteristic of the patient's inherent vitality that after seven years of masochistic slavery she found the strength to rebel and to leave her husband. Again under the influence of encouraging friends, she called her "good self" back from its exile. Seizing upon her adolescent interests, she went back to college, completed her studies, and soon made an astounding career. And at last, as a result of her treatment, she found personal happiness too in a new marriage.

VI

We have studied the conflicts and the defense processes underlying states of depersonalization, first in a group of normal persons under exceptional circumstances and then in different types of neurotic and borderline personalities. I shall recapitulate the impressions gained from this material and reformulate my conclusions.

Apparently, states of depersonalizaton always represent attempts at solution of a narcissistic conflict. Inasmuch as such states may be caused by sudden loss of love or of a love object, they presuppose object relationships of a narcissistic type. But this narcissistic conflict does not arise from a schism between superego and ego, as in depression. The conflict develops within the ego and has its origin in struggles between conflicting identifications and self images.

The material presented suggests that even normal people may respond with transient states of depersonalization to traumatic or even to simply unusual events. I had mentioned the mild, fleeting experiences of depersonalization which may develop when persons suddenly find themselves in a strange, unfamiliar environment. It is significant that such states may be caused by changes to fascinating new surroundings, to which we certainly can relate and respond very vividly and pleasurably. But delightful as it may be, we feel that we do not "belong" to this lovely new world. Evidently, it invites new identifications which the ego refuses to accept immediately. This indicates that the primary cause of the disturbance is not necessarily a disruption of object relations, but a narcissistic conflict caused by discrepancies between opposing identifications.

Probably, fleeting states of depersonalization of this type do not arise on the same premises as truly pathological states, such as I have described above. (It is interesting, though, that in patient B. feelings of depersonalization recurred "in milder ways" when he was transplanted to unfamiliar surroundings—marked by the temporary loss of home and family and friends.) It seems that the latter develop in situations of sudden threat of severely regressive processes involving the ego and superego, with drive defusion and pregenital drive invasion into these structures. Such processes may be induced by traumatic external events or by experiences which for inner reasons have a traumatic effect. They may be of brief or longer duration and may tend to recur in persons predisposed to such regressive relapses by an uneven, contradictory ego-superego structure. Furthermore, they may be indicative of a psychotic disorder.

In patient G., the narcissistic conflict situation was the least complicated. The intense hostility, aroused by the castration shock and warded off by her withdrawal from the child, certainly points to a sudden drive defusion and narcissistic regression provoked by the trauma. In her case, however, the conflict remains limited to a struggle between two contradictory self images which reflect opposing fantasies of identification with the adored phallic and the degraded, castrated daughter. This is why her experience of depersonalization is so acute, of such brief duration, and does not repeat itself.

In the other patients and in the prisoners, the emotional situation is different because the superego is involved in it. I emphasized above that the conflict leading to depersonalization is not between superego and ego, but within the ego. This does not imply, however, that the superego may not play a most significant part in the development of the conflict. Of this we found sufficient evidence in the clinical material. In all cases excepting Mrs. G., the instability or weakening of the superego structure and the resulting contradictions were the reason for drive intrusions into the ego. They caused a real split in the ego between the part that tried to restore and maintain a normal level of behavior, resting on stable identifications, and the part that had temporarily regressed and yielded to infantile, sadomasochistic, pregenital identifications and object relations. This is why in three of the patients and in the prisoners we found periods of manifest vacillations between opposing—normal or regressive—ego states, which led either to brief but recurrent or to more enduring states of depersonalization.

The specific defensive operations which induce such states are directed against the unacceptable identifications. They can be defined as attempts at undoing them by virtue of disowning and denying the undesirable part of the ego and of the corresponding self representations. Hence, this defense bears all those landmarks of primitive defense processes which I described in the preceding chapter. In the example of the prisoners, we could see that as long as their superego and ego remained intact, repression could operate against the specific, unacceptable id impulses aroused by the seductive situation. But insofar as their superego structure was impaired and repression failed, the prisoners found themselves struggling against relapses into a "delinquent" ego state in which they felt—and actually were—identified with the hated, worthless criminals. Then the defense was directed no longer against bad impulses, but against bad body parts or against the "criminal" self *in toto,* whose images were split off and put out of existence.

In Chapter 4 I also discussed the hypercathexis of perception, which in depersonalized states becomes evident in the watching ego. I described Mr. F.'s craving to observe the woman's delighted facial expression during intercourse. Whereas his watching was intended to undo and deny female castration, his original sadistic wish to expose the defect occasionally broke through. During actual intercourse he hardly ever gratified his desire, but, instead, became depersonalized and "watched" himself perform. Here we can see that the self-observation in depersonalization absorbs and transforms the original sadistic-voyeuristic impulse toward the woman and, turning it to the self, employs it for a denial of the identification with this castrated object and its image.

Oberndorf (1950) also laid much stress on the superego pathology in such patients. I am inclined to accept his assumption that their superego frequently shows a lack of uniformity and stability. But his thesis was that the superego shows discrepancies because of unacceptable superego identifications with the parental figure of the opposite sex. My observations do not wholly confirm this opinion. In Mrs. G.'s case the depersonalization certainly arose from the conflict between her phallic and her unacceptable masochistic identification with the "castrated" child. Inasmuch as they were expressive of a masculine-aggressive versus a feminine ideal, Oberndorf's assumption seems to be applicable. But I believe that the contradictory qualities of the superego in such patients are caused by discrepancies arising from drive intrusions into the ego ideal. In all my cases, these contradictions developed under the influence of a defective parental superego; but this may not be so in general.

This leads us to the relationship between depersonalization and (melancholic) depression and the different identification mechanisms in these two states. Both develop from narcissistic conflicts and both seem to presuppose object relations of a narcissistic nature. But the conflict in depersonalization certainly is quite different in structure from the conflict in depression. In both depression and depersonalization, identification processes bring about an inner schism. In depression, however, the schism develops between the punitive, sadistic superego and the ego or the self image. In depersonalization the superego need not even take part in the conflict, as was shown by the case of Mrs. G. But in many of these patients, contradictions in the superego apparently lead to a schism in the ego and in the self representations. Instead of a punishing superego accusing the worthless self, we find in depersonalization a detached, intact part of the ego observing the other—emotionally or physically dead—unacceptable part.

We remember that Nunberg (1932) could interpret the complaints of severely depersonalized patients as castration complaints, and that he pointed to the equation of the ego with the genital. This is in harmony with my findings, which show in addition that the deflated, castrated part of the self image becomes estranged, dead, because it is identified with devalued, castrated object images. In depression the superego directs the hostility against the whole ego or the self representations. In depersonalization a part of the ego employs aggression for the elimination of the "bad" part of the ego and the corresponding self image. This again confirms Oberndorf's (1950) statement that depersonalization means "playing dead." We may ask how, under such circumstances, depersonalization can develop in the frame of depression, but the answer is not difficult. The superego and part of the ego can easily join forces in their fight against the worthless, degraded, infantile self. This had been emphasized by Bergler and Eidelberg (1935). They believe, however, that in depersonalization part of the ego always offers its services to the superego and that the ego uses its own weapons to defeat itself. In my opinion, this view is valid only in special cases. I think that my conclusions are in agreement with the views expressed by Blank (1954).

One more remark concerning states of depersonalization in schizophrenics. It is my impression that in the case of chronic schizophrenic processes, experiences of depersonalization, which mostly occur in the beginning of the illness, are indicative of sudden mobilizations of regressive processes. The opinion has been voiced that depersonalization represents a restitutive process. I believe that even in psychotics it must be regarded as a defense of the ego which tries to recover and to maintain its intactness by opposing, detaching, and disowning the regressed, diseased part.

PART II

6

On Depressive States: Nosological and Theoretical Problems

Part II deals predominantly with the clinical, theoretical, and developmental problems which we encounter in the treatment of severely depressive—borderline or ambulatory psychotic—patients of different varieties. Some of the chapters are again comparative studies, with special emphasis laid on differential-diagnostic criteria. Extensive case material is presented in support of the theoretical assumptions.

Before approaching these problems, however, I must discuss some issues the clarification of which I regard as a prerequisite for the psychoanalytic investigation of depressive cases. During the last forty years I have observed, treated, and followed up quite a large group of severely ill patients who suffered from recurring, periodic or chronic depressive states. The study of these cases and of the psychoanalytic literature on depression[1] made me feel that our past and current concepts of depression, and specifically of psychotic depressive states, are still fragmentary, inconsistent, and even contradictory. It was this state of affairs which called my attention to the

---

This chapter is based in part on some ideas expressed in an unpublished paper on "Primary and Secondary Symptom Formation in Endogenous Depression." Read at the Midwinter Meeting of the American Psychoanalytic Association, New York, December 16, 1947. Most of it, however, was written recently and has not been previously published.

[1] I shall not attempt to review the whole psychoanalytic literature on depression, since several such reviews have already been published by other authors (see, e.g., Bellak, 1952; Grinker, 1961; Mendelson, 1960; Ostow, 1970; Rochlin, 1965).

study of affects, of normal and pathological moods, in general, subjects which I discussed in Part I of this volume.

The problematic nature of the psychoanalytic theory of depression reflects, in part, the changes in theoretical thinking: the introduction of Freud's last anxiety theory, his ideas regarding the role of aggression, the beginning of structural thinking, and the development of psychoanalytic ego psychology. In addition, the current psychoanalytic and psychiatric literature on psychotic types of depression and psychoses in general shows the surprisingly good results achieved by psychoanalytically oriented psychotherapy and even psychoanalytic treatment of psychotic patients. These results are not only interesting and promising, they also demonstrate the significant role that psychogenetic factors play in the development of psychoses. Unfortunately, however, this "dynamic" approach to the psychoses has also supported the tendency to blur the strict demarcation lines between the neuroses, the borderline cases, psychoses, and between the various types of psychotic disorders. I believe that this has interfered with a sound clinical orientation in the field of psychoses and created diagnostic, nosological, terminological, and theoretical confusion.

A characteristic example of this confusion is the frequent equation, in the general psychiatric literature, of "neurotic" with "reactive" depression—an old but useful psychiatric term. It refers not to neurotic, but to the kind of psychotic depression which, in contrast to "endogenous" depression, clearly develops in "reaction" to a precipitating event.

From the etiological point of view, this tendency has promoted a disregard of Freud's "complementary series of causal factors" which admits the part of constitutional and hereditary factors even in the transference neuroses. As regards the affective disorders, these trends to abandon the strict demarcation line can be traced back to Abraham. He was the first analyst who took manic-depressive patients into psychoanalytic treatment and achieved remarkable therapeutic success. Abraham was an outstanding clinician and his case material is most instructive. In contrast to Freud, however, he dealt with the affective disorders as though they were neuroses. His analytic results with such psychotic cases may have induced him to view them as essentially psychogenetic conditions. We also must not forget that his remarkable contributions antedated the introduction of Freud's new structural and drive theories, the beginnings of which can be detected in "Mourning and Melancholia" (1917). Accordingly, Abraham's distinction between manic-depressive and neurotic conditions was based mainly on the differences in the depth of pregenital-narcissistic regressions and, with regard to the hereditary factors, on the question of drive constitution. He did not yet have an ego-psychological orientation. Although he called attention to the development of object relations in the child, he did not focus on the child's ego-superego development, on its arrests and regressions to early levels of object relations, superego functioning, and ego defenses in psychotics.

Abraham made his contributions about fifty years ago. But even such an outstanding modern psychoanalytic author as Edward Bibring, who tried to develop a new ego-psychological theory of depression, used familiar psychiatric terms of the past incorrectly, and reduced the differences between grief, normal, neurotic, and psychotic types of depression to questions of "content." I shall discuss his opinions later on.

Many authors haxe expressed their dissatisfaction with the various existing nosologies, and some have attempted to develop an improved "psychoanalytic" nosology, most recently Rangell (1965). I appreciate his criticism of our current classification, his emphasis on "a careful evaluation of ego functions" as a prerequisite for an improved psychoanalytic nosology, and several other suggestions, but I have some doubts about his examples (p. 141). I do not believe that a "violent, adolescent, neurotic hatred" can "become delusional." Hatred is an affect and as such neither neurotic nor psychotic. Its quality and intensity may suggest that its ideational content may become delusional. As to Rangell's "summary evaluating statement": "in character qualitatively hysterical, in her functioning borderline, and symptomatically depressive-addictive" (p. 152), I believe that it does not essentially improve upon the simple, old clinical terms. Diagnostically, I should consider this patient a case on the borderline to schizophrenia. She shows hysterical character traits, as so many schizophrenics do; she suffers from depressive states, and, in contrast to manic-depressives, because of her depressions tends to have addictions.

My remarks display my discontent with any new suggestions—nosological or otherwise—which tend to obscure clinical observations and facts and to neglect important differential-diagnostic criteria. In my opinion, these tendencies do not support our efforts to gain an improved clinical and theoretical understanding of the psychoses. Besides, they do not act as an incentive to a sound collaboration of psychological-psychoanalytic and somatic-neurophysiological research on the problems of psychoses.

To some extent, this lack of collaboration is caused by psychoanalysts who have no interest in somatic research problems (i.e., problems of a nonpsychological nature), or else by scientific researchers who are not well versed in the field of psychiatry and even less in psychoanalysis. Neurophysiological studies of the psychotic disorders presuppose careful differential-diagnostic considerations. It is futile, for example, to do physiological research on "endogenous" types of depression with a group of patients consisting of neurotic, manic-depressive, and schizophrenic patients.[2] This kind of research cannot yield scientifically correct, acceptable results.

Fortunately we find remarkable exceptions, such as the opinions expressed by Reiser in his paper "Toward an Integrated Psychoanalytic-Physiological Theory of Psychosomatic Disorders" (1966), or by Bellak (1958) and Weiner (1958) in the book on *Schizophrenia: A Review of the Syndrome* edited by Bellak. This book demonstrates that differences of opinion are not to be equated with confusion. It is not accidental that these three authors have all had thorough somatic psychiatric, and psychoanalytic training.

Bellak refers to his "multiple-factor, a psychosomatic theory of schizophrenia [which] permits one to understand schizophrenia as the common result of a variety of individually differing etiologic factors" (p. 5). It may be questionable whether we can speak in these terms of a "theory" of schizophrenia, but I believe that this "multiple-factor, psychosomatic" approach is a sound beginning toward the development of a comprehensive theory of schizophrenia and the affective disorders.

The hypothesis that psychoses may involve an as yet unknown psychosomatic process is well founded. For this reason I regard Bellak's approach as a prerequisite for a sound theory of depression. Inasmuch as such a theory deals with the psychological aspects of

[2] Dr. Edward J. Sachar, a clinically and psychoanalytically well-informed researcher, confirmed in a personal communication that this is precisely what happens.

depression—neurotic or psychotic—I take it for granted that it will use the psychoanalytic theory. I believe indeed that we can make an inroad into the psychology of the psychoses only by studying, from the psychoanalytic perspective, the individually different, specific, psychogenetic factors; the specific structure and nature of the conscious and unconscious psychotic conflicts; the characteristic affective and mood conditions; the specific defenses and restitution mechanisms in each group of psychoses. This belief is at the basis of my approach to the problems discussed in this book. The value of such an approach for diagnosis, prognosis, and therapy is clearly exemplified, e.g., in Kernberg's papers, especially in his articles on borderline patients (1967, 1968).

I

In this section I shall report some clinical observations on the basis of which I formed my theoretical assumptions. To complement my statements, I shall discuss three outstanding psychoanalytic papers on depression (E. Bibring, 1953; Mahler, 1966; and Rubinfine, 1968).

We remember that after Freud introduced his new structural distinction of id, ego, and superego, he defined neurosis, melancholia, and schizophrenia as the results of conflicts between ego, id, superego, and reality (1924a). From that time on, psychoanalysts focused their studies of melancholic depression mainly on the structure and the infantile origins of the conflict between ego and superego. Although this trend brought forth most valuable clinical and theoretical contributions, in some respects it narrowed the road of the psychoanalytic approach to depression.

In observing cases belonging to the manic-depressive group of disorders (patients with recurring periods of endogenous depression, partly alternating with hypomanic states), I realized as early as 1943 that the emphasis laid upon the guilt problem as the core of the conflict did not do justice to all the cases. I am referring here not to those which ultimately turned out to be schizophrenic, but to patients who undoubtedly were and remained manic-depressives.[3] In

[3] I do not believe in the continuity between manic-depressive and schizophrenic conditions. I have kept track of a series of cases that always remained affective disorders

most of these depressive patients the guilt problem was not even the predominant clinical feature. In some, a severe, but neither typically "melancholic" nor delusional, guilt conflict presented itself or came to the fore in the course of treatment. What characterized the emotional picture in the other patients were—apart from dejected mood, inhibitions in thinking and psychomotor retardation, etc.—anxieties, feelings of blankness and detachment, of inner weariness and apathy, a mental and physical inability to enjoy life and love, sexual impotence (or frigidity), and feelings of deep inferiority, inadequacy, and general worthlessness. These feelings corresponded to the impoverishment of their egos, their inability to relate to people, and their general loss of interest. As I mentioned in Chapter 3, some of the patients who complained about their lack of feelings did not experience "sadness"; they were even longing for it. Some patients showed paranoid traits; some suffered from fears of monetary impoverishment; others belonged to the hypochondriacal type: their complaints and fears revolved around intellectual disturbances, such as "stupidity," physical defects or physical and psychosomatic symptoms, mainly gastrointestinal or heart conditions.[4] In most of the latter patients, especially those who were unaware of any emotional experience of depression, the depressive nature of their illness had not been recognized either by themselves or by their physicians. In several of these patients the suspicion of an underlying schizophrenia was justified, but not one of them, to my knowledge, ever developed a schizophrenic picture.

According to the common psychiatric terminology, most of these patients had a "simple" depression rather than the "acute" clinical syndrome.

Great clinical psychiatrists, such as Kraepelin and Bleuler, have pointed to the large number of cases of "simple depression" which do not manifest psychotic symptoms in the sense of delusional ideas or hallucinations, but which nevertheless belong to the manic-de-

[4] I am aware of the fact that my views are not in accord with those of Beres (1966). I agree with his opinion that we should carefully distinguish between the depressive and other related, but different aspects. But my clinical experience does not confirm his assumption that in the absence of guilt we are dealing not with depression but with other affects, such as sadness, apathy or disappointment. Nor do I find his case example (p. 481f.) convincing because in nonpsychotic types of depression the morning depression frequently lifts spontaneously after breakfast.

pressive group.[5] If these cases are mild states of depression, they are easily mistaken for neurasthenic or psychoneurotic, somatic or psychosomatic disturbances, and hence may be referred to the analyst. Such patients are frequently amenable to psychoanalytic therapy, even while they are in a depressed or hypomanic state, provided, however, that we know we are dealing with a basically psychotic case. From the therapeutic point of view a correct diagnosis will guide our choice of treatment methods; and scientifically, it will deepen our understanding of such cases.

To be sure, in cases of depression a clear differential diagnosis may often be difficult or impossible. The case I shall present in Chapter 8 demonstrates these difficulties only too clearly. But valuable diagnostic criteria may be gained by focusing on the psychosomatic, "endogenous" features in the questionable syndrome. I refer not only to the symptoms that impressed even Freud as having somatic rather than psychological origins: the insomnia, the anorexia, the amenorrhea, the loss of weight, the vegetative and metabolic disturbances, and the frequent gastrointestinal or cardiovascular psychosomatic symptoms.

What I wish to emphasize especially are the psychosomatic features in the depressive retardation which color the quality—not the content—of the depression. True cyclothymics experience their slowing up quite differently from the way depressive neurotics experience their inhibitions. Cyclothymics seem to be aware that there is a somatic quality to this phenomenon. They commonly feel that the retardation, as well as the keyed-up state, befalls them like a physical illness. They experience it as strange to their nature; as something the sound part of their personality may watch with some detachment and even control to a certain point. One such patient, a female physician in her forties, said: "You know, this is a real 'illness.' One morning I wake up and have no appetite. I cannot

[5] Katan (1954), who reserves the term "psychotic" for conditions that show definite signs of a break with reality, would probably characterize such patients as remaining in a prepsychotic stage. In view of the fact that they manifest primarily the typical triad of symptoms—periods of depressed mood, of inhibition of thinking, and of psychomotor retardation, or the opposite—I have found it useful, and furthermore in accordance with clinical psychiatry, to emphasize the psychotic nature of their pathology. My use of the term prepsychotic applies only to the characterological predisposition to this disease.

think, I cannot move, but I can control it enough to be able to work. And then, one day I wake up and I know it is over."

Frequently these patients, unaware of their depressed affective state, complain only about their mental and physical fatigue and exhaustion. They may compare the slowing up to a fog settling down in their brain; to a veil drawn over their thinking; to insurmountable walls blocking their feelings, their thinking, and their actions. Other patients, especially those suffering from involutional depression, show and complain about restlessness. They may run away from their family and go to their own room where they can pace up and down, up and down. They may express anxiety—but not panic—along with their restlessness. So far as I could see, the subjective inner awareness of an endogenous process is often more pronounced in simple depression than in manic-depressive cases with blatant psychotic symptoms, because in the former the ego is not so fully immersed in the pathological process.

When we combine clinical observations of these "endogenous" phenomena with a comparative psychoanalytic study of various neurotic and psychotic types of depression, we come to the following conclusions: (1) that not only the content but also the quality of the depression is different in neurotic and psychotic states; and (2) that it is correct to regard the simple and the acute psychotic types of depression as a nosological unit which should be distinguished from the great variety of neurotic depressive states. (I shall discuss the differences between cyclothymic and schizophrenic depressive states in Chapter 11.)

The clinical facts to which I referred bring back to mind Freud's (1917) surmise of a primary ego disturbance—either because of a narcissistic injury or on purely somatic (toxic) grounds—in some forms of melancholic depression. They also remind us that in schizophrenics Freud (1914) distinguished between symptoms expressive of the psychotic process as such, those representing neurotic defenses, and those developing in the service of restitution. Following this track, it becomes feasible to make the same distinction in the affective disorders. In manic-depressive states of depression we might then distinguish symptoms expressive of the psychotic-depressive process proper from those which represent secondary attempts at defense and restitution.

This distinction enables us to bring the various types of cyclothymic depression under a common denominator. "Simple," especially "endogenous," states of depression may show predominantly the ego disturbance expressive of the psychotic process. Symptoms ensuing from a psychotic guilt conflict, such as ideas of sinfulness, (delusional) self-accusations, suicidal impulses and actions which, in the typical case of "acute" depression, are commonly in the foreground, may be the result of failing attempts at restitution.[6]

Such a distinction lends itself to the "multiple-factor" approach to psychotic depression of which I spoke above. It allows consideration of underlying constitutional, hereditary, somatic as well as psychological causal factors whose role might be quite different in different individuals.

It also makes it easier to understand why in blatant delusional cases we usually do not question the psychotic nature of the illness. But states of "simple" depression—especially those which develop in "reaction" to experiences of loss or disappointment—may easily be regarded as neurotic or may even be equated with grief.

II

This leads me to Bibring's paper on "The Mechanism of Depression" (1953). In a brief review of the psychoanalytic literature on depression, Bibring describes two different approaches to the problem. There are authors who distinguish two types of depression:

> . . . the first type (called simple, essential, endogenous, mild, blank, etc.) is represented on the one hand by the uncomplicated grief reaction (Freud), on the other hand by the depression primarily due to exhaustion of the "ego energy." . . . The second (severe or melancholic) type is characterized by . . . narcissistic injury, oral mechanisms of recovery, such as identification via incorporation and the concomitant turning of the aggression from the object against the self. According to the second approach, a loss of self-esteem is common to all types of depression. Consequently the clinical differences (ranging from simple sadness to the severe forms of melancholia) are explained by additional predominantly oral-aggressive etiological mechanisms

[6] This is not really a new conception. In his paper on depression Rado (1928) described the development of the melancholic guilt conflict as a grandiose effort toward recovery.

which are employed in the course of the struggle for readjustments" [p. 20].

These formulations show first of all that in contrast to the authors to whom he refers (Freud, Abraham, Federn, Weiss, Jacobson), Bibring employs the term "simple" (or "mild" or "endogenous") in reference to any kind of depression in which the guilt conflict does not dominate the clinical picture; i.e., to grief, to normal, to neurotic, and to "simple" psychotic depression. As a consequence he tends to misunderstand other authors' statements, e.g., my own.

In his remarks on such writers as Fenichel and Lewin, Bibring criticizes their emphasis upon the intense fixation or regression to orality as creating a narcissistic vulnerability predisposing to depression. Unfortunately, it is quite true that Fenichel as well as Rado stressed the role of orality in all kinds of depression and considered the mechanism of depression always to be the same. Lewin (1950) also heavily underscored the role of orality, but he never regarded the state of elation as a "narcissistic neurosis." Freud applied this term only to melancholia, i.e., to psychotic depression, which he carefully distinguished, especially with respect to the narcissistic identifications in melancholia.

The essence of Bibring's views is the thesis that "depression is an ego-psychological phenomenon, a 'state of the ego,' an affective state" (p. 21). From some clinical examples he concludes: first, that depression is the emotional expression of a state of helplessness and powerlessness of the ego; second, that it results from the tension between highly charged narcissistic aspirations and the ego's awareness of its helplessness and incapacity to live up to these standards.

As regards the first point, according to my clinical experience a state of helplessness does not always result in a state of depression. To be sure, it can be frequently observed, e.g., in children, in masochistic patients with paranoid trends, and especially in borderline patients or paranoid schizophrenics suffering from depressive states. These patients tend to complain bitterly about their feeling of helplessness. It is caused by their masochism which prevents them from establishing control and power over their environment and their own instinctual life.

Bibring assumes that depression is primarily determined by an intrasystemic conflict, a tension within the ego itself. I would certainly agree that in the cases of "simple" (psychotic) depression I described above, the narcissistic conflict is a conflict within the ego. This is also valid in many schizophrenic states of depression, as well as in those neurotic or even normal kinds of depression in which feelings of inadequacy and inferiority play the main role. In such cases the conflict is between the wishful self image and the image of the failing self. But in many of these cases the underlying guilt feelings may be covered up by the feelings of inadequacy. I may here emphasize that in contrast to patients who suffer from "simple" psychotic depression, obsessional-compulsive depressives usually complain about their guilt feelings and rebel against them (Freud, 1923, Chapter 5).

In a summarizing statement, Bibring then distinguishes four basic ego states which "cannot be reduced any further" (p. 34): the secure, the elated or triumphant, the anxious, and the depressed ego; corresponding to states of balanced narcissism, of exhilarated self-esteem, of threatened narcissism, and of broken-down self-regard (p. 35f.). According to him, anxiety and depression are diametrically opposed basic ego responses.

Hence, the predisposition to depression is not always caused by "oral fixation," but is attributed to "the infant's or little child's shock-like experience of and fixation to the feeling of helplessness" (p. 37). It is "*a basic reaction* to situations of narcissistic frustration . . . just as *anxiety represents a basic reaction* of the ego to situations of danger" (p. 40). Bibring regards depression as "essentially independent of the vicissitudes of aggression as well as of oral drives" (p. 40). He is convinced that "the oral and aggressive strivings are not as universal in depression as is generally assumed" (p. 41).

It is certainly correct that in neurotic states of depression the depressive conflicts are of a different nature than those in psychotic depression. In contrast to psychotic depressives, neurotic depressive patients do not tend to regress to such an early developmental level. But here the question arises what Bibring means by the little child's "fixation" to the feeling of helplessness in response to narcissistic frustration. Evidently, this "fixation" refers to an ego state at an early developmental level, i.e., the infantile narcissistic stage of ego development. From the instinctual point of view, the child during that phase is at a pregenital level and suffers from marked ambivalence. This leads to the problem of the role of aggression in depression.

It is conspicuous that Bibring refers to the turning of aggression from the object to the self as "complicating the structure of depression" in certain cases (p. 41). He does not regard the intensity of the ambivalence conflict as generally predisposing to depression. This is not in accordance with other authors' and my own clinical experiences. What Bibring describes as basic ego responses are actually characteristic states of normal or disturbed narcissistic equilibrium, which can be observed in early childhood. He admits that depression arises in reaction to frustration, and is expressive of an (intrasystemic) conflict between narcissistic goals or expectations and the ego's inability to achieve or gratify them. But he forgets that people commonly react to frustration with aggressive, angry attempts to live up to their narcissistic goals and expectations, and in case of failure experience a loss of self-esteem that involves a hostile deflation of the self image. This also applies to conditions which we might consider states of libidinal exhaustion. Such patients usually spell out their self-derogation very clearly.

While Bibring minimizes the role of aggression in depression, he maintains that he observed cases of self-hate without depression. While this is true, he uses his observations for a wrong argument. People may develop guilt feelings or feelings of inadequacy, or even self-hate, without depression. But in this case the feelings refer only to specific impulses, attitudes, or actions, without the generalization which, as I discussed in Chapter 3, leads to a mood.

At this point I may underline the fact that Bibring does not carefully distinguish between moods and emotional responses—pleasurable or unpleasurable, depressive, elated or anxious. The latter, which I tried to define in Chapter 3, are generalized affective ego states that extend over a period of time. I believe it is useful, for clinical and theoretical reasons, to distinguish between passing emotional responses to specific experiences and moods. Anxiety is a reaction which may turn into a mood; depression and elation are commonly regarded as moods, but they can also develop as rather transitory, brief emotional reactions. Bibring's lack of distinction between an affective response and a mood here deprives him of the required explanation.

Moreover, in some borderline schizophrenic cases I observed self-hate seemingly without depression, which turned out, later on, to have been denied.

But if it is correct that depression is the result of the ego's inability to achieve narcissistic gratification, leading to a loss of self-esteem caused by self-derogation, can we call it a basic ego response, i.e., a reaction that cannot be reduced further? Strangely enough, Bibring does not seem to regard feelings of love or hate which are centered on objects as "basic ego responses," although they are not caused by a conflict, as is depression. What he means by basic ego states seems to have reference only to feelings indicative of the state of narcissistic balance.

Of course, in the case of feelings of love or hostility we think in terms of the underlying sexual or aggressive drive. This is precisely what Bibring avoids, even though he speaks of narcissistic injuries and the like. But as long as we maintain the psychoanalytic drive theory, we must view all psychic manifestations, including the "basic ego reactions," in terms of the underlying cathectic and discharge processes which involve self- and object-directed, sexual and aggressive or neutralized drives. It is true that in the case of anxiety, Freud was no longer concerned about the nature of the underlying drives. But anxiety differs significantly from depression: it is not the result of a defense, it is the central motor of defense. I believe that this essential difference was the reason for Bibring's disregard of the ambivalence conflict that is inherent in all depressions.

The main value of Bibring's paper lies in his putting the focus on the ego and in making clear that in depressive states the underlying narcissistic conflicts may, but need not, be conflicts between superego and ego. They may be intrasystemic conflicts within the ego.

It is unfortunate that Bibring neglects the role of object relations, of aggression, of the drives in general, and of the underlying hostility conflicts that can be observed even in early infantile depressions (Mahler, 1966).

Let me here turn to the child analyst for further information. At first sight, Mahler's (1966) observations on toddlers appear to confirm Bibring's assumptions; actually they point up the problems involved in his way of thinking. Mahler and her collaborators found

> . . . unmistakable evidence for the belief that a basic mood [i.e., an individually characteristic affective responsiveness] is established during the separation-individuation process. [But then she speaks correctly of] a loss in fantasy—that is to say, *intrapsychic conflict* of a particular type . . . which is the genetic cause for

> the occurrence of depression as an affect, as a proclivity toward a basic mood [p. 156]. [As to the first subphase of differentiation, Mahler emphasizes that] the momentum of libidinal responsiveness is greatly augmented . . . by the "dialogue" with the mother. . . . *Elation* seems to be the phase-specific or basic mood during the second subphase of individuation (the "practicing" period) [p. 158].

In her discussion of the next subphase, that of "rapprochement," Mahler describes very clearly that the lack of acceptance and of "emotional understanding" by the mother seems to diminish the child's self-esteem, and leads to ambivalence ("ambitendency") and "especially aggressive repetitive coercion" of the parents. These attitudes result in a turning of aggression against the self and in "a feeling of helplessness, which . . . creates the basic depressive affect" (p. 162).

I have quoted Mahler's paper so extensively because it points very clearly to what I want to show: that this so-called basic depression is the outcome of an aggressive conflict, caused by a lack of understanding and acceptance by the mother that reduces the child's self-esteem. Although there are early, preverbal forerunners of this mood, it is of interest that according to Mahler, elated mood develops prior to the time at which depressive responses can be clearly observed.

I now turn to Rubinfine's recent paper on depression (1968). After praising Bibring for his brilliant effort toward an ego-psychological theory of depression, the author points out that Bibring does not explain, or even raise the question, "why certain people achieve a mastery of depressive affect while others succumb to depressive illness." In this connection, he states: "In the abstract, a purely ego-psychological theory of depression should not derive explanatory power from drive theory" (p. 402). This, I believe, is quite a regrettable misunderstanding which supports the current tendency to eliminate the drive theory. But then Rubinfine discusses Bibring's emphasis on narcissism and self-esteem—i.e., the libidinal drives—in depression, and also points to Bibring's omission of aggression. He reminds us of the infantile rage in response to prolonged frustration, a response that precedes exhaustion and helplessness (depression). We are all familiar with the role these reactions play in depression. But then Rubinfine makes some rather simplified statements regarding the factors predisposing the child to psychosis, to psychosomatic illness, and to depression—problems which had previously been discussed by other authors, e.g., by Schur and by myself.

He correctly points out that aggression as such "does not provide an answer." He sees as "the two primary factors . . . sequence and timing and the modifying principle of degree: in other words, the order, the era, and the amount of frustration encountered" (p. 404). Rubinfine believes that these two factors of sequence and timing create the predisposition to the three groups of illnesses in the first year of life.

In this connection, Rubinfine makes some important comments on psychotic depression, which he regards as more closely related to the sequence type of disturbance. He believes it is characterized by dedifferentiation, bad reality testing, thought disorders, fragmentation of self and object representations.

Here we see the damaging effect that our terminological confusion has on our clinical and theoretical thinking. Rubinfine categorizes the psychotic depressions as resembling depression, but in their structure as identical with schizophrenia (p. 405). This is quite correct inasmuch as the kind of psychotic depression which he describes makes its appearance in schizophrenics. But simple or acute (delusional) depressions belonging to the manic-depressive group are likewise "psychotic" depressions, a term which Rubinfine does not use when discussing "depressive illness." The latter is the broad term employed by Zetzel (1965). It too is not sufficiently specific.

In other words, Rubinfine follows Bibring's lack of distinction between neurotic states of depression and those which belong either to the manic-depressive or to the schizophrenic group of disorders. His discussion of the narcissistic fixations in patients with "depressive illness" and his conclusions undoubtedly refer to psychotic types of depression, manic-depressive or schizophrenic. He emphasizes the narcissistic fixations of such patients in terms of arrest at a state of narcissistic unity with the mother. This is too generalized. It is true specifically for symbiotic types of schizophrenics; but it does not apply to manic-depressives, in whom the situation is more complicated (see Chapters 9, 10, and 11).

Rubinfine mentions, furthermore, that "The depressive person obviously suffers from a failure to achieve object constancy" (p. 416). This is again in accord with what we observe in schizophrenics, but is incorrect with regard to the simple or acute manic-depressive states of depression. In other words, Rubinfine obscures matters by making no distinction between the two main types of psychoses.

I share his opinion, however, that the depressive never gives up hope, even in suicide. I also agree with his distinction between depressive affect and guilt feelings, although not with his explanation. As I pointed out above, there are superego-ego conflicts which cause guilt feelings but not depression, because they refer to specific, object-directed, forbidden impulses. As I stated in Chapter 3, the guilt feelings in depressive states are generalized. They are caused by the patients' severe ambivalence toward all objects and morally condemn the whole self. The patient feels not that he has a forbidden impulse, but that he is an "evil person." At the end of his paper Rubinfine agrees with Zetzel (1965), as I do, "that the capacity to bear depression and anxiety represents an important measure of ego strength" (p. 417).

Having criticized the work of others, I must now reformulate clearly and specifically my own views concerning depression or, rather, the various states of depression.

I repeat once again that I consider a clear distinction between neurotic, borderline, psychotic, and between the different types of depressive states, as a prerequisite for both psychoanalytic and neurophysiological research on depression.[7]

Applying ego psychology to depression, I think of feelings of security, depression, and elation not in terms of basic ego states, but as characteristic states of normal or disturbed narcissistic equilibrium. I agree with Mahler (1966) that elated and depressive responses can be found at an early age as a result of experiences of narcissistic gratification or frustration. That these responses may turn into indicators—mainly into stop or go-ahead signals—I do not doubt; but their signal function is not comparable to that of anxiety, the motor of repression.

An ego-psychological approach to the problem of depression would, however, not be psychoanalytic if it neglected the drive theory. Actually, the clinical facts point to the involvement of the drives. Even in the infantile types of depression, there is clear evi-

[7] Arlow and Brenner (1964) maintain that there are only quantitative differences between neurosis and psychosis. I believe, however, that at a certain point quantitative differences turn into very essential qualitative differences.

dence of a basic underlying "conflict," as Mahler (1966) amply demonstrated. This basic conflict seems to be of the same order in all depressed states: frustration arouses rage and leads to hostile attempts to gain the desirable gratification. When the ego is unable (for external or internal reasons) to achieve this goal, aggression is turned to the self image. The ensuing loss of self-esteem is expressive of the narcissistic conflict, i.e., a conflict between the wishful self image and the image of the deflated, failing self. The nature of the mood condition that then develops depends on the intensity of the hostility and the severity and duration of frustration and disappointment. But this still does not fully answer the question of what distinguishes the various groups of depression from each other.

To be sure, this is not only a question of "content." Freud beautifully described the different mechanisms operative in the depressive states of compulsive neurotics and melancholias. And with regard to psychotic depressions I have conjectured that their very special qualities may be determined by the underlying neurophysiological pathology. A sound psychoanalytic theory of depression presupposes a "multiple-factor" genetic approach. It must take into account the nature and intensity of the drives involved in the conflict, the instinctual constitution; the qualities of the drives in terms of deneutralization and defusion, the special drive fixations and regressions, the nature of the cathectic conditions; the drive discharge processes, and the changes in the cathexes of the self and object representations, since all these factors have a bearing on the level of ego functioning.

A psychoanalytic theory of depression must also deal with the problem of the individual ego anlage, the ego-superego arrests or regressions, and their influence on the ego's functioning. The structural differences in the depressive conflict situation in various groups of depression as well as the different mechanisms of defense or restitution must be given due consideration.

Moreover, a sound theory of depression must not ignore the developmental psychogenetic aspects, including the factors of sequence and timing, which, combined with the study of the regressive processes, may clarify the problem of the "content" of the depression.

Finally, I reaffirm my belief that the differences between neurotic and psychotic states of depression rest on constitutional neurophysiological processes. Considerations of this order must complement the psychological—i.e., psychoanalytic—assumptions.

Both must be based on the careful clinical observation and psychoanalytic exploration of the different clinical pictures found in various groups of depressive states. Only a combination of all these factors can assist us in developing what I should like to call, not "a" theory of depression, but sufficiently sound theoretical assumptions concerning the nature of infantile and adult, neurotic and psychotic states of depression.

7

A Special Response to Early Object Loss

This chapter deals with a special reaction to early object loss, which was observed in three patients suffering from neurotic depressive states.

In the course of my psychoanalytic practice I have treated quite a number of patients who in early childhood had lost either both or one of their parents. From the multifaceted problems which such patients present (Bonaparte, 1928; Meiss, 1952; Tarachow and Fink, 1958; Neubauer, 1960; Pollock, 1961; Fleming and Altschul, 1963), one specific response to the early object loss has been selected for discussion. It is a response that played a decisive role in their propensity for states of depression.

This response was also related to the well-known family romance which so many children develop. In fact, almost all of the orphaned or semiorphaned patients had built up a florid family romance in their childhood. It involved daydreams about admirable families or persons—wealthy, gifted, and of noble origin—who would turn out to be their real parents, from whom they had once been forcefully separated, and with whom they would one day be reunited.

In the course of adolescence these patients modified their day-

---

This chapter is based on a paper, "The Return of the Lost Parent," first published in *Drives, Affects, Behavior,* Volume 2, edited by Max Schur. New York: International Universities Press, 1965, pp. 193-211.

dreams and, bringing them closer to reality, tried to search for families or persons to whom they could attach these fantasies. They looked for superior, "worthy"—and frequently wealthy—people who might be willing, as it were, to "adopt" them (Lehrman, 1927; Greene, 1958). Naturally, such attempts were bound to fail. The persons they selected could not live up either to the part they were supposed to play or to the patients' glorified imagery. The patients then reacted to their disappointment with depression, after which their search often started anew.

The three patients to be presented reacted to the loss of the patient with fantasies of this kind which led to particular complications in their adult life.

The predominant feature in their reaction to the early object loss was their stubborn refusal ever to accept the reality of the actual events. They remained doubtful about them, distorted them, or even denied them altogether. In "A Type of Neurotic Hypomanic Reaction" (1937) Lewin described such patients in terms of their glorification of the lost parent, their unconscious belief that he did not die, and their particularly intense ambivalence conflicts with the surviving parent. These traits were characteristic of my patients, too. My patients, however, carried their denial to the point of preconsciously, or at times even consciously, expecting that one day the lost parent would reappear. Their fantasies and expectations of a return of the lost parent were mostly coupled or alternated with daydreams of the familiar family romance type.

In the first case to be reported, the patient's hope to find her lost father had a more realistic basis than in the others, since her father had not died: he had deserted her mother before the patient was born, and to all practical purposes had disappeared forever. In this patient as well as in the two others, the attitudes and the behavior of the surviving family were apt to support the denial of the significant real events. The other two patients suspected, indeed, that the parent had not died but had abandoned the family and lived faraway in some other place. In the minds of all these patients this—actual or supposed—desertion had not been the fault of the lost parent, who they were sure had been a wonderful person. It has been caused by the surviving parent's intolerable character or moral worthlessness.

CASE 1

From the clinical point of view, the most impressive of the three cases was that of Mary. She entered treatment because of a monosymptomatic hysteria and a depressive state of about two years' duration. Her history showed that she also suffered from a "fate neurosis" that threatened to ruin her life.

Mary K. was a thirty-year-old, rather attractive, unmarried secretary. She lived together with an older spinster sister, who had a similar job. This sister exercised a considerable influence on Mary's opinions and decisions, and never separated from her even for a single day.

However close the sisters were to each other, there was an area in Mary's life about which she had been secretive. She had never mentioned it to her sister, her friends, and the various physicians whom she had consulted before she came to me. The reason for her previous consultations and treatments had been her main symptom, which had been caused by an accident. Mary had fallen down the subway stairs without suffering any serious physical injury. But at home, when she tried to use her hands, she discovered that her right index finger became stiff, erect, and could not be bent. Treatment by several orthopedists and physiotherapists did not help. She was finally sent to a psychiatrist who, after a brief period of psychotherapy, referred her to me for psychoanalytic treatment.

Mary wept when she told me her story and complained bitterly how much this symptom interfered with her secretarial job. But when I questioned her more specifically, I discovered that for many years she had actually worked as an executive secretary and had a sufficient number of typists at her disposal. At this point Mary became very embarrassed and responded as if I had caught her in a lie. At last she began to tell me the "true story," which she had carefully managed to conceal.

In her early twenties, Mary, who had a remarkable musical talent, had decided to obtain serious training as a pianist in her free time, and to become a professional musician. In her daydreams she would see herself as an admired successful concert pianist, in close contact with other prominent musicians. To some extent Mary had carried through her plans. She had vigorously practiced every night, and regularly attended concerts and rehearsals, where she was introduced to a number of musicians. On such an occasion she had met Karl, the concertmaster of a well-known symphony orchestra.

Karl was about twenty-seven years her senior. He was married and had two daughters who were close to her age. A strange friendship developed between Mary and Karl, whom she told about her vocational plans. It was understood that every week after the last big orchestra rehearsal they would secretly spend a few hours in a little restaurant with each other and talk—mostly about music. This was all. Karl never tried to make passes at her or to change their relationship in any way. But in spite of the very limited gratification which such a friendship could offer, Mary devoted herself completely to it. She loved Karl very intensely. When at concerts she saw his family in a box, she felt terribly jealous—not of his wife, but of his two daughters. She did not look at any other man and rejected the idea of marriage, now or in the future. She wanted nothing but this friendship and her piano.

One night, after a friendship of about six years, Karl at last expressed the desire to play sonatas with her in her home. Mary became anxious, evasive, finally angry, but her friend insisted and they made a date for one of the next days. On that day, on her way home from work, Mary suddenly began to feel very dizzy. Walking down to the subway platform, she fainted, lost her balance, and fell down the stairs. When she came to, she immediately thought, with a feeling of relief: "I broke my arm, so now I cannot play with Karl." Actually, she had not suffered any physical harm except for a few bruises. Hurrying home in a state of shock, she sat down at her piano. Trying to clap down her fingers she found that her right index finger could not be used. She was unable to play. Mary immediately called up her friend, reported what had happened, and canceled the date. He responded with an expressive silence, and from then on never again attempted to visit her in her home. Since her symptom did not subside, it naturally prevented her from continuing her piano studies. But her daydreams did not break down completely. She went on hoping for a cure, keeping her interest in music alive and seeing Karl every week, who accepted the situation on this basis as he had done before.

To the analyst, this story of a girl's hopeless love for a married man old enough to be her father, and of her symptom formation under the threat of a sexual temptation, sounds rather transparent.

But no analyst could have guessed this patient's unusual infantile history and exceptional experiences which were actually responsible for the development of her neurosis.

Mary's life as a musician had not been her only "secret." What she had also tried to conceal all her life was the fact that she had been adopted and was the illegitimate daughter of a peasant girl who had put the baby into a foster home a few weeks after birth. The foster parents, very nice, lower-middle-class people who already had one little girl and had another one a year later, nevertheless fell in love with this pretty baby and decided to adopt her. The real mother seemed glad to get rid of her. She became a seamstress, settled down nearby in the same city, and never married. From time to time she visited Mary, brought her a little gift, but never showed any signs of genuine interest or tried to gain her love. Mary regarded her as a "stranger." During latency, when Mary learned from other children that she was an adopted child and this woman was her mother, she began to despise her more and more and to detach herself completely from her. In these years her denial mechanisms began to flourish under the influence of her parents' attitude and of their silence about her background. She developed what one might call a special version of a family romance. Being so clearly the "favorite" child, especially of her father, made her feel that they must be her true parents, while her real mother might once have been her nurse.

In her adolescence, Mary's fantasies took a new turn. She and her older sister had always been as serious, strict, and moralistic as her adoptive mother. But the youngest girl, for whom they never had had much respect, showed increasing signs of waywardness. Thus Mary developed a fantasy, which returned to awareness in her analysis, that perhaps *this* girl was actually the adopted one and was really the seamstress's illegitimate child. Evidently, Mary repressed this fantasy after her adopted mother, quite unexpectedly, had given her serious warnings regarding her relations to boys. They implied that her adoptive mother was afraid Mary might repeat the misdeeds of her real mother.

The girl reacted with feelings of shock and confusion, of hurt and resentment, to her mother's revelations and implied lack of trust in her. But she soon managed to re-establish her self-esteem and her good relationship with her mother by displacing her anger and contempt to her true mother and her younger sister; they were the ones who needed moral guidance. When at the age of eighteen this younger sister became engaged to a rather attractive though not very solid young man, the whole family felt relieved. But in Mary's opinion, this worthless girl did not deserve a husband, since like her real mother she was no better than a prostitute. These hostile, derogatory thoughts made Mary feel guilty. She began to suspect that she might possibly be jealous of her sister and might want as much sexual freedom as this girl and her own mother had permitted themselves.

What happened next was that one day when nobody but Mary was home, her sister's fiancé dropped in, made passes at her, and tried to seduce her. At this moment her defenses broke down, and so did her identification with her adoptive mother's and her older sister's virtues. If this man behaved toward her as to a prostitute, she must be the true daughter of her real mother. Whereupon Mary yielded to the seduction. When the incident was over, Mary felt guilt-ridden, sinful, depressed, and disgusted at this boy and at herself. Neither she nor the boy ever confessed to anybody what had happened. But she made a solemn vow to herself that she would never again let herself be seduced by a man. She kept her vow, and renounced sex and young men in general. A few years later Mary lost first her adoptive mother, then her father. The younger sister had married, and she was left with her older sister as a moral guardian.

In her analysis Mary described how, after a period of sincere grief, she had begun to plan to take up music as a profession and started to develop daydreams about her future career. At this point she suddenly mentioned a strange screen memory, which turned out to be of singular significance. She remembered that at the age of about five or six she had been visited by a wonderful stranger who had brought her candies. He held an odd big gadget in his arm that he put in a corner. She had never forgotten it.

Now Mary learned from her sister that this man had been her true father and the mysterious gadget had been a musical instrument, a trumpet. Her father had been a trumpet player in a military band stationed in her mother's hometown. Mary reacted to this revelation with the feeling that she had known this all along. It turned out that after the loss of her adoptive parents, she had built up a daydream which was unconsciously centered about a glorified image of her lost musician father. She remembered having had fleeting fantasies during that period about actually meeting her real father one day. Her repression of her father's vocation permitted her to keep these thoughts apart from her plans and daydreams about her musical career, and from her relationship with Karl, the married musician old enough to be her father.

With great anxiety Mary now began to realize that her musical interests had been in the service of her secret search for the lost father. It finally occurred to her that Karl's affectionate attachment and secret relationship to her might have a special reason: he might actually be her father who, in his turn, had searched for her and found her. In fact, as with her adoptive father, she felt he preferred her to both of his legitimate children, who had not inherited his musical talents. In regard to this identification with her real father, the analysis finally disclosed the idea that her real father might have married her real mother if the latter had been decent, or else, if Mary had been a boy. Her adoptive father, too, had been sorry that none of his children was a boy. Only by being musically gifted and more intelligent than the others, which meant closest to being a boy, had she become his favorite child.

Only now can we understand the causes for Mary's symptom formation. In her mind a sexual relationship with Karl might have been potentially a real incestuous act. Thus Karl was not, or only partly, a "transference" object. She suspected him of actually being her lost real father who had abandoned her and her mother, married a "decent" woman, but had secretly looked for her and finally found her. She could regain him and keep him forever if she could prove to him and to herself that she was worthy of him: indeed, his worthiest child, the opposite of her prostitute mother, and even better than his legitimate children. Since "playing" sonatas with Karl in her home meant to Mary a sexual play, her friend's suggestion threatened to destroy her idealized father image as well as that of her virtuous self. For this reason she reacted to his proposal not only with great anxiety but with intense anger at him. When he calmly accepted the results of her accident, her anger subsided, but she became depressed.

Going back to Mary's various fictional stories and the denial and projections on which they rested, we can at last define their main defense functions. They were not merely supposed to keep alive and even gratify her desire to regain the lost love object. They were also attempts at mastery of the castration and guilt conflicts, whose normal vicissitudes and solution her special situation had precluded. Undoing the narcissistic injury of her illegitimate birth and adoption, Mary's stories served especially the warding off of her unacceptable unconscious identifications with the sinful (castrated) "prostitute" mother who was responsible for the harm done to her. At the same time her fantasies aimed at the solution of the guilt conflicts arising in part from these very identifications and in part from the severe hostility toward her real mother. Needless to say, Mary's illusory fantasy productions and the primitive defenses which they employed did not have the desired effect. They brought about an untenable situation and led to neurotic symptom formation, including depressive states.

I conclude my report of this case by adding that Mary's analysis gradually helped her to liberate herself from her masochistic enslavement to her musician friend and from her puritanical attitudes in general. She began to look for a suitable partner, started a sexual relationship, and became more independent of her moral guardian, the sister, who promptly followed her example. After her symptoms subsided, Mary took up her piano studies again, but gave up her ideas of a musical career.

In the other two cases, the denial was of quite a different order. While Mary had refused to accept the fact that she was an illegitimate adopted child and the daughter of her seamstress mother, these two patients, who were semiorphans and also suffered from depressed states, could not admit that their parent had really died.

CASE 2

Robert H., a married man in his thirties, had lost his mother when he was at the end of his oedipal period. She died while giving birth to a boy, who died on the same day.[1]

In the first years of his life Robert had been very closely tied to his mother and had been thoroughly spoiled by his nursemaid. When his mother tried during her pregnancy to send him to kindergarten,

[1] I discussed this case from a different perspective in Chapter 5.

he developed such separation anxiety that she finally had to take him back home.

When the tragic event occurred, the child was completely ignored. He knew that his mother had left for the hospital to have a baby, but nobody informed him about what had happened. The next day he was taken to relatives, where he stayed for some time. Suddenly deprived of his mother and his nursemaid, of his home, and for some time also of his father, placed in a new environment with grieving adults, the little boy went through a period of anxiety and helpless confusion, and then of deep loneliness and depression, with feelings of self-estrangement.

Neither his father nor his relatives ever gave Robert an explanation of his mother's disappearance. Later on, whenever he asked his father what had happened to his mother, the only answer was: "Your mother was an angel." Unsatisfactory though it was, this answer helped the child to create an utterly glorified, rather mystical picture of his lost "angelic" mother. Thus his hostility could be readily diverted to the surviving members of the family.

Robert's former nurse became a special target for his negative, derogatory feelings. When she came to visit him, he found her "disgusting," turned away from her, and completely detached himself from her.

Robert's father did not remarry. He moved with his son into his mother's home. But even though in general he took loving care of his son, neither he nor the grandmother—a gloomy, overly strict woman—was able to gratify the child's emotional needs. Robert's conflicts increased when his father took a city apartment, where he would spend his evenings with various mistresses. The situation became even worse when he introduced his son to some of them. There was again an unpleasant aura of secrecy and mystery about these women, their role, their appearances and disappearances. As soon as Robert began to guess the nature of his father's relationships with them, he became very critical of his father's immoral and materialistic attitudes, and began to build up a reactive, overly strict superego and high ego ideal, modeled after the image of his "saintly" mother.

During this period, the lonely child began to develop a family romance. It revolved around fantasies of being the son of an aristocratic British family. In his family romance, a mother figure did not play a particular role. It is of interest that these fantasies had a considerable influence on his appearance, bearing, and behavior, which suggested a British upper-class background, and also on his choice of a marital partner.

When Robert lost his father in his early twenties, he immediately married a well-bred, very intelligent girl who came from a family socially higher than his own. His rather large inheritance actually permitted him to live the life of a gentleman. He detached himself from his less educated, simple, and simple-minded relatives, and accepted his wife's family as his own. Subsequently, being a very gifted man with broad intellectual and aesthetic interests, he made a successful career in a vocational field related to that of his father-in-law.

Up to the time of his marriage Robert had never had any sexual affairs. Like Mary, he was and remained a puritan in his convictions, his attitudes, and, with certain exceptions, also in his actions.

Robert sought treatment for his recurring states of depression and depersonalization. Their analysis revealed an intensely vested sadomasochistic fantasy life, which had its origin in violent primal scene fantasies aroused by his mother's pregnancy and death. He had managed secretly to gratify these unconscious fantasies, especially in repetitive stormy scenes with his very charming and intelligent but temperamental wife and his impulsive children. Having totally idealized both his marriage and his particular aesthetic interest, Robert was very disturbed by the discovery that under the guise of his ideals his strivings had found expression in his fantasies and behavior.

As in Mary's case, this made him feel that he was actually no better than his "immoral" father. The analytic material showed that Robert's sadomasochistic fantasies were linked up with unconscious suspicions that his father killed his wife and child in the sexual act. These fantasies were so unacceptable that they had to be warded off by a denial of his mother's death. The secrecy that surrounded her sudden disappearance could be explained just as well by the assumption that his mother had left his father because of his immorality and worthlessness. This interpretation still held the father responsible for the loss of the mother, but it did not make him a sexual murderer, and the mother a victim of her sexual passion for the father.

How firmly Robert believed this story became clear when he

told me that every morning he would run down to the mailbox, expecting to get a "special" letter. Each time he would return very much disappointed that again "the letter" had not arrived. The mysterious letter, for the arrival of which he had stubbornly waited as long as he could remember, was a letter from his mother and brother who, he suspected, lived somewhere in a faraway place and would one day write and return to him.

It is noteworthy that Robert's family romance about being the son of a British nobleman was completely disconnected from the set of fantasies which denied his mother's death and sustained his hope for her return and their final reunion.

The first was a conscious daydream, expressive mainly of his wish for a worthy, ideal father with whom he could identify. The patient had always been fully aware of the fantastic quality of this part of his family romance, despite its influence on his ego and superego development and on his object relations. The ideas about his mother's and brother's survival were of a different nature. They were not daydreams but vague suspicions, hopes, and expectations, which would only occasionally come close to awareness. Reflecting Robert's ambivalence toward his father and grandmother, they had been provoked by their secrecy about his mother's death. Later on they found support in the mysterious sudden appearances and disappearances of his father's mistresses, and in the latter's partly exhibitionistic, partly secretive "bad" sexual behavior.

Of course, Robert's unconscious denial of his mother's death, and his expectation of her return in some distant future, helped him to keep up the illusory belief that he might get back his first love object to whom he had been so closely attached. But in particular they served as a defense against his murderous primal scene fantasies, his identifications with his sinful parents, and the guilt feelings aroused by these sadomasochistic identifications. His belief certainly enabled him during those unhappy, lonely years in his grandmother's home to maintain a certain optimistic, hopeful outlook on life and himself. Later on, it found expression in mildly elated states of mood which alternated with his depressions. His optimism probably, had its origin in the ineradicable happy memories of his early childhood years. But being quite illusory, his optimistic expectations failed in preventing the development of recurring depressions, which repeated his original response to his mother's sudden death and remobilized the guilt conflicts caused by his hostile reactions to her pregnancy and his death wishes toward his future rival.

CASE 3

The third case is that of Paul L., a married man in his late twenties. His severe depressive episodes, with an occasional hypomanic bout, had started in the latency years and probably even earlier. His father had died a short time before he was born. But even though the patient did not undergo the traumatic experience of early object loss, he could not escape the fate of a fatherless child. His father's illness and death had exhausted the financial resources of his mother and compelled her, after Paul's birth, to take over the support of the family. She first worked at home and, as Paul grew a little older, held regular jobs. Her oldest sister, likewise a widow, moved in and took care of the home and the two children—of little Paul and his sister who was several years older. Thus Paul was brought up with three rather aggressive females around him. The old aunt, who was quite a character, was the most loving of the three. But both she and her sister did not seem to care much for the other sex. Neither of them ever talked about their past lives or seemed to want a second marriage. Both showed little respect for Paul's uncle, their brother, who frequently visited the family on weekends.

Thus, the little boy's situation at home was not a very happy one. In his preschool years he was very lonesome. None of the three females seemed to be aware of his needs; they never played with him. Paul's mother, a very dutiful mother but a rather narcissistic, compulsive, depressive person, constantly complained about her hard life. She impressed on him very early that she expected him to compensate her for all her losses and sacrifices and to assume the responsibilities of a "man" in the home. At the same time she did her best to tie him to herself and to prevent his ever becoming independent. In response to these contradictory maternal attitudes, Paul developed the conviction that as a fatherless boy he had no chance of ever becoming a real man. On entering school, he felt different and rather estranged from other boys who had "normal" families.

His uncle tried to play the role of a father, which Paul eagerly accepted for some years. Once the uncle invited Paul for a vacation with his own boys in his home in the suburbs. Paul immediately began to hope that the uncle might keep him forever in his family. He was very disappointed when his uncle did not "adopt" him or ever invite him again. Later on, this uncle became very critical of him, evidently out of jealousy that Paul was much brighter than his own sons. His uncle's behavior did much to lower Paul's self-esteem still further.

Some years later Paul began to develop a series of friendships with boys who seemed to have admirable, loving parents. Trying to establish himself as a member of their families, Paul spent as much time as he could in their homes. During this period he began for the first time actively to compete with other boys. But in the end his renewed efforts to find a family that would adopt him proved to be as futile as the attempt with his uncle. Each time they ended with disappointment and depression.

In his own home, the situation had become intolerable. The three women constantly fought with him and with each other, playing off one against the other. The atmosphere became even more hostile when Paul began to rebel, to assert his masculinity and independence, and to show the three women his physical and mental superiority.

Paul was in fact by far the most gifted member of the family. He was a brilliant, ambitious boy, but forever doubtful about the extent of his physical and intellectual abilities. This did not change when he became financially independent. After working his way through college and law school, he attained a very good position in a law firm and married. At this point, in his early twenties, Paul at last felt able to detach himself from his family in the same way as Robert had done.

Paul soon made a successful career, financially and professionally. He had a charming, devoted wife and a lovely, bright child. In reality, he had accomplished everything he could have wished to attain at this age, yet he was constantly dissatisfied and depressed. Although his wife and his law firm gave him all the freedom he wanted, he felt as much trapped in his professional and marital situation as he had once felt at home with his mother.

He continuously complained about his wife, his firm, his jobs, and his own work. At the same time he daydreamed about drastic changes in his life in the future. In fact, he was forever in search of the right people and work to help him find at last his real self.

This leads to Paul's fantasy relationship to the father he had lost before he was born. In Paul's case the family behavior had not supported any glorification of the late father. Paul knew the bare outlines of his father's background, of his vocation, and of his fatal illness and death. Even this account had been incomplete, confusing, and contradictory. His mother had never talked with him about his father as a person. She had never arranged for him to meet any of the surviving members of his father's family. As far as she was concerned, Paul's father seemed never to have existed. His mother's eloquent silence about her late husband profoundly affected Paul and caused him to create a myth about his father. He built up a highly glorified but rather lifeless, abstract paternal image. Since he had no personal memories of his father and did not even hear stories about him, Paul himself thought that his image of a brilliant, great man might have nothing to do with his real father. He thought it might be a product of his own imagination and even felt quite triumphant about the fact that he had not needed a realistic model but had created his goals and ideals, which this image reflected, independently and out of himself.

This spiteful feeling, which denied his urgent need for a father, was an expression of his rejection of the mother's attitudes and behavior, and especially of her hypermorality and her scales of value in general. His reactive ego ideal and his ambitious ego goals were in fact the product of a permanent struggle against his unconscious identifications with her and with his sister and aunt (Greenson, 1954),

Unfortunately, this struggle had resulted in marked identity conflicts and prevented Paul from ever developing a feeling of continuity and firm direction. But his constant search for an identity did not simply reflect his need for a realistic parental figure whom he could accept as a model for himself. Apparently no person—man or woman—had ever been acceptable in this role, since Paul expected his real father to return and take over the part of the model that he had so urgently needed.

Whereas Paul had greater doubts than Robert about the correctness of this assumption, he was far more specific in his elaboration of the story about his father. He wondered whether his father had not left his intolerable, hostile wife and founded a new family on the West Coast where his relatives lived. Moreover, he thought that probably for this reason his mother had never let him meet his father's relatives. He suspected that she always kept him so close to herself because she did not want him to discover the truth and to find and join the father and his new family. There was also a vague implication that he might not really be his mother's son. While Paul never made the slightest move to write to these relatives or to see them, it turned out that he had developed the same habit as Robert. He too expected every morning to get an exciting "special" letter, which never came: the letter from his father. And he also continued to hope that one day in the future his father would write to him and they would be reunited.

The intensity of Paul's hopes for his father's return was illuminated by his acting out during his analysis. He developed a sudden, very strong emotional involvement with an impressive, much older lawyer, until he found out that this man closely resembled the only picture of his father that he owned. For a brief period he had evidently hoped that this man might actually be his real father.

Paul's suspicions about his father's desertion of his family and his life in California had always been on a preconscious or, at times, even conscious level. What he had not known, however, was that his feelings of being trapped, his compulsive urge to run away from his mother, his wife, from jobs and superiors, and to look for the right persons and the right work, were an expression of his search for his father and of his wish to join him and his new family.

His father's supposed new wife did not play any part in his conscious fantasies. Her role in his unconscious became clear from his fantasies about certain older married women who might be able to give him something very "special." The "special" gift he expected to get and never could get from them was obviously his real father, and hence his real own "manly" self.

All these fantasies, hopes, and expectations, which we may call a family romance, centering on the figure of his real father, began to develop in his latency period. They arose concomitantly and were interwoven with his desires and his disappointing attempts to be "adopted." Paul's illusory ideas were predominantly in the service of his attempts at a solution of his narcissistic conflicts. Since the loss of his father was experienced as a narcissistic injury, in fact as a castration, the survival and future return of his father meant to him a potential recovery of his own lost masculine identity.

As in Robert's case, however, the additional function of his myth was to ward off deeply unconscious fantasies about his father's violent death. Sadomasochistic primal scene material involving Paul's mother disclosed fantasies—similar to those of Robert—that his mother might have revengefully killed his father when the latter tried to rape her. Paul remembered that at the age of six he had developed fantasies in which his mother was assaulted and disrobed by a man on the street. Being a helpless little boy, he could only watch the scene but do nothing to help his mother. As he grew up the fantasy changed, inasmuch as he now tried to save her by attacking the aggressor. The analysis of his fantasies, which showed the underlying hostility toward his glorified father, revealed that Paul was clearly identified with both partners' roles and crimes. He suffered indeed from guilt feelings loaned from both parents. Since Paul felt that his mother had wanted and tempted him to usurp his father's place, he felt in particular that he shared the responsibility for his father's death with his mother.

DISCUSSION

A comparison of the three cases shows rather striking resemblances and also interesting differences, not only in the patients' direct responses to the object loss but also in the broader psychopathology which they gradually developed on the basis of this loss.

It was not accidental that all three patients entered treatment in a state of depression. But it is significant that Mary's depression was of a hysterical type and showed conspicuous features of true grief. Its obvious cause was the sad recognition that she could no longer anticipate any satisfaction or happiness in the future, either as a woman or as a musician. Her conflicts were of a hysterical rather than of a profoundly narcissistic type: they revolved essentially about her incestuous problems. Of course, the fact that Mary was an adopted, illegitimate child was a severe narcissistic injury. It readily directed all her hostility to the "prostitute" mother, who had abandoned her.

But we must not forget that since early infancy Mary had been brought up by very loving adoptive parents. Her readiness to act out her incestuous impulses was probably caused by the very fact that her adoptive father had been less inhibited in giving physical affection to her than to his own children. The love she received could not prevent the development of a fate neurosis that cut her off from a normal heterosexual love life. But Mary's general capacity for object relations had not been seriously affected. The disgraceful fact of her illegitimate birth and adoption was so intolerable to her that she built up fictitious stories which not only denied this fact but projected it onto the younger sister, thus reversing the situation. Despite the extent to which her denial and projection mechanisms went, they remained limited to this specific problem. Her secrecy about her vocational plans and her friendship with Karl were also linked up with that.

While Mary did not deny the loss of her father but denied only the fact of her illegitimacy and adoption, the two semiorphaned patients had to resort to a denial of their parent's death. Both of them had a rather lonesome, unhappy childhood. Robert at least had memories of his happy early childhood years, even though his happy life had ended with the traumatic experiences which were described. This accounted for the fact that except for recurring states of depression and his prolonged adolescence with detachment from his relatives, he developed stable emotional relations and interests and was able to enjoy life. Robert was basically a hysterical personality, though with obsessional-compulsive features. His narcissistic vulnerability was caused by the abrupt traumatic change from the life of a protected, overindulged child to that of a motherless, emotionally deprived one, too young to cope with his losses by means of truly grieving.

There were striking resemblances in the cases of Robert and Paul: their surmise that the parent had not died but deserted the unworthy partner and lived in another city, and their expectation of a confirming letter and a future reunion. In both cases, the denial of the lost object's death had been provoked by the surviving parent's refusal to talk about the dead partner. And in both patients their strikingly similar story served the same function: to ward off not only the intolerable fantasies that the lost objects had been killed by their partners in the sexual act, but in particular the guilt feelings caused by the patient's unconscious fantasy identification with the surviving parent's supposed hostility and criminal acts.

In Robert's case, the murderous primal scene fantasies had been provoked by his knowledge that during childbirth something terrible had happened to mother and infant. Paul's corresponding fantasies had been stimulated by the close temporal link between his own birth and his father's illness and death.

In view of Paul's early emotional deprivations, it is not surprising that, in contrast to Mary and Robert, he became an obsessional-compulsive, chronically depressive person with marked identity conflicts.

The differences in the personalities of these three patients, and in the structure of their conflicts provoked by the early object loss, were intentionally pointed out.

With regard to the similarity of Robert's and Paul's stories and the hope of all three patients for the return of their lost parent, it appears to be of utmost importance that in all three cases the stories were, above all, supposed to aid the patients in the mastery of the narcissistic injuries caused by the early loss of the glorified object, and to help them in the solution of their hostility, castration, and guilt conflicts. Their expectation of getting back the lost object in the distant future is certainly reminiscent of the little girl's hopes of getting back the lost penis. One feels tempted to speak in these patients of an "illusory parent," in analogy to women's "illusory penis."

Evidently, children experience the loss of a parent in early childhood not only in terms of loss of love or of a love object, but also as a severe narcissistic injury, a castration. Since children in their first years of life depend on their parents for narcissistic supplies and participate in their supposed grandeur, to be fatherless, motherless, an orphan, or an adopted child is felt to be utterly degrading. The fact that in such children the hostile and derogatory feelings caused by their losses are so commonly diverted to the surviving parent or the parent substitutes, while the lost object becomes glorified, tends to raise that object's narcissistic value and meaning to the point of turning it into the most precious part of their own self which has been lost and must be recovered. This is the reason why so many of these children refuse to accept and to identify with their surviving (castrated) parent or the parental substitutes, and are apt to have illusions about the lost parent's grandeur and even to develop a florid family romance serving their own aggrandizement.

In Mary, the disgraceful fact of her illegitimacy and adoption, and of her father's desertion of her mother, had indeed been unconsciously considered a castration, a punishment for her mother's—and her own—sexual sins. Her struggle against her unconscious identification with her true mother and her hope for the return of the lost father—and the lost penis—rested on her unconscious expectation of getting them back as a reward for her outstanding sexual virtuousness.

Although Robert had lost his mother, he also regarded this loss, which compelled him to live with his grandmother and his "immoral," sinful father, as a degradation and, unconsciously, as a castration. The glorified angelic mother was in his unconscious the most precious part of himself, the penis which he and his father had lost as a punishment for their sinfulness. As in women's denial of castration, his denial of the mother's death and his hope for her return were intended to assert that this most valuable part of himself had not really been lost, that he would get it back as a reward for his saintliness.

In Paul's mind, the loss of his father was even consciously equated with his supposed lack of manliness. His doubts and his fantasies about his father's greatness, about his death or survival, were interchangeable with his doubts about his sexual identity. His supposed castration was considered to be a punishment for his unconscious sadomasochistic identifications with his parents, against which he had so desperately struggled. His search for his glorious father—and the latter's worthy second wife—reflected his unconscious wishes for a mother who, being able to be both father and mother to him, could have turned him into a powerful, great man.

The young child's inability to go through a true mourning process[2] and to resolve the narcissistic and ambivalence conflicts with the surviving parent or parental substitutes by means of illusory fantasies is apt to predispose such children to depressive states.

[2] I am aware of the current controversy concerning the young child's ability to mourn. I fully agree with Anna Freud and Dorothy Burlingham (1944,), Anna Freud (1960), Nagera (1970), Wolfenstein (1966), who question the views of Bowlby (1960, 1961, 1963) and Furman (1964a, 1964b). The fact that children's grieving differs from that of adults (Rochlin, 1965) is also borne out by such case reports as those of Root (1957) and Laufer (1966).

8

The Influence of Infantile Conflicts on Recurring Depressive States

This chapter deals with those aspects in the early infantile history of a female patient which appeared to have had a decisive influence on the development of her personality, her object relations, and her recurring depressive states.

A series of circumstances made this case rather unique. The analytic treatment of this patient permitted insight into the development of depressive states. In her case it uncovered a "primal" depression at the age of three and a half.

While the patient was in psychoanalytic treatment with me some thirty years ago, I have been able to follow her subsequent development until now. This fortunate circumstance has enabled me to review the treatment material in the light of knowledge and information gained since the time of treatment.

This prolonged follow-up, moreover, has been of crucial im-

This chapter is based on two interrelated papers first published as "Depression: The Oedipus Conflict in the Development of Depressive Mechanisms." *Psychoanalytic Quarterly*, 12:541-560, 1943; and "The Effect of Disappointment on Ego and Superego Formation in Normal and Depressive Development." *Psychoanalytic Review*, 33:129-147, 1946; and *The Yearbook of Psychoanalysis*, 3:109-128. New York: International Universities Press, 1947.

Since these papers dealt with the same case material, they have been considerably revised and condensed into one chapter.

portance in throwing into relief the differential diagnostic problems presented by such cases.

The patient, Peggy M., a twenty-four-year-old teacher, came for psychoanalytic treatment because she felt very depressed and suffered from phobic fears. She remembered that since the age of three to four, she had always been a rather unhappy child. In her late adolescence, however, she had suddenly developed a profound depression of prolonged duration. In her beginning twenties she had gone through several briefer and milder depressive states, until this last severe depression and the development of agoraphobic and claustrophobic symptoms compelled her to look for help.

Between her depressive periods the patient seemed to have been in a mildly hypomanic mood. Because of her symptoms and attitudes I was inclined in the beginning of her treatment to regard Peggy as a neurotic patient, a case of preoedipally fixated anxiety hysteria. She showed a rather well-developed sense of reality and had surprisingly good insight. She was able to cooperate and to develop an excellent therapeutic alliance. In general, the synthetic strength of her ego, the productiveness of her free associations, her capacity to sublimate and build up her personality tended to bear out the assumption of a neurosis. Her tendency to magnify, to dramatize, and sometimes to "act out" her recollections had a hysterical quality.

The diagnosis of a neurosis had to be given up because in the course of her analysis Peggy began to develop definitely psychotic transference manifestations. During a period of severe depression she began to suffer from experiences of depersonalization. At that time I began to think of her as a manic-depressive case, especially when she recovered memories of a "primal depression" at the age of three and a half. I was not yet aware of the fact that borderline and schizophrenic patients who suffer from depressive states also may have retained or subsequently uncover memories of such early depressions. In any event, the discovery of Peggy's "primal depression" was not really of any diagnostic help. To be sure, her depressions were severe and genuine; they led to a deep narcissistic regression, a dangerous weakening of her object relations, and suicidal impulses. While the depressive states were "reactive" in that they were provoked by current conflicts and could be traced back to underlying infantile conflicts, their succession by a more or less elated condition was sudden and hardly intelligible as to its motivation.

But as the analysis advanced further, the picture changed again. At a stage when deeply repressed unconscious material suddenly came to the surface, Peggy developed severe anxiety attacks and a few times went through brief states of confusion. Her fantasies became so frightening as to appear delusional, and certain body sensations also seemed to be schizophrenic in nature. In rereading the material I felt that the patient had developed a transference psychosis.

In spite of these psychotic manifestations, the patient's emotional responses were never shallow or inadequate; they were intense and vigorous, even though she was at times somewhat cold and detached. The states of depersonalization were brief, and the few acute attacks of confusion and panicky anxiety were followed by a quick return to reality. Moreover, there was no sign of psychic disintegration during a period of three and a half years, and these alarming reactions did not recur after termination of the treatment.

When I presented this case to the New York Psychoanalytic Society many years ago, I pointed to the diagnostic problem but expressed my assumption that the patient's illness probably belonged to the affective disorders. Gregory Zilboorg, who was an excellent and very experienced psychiatrist, responded to this by saying that he would make a bet any time that in some years this patient would end up in a state hospital, and would stay there forever. Evidently he regarded her as a rapidly deteriorating case of schizophrenia. This is worth mentioning because Zilboorg's gloomy predictions proved wrong. So far as I could learn from Peggy, with whom I last talked in the spring of 1969, she had been clinically healthy since the time of her marriage soon after the end of her treatment, except for three brief periods of mild depression.

The first of these was precipitated by an impulsive separation from her fiancé, to whom she returned after a long talk with me; the two others developed following spontaneous abortions. During the last depression she came back to New York again for some days to get help from me. Except for these disturbances, Peggy has remained clinically healthy.

At times she was in a mildly hypomanic state. (Her coworkers used to call her "our little sunshine.") In general, however, she was and still is a gentle but somewhat aloof person, who functioned surprisingly well, both in her professional and private life. From the standpoint of her masochism, it is worth mentioning that she chose a partner who had a physical handicap. But her marriage has been happy, and her son developed well.

Unfortunately, the good therapeutic result does not help us to clarify the diagnostic problem. Peggy's illness might currently be regarded as "schizoaffective." I am now inclined to consider her a borderline patient who during her analysis developed a passing transference psychosis, very much like the type of patients described by Knight (1953) and Kernberg (1967).[1]

CASE REPORT

Peggy believed that her depressive states had developed in reaction to difficulties in her love and sex life. After various unhappy love affairs, she had started her first sexual relationship with Sidney, a teacher and her superior, some months before she came to analysis. Foreseeing the inevitable end of this relationship, she fell into a deep depression. Her work deteriorated to such an extent that she was afraid of losing her job, the only area where she had been successful. It was in this predicament that she turned to me for help.

The patient was a tall, attractive, and intelligent-looking girl, whose movements were retarded and who had a sad expression. Her friendly, gentle manner lacked spontaneity and warmth.

Her father, a cold aggressive man, had for years been mentally disturbed and unable to work. His depressions were accompanied by fears of impoverishment and compulsive symptoms. His handwashing compulsion was linked particularly to Peggy, from whom he refused to take food because she might have touched it with dirty hands. Peggy's mother, a warm but domineering woman, had always babied her daughter and protected her from life, i.e., from the aggressive father. Very early, she had disclosed the fact that her husband had destroyed their home life by his unpleasant behavior.

Peggy was an unhappy child who always tried to be "sweet and nice." This attitude as well as her obedience and her scholastic

[1] See also Frosch (1967b), Ross (1967), Atkins (1967), Peto (1967b), Wallerstein (1967), Dickes (1967), and Khan (1960, 1964).

achievements were in the service of her competition with a brother who was three and a half years younger than she. He was a charming, handsome, but rebellious and unstable boy, a bed wetter and poor student, who later could not establish himself in any kind of work. Peggy remembered that during her adolescence she had envied and resented her brother's aggressive, uninhibited behavior; she could not allow herself even the slightest sexual liberties. She clung and looked up to her attractive and efficient mother.

At the age of seventeen when Peggy tried to liberate herself from her family, she went through her first depressive period. Her intellectual ambitions broke down. She could not work, slept badly, felt physically weak, and suffered from various hypochondriacal and phobic symptoms. After her recovery, she did not resume her intellectual interests but began to have dates with boys. This situation did not last, however. At that time, she blamed her father for her failure because he interfered with her love affairs.

At twenty-four, after some disappointing love experiences followed by brief states of depression, Peggy suddenly underwent a definite change in her attitude toward mother. Influenced by girlfriends, she started her first sexual relationship with Sidney, the teacher already mentioned. She developed an almost paranoid hostility toward the previously adored mother, whom she now held responsible for her sexual failures because "she made me so dependent and weak." At this point Peggy decided to separate from her parents. She moved into the home of a divorced woman who was living with a lover and who resembled the patient's mother in many ways.

Peggy was a jealous observer of the happy couple, but her own love affair did not work out. She became so depressed that she sought analysis. She knew that Sidney still maintained an earlier relationship with another girl. Peggy saw him rarely and doubted his love. She became depressed whenever he left her, expecting never to see him again. She indulged in fantasies of his betrayal and her revenge for his cruelty. When he returned, however, she was unable to express her feelings and could only comply with his wishes.

Their relationship appeared to be founded primarily on sexual interests. Prolonged intercourse gave her a mild vaginal pleasure. Although Peggy insisted that intercourse was "the only valuable thing in life," she had never had an orgasm, nor did she desire it, for to her orgasm was "the end," and she hated the end.

One day Sidney informed her that his other girlfriend was pregnant and that he felt obliged to marry her. For the first time they had an intimate talk. Very much to her surprise he confessed that he had been more attached to her than he had let her know. She was reminded of her father's attitude: in the midst of treating her badly, he would occasionally reveal the fact that he did love her. Before Sidney's departure, they had sexual relations which ended in a violent emotional outburst on Peggy's part. She cried: "Don't go away, don't take it away, don't leave me!"

At the beginning of the ensuing depression, the patient cried desperately and complained that all women took away men from her. She was not worth loving. She hated all married women whose husbands might have been hers. This agitated phase passed into a paralyzing depressive period with feelings of emptiness and some depersonalization. "I have lost my sense of time. It passes so slowly, it never has an end. For me everything is over. I shall never love again. Life is senseless, melting away. I am dead already. My blankness is nothing—like death. I am also mixed up with space. Sometimes I feel alone in space, with everything else empty, and I the only person in the world. In a fleeting moment I believe my lover to be in the room, but then it is all blank. Only a dead world is left, that is eternity."

The patient had suicidal impulses to jump out of the window or to throw herself under the subway train.

There followed a more anxious depressed condition during which phobic and hypochondriacal symptoms increased. She was afraid of losing her job and her money, of contracting tuberculosis or other diseases. She was scared of open closets. All doors must be closed. Attacks of anxiety occurred in the theater or at the movies or in enclosed rooms, e.g., an elevator. She was afraid that "something might crush her." Her main anxiety concerned riding in the subway. When the train stopped, she became very frightened. "Everyone seems to look like wax, all frozen. The next moment something terrible will happen. There will be a crash, and everything will end up in death and destruction."

After several weeks of depression, Peggy suddenly became elated and abruptly started another love affair, which soon broke up again and was followed by another depression. This pattern repeated itself several times throughout the analysis. In an elated condition she would start a love affair and throw herself passionately into the new bondage. There was always the same change from initial hopeful, exaggerated expectation to deepest disappointment and despair. It soon became evident that the rapid change of her partners' attitude was due to the patient's own behavior. After a few successful meetings, she became depressed whenever she expected her lover. Haunted by jealous fantasies, she was so cold and detached that she frightened the man to a point where he lost interest in her.

Despite her severe illness, Peggy behaved surprisingly well in everyday life. During the first two years of analysis—a period of depressions alternating with elations—she never missed her sessions and maintained her work except for a few times when she collapsed so completely that she was compelled to stay in bed for some days.

It is my intention to describe the infantile conflict preceding the primal depression, as it was revealed in fantasies and recollections and "acting out," particularly in the patient's love life, which in this case was the nucleus of the pathogenic conflict.

The analysis of Peggy's love life led directly back to the decisive period of her childhood when her brother was born, and she herself was three and a half years old. Until the age of three Peggy had evidently been a well-balanced child, loved by both mother and father. She remembered that her father and she used to take walks together, talking and playing affectionately. Suddenly "everything was over and gone, and I had lost everything." She felt "as if I had died at that time. Life has been empty ever since."

What had happened then?

Peggy remembered that before her brother was born, her mother went to the hospital, while she and her father stayed with her maternal grandmother near New York. Apparently, the first great conflict between the parents had arisen at this time. Her father was in a very bad mood. He ignored Peggy, quarreled with his in-laws, and finally went back to New York. The child was left alone, disappointed by her father and eagerly awaiting her mother's return. When the mother did return, it was with the baby. "This was not my mother, it was a different person." The mother was ill at first. Then she neglected the older child to take care of the sickly baby. "The baby could not talk or walk, but he got all the love from mother." Peggy was unable to re-establish the relationship with her father. "He was so proud to have a son that he did not care for me anymore." The little girl broke down in her first depression.

What made the baby, "this insignificant little bit of a nothing," so important? It was his penis. This organ allowed him "to take pleasure aggressively, though he did not deserve it." It was "a magical, powerful instrument which makes men independent and aggressive." True, she hated and envied men for having an organ which "is dangerous but can also give the highest pleasure." Yet she did not want to be like a man. What made intercourse sacred to her was that she was entirely passive and receptive. Out of this same passivity, she refused to masturbate. Only a man should give her this pleasure. She always had "a feeling of emptiness in the vagina, like being very hungry. There is something sad about this emptiness like about an empty life." A man could temporarily "fill up this defect by the presence of his penis."

This clarifies Peggy's outburst when Sidney left her. Whenever she was deserted by a lover, the patient saw images of penises, "very large like those of horses." Thereby she had "a sort of tickling at her lips, like a sexual irritation." These pictures, shes aid, "attract and frighten me like the devil." She wanted her partner to return to her, and yet in her fantasy she would "send him back to hell where he came from."

Why did she want to hold him if she hated and feared him so much? "To have a penis in the vagina, even though it might destroy me." The penis which she hated and craved so much appeared at first to be her brother's. During puberty she had occasionally dreamed of intercourse with him; she imagined herself a small child, breaking off his penis. Later material suggested that she might actually, at an unguarded moment, have attempted a sexual attack on her baby brother. She certainly had envied him and wished to deprive him of this organ as well as of the pleasure derived from the mother's breast.

Peggy remembered the baby nursing, grasping the breast greedily and aggressively, while she herself had to eat alone at her table. He could take what he wanted because he had the penis which once had been hers. "Mother must have taken away my penis and given it to him just as he got my mother's breast. I was not even allowed to suck my thumb." At this point, nausea, anorexia, and fears of food poisoning developed. They were not really delusional ideas of being poisoned, but they seemed pretty close to it. Peggy remembered how her mother had forced physics into her mouth at the age of two or three, after wrapping her body tightly and closing her nose while she struggled. Her mother had compelled her to give up thumb sucking by tying her hands to the bedposts and smearing bitter stuff on her fingers. The child would cry: "Please let me do it, please let me do it!"

Masturbation was similarly suppressed. Both she and her mother were ill when Peggy was five; a harsh, disagreeable nurse took care of her, and once caught her masturbating. The child was suddenly stopped and spanked. Her hands were tied up and her body was wrapped tightly in her sheets. The patient re-enacted the resultant state of tension in attempts to masturbate. Trying desperately to get a vaginal orgasm, she burst into tears and begged herself: "Please let me do it, let me do it!"

Her appeal was in vain. Her sensations stopped short of the orgasm. Anxiety arose, as if she were "locked up in myself and could not let myself get out." This was like being imprisoned in an enclosed room or in an elevator or subway. Emotions and sensations suddenly faded, for otherwise there would have been a terrible outburst which would have destroyed as well as liberated her. "It would be like suicide," she said.

While Peggy felt tempted to jump out of the window, she understood that one aim of this act would be to liberate herself. She fantasied flying into the open air and escaping into freedom, thereby killing herself. This fantasy reflected her impulse to escape the overpowering psychic and physical tension of masturbation which stopped short of the climax. As if from a threat of suicide, she had to hold herself back on the verge of orgasm to avoid destruction. She had to let her sensation die in order to save herself from death. Why did the patient crave orgasm as her liberation and yet fear it like death?

In masturbation she saw herself threatened by growing impulses to urinate or defecate, which disgusted as well as frightened her. Since her earliest childhood she had disliked these functions, which her mother had suppressed as severely as thumb sucking. The child was so strictly trained that she was clean at the age of one year.

Since then she had never been able to urinate or defecate outside her home; she had acquired severe constipations. Resentfully, she remembered how her mother had coaxed her to give up her stools. "She fooled me and deprived me of my bowel movements for her own pleasure."

Peggy's stubborn overobedience had helped her to gain her mother's favor over her brother, who was greedy, aggressive, and a bed wetter. The mother gave her enemas for years, a procedure as much feared as liked by the little girl. But it was her only remaining sexual outlet; and it secured for her a long-lasting, secret, passive homosexual relationship with her mother, which she carried on in anal games with a girlfriend at the age of six to seven. In adolescence she felt uneasy when she had to sleep in the same room with her mother or girlfriends; anxiously, she avoided any physical contact; she was deeply disgusted when her mother tried to fondle or kiss her.

Her homosexual wishes developed early in the transference to the analyst and other mother substitutes. The analyst was supposed to extract ideas from her brain, to coax her to think. Peggy could not think alone. Thinking created a feeling of tension in her head as if it might burst. She then demanded active help to liberate her thinking.

The analysis took an important turn when we learned how her emotional detachment had grown out of the severe restriction of her excretory functions: she was not allowed to reveal her feelings of either love or hate; she had to hold them back like stool or urine, to deny that they existed. Otherwise she would be overwhelmed by her emotions. Her cold detachment was modeled on that shown toward her by her father. She had certainly tried to "give" him her emotions. Yet he, like her lovers, did not accept what she offered, and had treated her badly. Only her mother had given her real "values" which could be accepted.

Peggy thought of her mother giving her breast to the baby or giving away the baby in childbirth. Shortly before the menstrual period, Peggy's breasts began to swell. She was afraid they might burst. She had cramps and kept back her menstruation for weeks. Ideas of childbirth came up. She feared she would die producing a child who would be "myself and yet another person." When her mother had come back from the hospital, she had been sick and then changed. She was never again as gay and happy as she had previously been. This no doubt was a correct observation, since the mother's relationship with her husband deteriorated at that time. But Peggy held the birth of the baby responsible for this change. "Delivery must be a terrible fight between baby and mother." She dreamed of her mother with dirt, mud, and blood splashed all over her face. So must her genital have looked after delivery. "Otherwise this child coming through the anal canal would have been crushed into pieces and liquefied like feces." Her brother came out victorious, because he had a penis, while she herself was defeated in that fight and lost her organ.

Peggy had the idea now that she had a penis inside her (perhaps the cervix), which might come out during orgasm. In an anxiety spell she imagined how during orgasm everything that was inside her might pour out—penis, feces, urine, and blood—in an outburst similar to the explosion she had experienced when given an enema by her mother. During masturbation she finally gave way to the impulse to urinate and defecate, thereby experiencing a relief which she felt was the equivalent of an orgasm.

At the same time, however, she had growing sensations of an "inner emptiness" throughout her body, "so deep that nothing could reach it." She would have liked "to take in something enormous that might fill the body up to the stomach." This wish was associated with her recollection of the enemas. She recalled the sensation when the nozzle had been pushed into her anus and the water would fill up her intestines. She wanted a similar experience with a man in intercourse. When she masturbated, she had peculiar, vague images of her father. She dreamed of being in bed with him. Real contact between a child and an adult would mean complete demolition. She fantasied a three-year-old child receiving the penis of a real man, a penis "so big and powerful that it would split her in two."

Eventually the patient uncovered an experience dating back to the age of three. In a severe anxiety attack with detachment and confusion, with nausea and the need to vomit, urinate, and defecate, she saw herself sitting astride her father's lap in bed, playing seesaw with him. On that occasion, she thought, she must have felt her father's erect penis and must herself have been genitally aroused. Peggy fully revived her feeling of overpowering excitement and horror, as well as her wish to take in the gigantic penis. She understood that the magnified pictures of this organ, which was equated with the man's whole body, reflected the tremendous intensity of her anxiety mixed with desire which had threatened to overcome her weak ego while playing the seesaw game. She imagined the penis entering her and discharging, and she felt an unbearable tension throughout her body. She had to throw the penis out and yet hold it in. In the greatest anxiety she fantasied how she would take this organ through her anus, genital, or mouth, pulling it out with her teeth until she herself would burst.

This fantasy reflected her childish ideas of pregnancy and delivery. Peggy saw pictures of a pregnant person much bigger than she, large and powerful "like a mountain." So must her mother have appeared to her. She also saw large breasts with red bleeding nipples and large dark spaces containing penises like black snakes with red heads, such as she had seen in her grandmother's country home. They might be penises, intestines, or little babies. All swellings represented dark spaces containing these slippery snakes that might burn her, eject poison on her, strangle or choke her to death.

Peggy's subway fears increased, and breathing difficulties arose. A frightening scene from the time of her mother's pregnancy emerged, which was confirmed later on in the analysis. For two weeks her mother had employed a schizophrenic Negro housemaid. One night, when the parents were out, this girl had entered the child's bedroom, carrying a knife and hallucinating dead persons who were persecuting her. Peggy remembered her fright at seeing the black girl with her wide-open red mouth, her white teeth, and her hand holding the knife.

The little girl had related this experience to her own sadomasochistic wishes and fears concerning her mother's pregnancy. She imagined that her mother might take her and put her inside her stomach instead of the brother. There she would stay in a hellish prison and be tortured to death. "Mother might snatch up all children and penises around, and swallow them. That is how a woman gets pregnant." She imagined her mother taking in the father's penis and "carrying it around as a source of her power and strength." She wanted it also from her father, or, since he would not give it to her, from another man, such as her brother or her uncle whose penis she had once seen in the toilet.

If only her mother had peacefully given her what she wanted, if she had shared what she received from the father—the baby—the problem might have been solved. Peggy felt she might have learned to love the child and to love men later on. Her relationship to her brother began to improve. She felt that her mother had taken away both brother and father. She had caused Peggy to build up the concept of bad, dangerous men and to love only her mother. But what had she ever gotten from her? Nothing! Her mother had taken everything away and kept it all for herself. "She must have had special organs that give continual pleasure, safety, and self-sufficiency."

At this time Peggy had impulses to kiss a woman's genital and anus. She fantasied revenge on her mother for all the deprivations. She might attack her, beat her down, and obtain all the things her mother possessed. She might take a knife, cut open her stomach, enter her abdomen, and destroy its contents. She would have to take little parts of her, bit by bit, and swallow them up. Thus she might become her mother. "Mother and I cannot both live," she said. "One of us has to die."

When the mother had gone to the hospital to have the baby, she should never have come back; she should have died. Then the patient could have taken her place and acquired both the father's penis and the baby. But the father would not give her what she wanted. Indeed, he left her forever. So she wished her mother back, ruefully; but when she came, it was with the baby, and again the patient felt abandoned.

Her reactions to this double abandonment became clarified in her analysis. When Peggy was depressed, she would express complaints of being utterly "changed" physically and emotionally: she felt she had turned into a homely and untidy-looking, weak, inferior person; her initiative, her intelligence, her emotions had died. The feeling of such changes in her personality linked up with recollections of that decisive childhood period. Then, she had imagined that her parents had definitely "changed" their personalities. "After that quarrel with my relatives," Peggy said, "father was a different person. He appeared cold and detached, and he never was the same afterwards. When my mother came back from the hospital with the baby she had changed. This was not mother; it was a different person, as if my real mother had died."

These experiences repeated themselves vividly in the transference situation. Once the treatment had to be interrupted for weeks because I fell ill. Peggy had been informed of my acute illness by a physician when she came for her analytic session. While her main reaction to the analyst's sickness was that "she was mean to leave me alone, and is of no further value to me," she built up in her fantasy the picture of this man who might be my husband. As I became the object of intense jealousy, Peggy indulged in glorious fantasies about him. She imagined how she might take revenge on me by getting this man for herself. When her disappointment grew that she could not meet him anymore, she began to depreciate him and to look forward to seeing me again. He suddenly seemed changed to her, not worth her interest, since he now appeared unpleasant, cold, and detached like her father.

The patient repeated this pattern more than once during the analysis by starting love affairs and playing them against the analyst whenever she felt disappointed.[2] The unhappy ending of her love relationship would turn her love demands back to me. This fluctuation was always accompanied by complaints of a sudden change in me or her lover, which would be brought up later, in her depressive periods, in the form of self-accusations. In other words, when the patient felt disappointed and deserted by the analyst, she devaluated me, but reanimated a glorified father concept which she then pinned onto the man to whom she attached herself. As the paternal image collapsed, she returned to the maternal ideal as represented by the analyst.

When Peggy's disillusionment reached its peak, she felt deserted by both parent representatives, and consequently fell into a full-fledged depression with deep narcissistic and sadomasochistic regression. During the initial phase she frequently went through an intermediate stage of rebellion. Detaching herself from the analyst as well as from her friends and her family, she indulged in spiteful fantasies of living alone without love, which were in striking contrast to her actual feeling of ego impoverishment. During this phase she would start long, affectionate dialogues with herself, playing a mother soothing and caressing her baby. At the same time her aggression toward the analyst would break through: she wished to terminate the analysis and to prove that she did not need it any

[2] Her wishes for a betrayal of the disappointing love object accounted for her paranoid trends. This problem will be discussed in Chapter 13.

longer. What then appeared to her as the accomplishment of her wishes was to leave the analyst triumphantly behind as an inferior being, whereas she herself, instead, had become superior and powerful. The roles would be changed.

At such times Peggy's aggression against both her parents became intense and alternated with short periods of depression accompanied by anxiety, guilt, and self-depreciation. Her jealousy toward her current lover and his girlfriend increased while her fantasies were focused on the relations between father and mother. Vaguely at first, then more distinctly, she recalled a primal scene.

Until she was two and a half years old, she had slept in her parents' room. At the age of three she used to leave her own room and run to the parents' bedroom "just to peek in." Once she must have entered it and watched something terrible. She remembered that it had ended with her father getting up naked, very angry, and chasing her out.

During an anxiety attack, the patient saw two persons undressed, breathing noisily and moving violently as if they were fighting each other; then sudden stillness, a complete stop. At this moment in the analytic hour she experienced extreme anxiety, dizziness, difficulties in breathing, and a feeling of "sinking like dead." The picture of a woman appeared to her with her head back, her mouth open, gasping for breath, and sinking as if she were dead.

This version was a fusion of the primal scene and two later experiences. At the age of five, Peggy had seen her mother, who had pneumonia, breathing heavily, almost dying. About two years later, the child's tonsils were taken out under an anesthesia that gave her the sinking feeling, the anxiety, the breathing difficulty, and choking. When she woke up she saw the doctor, as if at a great distance, holding an instrument with a bulky, bleeding mass. These memories and associations showed Peggy identified with her mother—sick, close to death—defeated in the nightly fight with the father.

At the same time the patient began to pity her poor mother who had always been so unhappy; her husband had ruined her life, and Peggy shared his guilt. But this pity and guilt, like her love, soon encompassed both: not alone her mother, but equally her father who was hardly better off. Perhaps he suffered even more than his wife, who like his daughter did not really love him. A dream showed her girlfriend's father desperately ill in bed, while she and mother joyfully prepared for his funeral. Thus Peggy switched her regrets and guilt feelings from one parent to the other.

As the primal scene was related to her triangular love situations, Peggy's destructive impulses gradually rose up to the surface, culminating in a sadistic outburst. She imagined helping her father "tear down" and kill her mother. She would suck out not only her mother's genital but her whole body and take it into herself. Then she would fight her father. She would kill him, too, pulling off his genital with her teeth and devouring his intestines.

The gist of these fantasies, which the patient eventually formulated, was this: "After becoming like my mother by taking her in, I might become like my father too. Then there would be three persons in one, in me." This general destruction would mean the end of the object world: "nothingness." There would be "no more danger left outside and no pleasure either. My wish for absolute self-sufficiency might thus be fulfilled."

During this analytic period, Peggy had a dream in which she made love to another girl "who is somehow myself." She woke up with disgust and nausea. The dream meant that she wanted "to give everything to myself, to have myself in myself." She felt autoerotic impulses: to stroke and caress herself, to admire and kiss her own genital, to dig in her genital and anus, to eat her stools. She wished to be a man and a woman, to have a penis and a vagina. Thus she would triumph in her utter independence over father and mother, both of whom had left her alone. She would be able to give everything to herself and take it from herself—physical pleasure, love, appreciation. Independent of the criticism of the world, she would be her own judge, controlled only by rules of her own.

The destructive fantasies and urges of this period were expressed with feelings of desperate yearning, which broke down in states of profound depression and unbearable, helpless anxiety. At that time Peggy presented the picture of a schizophrenic psychosis. She expressed increasing fears that, as a result of her sadistic wishes, the power with which she had endowed the analyst might actually vanish. Then she would collapse. She preferred being afraid of power to the feeling that the analyst might shrink into nothingness, since she depended on the latter as on her "only value." In a frantic effort she tried to build up the image of the analyst again, and to cling to it as to the omnipotent goddess who might protect her from her archaic, threatening superego which persecuted her with magic fears of destruction. During short periods of deepest regression her relationship with the analyst would disintegrate, too, and would be no more than a reflection of her inner conflict.

What was impressive during such phases was the temporary regressive transformation of her superego into frightening "introjects." I described above her oral-sadistic fantasies. She would feel that the objects which she had physically incorporated, in fantasy, threatened to "destroy her from within." At the same time she would say, "My fears are the only value left over. I have to keep the dangers alive: they are better than blankness, they are at least emotions. If I would get over my fears, my own self would die. There would be no danger left, but no pleasure either. They are dangers left alive, but dangers promising possible future pleasure."

What Peggy meant was that the "dangers" were the only distorted remnants of her demolished love objects, to which she held on because she still depended on them. In fact, her masochistic submission to her anxieties represented what was left over from her love relationships. Hence her ego still felt alive in the struggle with her cruel superego introjects, and there was hope for future reconciliation and reunion with it.

There was one way to ward off the horrible threat of her inner danger: She must "put out what is inside of me," in an overwhelming orgastic outburst which she felt would liberate her. Giving away all she possessed would be a rebirth of the incorporated world, which would make good her guilt. It would be her own rebirth, too, her reconciliation with a good world of love and pleasure. But something else could happen instead: she "might stand up to those inside dangers, kill and throw them out or be overpowered and die." Instead of being reborn and re-creating a good world, she would complete either its destruction or her own self-destruction.

When Peggy came close to the desired outburst, she was terrified of becoming insane, of committing homicide or suicide. At the climax, a four-hour session with the patient became necessary. Caught between her opposing impulses, unable to fulfill her desire for reconciliation with herself and with the world or to carry out her aggression, she had reached an impasse. Her defense was to avoid destruction by "neither taking in what is outside nor giving away what is inside." This situation came about whenever she was endangered by an overwhelming aggressive and libidinal tension, as in coitus.

When she reached the inner point of danger, there was a sudden stop, i.e., a denial of any emotion or sensation, and a complete paralysis of all activity. Anticipating destruction, she pretended that she herself or the object world was dead, thus avoiding her real psychic and physical destruction. This defense, the infantile magical mechanism of denial (discussed in Chapter 4), had achieved its purpose in the genital seduction by her father and in the observation of the primal scene, and had attained its height in the traumatic interruption of her masturbation. It accounted for the detachment and coldness toward the love partner, the fading of sensation during intercourse, and the periods of blank depression with the feeling of complete inner death, of nothingness. Then it seemed as if her demolished ego had lost even the power to react with anxieties as last representatives of the object world.

The critical stage in Peggy's analysis was reached when she understood that the state of detachment acted like a protective screen over her dangerous fantasy life. The more her sadistic impulses lost ground in favor of the libidinal elements, the more obvious became her tendency to dramatize and enjoy her fantasies. Only then did her ambivalent emotions toward the analyst break through directly, while at the same time she tried to build up the first real love relation in her life.

Her partner was the man who subsequently became her husband. She ended the treatment when he moved to the West Coast and she was able to find a good position in the same city. Since he did not propose to her as long as he could not support her well enough, she repeated once more her acting out of the past: she suddenly left him and came back to New York, i.e., to her mother, who had encouraged her return. She came to see me immediately. After one session with me—and her mother—Peggy went back to her partner, and soon they married.

DISCUSSION

I shall first summarize the history of the patient's infantile depression. Here we see a child with a loving but domineering mother, whose early sexual and aggressive prohibitions and strict cleanliness training had tended to create a submissive, overobedient, masochistic little girl, albeit with signs of passive aggression. Frequent enemas had played their role in the development of anal-sadistic, homosexual fixations.

In spite of this, we find the child at the age of three in the beginnings of a normal oedipal situation. An affectionate relationship with the father was being established. According to the family history, the father seemed to have been emotionally undisturbed till the birth of his second child. From then on, apparently, he suffered from a depressive-psychotic disorder which subsided or at least greatly improved after the patient left home and married. This suggests that the father was very jealous of the close relationship between mother and daughter. While I do not know the nature and the causes of his depression, there is no doubt that the father's sudden breakdown and withdrawal when his son was born, and his pathology since that time, exercised a decisive influence on her development.

Peggy remembered her first years of life as a brief happy period, which proved to be spurious. Then she suffered a series of traumatic experiences, which led to a severe depression at the age of three and a half:

On the verge of advancing from her preoedipal and pregenital fixations to a genital position, which in girls always starts with wishes for the father's penis, Peggy felt her father's genital during a seesaw game in bed. This not only aroused her genital sensations intensely and prematurely, but mobilized her pregenital fixations. She expected from her father a gratification similar to that of the enemas given by the mother. In other words, the general arousal by the father, which occurred too early to be mastered, had a traumatic effect. It interfered with the further establishment and acceptance of a feminine genital position, and supported the survival of pregenital sadomasochistic introjection and projection mechanisms.

Unfortunately, the scene with her father was followed shortly by her mother's pregnancy. During this difficult time she had a traumatic experience with the psychotic Negro maid. Earlier observations of her parents' sexual life were reactivated and interpreted according to her present knowledge. Concluding that the mother had acquired the father's penis by incorporation during a bitter fight, she reacted with deep hostility to her mother's pregnancy.

She wanted to kill her, to enter and destroy her abdomen, and also to have the baby herself. When her mother left for the hospital, the child wanted to take her place, hoping for the desired gratification from her father. But he disappointed her and left her, never to love her again. It is significant that her reactions during the analysis showed that Peggy responded to the separation first from the mother, then from the father, less with "separation anxiety" than with feelings of being rejected, leading to disappointment and hostility. Thus, in bitter hate, Peggy turned ruefully back to her mother, only to feel abandoned once more: the mother gave attention only to the sickly baby. Peggy tried to escape into a narcissistic withdrawal. She decided to kill her need for love and to become self-sufficient and independent.

In this goal she was bound to fail. Not only was she too young to resolve her intense ambivalence conflicts, but her attempt at an autarchic independence had the opposite effect. It led to an even more masochistic, regressively symbiotic leaning on her love objects, which did not sharpen the distinction between self and object representations but impeded its development. Since her attempts to rebuild her love relationships to the "good" parents and to identify with their "good" images were not successful either, the outcome of the infantile conflicts which she re-enacted in her triangular love affairs was her "primal depression." From then on her relations to her family remained affected by her ambivalence. She found some security in her dependent but reliable bondage to her mother, competing with her brother by being the good, oversubmissive child, and courting her father's appreciation by her intellectual superiority.

Unfortunately, her adolescent problems were apt to revive her early infantile conflicts. They resulted in depressive states whose basic pattern had been established in her "primal" childhood depression.

In the ensuing discussion I shall focus more thoroughly on Peggy's personality, the nature of her object relations, and her ego-superego functions.

Obviously, Peggy had not developed to a mature level but showed strong preoedipal-narcissistic characteristics in her attitudes and love relationships. She wanted to attach her love demands intensely to persons, male or female, upon whom she might depend and lean. Her anxious-masochistic submissiveness barely disguised a demanding and possessive attitude toward love partners and friends, and failed to protect her sufficiently from her underlying, passionately jealous and envious, hostile impulses toward men and women alike. Unfortunately, she projected her high standards onto her friends and love partners, whose superiority she regarded as a yardstick for her own value. For this reason she tended to put them on a pedestal and expected them to embody the ideal qualities with which her fantasy had equipped them.

Hence her love objects represented glorified parental images with which she identified through participation in their superiority. To be loved and to find recognition by them served the purpose of supporting her self-esteem, which was forever threatened by the overstrictness of her standards and the intensity of her ambitions. It is significant that Peggy did not tend to "borrow" the ego or superego of her love objects, as certain schizophrenics will do. What she needed was respect for them and love, praise, emotional support from them. As she glorified and admired her love objects, her relationships reassumed narcissistic characteristics congruent with the stage of development when she had broken down in her first depression at the age of three and a half.

Since her self-esteem depended upon the high value of her love objects, disappointment caused not only their devaluation but also a deep narcissistic injury which threatened to undermine the respect for her own self. Whenever this happened, she tried to regain her narcissistic balance by leaning on a different person, whom she equipped with the desired characteristics, until she felt disappointed again. Her acting out showed that she alternately chose a mother and a father representative. Her self-esteem dropped along with the deflation of such a parental representative, and was recovered as she rebuilt the good, superior image of the other parent, which then again was pinned onto a real person.

The depression started when Peggy became disillusioned in both these objects. Since at the time of her first depression the whole object world was still represented by her parents, her disappointment in both of them led now, as then, to a general disillusionment with life which did not fulfill her exaggerated expectations.[3] The

[3] See my remarks on the role of generalization in the development of moods (Chapter 3).

far-reaching break of her love relationships shifted the scene of conflict into her ego.

Her narcissistic withdrawal from the deflated love objects, upon whom she depended, threatened her own image with collapse. She tried to escape this danger by reanimating and setting up the powerful parental images in herself. In these short, rebellious phases, frequently preceding her complete depressive breakdown, she indulged in wishful fantasies of autarchic independence. Trying to fight her hostility, she succeeded for some time in taking over the role of the "good" powerful parents, lavishing love on herself. But owing to her growing hostility, this illusory wish fulfillment soon had to be given up. She preferred submitting to a punishing superego, which promised future reconciliation and happiness, to a fatal liberation of her destructive impulses. The less she could find her way back to a deflated object world, upon which she could no longer project her images, the more her inner pressure increased. As self-love turned into anxiety and self-hate, her superego assumed the archaic characteristics of evil demons pouring fears on her and carrying her self-destruction further.

In this pathological process the originally recuperative function of her superego became reversed, as the cleavage between ego and superego could no longer be bridged. Their union had to be prevented as a twofold danger: the one being a homicidal manic outburst, the other a suicidal victory of the superego. Both avenues would have led to self-destruction.

I have described how the depressive conflict developed in this case. The analytic material presented by Peggy corresponded in its essential elements to that of other patients with borderline or psychotic depressive conditions.

The case material permitted insight into the disturbances caused by experiences of disillusionment and abandonment at an early infantile stage. It should also be stated, however, that the effect of early frustrations and disappointments may be so devastating only in persons who tend to respond to them with uncommonly intense hostility. In the case of Peggy, the primal childhood depression was precipitated by certain traumatic events followed by severe disappointments in both parents in the beginning of the oedipal period. Such general disillusionment at a phase when the boundaries between object and self images are not yet firmly established, and when the infantile love relationships still have the preoedipal-narcissistic characteristics described above, may lead to a severe pathology in the development of both object relations and narcissism.

Peggy's case showed that after recovery from the primal depression, the child again reached out for the lost love objects. Narcissistic libido was thereby partly retransformed into object libido, as ego and superego (or its forerunners) regained more normal functions. Since the oedipal development was disrupted at the beginning genital stage (Gero, 1936), before ever reaching its peak, the fragile object relations retained the earmarks of preoedipal-narcissistic dependence and submission. There was overexpectation, with regard to the love objects as well as the self, which could not be gratified. The love objects were overvalued and idealized; the wishful self images and the ego ideal were too high to be reached.

Since the narcissistic coloring of the personality is not fundamentally changed, any new disappointment may break up the brittle relationship and lead again to a denigration of the love object in which the self image participates.

This I consider the basic depressive process in this type of patient.

The pathology of the superego functions I regard as due to a restitutive effort to repair the narcissistic hurt by means of replacing the deflated love objects by an introjection of their glorified, omnipotent images into the superego. Rado (1928), who pointed for the first time to the double introjective processes in melancholia, stated, "The 'good object', whose love the ego desires, is introjected and incorporated in the super-ego. There, . . . it is endowed with the prescriptive right . . . to be angry with the ego—indeed, very angry" (p. 434f.). My assumption modifies this statement by underlining the distinction between the introjection of the deflated, bad, worthless parents into the self image and of the inflated, good or bad, punishing ones into the superego. The child can still hope to gain back love, praise, security from the punitive, godlike parents. But he can no longer expect anything from the devaluated parents. This restitutive attempt must fail, however, and the boundless hostility turned to the self may lead to self-destruction.

As for the problem of mania, I can merely contribute a few remarks about the distinction which might be made with regard to a certain type of hypomanic conditions. Peggy's case revealed that hypomania can be a temporary successful conflict solution, within the frame of a basically ill personality, by way of a true reconciliation between ego and superego. While in some types of hypomanic and manic conditions the ego escapes into an illusion of power by alliance with the id, but actually gives up its essential functions, in other forms of hypomania the condition represents a victory of love over destruction, leading to a true expansion of the ego along social and cultural lines.

It is well known, for instance, that there are creative people suffering from cyclothymia who are most productive during seemingly healthy intervals which are actually hypomanic conditions. In two patients I could observe how in the stage of slow recovery from depression and the transition into hypomania, the punishing superego gradually lost its destructive features, while exalted ideals, social interests, cultural strivings, and love relationships were built up again, which the strengthened and elated ego then pursued successfully and enjoyed intensely. Peggy seems to provide a good example of such a vicissitude.

9

On the Psychoanalytic Theory of Cyclothymic Depression

In contrast to neurotics, psychotics seek a solution to their emotional and instinctual conflicts in a regressive escape which involves not only instinctual regression but a severe regressive process in the whole personality organization. As a patient after recovery from a schizophrenic episode put it drastically: "I ran and ran, back to the womb." As a result of constitutional and environmental factors (early infantile emotional deprivations and instinctual overstimulation and/or frustration), these patients are evidently predisposed to such a profound regressive process by an arrested, defective ego and superego development.

It seems to me that the central element in this predisposition is an insufficient neutralization of libidinal and aggressive forces. We may speculate that the underlying psychosomatic processes in psychoses result in a reduction and exhaustion, or else in an insufficient reproduction, of libidinal and possibly in an overproduction of aggressive drives. This would change the proportion between libido and aggression in favor of the latter, and promote defusion and deneutralization of the drives. Whatever the nature of these pathogenic processes, they do not permit normal maturation to take place and thus interfere with the development of lasting libidinal cathexis

---

This chapter is a shortened version of the paper "Contribution to the Metapsychology of Cyclothymic Depression," first published in *Affective Disorders*, edited by Phyllis Greenacre. New York: International Universities Press, 1953, pp. 49-83.

of object and self representations and the maintenance of stable object relations and firm ego and superego identifications.

In the prepsychotic personality the self and object representations and the ego ideal are not sharply separated; they retain attributes of early infantile object and self images, and thus are carriers of primitive, infantile, magic values. The superego is not a firmly integrated system. It is personified, unstable in its functions, and tends either to assume excessive control over the ego or to disintegrate, dissolve, and merge with object and self representations. It is easily reprojected onto the outside world. The superego and the object and self representations are prone to regressive fragmentations, on the one hand splitting up again into primitive early images and on the other fusing with one another. There is then a tendency to react to conflicts with the object world not by ego defenses against unacceptable strivings but by withdrawals and shifts of libidinal and aggressive cathexis, not only from one object to another and from personal object to thing representations, but from the object to the self representations and the reverse.

The onset of the psychosis proper is characterized by a dangerous, irresistible defusion and deneutralization of the instinctual drives. This unleashes a furious struggle for supremacy between the libidinal and the destructive forces. Whatever sets it going, this struggle may lead eventually to a fatal libidinal improverishment, an accumulation of sheer aggression, a destructuralization, and a dispersion of the defused drives in the whole self. I suspect that the "endogenous" psychosomatic phenomena in psychosis, to which I pointed in Chapter 6, arise with the development of such a state.

Psychologically, the psychotic process is probably set in motion by a reactivation of infantile conflicts centered primarily around both parental love objects or their substitutes, but then spreads to the whole object world. The defective ego of the prepsychotic is unable to master these conflicts with the help of neurotic defenses. It attempts to resolve the conflicts by shifts, first of the libidinal, then of the aggressive, cathexis from the object to the self representations; by renewed efforts to recathect the objects; and finally by increasing fusions of object and self images. This goes along with a severe regressive distortion of the object and self representations, a process that leads to their breakdown and eventual dissolution and splitting into primitive images. The ego and superego identifications disintegrate and are replaced by "narcissistic identifications," i.e., by regressive fusions of superego, self and object images. The result may be a collapse of the total psychic system. These psychic events find expression in the schizophrenics' experiences of "the end of the world," his loss of identity, and feelings of having died.

In such psychotics secondary process thinking breaks down and they show severe disturbances of their sense of reality, i.e., in the perception of and the judgment regarding the object world and their own self. The ego functions and the emotional relationships with the real personal and inanimate objects deteriorate; misinterpretations of and inadequate responses to the object world abound.

The psychotic defense mechanisms aim at the maintenance and/or restitution of object and self representations. First, the real object world is used for this purpose. As I described in my Freud Anniversary Lecture (1967), the psychotic attempts to save himself by seeking support from without. He tries to buttress his ego functions by looking for emotional and ideational stimulants in the outside world. Using introjection and projection mechanisms, he borrows the ego and superego of other persons and projects parts of his own self onto certain objects in whose actions he can magically participate. If these efforts fail, he retreats from the object world. Regressively revived primitive object and self images, which have found their way to consciousness, then merge and join with remnants of realistic concepts to form new units. In this way, delusional object and self representations are built up, in disregard of reality, and are again reprojected onto the outside world.

Possibly, it is the depth and the nature of the regression that determine the development of a manic-depressive or a paranoid schizophrenic psychosis. Manic-depressives seem, at some point, to have reached a higher level in the differentiation and integration of the psychic systems. Consequently, the acute regressive process during their episodes does not go so far as in schizophrenics and is of a different type. Usually, it does not lead to a complete disintegration of the personality, but is reversible. It stops at a point that still allows a rather complete recovery. Bleuler (1911) described as a characteristic difference between the schizophrenic and the manic-depressive that the fears of the former refer to disasters occurring at the present time, those of the latter to future catastrophes. I believe that from the metapsychological point of view, this difference indicates that in the schizophrenic the object and self representations in the system ego actually break down to the point of dissolution, whereas the manic-depressive only feels threatened. His anxieties may be severe, but they are not true states of panic. The delusions in manic or melancholic states show characteristic differences from schizophrenic delusions, which, I believe, prove this point.[1] As to the suicide of the melancholic, we recall Freud's statement (1917): that the love object is shown to be more powerful than the self. I would add that in the suicidal act the self, too, regains a feeling of power and achieves a final, though fatal, victory.

CLINICAL FEATURES OF THE MANIC-DEPRESSIVE PERSONALTY

When we have an opportunity to observe cyclothymic patients before their break or during free intervals, we are often impressed by the richness of their sublimations. We are also surprised to see that as long as they are not ill, they may be delightful companions or marital partners, a feature that Bleuler mentioned especially. In their sexual life they may show full genital responsiveness, and emotionally, in contrast to schizophrenics, a touching warmth or, sometimes at least, an unusual, affectionate clinging to people they like. No doubt these persons have developed intensely vested emotional object relations and are potentially able to function extraordinarily well. Although they do not manifest a lack of inner resources, they seem to suffer from a specific ego weakness, which shows in their remarkable vulnerability, their intolerance of frustration, hurt, and disappointment.

Freud (1917) underlined the contradictory fact that these persons show simultaneously the tendency to too strong fixations to their love object and to a quick withdrawal of object cathexis. He pointed to Otto Rank's remark that the object choice of these persons must have been, to begin with, on a narcissistic basis, which permits them to regress easily to the narcissistic identification with the love object described in "Mourning and Melancholia." This is true, indeed; and we now know that it also applies to schizophrenics, although they seem to be arrested at a different narcissistic level.

Manic-depressives show a special kind of infantile narcissistic

[1] Further differences between cyclothymic and schizophrenic states of depression are discussed in Chapter 11.

dependency on their love object. They require a constant supply of love and moral support from a highly valued love object, which need not be a person but may be represented by a powerful cause or organization of which they feel to be a part. As long as their "belief" in this object lasts, they are able to work with enthusiasm and high efficiency. Actually, however, these patients tend to make a masochistic choice of their partners or "causes" and to establish a life situation which sets the stage for their illness in that it is bound to disappoint them. Gero (1936) pointed out that manic-depressives belong to the masochistic personality type. When we have an opportunity to observe both the patient and his partner, we frequently find that they live in a peculiar "symbiotic" (Mahler, 1966) love relationship to each other. They feed on each other, but in a way that differs greatly from what we find in schizophrenics. In some instances, both partners are manic-depressives and break down alternately. In others, the partner of a manic-depressive may be an oral type of a different variety.[2]

As a point of departure for the clinical study of the depressive conflict, the defenses, and the restitution mechanisms, I have chosen a short dream of patient N., a physician who was at the beginning of a depression. It had been precipitated by the alarming news that his mother had cancer of the uterus which required an immediate operation. During the preceding years N. had developed depressive states with a paranoid tinge, feelings of tiredness and exhaustion, and a series of psychosomatic and hypochondriacal symptoms and fears. They were initiated by his discovery that his wife had to undergo a gynecological operation which might affect her fertility.

N. dreamed that he had lost two of his "excellent" teeth. As they fell out, a fine thin silver cord that had held them together went to pieces. N.'s immediate interpretation was that the two teeth represented himself and his mother, and that the connecting structure was the umbilical cord by which he was still attached to her. If his mother should die, he would feel as though he had lost his own self. The silver cord also represented his weak personality which, in the case of her death, would break down.

When this patient was not depressed, he manifested a rather conspicuous self-inflation. He expressed his feelings of being very

[2] The object choices of depressive patients and the types of interaction with their partners are further discussed in Chapter 12.

good-looking, bright and smart, as "excellent" in his field as his teeth were. In these states he also talked incessantly of his worship of his mother, of her unending kindness and generosity, her great intelligence, her physical and mental strength. He had married his wife because she seemed to resemble his mother. Neither woman in any way corresponded to this ideal picture. They were neurotic, over-anxious, clinging women, and, as mentioned above, both suffered from gynecological conditions. The patient had managed for years to deny their weaknesses, including their physical handicaps. He himself had gone through several serious illnesses to which he had regularly responded with a depressive state and hypochondriacal complaints and fears. At other times, the patient exhibited unusual pride in his body.

His dream of the loss of his teeth referred to an experience in his adolescence when he had lost a tooth because his mother had neglected to arrange for adequate dental care for her children, in the same way as she had neglected her own present illness until it was almost too late for help. At the time of his tooth trouble, the boy had had to take matters into his own hands. He found a dentist who extracted the tooth, supposedly because it could not be saved. I may interject here that N. went into medicine because his mother's only brother as well as his own brother, a father substitute, were physicians; he had greatly admired these men. Hence his vocation, medicine, represented an ideal derived from both parental love objects, for his mother had told him repeatedly how she had nursed and cured him during his early childhood diseases. But an outstanding early childhood trauma had been the death of his maternal grandmother whom neither uncle nor brother had been able to cure. And both, uncle and brother, had been very gifted and promising young men who failed completely in their careers.

During the dream session the patient began to express his deep resentment of his mother's and his wife's inability to take proper care of their own health and that of their children. He blamed his mother for his severe childhood diseases, which had probably been neglected as much as his teeth. As the session proceeded, the patient started derogating the whole medical profession for its utter impotence. He talked of prominent but incompetent doctors who drew a fortune from their patients' ignorance. Finally, he indulged in severe self-reproaches. He blamed himself for being an incompetent, neglectful physician, uninterested in his patients and unable to cure them. He ended the session with an expression of deep guilt feelings toward his mother, whose sickness he had ignored and neglected, and diagnosed too late to save her. He left in a very depressed state.[3]

The dream and dream material, and the corresponding emotional reactions during this one session, show in a nutshell the prerequisites for the depressive conflict and its development.

The superficial symbolic interpretation offered by the patient immediately informs us about the pathogenic core of the manic-depressive personality. The thin, fragile silver cord in the dream indicates the weakness of his ego, resting on the intimate bond between himself and his mother. The two teeth are symbols of his love object and his self representations. The one tooth, representing his mother, is his own. The two teeth are connected. In other words, we see what I regard as characteristic of these patients: the insufficient separation between the representations of the love object and the self. There is a lack of distinct boundaries between them, which accounts for the patient's too strong fixation to the parental love objects. The self representations extend, so to speak, to the object representations; both show insufficient maturation and stability.

The patient gauges his love objects and himself by infantile value measures, predominantly by their omnipotent physical power and invulnerability. These standards are embedded in his high-flung ideal of a competent, in fact, omnipotent, physician who devotes his whole life to the rescue of his patients. In the patient's associations, we also observe the personification of his ego ideal, its insufficient distinction from the ideal parental image. He talks indiscriminately of the value or worthlessness of the whole medical science and profession, and of the individual physicians who represent parental images.

His example shows, furthermore, how in manic-depressives all ambitions and pursuits revolve only about representations of the overvalued parental love objects, which extend, as it were, to the whole world. This is why all their ego functions fail when the love object becomes disappointing and is depreciated. Frequently we observe that manic-depressives live on their ideals or their idealized partners rather than on their own ego. They exhibit an unusual pride

[3] The patient's mother is still alive, but she suffered from a severe senile depression which required shock treatment.

in their idealizations, as though their own idealism would per se turn them into valuable human beings. I may add that the "idealism" of the manic-depressive differs greatly in type from that of the schizophrenic. The latter is more abstract, removed from personal objects; the former, as in the case of N., is mostly attached to a personal representative object. This accounts for the seeming "realism" of the manic-depressive, which clinical psychiatrists, such as Lange, have described.

THE DEVELOPMENT OF THE DEPRESSIVE STATE

Clinically, this patient's depressive states were always "reactive" in nature. This time his depression was precipitated by his mother's illness, but at other times it had developed when he himself became ill or met with failure in his work, with financial difficulties or with disappointments in his love life. In other words, his depressive states would be precipitated by a failing either of his love object or of himself. But the analysis showed that, in either case, he felt hurt and blamed the love object for it. In fact, this patient expressed with unusual clarity his feeling that all his achievements or failures were due to the effectiveness or failure of his "intuition"—in German, *Eingebung;* that is, all achievements or failures were the result of what had been given to him. He regarded his ego functions not as his own productions but as reproductions of what he had received.

We understand that in disregard of his potential abilities, his self representations retained the infantile conception of a helpless self drawing its strength from a powerful, ideal love object. He tried to keep the image of this love object hypercathected, by constantly depriving the self image of its libidinal cathexis and pouring it on the object image. He then had to bolster his self image again by a reflux of libido from the image of his love object. These continuous cathectic fluctuations found expression in corresponding emotional vacillations. In his actual attitudes he would show a mixture of conceited and humble, sadomasochistic and protective behavior to the love object, and simultaneously demand continuous evidence of the latter's value, power, and devotion.

This position is inevitably unstable and facilitates easy, rapid, and cathectic changes on the slightest provocation. The manic-depressive protects himself against this danger by strong pathological safeguards, essentially by the denial mechanisms which I discussed in Chapter 4 and which were so beautifully described by Lewin (1950). He can maintain a lasting libidinal overcathexis of the love-object image only by constant efforts to deny both his own intrinsic value and the weaknesses of the real love object, i.e., by a continuous illusory overestimation of the love object and an equally illusory or even delusional under- or overestimation of himself. If he meets with disappointment or failure, the denial mechanisms will either break down or have to be so fortified that the patient may go into a manic state.

In contradistinction to schizophrenic feelings of grandeur, the manic state represents, I believe, a state of lasting participation of the self in the imagined omnipotence of the love object. The manic can afford to discharge his aggression fully and diffusely. Since, by his denial of the existence of unpleasure and destruction, the whole world becomes a valley of unending and indestructible pleasure, his aggression can do no damage.

To give an example: A patient in a hypomanic state, which terminated a nine-month period of depression, told me that she felt so voracious: she would like to eat up everything—food, books, pictures, persons, the whole world. When I jokingly and with deliberate provocation remarked that this seemed to be quite bad and dangerous, what would she do if everything were eaten up, she said, highly amused: "Oh no, the world is so rich, there is no end to it. Things are never finished. I cannot hurt anybody or anything."

If the denial mechanisms fail, the patient's first reaction will be to master the narcissistic injury and build up his self-esteem by disparaging the love object in a way as illusory as he had previously glorified it. He will try to repair the hurt by switching the whole aggressive cathexis to the object image and the libidinal cathexis to the self image. In adolescence this mechanism was still effective in my patient: he asserted himself by derogating his neglectful mother and by reactive identification with her ideal image. Thus he went ahead and took care of his tooth, instead of and in spite of his mother. But he indicated in his dream that unconsciously he regarded his success—for good reasons—as a failure; he actually lost his tooth, which in the dream was equated with his own self and his mother. In fact, manic-depressives may react to success in love or work in the same way as to failure: with either a hypomanic or manic state or with a depression. Their reaction depends on what the success means: an aggressive self-assertion by derogation and destruction of the love object, or a present from the powerful love object. Their inability to accept success is not always or not only an expression of their moral masochism and of their guilt conflict.

One of my depressive patients regularly responded to achievements by a struggle between feelings of tremendous pride and of rising anxiety and emptiness. He felt as though the most precious thing in life were gone; life would be empty forever. He lost his interest in his previous endeavors and finally felt that his whole work had been worthless anyhow. This response is merely more intense and pathological than the well-known attitude of narcissistic people who value an object so long as they cannot get it, and depreciate it as soon as they have got it.

The manic-depressive cannot bear a self-assertion through derogation of his love object. He tries to avoid such a situation by keeping the valued love object at a distance, as it were, which protects it from deflation. The simultaneous libidinal hypercathexis of the object clearly distinguishes this attitude from the schizoid remoteness. Since the love object has to stay unattainable, he may avoid success by delaying a final achievement or the real consummation of a love relationship, for which he has desperately struggled.

Evidently, he is so afraid of a lasting self-inflation at the expense of the love object because it might lead to a complete libidinal withdrawal and unleashing of all his severe hostility on this one object. His fear of a "loss of the object" is fear of a destructive absorption of the "good, powerful" object image by the self image. Here is a situation that induces an immediate and intense need to retrieve his old position. He will be overperceptive of any flaw in his achievements, and use it to confirm his own weakness and to reinstate the strength and value of the object. This is why success afflicts the manic-depressive in the same way as failure. Both may arouse an initial hostile derogation of the love object, which cannot be tolerated, and which yields to a rapid reversal, undoing, and denial of the previous situation.

There will be an immediate, increased reflux of aggression from the love object to the self image, but by this time the pathological process may have proceeded so far that the patient is too depleted of libido to recathect the object sufficiently. All he can achieve may be an aggressive devaluation of both: of himself and of his love object. He will return to his position of participation, but in the worthlessness instead of the value of the love object. Many patients, especially those with chronic "simple" depressions, and many depressive children may represent this picture. They manifest a general pessimism, disillusionment, and lack of interest in life and in themselves. Everything has become worthless, unpleasurable, or empty. They maintain a continuous denial of the world's and their own value.

In Chapter 6 I stated that I regard this as the primary depressive disturbance, which may be distinguished from the secondary attempts at defense and restitution. Some patients give evidence indeed of very intense efforts to recathect and build up the love-object image again, and to regain their original unstable equilibrium.

We will now investigate the defenses which the patient uses for this purpose. Since his libidinal resources are fading, his first line of defense will be to turn to the real object world for support. He will try to resolve the inner conflict by help from without (Jacobson, 1967). He wants to use the love of an outside person, to whom he has attached his ideal object image, as a stimulant for his failing ability to love. This is the stage when the patient, in his frantic endeavor to stop the depressive process, persistently and increasingly clings to the person he has chosen for this purpose. He gathers all his available libido and pours it on this one person, in a desperate appeal to give such convincing evidence of unending love and indestructible power and value as to evoke a libidinal response in himself, and in this way enable him to re-establish an ideal object image that cannot be deflated and destroyed.

It is a phase of acting out that we can well observe in the treatment of depressives in the transference situation. The patient exhausts himself in efforts to concentrate on the analyst whatever love is still at his disposal. He behaves in an extremely submissive, masochistic, and at the same time sadistic way: he gives himself up to the analyst, but expects the impossible in return. He desires the analyst's constant presence and tries to blackmail him into a continuous show of omnipotent love, value, and power.

Much depends, at this stage, on the analyst's handling of the transference situation.[4] As the depressive episode develops, things may get out of hand. The analyst may no longer be able to live up to the patient's expectations. Analyst and patient will be in a trap. The patient will be less and less able to tolerate the analyst's warmth and sympathy, which, failing to elicit an adequate libidinal response, will only increase the disappointment and the hostile claim for a more powerful love. In his fear of a complete breakdown of the object image, the patient regresses a step further. We realize that the deserted child prefers an aggressive, strong love object to its loss. Correspondingly, the patient may now attempt to hold on at least to the reanimated image of an omnipotent, not loving, but punitive, sadistic object. This manifests itself in the patient's increasing, masochistic provocations of the analyst's anger, to a show of aggression, which may bring temporary relief but will actually promote the pathological process.

If the outside world has failed to help the patient in the solution of this conflict, he may turn to his last line of defense: retreat from the object world. The conflict may become fully internalized and an acute, blatantly psychotic depressive syndrome may develop.

Before I turn to the problem of melancholia, I should like to interpolate that for reasons of simplification I have so far deliberately neglected the superego aspects of the depressive conflict.

The melancholic introjection mechanisms seem to represent the last failing attempt at a recovery of the lost original position. What they achieve is at least to restore the powerful object image by making it a part of the self. What happens is, briefly, this:

The patient's final escape from the real object world, first of all, facilitates a withdrawal of cathexis from the realistic part of the object representations. Consequently, the object images are split up. During the last phase of the conflict the archaic wishful image of a powerful, but punitive, love object was built up—as against the image of a weak, bad love object. This reanimated, inflated wishful image is now dissolved as a representation in the system ego and is absorbed by the superego, whereas the deflated worthless object image merges with the self representations. A dangerous schism develops, which still reflects the patient's efforts to rescue the valued object by keeping its wishful concept protected from his destructive

[4] The broader transference problems in the treatment of depressives are discussed in Chapter 12.

impulses at an unattainable distance from the denigrated self image. Accordingly, the aggressive forces accumulate within the superego and cathect the self image, while the ego gathers the reduced libidinal forces and surrenders to the assault.

Thus the patient succeeds in rescuing the powerful love object, but only by a complete deflation or even destruction of the self. The incessant complaints and self-accusations of the melancholic, his exhibition of his helplessness and his moral worthlessness, are both a denial and a confession of guilt: of the crime of having destroyed the valuable love object. Both indeed tell the truth: the powerful image has collapsed as an object representation in the ego, but it has been reconstituted in the superego.

These introjection processes differ from normal or neurotic ego and superego identifications. In normal and neurotic superego identifications, the object representations in the ego system are maintained, whereas the melancholic introjection of the idealized (powerful, but punitive) object image into the superego goes along with a giving up of the "good" object representations in the ego, and leads to their merging with and a personification of the superego. This is facilitated by an insufficient initial separation between the wishful object image and the ego ideal. The introjection mechanism in the ego, on the other hand, leads not to an identification of the ego with the love object but to a merging of the "worthless" object image with the image of the self. The ego does not assume any characteristics of the love object; the self is perceived and is treated by the superego as though it were a deflated love object. (This will be discussed further in Chapter 10.)

My discussion and metapsychological description of the problem of depression have been of necessity one-sided and schematic. I have deliberately left out of consideration the corresponding instinctual processes. In the frame of this chapter it has seemed to me to be of lesser importance that the melancholic divulges cannibalistic incorporation and anal-sadistic ejection fantasies. All psychotics, schizophrenic and manic-depressive, manifest such deeply regressive id material, which corresponds to the processes I discussed: the threatening destruction of the object and self representations and their restitution by their partial merging.

The questions I have tried to explore in this chapter are: where, in psychotic depression, these fusions, i.e., introjections, take place from the structural point of view, and what they mean with regard to the pathology of the ego and superego functions. This is why I wished to concentrate on the following issues: on the importance of the concepts of self representations and of wishful, good and bad, object representations for an understanding of the depressive type of identifications; on the cathectic fluctuations and shifts from self to object representations and the reverse, and their fusions; on the struggle of the manic-depressive to maintain and recover his position of participation in the power of his love object; on the defensive function of the patient's clinging to the real, outside love object during the depressed period; and finally, on the melancholic symptom formation as an expression of his last, failing attempts at restitution of a powerful love object in the superego.

Naturally, the phases in the development of the depressive conflict and its pathological solution are interwoven and cannot be distinguished so clearly as they are in this description. Even during the free intervals we usually find that the manic-depressive shows more or less continuous vacillations in his mood and efficiency, and tries to recover his narcissistic equilibrium once by clinging to his real love objects and by claims for support from without, and then again by temporary retreats into a pseudo self-sufficiency and attempts to resort only to his own superego standards. This is why I consider it not quite sufficient to say that during his free intervals he shows compulsive attitudes. Paranoid schizophrenics, too, may develop compulsive attitudes; they are conspicuously rigid. The main difference between the attitudes of the manic-depressive and the compulsive personality, however, seems to be the former's simultaneous or alternate leaning on an idealized love object and on his own superego. He suffers from a mixture of pseudo independence and dependency, which true compulsives do not show.

10

Psychotic Identifications

In *The Ego and the Id* Freud (1923) started his discussion of ego and superego identifications with a reference to melancholia in which a lost object is set up again in the ego and thus an object cathexis is replaced by an identification. He states: "When it happens that a person has to give up a sexual object, there quite often ensues an alteration of his ego which can only be described as a setting up of the object inside the ego, as it occurs in melancholia" (p. 29).

As in many other instances, the exploration of pathological phenomena proved to be exceedingly fruitful for the understanding of normal psychological development. For the further study of psychotic identifications, however, it may be of equal value to carry Freud's comparison further by a closer scrutiny of the differences between normal ego and superego identifications and the corresponding mechanisms in psychosis.

It is noteworthy that Abraham (1911) failed to detect some conspicuously different features in the melancholic reactions and the identifications in normal grief to which he had called attention. Abraham referred to himself as an example of the latter: to his hair turning gray like that of his father, right after his father's death. We all know of instances when such identifications after the loss or death of the love object set in; these may not bring about a body change, as in Abraham's case, but result in striking changes of the

---

First published as "Contribution to the Metapsychology of Psychotic Identifications" in the *Journal of the American Psychoanalytic Association*, 2:239-264, 1954.

personality. For example, after the loss of her husband a woman takes over his business which becomes the leading ideal and pursuit of her life. She turns into an efficient business woman emulating not only her husband's interests but his ways, his attitudes, his methods in handling his business.

The outcome of such a normal identification process is indeed quite different from that of depressive identifications. If a woman were to develop a melancholia depression after her husband's death, the shadow of the object would fall upon her ego, as Freud (1917) expressed it so beautifully in "Mourning and Melancholia" (p. 249). Instead of taking over his ideals, pursuits, or character traits, she would blame herself for her inability to carry on his business or even for having ruined her husband, unaware that her self-reproaches unconsciously refer to her husband. We know, of course, that her severe unconscious hostility toward her late husband prevents her from responding to his death as did the loving wife in the first example. The result of her conflict is that instead of achieving realistic likeness with him, she treats herself in her pathological state "as if" she were the "bad" husband.[1]

This term reminds us of a quite different, the schizoid "as if" type of personality, which H. Deutsch (1942) has so brilliantly described. She discussed personalities who, unable to have true feelings and interests and to develop lasting ego and superego identifications, behave "as if" they had done so. Not rarely, the prelude of a delusional schizophrenic state is a stage during which the patient imitates idealized persons. A boy of eighteen, in a beginning schizophrenic development, for example, tried, whenever he was afraid and unable to handle a situation, to think of a big, powerful, admired friend and, literally "inhaling him," to imitate his appearance, gestures, behavior. Thus, he felt he "had become his friend" and could safely control the situation. We realize: while the melancholic *treats* himself as if he were the love object, the schizoid or preschizophrenic patient imitates, he *behaves* as if he were the object. And in a delusional schizophrenic state the patient may eventually consciously *believe* himself to be another object.

[1] I need not emphasize that even though it is useful from the theoretical standpoint to make such a clear distinction between identifications in normal grief and in depression, practically we may find in grieving persons all kinds of transition from the one to the other type of reaction.

This outlines the problems which I wish to scrutinize further. In both groups of psychotics, in schizophrenics and in manic-depressives, regressive processes of identification are induced by the breakdown both of object relationships and of normal identifications. The question arises whether we cannot find criteria for a comparison and distinction between the identification mechanisms to be observed in schizophrenics and those formed by manic-depressives; and, furthermore, whether the characteristic differences between psychotic identification mechanisms and normal ego and superego identifications cannot be more precisely defined.

The "as if" type of personality reminds us of an infantile period where such behavior does not yet have such an ominous meaning. I refer to the time when the little boy likes "to play father" by snatching his father's hat and cane, by imitating his way of talking and walking. He, too, pretends to be—he behaves "as if" he were—the father.

Even though such playful make-believe activities may continue far into the latency period, they are founded on identification mechanisms characteristic of the preoedipal stage, a period during which the boundaries between self and object representations are gradually built up.

During the early preoedipal phase "good" and "bad" images of the self and of the love objects begin to be formed; far from depicting reality, they are not yet clearly distinguished from each other and show the tendency easily to merge and split again. We know that for some years the child still feels himself to be only an extension of the mother and participates in her imagined omnipotence or, the reverse, regards the mother as a part of his own omnipotent self. He is also inclined in fantasy to equate or blend significant maternal and paternal body parts, such as breast and phallus, to attach the latter to the mother and, in general, to forge from maternal and paternal images combined parental image units. The child's reluctance to give up such magic fantasies is, of course, expressive of his desire to evade the painful intrusion of reality by maintaining or by re-establishing his lost unity with his earliest love object, the powerful mother.

The baby's wish for oneness with the mother, founded on fantasies of oral incorporation of the love object, easily brings about refusions between self and love-object images whenever the child experiences gratification, physical contact, and closeness with the mother. Evidently, such experiences of merging with the love object are always connected with a temporary weakening of the function of perception—i.e., of the awakening sense of reality—and with a return to the earlier, undifferentiated state. But as early as during the first year of life, the child strives to achieve his goal not only passively by way of gratifications from the outside, but by active imitation of his parents. Although these imitations represent a transition to ego identifications and are indicative of the beginning process of ego formation, they still have a magic character. At first merely formal activities, without ideational content and functional meaning, they appear to serve only the one purpose: to bring about the desired experience of a merging of the self with the love object.

Later on, imitation may play a significant role in the development of the ego. We only have to remember the function of imitation in learning. Gaddini (1969) has discussed the problem of imitation in an excellent paper.

The further advance from the stage of imitation of the parents to that of identification with them in the ego presupposes, indeed, that the child with increasing perception and distinction of the object world and of his own self begins to develop more realistic self and object representations in the system ego, and to set up firm boundaries between them. His desire for complete oneness with his love objects is now gradually relinquished in favor of active strivings to become *like* the love objects in the *future;* these changes correspond to the progress from the state of total to that of partial identification. Only at this point does the child begin to emulate his parents by taking over meaningful attitudes and behavior, thereby gaining true interest in their pursuits. In the course of such essentially unconscious identification processes his ego actually assumes characteristics of his love objects. As his self image becomes a more faithful mirror of what he really is, he can now achieve a partial blending between self and love-object representations, on the basis of realistic likeness.

These brief remarks may suffice for the purpose of defining the essential differences between ego identifications and the early infantile identification fantasies. The first are realistic insofar as they result in lasting changes of the ego, which justify the feeling to be at least partially like the love objects. The latter are magic in nature;

they represent only a temporary—partial or total—blending of magic self and object images; they are founded on fantasies or even on the temporary belief of being one with or of becoming the object, regardless of reality. Of course, unconscious, short-lived, partial identifications of this early preoedipal type normally survive in our empathic understanding of other human beings as an important element in our social and love relationships. My clinical material, however, will demonstrate that in psychotic processes of regression, normal object relationships and identifications disintegrate and are replaced by preoedipal, magic types of identification.

Before discussing these processes I must point to the one area in the ego where the child's magic identifications with his love object normally find a safe, lasting refuge: the ego ideal and superego. In fact, the core of the ego ideal is composed of idealized images of the parents blended with archaic, aggrandized images of the self. It must be added that it takes years for the child to develop more or less realistic self representations which are firmly differentiated from his magic, wishful self images and his ego ideal. Superego formation is indeed a good example of the constructive use of regressive mechanisms in the service of the ego. Undeniably even the mature superego still has a magic character; it even represents a magic wish fulfillment, but the ego is aware of it. This awareness is reflected in our realization of the discrepancies between our ego and superego standards. In the eternal struggle for harmony between them, the unending desire for union with the oedipal love objects thus continues to find expression.

We know that the constitution of the superego system signifies the final solution of the oedipal conflicts. In view of the melancholic pathology I re-emphasize that these grandiose reaction formations achieve not only the renunciation of the infantile sexual desires in favor of social and cultural pursuits, but, as Freud (1914, 1921) stressed, also are of the greatest significance for the solution of the child's narcissistic and ambivalence conflicts. Counteracting the child's tendency to derogate his parents, the processes of idealization and ego-ideal formation transform the bad, sexual, aggressive, weak, dirty, castrated parents into aggrandized, good, strong, asexual model figures. The child's endeavors to identify with them find the most powerful support in the internalization of the demanding and prohibiting, the disapproving and rewarding parental attitudes.

The development of self-critical and self-approving superego functions promotes the neutralization of libidinal and aggressive forces, and helps to veer them away from the love objects to aim-inhibited ego interests and ego functions. Thus, the constitution of the superego becomes instrumental in the ego's attempts to overcome the narcissistic injuries which instinctual frustration, disappointments, and the impact of reality, in general, inflict upon the infantile self.

These three essential aspects of superego formation make us realize that a simple statement, such as that ego and superego identifications *replace* the lost sexual love object, is not comprehensive and precise enough. The fact must be understood that, quite contrary to psychotic identifications which arise with the breakdown of realistic object and self representations, of object relations, and of ego functions, the child's object relations profit greatly from the building up of ego and superego identifications. The latter neither destroy nor replace, they only transform and change the nature of object relations.[2] By reinforcing the processes of drive neutralization, by reducing the sexual and aggressive object cathexes in favor of affectionate love relations and ego interests, these developmental identifications contribute indeed very much to the establishment of firmly cathected, realistic, and enduring object and self representations and of stable object relations and ego functions.

After having briefly examined the nature of primitive magic (primary) identifications in contrast to (secondary) ego and superego identifications, I shall now present two brief vignettes: a case of depressive and a case of schizophrenic psychosis. With the help of these clinical examples we shall study the regressive revival of magic identifications in psychosis, and try to define some important differences between the manic-depressive and the schizophrenic identification mechanisms.

CASE 1

Some years ago I treated a forty-year-old woman who was then suffering from her fourth depression. This patient, Mrs. O., was one of the rare cases that display, right on the surface, the development

[2] I discussed these developmental processes more extensively in *The Self and the Object World* (1964).

of the depressive conflict and the psychotic mechanisms with which we are concerned here.

Each time her depressive state was preceded by a period of increasing irritability and hostility toward her husband and children. As in the course of some weeks her manifest hostility subsided, she developed a typical depressive state, characterized by insomnia, anorexia, loss of weight, severe anxieties, retardation, withdrawal from all activities and social contacts, and continuous self-accusations.

The patient came to see me in a state of transition from the first to the second stage of the illness. At first the hours were filled with endless complaints about her husband. She talked about his inefficiency and his unloving, selfish attitudes, his greed and his aggressiveness, his moral worthlessness. Quite insidiously the subject of her complaints began to change. She herself became the center of her attacks. She now expressed precisely the same criticisms about herself as she had previously in regard to her husband.

One day, during this phase, she suddenly interrupted her alternate attacks on herself and her partner, and said: "I am so confused, I don't know whether I am complaining about my husband or myself. In my mind, his picture is all mixed up with that of myself, as if we were the same person. But that is not true at all. I know he is quite different from me. We are alike only in our overdependence on each other. We don't love each other. We cling to one another like two babies, each expecting the other to be a good mother. I don't know anymore what sort of person he really is or what I am like. I think previously I have always been generous and giving, whereas he is stingy and selfish, expecting me to give myself up for him. Now I cannot give him anything either. All I want is to be taken care of. Maybe this is why I have become sick. I want Irving now to do everything for me. I have felt powerless to change him, but my sickness will not make him love me either."

Although the patient's outburst touches on many problems in depression, I shall focus mainly on the nature and functions of her depressive identification mechanisms.

This woman clearly displayed her severe ambivalence conflict with the husband, which threatened to destroy their relationship. Her aggressive devaluation of her partner was not without realistic foundation. My own impressions had confirmed her assertion that he was selfish and stingy, an overdependent and overdemanding person, whereas the patient had normally been a compulsive, domineering, nagging, but also a warm, generous, and self-sacrificing wife. Quite characteristically, these two people had always had a somewhat symbiotic relationship to each other. Each of them felt part of the other. But they were alike only insofar as he was basically a narcissistic, oral personality type. Characterologically, their pregenital-narcissistic pathology had developed in different directions, indeed complementary to each other.

I emphasized in the beginning that the melancholic treats himself as if he were the worthless love object, without actually assuming its characteristics. But in her depression this patient had certainly become as self-centered and ungiving as she described her husband. These attitudes, however, expressive of the regressive process and common in all melancholics, are certainly not ego identifications with the love object. Due to the pathological, narcissistic, and frequently very masochistic choice of their partners, the unloving but clinging attitudes of such depressed patients may, as in this case, actually mimic their partners' behavior. This is quite different from what we find in certain neurotic depressive patients.

Charles Fisher observed a number of female depressed patients who, at the beginning of their depressive state, actually behaved in a way characteristic of their first love object, the mother; they had previously severely criticized this very same behavior.[3] I have made similar observations in my depressive-compulsive patients. In such cases we see a real, though transitory, ego identification with the ambivalently loved object, which justifies the severe self-reproaches.

The psychotic depressive patient disclosed, in the outburst I recounted, the nature of her identifications, of which melancholics are usually quite unaware. "I don't know," she had said, "whether I am complaining about myself or my husband." She admitted that she could no longer perceive either him or herself in a realistic way, or clearly discern and evaluate their different personality features. This was an overt expression of her impaired sense of reality, of the replacement of realistic by distorted object and self images, and of the pathological fusion and confusion between the image of her devaluated, "bad" partner and the concept of her own worthless

[3] Personal communication.

self. The patient also clearly demonstrated the extent to which her fixation at the infantile stage of magic participation in the power and value of an idealized love object had predisposed her to this regressive process.

The beginning of her pathological state had announced itself by denunciations of her husband's character. The reproaches resembled those of a disappointed little child. Whereas the child is capable of rapidly changing the good and bad images of his love object, her disappointment in her partner had kindled a profound hostility which made her look at him as through dark glasses only. Her mind had transformed him into the image of a worthless weakling. Within some weeks, however, her efforts to maintain her affection for her love object, her fear of annihilating the "good" image on which she depended so greatly, had increasingly turned her hostility toward herself. This permitted her to cling more and more tenaciously to her husband. A pathological identification had been induced. This process can best be described, not as an introjection of the love object into the ego, but as an introjection leading to a gradual absorption and replacement of the "bad husband" image by the image of her own worthless self.

In view of Melanie Klein's opinions and those expressed by Schafer (1968), in *Aspects of Internalization,* I should like here to insert some remarks on the meaning of the terms internalization, introjection, and introjects. Schafer uses the term "internalization" more broadly than Hartmann, Kris, and Loewenstein and I myself did. Since this term is descriptive and becomes meaningful only in its specific application, I have no objection; but I have doubts about Schafer's use of the term introjection "in the sense of setting up an introject" (p. 17).

In many near-psychic or psychotic cases where the normal boundaries between self and object representations are dissolving or where the superego system is regressively repersonified, we find symptoms and fantasies that relate to "introjected objects," sometimes to "body introjects," such as described by M. Klein. These "bad" introjects may be experienced as the bad, worthless part of the self, or again maintain the character of dangerous objects which threaten to destroy the self. It is M. Klein's great merit to have observed and described fantasy material of this type in small children and in psychotic adults.

But to equate the establishment of "introjects" with introjection does not seem to me to clarify the issue. Moreover, Schafer stressed the role that "introjects" play in the life of normal people. I have found no confirmation of this idea in my clinical material. In general, I have avoided the term "introjects" in my writings because various authors used it in very different and confusing ways. The term, as coined by Klein, refers to feelings of having incorporated objects, whereas introjection as well as projection are mechanisms that can be used on a more corporal or more abstract level. Both "introjection" and "projection" are very useful terms—if applied as they have been in the past—because the psychological mechanisms or processes to which they refer can be clinically validated as easily as their role in the building up of identifications. A good example is my case, to which I want to return.

I had spoken of the introjective identification with the "bad husband" whose image the patient had set up in her self image. Careful observation of this stage frequently shows that for some time such patients may even unduly praise the love object for what were actually their own lovable character traits in the past. Hence, to the extent to which the self is experienced as the "bad object," the "good self" may be projected onto the object in exchange. Especially in melancholic depressions, after the death of a love object, the latter may be ostensibly glorified by the patient by dint of such projective mechanisms.

During one session Mrs. O. interrupted her repetitive self-accusations and suddenly mentioned her mother. "When I listen to my endless self-reproaches," she said, "I sometimes hear the voice of my mother. She was a wonderful, strong woman, but very severe and disapproving. I was as dependent on her as I am on my husband. If he were only as strong and wonderful as she was." With her usual lucidity the patient not only indicated that unconsciously her husband represented the mother, but also realized that her superego had become so punitive through reanimation of a powerful, severe, aggressive mother-husband image. This points to the restitutive function of the superego changes during the melancholic period (see Chapter 9).

The first-described identifications resulted in the setting up of a deflated, bad love-object image within the self image, a process intended to maintain the libidinal cathexis of the love object. As these efforts for the solution of the ambivalence conflict fail, the withdrawal of cathexis from the real love object and, eventually, from the object world in general, continues further. The object relations become meaningless and attenuated, the ego functions inhibited and slowed up. Instead of the dissolving realistic object representations a powerful and indestructible, punitive and cruel love-object image is resurrected and set up in the superego, which thus becomes repersonified, deneutralized, and severely sadistic. Contrary to what can be observed in schizophrenics, however, the melancholic superego, even though regressively personified, archaic, and highly pathological in its functions, is maintained as a psychic system and even gains strength by taking the place of the fading object representations or the external love object.

As to the unfortunate results of the double introjective processes in melancholia, I wish to underscore only those points that are important for the comparison with schizophrenia. In the intrapsychic continuation of the struggle with the love object, the ego maintains its utter dependence on the latter. It becomes, indeed, a victim of the superego, as helpless and powerless as a small child who is tortured by his cruel, powerful mother. The inner experience of helpless inferiority is of course increasingly reinforced by the actual paralysis of ego functions caused by the withdrawal from the outside world.

A manic condition may or may not follow the depression. Such a state announces the end of the period of atonement by a magic reunion with the love object or superego, which now changes from a punitive into a good, forgiving, omnipotent figure. The reprojection of this all-mighty, all-giving object image onto the real object world re-establishes spurious object relations. The patient throws himself into an imagined world of unending pleasure and indestructible value, in which he greedily partakes without fear.

CASE 2

A twenty-seven-year-old woman, Mrs. P., a brilliant social science student, went into an acute catatonic episode at the time when her second marriage was going to pieces. Some years earlier, during her first marriage, she had been under my care for a prolonged period of time. The nature of her disease had then been established beyond doubt. This was her second acute breakdown. Prior to her first attack she had been a very ambitious girl, predominantly megalomanic, supercilious, cold, and brittle. She was forever in search of her own identity. She wished to be, and at times believed she was, a genius—an idea she shared with her schizophrenic mother, a severe dipsomaniac. When the patient was confronted with her realistic inner and outer limitations, she responded at first with increased ideas of grandiosity and a stubborn denial and refusal to accept facts until failure was unavoidable. Then she became depressed, stopped working, and, as she called it "got into a general mess."

Shortly before the onset of her acute condition, the patient had asked for an appointment. The reason for wanting to see me was her fear that her husband, Larry, "might have to commit suicide" if she deserted him, as she planned to do. When I pointed to her own disturbed state, she denied it completely. While expressing her concern about her husband, she assured me that she herself felt on top of the world, since she did not "need" Larry anymore. After the interview she flew into a rage at him. Then she suddenly calmed down, packed her things, coldly left her home, and moved to a hotel. Shortly thereafter she developed a severe state of excitement. She rampaged through the hotel apartment, took a shower at 2 A.M., singing and making a lot of noise. I rushed to her, quickly succeeded in establishing contact, and persuaded her to go immediately to a hospital.

In the course of my talk with her, Mrs. P.—a pathetic, beautiful Ophelia clad only in a torn nightgown—pulled me down to the couch where she had seated herself. "Let us be close," she said. "I have made a great philosophical discovery. Do you know the difference between closeness, likeness, sameness, and oneness? Close is close, as with you; when you are like somebody, you are only *like* the other, you and he are two; sameness—you are the same as the other, but he is still he and you are you; but oneness is not two—it is one, it is one, that's horrible.—Horrible," she repeated, jumping up in sudden panic: "Don't get too close, get away from the couch, I don't want to be you," and she pushed me away and began to attack me. Some minutes later she became elated again. "I am a genius," she said, "a genius. I am about to destroy all my books [on social science]. I don't need them, to hell with them. I am a genius, I am a genius." (Her husband was a social science teacher.)

When I took her in an ambulance to the hospital, she became calm, subdued, and depressed. "I am dead now. Larry won't kill himself," she said, taking out a little amulet, a tiny crab enclosed in a small plastic case. "This is my soul," she said, handing it to me. "My soul is gone, my self is gone, I lost it. I am dead. Take it, keep it for me till I shall come out." Then, in sudden panic: "I don't want to die," and she began to attack and to beat me, as though I had assaulted her, only to fall back again into her depressed, humble mood. When we got out of the car at the hospital and I lit a cigarette, she suddenly began to laugh, snatched it away from my mouth and smoked it herself. "Now you can go home, I don't need you anymore," she said, and in an elated mood she left me.

After some months of hospitalization, during the time of recovery, Mrs. P. accepted the suggestion of the chief psychiatrist, to whom she had become quite attached, to work as an attendant aide. In this activity she very conspicuously imitated his gestures and behavior. She played the psychiatrist. She repeated at that time what I had observed in her during her first period of treatment with me.

After her recovery she gave up this interest as well as her social science studies. She obtained a divorce and moved to the West, to be with her father and stepmother. There she did secretarial work for the father, cooking and baking with the mother. She lost her interest in her former life and studies so completely that she impressed a visitor as a person who had never done intellectual work. The grandiose, ambitious attitudes that she had shown prior to the breakdown seemed to be gone. Evidently, she had adjusted at a lower level, maintaining a rather clinging dependency on her parents and attempting to imitate their behavior and activities.

The patient is now in her fifties and lives in California. To some extent she has re-established her intellectual interests. She has had three more episodes and, each time, called me up when she felt she was getting ill and accepted my advice to go to a hospital. In free intervals she did secretarial work and lived with an alcoholic psychopath.

Mrs. P.'s acute breakdown had been precipitated by conflicts with her husband, previously her teacher. Her object relations prior to this episode were in many ways reminiscent of the "as if" type described by H. Deutsch (1942). They were quite different from those of the manic-depressive patient, which had been steady and highly discriminating, though overly close and too faithfully "clinging." In contrast, the love relations of Mrs. P. were indiscriminate and at an infinitely more magic, infantile ego level.

At first sight her marital relationship gave the impression of being selective and highly intellectual. Actually, it was completely unrealistic and lacked substance and true feelings. She simply chose partners to whom she could attach her own genius fantasies; although she herself was brilliant, her interests changed according to those of the current lover or husband. She began to devote herself to social studies after she had fallen in love with a social scientist who had impressed her as outstanding. When he did not respond, she easily displaced her fantasies and feelings from him to another man, and then onto a third man who eventually married her.

Quite different from the manic-depressive woman, Mrs. P. displayed, from the beginning of her marriage, violent, open ambivalence toward her husband. It is characteristic that, in rapid mood vacillations, she either denied her hostility and felt only kindly disposed toward him, or she denied her attachment and scorned and rejected him. Thus, she alternately praised and imitated his supposedly outstanding qualities, which automatically also gave her, as his wife, high stature, or played the woman of genius on whom this pathetic little creature depended. Between her two marriages she would occasionally, in a keyed-up mood, throw herself into precipitate, short-lived, senseless sexual affairs which left her emotionally cold and sexually unsatisfied. Her behavior was quite different from the sexual exploits of the hypomanic who may passionately and pleasurably consume and gaily dispose of one love object after the other.

In both her marriages the patient had been involved with her husbands' previous wives and mistresses. These triangular involvements were no more than faint shadows of past oedipal constellations. Her dreams and even her manifest fantasies left no doubt that the heterosexual and the homosexual love objects represented "units" to her; they were mixtures of infantile, omnipotent, paternal and maternal images as well as projections of her own grandiose self. In dreams and even in her conscious imagery, Mrs. P. easily exchanged these objects or merged them with each other and with herself. Evidently, these figures were fusions of split-up infantile object images which tended to be recomposed and distinguished only according to bisexual organ attributes representing either life, strength, omnipotence, or death, destruction, impotence. In this way she created omnipotent, male-female, breast-phallus figures and castrated, breastless, injured, dead figures, variously combining traits that lent themselves to her imagery.

The final break occurred when Mrs. P. was no longer able to bear up under the increasing compulsiveness of her husband. In the interview shortly before the onset of her episode, she implored me to save her husband from suicide. She explained that she had to desert him because she could not tolerate his imposing strict schedules for work and pleasure on her. He had insisted on her paying the taxes on time and "would not even let her have fantasies of getting a dozen children."

Thus, the episodes appeared to have set in with a situation of unbearable ambivalence, indicative of a process of irresistible instinctual diffusion; a situation of being enmeshed in a fatal struggle between extremely passive, masochistic strivings and severely sadistic, murderous impulses toward the love object. This conflict found expression in the fear that either the patient or the love object must die or commit suicide. The tearing up of scientific books (magic murder of her husband in effigy); the handing over of the amulet, the symbol of her self, to me—all this psychotic acting out reveals clearly the underlying conflict between wishful fantasies of either being destroyed by the object or of killing or having killed it.

The fantasy material presented by Mrs. P. prior to her episode, as well as that of other schizophrenic patients, disclosed that the ideas of killing or being killed correspond to fantasies of devouring, incorporating, or ejecting the objects, or vice versa. We are familiar with these fantasies from the work of Abraham (1911, 1924), M. Klein (1935, 1940), and Lewin (1950). The patient escaped from her intolerable conflict by a sudden break with reality and total regression to a magic, primary process level. The murderous fantasies developed rapidly into delusional ideas and fears of either the object's or her own imminent death. The belief in the object's death temporarily induced an elated mood and megalomanic attitudes and ideas, which quickly changed to panicky fears of imminent death, or to depressed states with experiences of losing the self or of inner death. Mrs. P.'s manifest ideas at the beginning of her episode enable us to understand the cathectic shifts and the processes of identification leading to these delusional experiences and ideas. Her philosophical elaborations described step by step, in an almost clairvoyant way, her regressive escape from the insoluble ambivalence conflict with the love objects: from object relationship, "closeness," to identification, "likeness," to magic, total identifications, first "sameness," and eventually "oneness," i.e., complete fusion of self and object images.

In metapsychological terms these processes may be described as follows. Long before the onset of the episode, probably since the age of nineteen when she had run away from college to marry her first husband, the patient's ego had operated at a profoundly magical level. Her reality testing had been impaired, her concepts of the object world and of her own self distorted by the invasion of highly irrational images and by the lack of boundaries between the different object representations, between the images of the objects and her own self, and between her wishful and realistic self images.

The episode announced itself by signs of increasing ambivalence and outbursts of fury toward her husband. The breaking point, however, was reached when her rage at him suddenly subsided as she coldly walked out on her partner. Evidently, the cessation of affects and the assertion of "no longer needing" the husband were expressive of a complete withdrawal of all cathexis from the object. Whereas the libidinal cathexis had veered away from the object to the self image, the aggression was first turned to inanimate object substitutes (the books) and, with increasing catatonic excitement, more and more diffusely discharged on the outside. A magic, total identification had taken place. As the object representations were dissolving, the image of the murderous, powerful object had been set up in the image of the self. This process found expression in megalomanic, aggressive self-expansion and the idea that the object had died. Fear and hate of the object had disappeared; the self threatened by the omnipotent object had been saved by the magic murder of the object.

This state, however, was only temporary and was soon followed by the reverse process which restored the object, though by magic destruction of the self. Apparently, the entire cathexis had now been called away from the self image and reinvested in the object image. A powerful, threatening object image had thus been resurrected, at the expense of the self. During my visit this image became immediately attached to me. Surrender (A. Freud, 1951) followed by panicky fears, feelings of loss of the self and of death, and renewed outbursts of rage toward me, as the murderous object, were indicative of the threatening dissolution of the self representations which had been emptied of libido and cathected with destructive forces.

Longer periods of observations show the enormous cathectic fluidity in schizophrenics and their inability to tolerate ambivalence, both of which were especially stressed by M. Klein. They tend to decathect an object completely and to shift the entire (libidinal or aggressive) cathexis not only from the object to the self image and vice versa, but also from one object image to another; or all the available libido may temporarily be invested in one object image, while another one or that of the self is cathected with all the aggression; furthermore, these processes may rapidly be reversed.

One of my patients, who had been excessively involved with his parents, "lost all feeling for them" when he married. They became "shadowy figures." He felt interested only in his wife and father-in-law. When during his treatment his feelings for his mother were stirred up for the first time, he said: "I cannot continue loving her. I feel that my self would be gone." Another patient, who had coldly assured me that his father was "dead" for him, very excitedly said when his feelings were rearoused: "I had locked him up in myself. He is coming out now, he is halfway out; that is terrible, I shall die"—and he began to shudder with fear. Soon his father "was gone," and he felt alive: "Now he is in again; I feel alive and strong."

In the further course of such psychotic episodes we often observe how the processes of restitution succeed in resurrecting new, more or less fixated, delusional self and object representations. I mentioned above the dreams and imagery of the schizophrenic patient. They had shown: first, the breaking up of realistic object and self representations into fragmented, archaic images; then, their refusion and merging with the remnants of realistic representations; and eventually, the attempt at their reorganization into new, composite, pathological image units.

As an example I mention the simultaneous persecutory and

grandiose delusions in the case of a schizophrenic social worker. He planned to set up an international social agency of his own, which would prevent war and save the world from destruction. He maintained the delusion of a secret adversary in the government who tried to ruin all his plans. This patient had eventually succeeded in setting up the image of an omnipotent, loving father-mother unit in the image of his self as the "rescuer of mankind." The omnipotent, destructive father-mother-self unit was split off and projected onto an imaginary outside object, his evil adversary in the government. He never attached this evil object image to a real outside object. In other cases such delusional new object images become reattached to real persons and lead to the re-establishment of pathological paranoid object relations. Since reality testing may temporarily still be effective in certain ego areas, relations to the outside world may then simultaneously operate on both a realistic and a delusional level.

COMPARISON BETWEEN MANIC-DEPRESSIVE AND SCHIZOPHRENIC MECHANISMS

In manic-depressives the regressive, magic identifications appear to reflect their fixation at the stage of magic participation of the child in the power and value of the idealized parents. In fact, they maintain forever standards for themselves and for their love objects which are far too high to be reached. For this reason, the personality of manic-depressives is characterized by their narcissistic vulnerability and their tendency to react to any slight hurt or disappointment with a profound ambivalence conflict. They suffer from an instability of their self-esteem, caused by this overdependency on the love and narcissistic supply from an overvalued, all-giving love object. The libidinal cathexis of their self representations thus depends on the maintenance of a continuous libidinal hypercathexis of the love object, designed to prevent its aggressive devaluation in which their self is bound to participate. Any arousal of aggression is apt to upset their precarious narcissistic equilibrium and to precipitate a regressive process which leads to a depression.

In the depressed state the attempt to safeguard the libidinal cathexis of the love object leads first to an increasing merging of the bad, worthless love-object image with the self image and sometimes even to a projection of the "good, worthy" self onto the object. The failure of this defense promotes the increasing withdrawal of cathexis from the realistic love object and the revival of infantile, "bad" parental images. Processes of restitution set in, resulting in the reanimation of a punitive, sadistic, but powerful and indestructible love-object image which is set up in the superego or in the self-critical parts of the ego.

Contrary to the corresponding process in schizophrenia, it is characteristic of manic-depressives that these double magic identification mechanisms succeed in maintaining the situation of dependence of the self on a powerful, superior love-object image. This statement is in agreement with opinions previously expressed, especially by M. Klein. In the endopsychic continuation of the conflict, in the melancholic state, the self passively surrenders to the sadistic superego—or to the self-critical ego—as it once did to the love object. But even in the manic state where the archaic, punitive love-object image or superego turns into a loving one, its reprojection onto the outside permits the self to feel part of a highly pleasurable, good, indestructible object world and to "feed" on it. The aggrandizement of the manic thus encompasses and depends on an illusory, grandiose world.

Comparing these mechanisms with the corresponding processes described in the schizophrenic case, we note that the regressive processes in schizophrenia go much further and are different in nature. They may lead to a loss of structural differentiation in the psychic organization and to a drive deneutralization far beyond what we observe in manic-depressives. We found that the schizophrenic patient's grandiose, elated states, as well as her states of depression and panic, were an expression not of conflicts or reconciliation and reunion between superego and self image, but of processes of total fusions between self and object images within the disintegrating ego-id.

In fact, many schizophrenics appear to have a severe intolerance to guilt feelings, coupled with their inability to ward off guilt-provoking impulses by normal neurotic defense mechanisms. Again, I refer to the case of the schizophrenic woman, whose final break came when she could no longer tolerate her husband's compulsiveness which played continuously on her guilt feelings. Pious (1949) also has called attention to the breakdown of superego functions in schizophrenia, and Kanzer (1952) has expressed ideas along similar lines.

Whereas in melancholics the superego, by absorbing punitive, powerful parental images, gains sadistic control over the self image, we observe the opposite in schizophrenic patients: an escape from superego conflicts by a dissolution of the superego and by its regressive transformation back into threatening parental images. The schizophrenic seems to be predisposed to such processes by his defective ego-superego formation. As in the case of the schizophrenic woman, we find in prepsychotic or latent schizophrenics and in borderline patients that their so-called ideals are actually ambitious daydreams and magic, wishful fantasies of sharing or even usurping the desired omnipotence of their love objects.

In the manifest psychosis these fantasies may become delusional. The superego fears are frequently replaced by fears of omnipotent, murderous object images which may be attached to body parts (body introjects) or to outside persons. Instead of guilty fears and submission to a destructive superego, as in melancholia, schizophrenics experience fears of being bodily destroyed or, as my patient did, of being influenced and persecuted, of dying or being dead, or of losing their identity. These fears correspond to wishful fantasies of passively surrendering, of being devoured and killed by murderous parental figures. In some cases we may observe that a seemingly compulsive superstructure, developed in early latency, which helped to keep the schizophrenia latent, gradually or suddenly breaks down and gives way to paranoid syndromes.

On the other hand, their grandiosity and elation, contrary to that of manic patients, is autistic in nature. Instead of feelings of owning and partaking in a world of unending pleasure, schizophrenics may show the grandiose belief of being the genius who does not need the world, or of being the omnipotent evil or good ruler of mankind who can control, destroy, or rescue a doomed world. Their outbursts of panic, their fantasies of *Weltuntergang* arising from an inner perception of their disintegration (Frosch, 1967a), of the breakdown of object relations and ego identifications, reverberate the processes of dissolution, both of the object and of the self representations. Split up into archaic images, they cease to be entities. The delusional ideas appear to develop from restitutive processes leading first to refusions of such fragmented images and subsequently to the resynthesis and recathexis of new image units which may be reattached to outside objects.

Within the frame of this pathology the schizophrenic identifications present themselves as introjective and projective processes of either dissolution, loss of cathexis, and immersion of the self images in omnipotent, devouring parental images, or of the opposite.

SUMMARY

In manic-depressives the regressive processes are different from those found in schizophrenia; they do not proceed as far and do not result in a return to the early symbiotic stage of "total identifications." They may result in fusions of bad or good love-object images with the self image and with the superego and eventually lead to a severe pathological conflict—or harmony—between the superego and the self representations. In schizophrenics the ego and superego systems deteriorate to a much more dangerous extent. The conflict between self image and superego may become retransformed into struggles between the image of the self and magic, sadistic, threatening love-object figures. The pathological identifications are the expression of alternating introjective and projective processes that lead to a more or less total merging between these self and object images within the deteriorating ego-id. Insofar as powerful, lasting object images are reconstituted and reattached to the outside world, the ego-superego conflict may change into homosexual paranoid conflicts, with impulses to kill and fears of being persecuted and destroyed by outside representatives of these terrifying figures.

I stated in the beginning that the manic-depressive treats himself as if he were the love object, whereas the schizophrenic behaves as if he were or believes himself to be the object. The meaning of this difference has now become clearer. It points to the manic-depressive's tendency and effort to submit to or to reconcile with the love object and to cling to it. He keeps it alive and maintains his own identity feelings. In contradistinction to this position, the schizophrenic tends either to destroy the object image and replace it by the self image, or to let the latter be annihilated and replaced by the image of the object. This difference is reflected in the fact that in the preschizophrenic, imitations of the love object and fears of loss of identity play such a paramount role, whereas all the manic-depressive needs and wants is punishment leading to forgiveness, love, and gratification from his superego or his love object.

11

Differences between Schizophrenic and Melancholic States of Depression

In this chapter I shall focus specifically on some characteristic differences between melancholic and schizophrenic states of depression. We know that depressive states can develop in the course of any psychotic or neurotic illness. Attempts to discriminate more carefully between different kinds of depression (Asch, 1966; Gehl, 1964; Grinker et al., 1961) are certainly desirable, since they may help us to establish a clear differential diagnosis. Unfortunately, in severe states of depression this may be very difficult (see, for example, the case described in Chapter 8).

We know that patients belonging to the manic-depressive group may show features indicative of a schizophrenic depression. In turn, schizophrenics may sometimes present the picture of a typical melancholia. The diagnostic difficulties increase in those schizophrenic disorders which have a circular course. Many patients originally diagnosed as manic-depressives develop clearly schizophrenic manifestations. In view of the problems that such patients present, I should like to call attention to some characteristic differences in the psychopathology of schizophrenic and melancholic types of depres-

---

This chapter is based on a paper first published as "Problems in the Differentiation between Schizophrenic and Melancholic States of Depression." In: *Psychoanalysis—A General Psychology*, edited by R. M. Loewenstein, L. M. Newman, M. Schur, and A. J. Solnit. New York: International Universities Press, 1966, pp. 499-518.

sion. These differences may easily escape the clinical observer, but may be of great help in a correct diagnostic evaluation and understanding of such cases and in our therapeutic approach to them.

Great clinical psychiatrists of the past, e.g., Kraepelin, Bleuler, and Lange, have thoroughly described the phenomenology of these various groups of psychoses. Lange (1928), for instance, said that we encounter "the greatest difficulties in the distinction between melancholic and schizophrenic depressions. . . . There are evidently clinical pictures which in the current episode as in the course of quite a series of attacks do not in any way make us think of a schizophrenic process in the future. Here only a schizophrenic heredity may arouse such a suspicion. On the other hand, we must not forget that cases which doubtlessly are circular melancholias can manifest ample additional catatonic features" (p. 198; my translation).

Bleuler (1911), too, refers to "the periodic and cyclic forms of melancholic and manic moods seen in schizophrenia" (p. 206f.). He emphasizes that "chronic as well as acute depressions are found more frequently in the beginning of an outspoken [schizophrenic] illness than any other syndromes" (p. 254). "Yet, we do find genuine states of melancholic depression even in schizophrenics of long standing." However, he points to "the typical schizophrenic stiffness, superficiality, and exaggeratedness," and to the "extreme form of monoideism which, in contrast to that seen in simple melancholias, may here be almost absolute." He also mentions that "Delusions and especially hallucinations are rarely absent [in schizophrenia]." Bleuler believes that "The 'hypochondriacal melancholia' of other authors is usually a schizophrenic melancholia" and that ideas of grandeur "may exist side by side with the most appalling fears and terrors" (p. 209f.).

Kraepelin (1913) presents criteria similar to those which Bleuler regarded as significant for the differential diagnosis between melancholic and schizophrenic depressive states. But he, too, points out that "it may be impossible to distinguish it [the depressive psychomotor retardation] from the lack of mental agility and of the will power, such as is characteristic of dementia praecox. In the beginning of a dementia praecox . . . one hears from them statements quite similar to those of manic-depressive patients" (p. 951; my translation).

Interestingly enough, we find an excellent and appreciative brief review of Freud's paper on "Mourning and Melancholia" only in Lange's monograph (1928). Although Lange wondered whether Freud had not thrown melancholic and hysterical cases together, he criticized not Freud but Jaspers for his psychological approach, for instance, to the manic states.[1]

I have deliberately referred to a series of outstanding psychiatrists of the past. All of them were brilliant observers who, with the exception of Bleuler, regarded any psychological approach, especially the psychoanalytic one, as scientifically questionable because they assumed a merely endogenous etiology of the psychotic diseases. To be sure, the hospitalized patients who were the predominant subjects of these authors' observations are likely to support this opinion, whereas ambulatory psychotics or borderline patients, who may desire psychotherapy or even analytic treatment and be accessible to it, are apt to show the significant role of psychogenic factors in the development of both neuroses and psychoses.[2]

Yet in these milder depressive cases that we so frequently see in our private practice, even more difficult differential diagnostic problems arise, since we may have doubts regarding the neurotic or psychotic, either manic-depressive or schizophrenic nature of the depressive illness. In certain mildly schizophrenic-hypochondriacal or cyclothmyic patients who show a predominance of somatic autonomous (Campbell, 1953, pp. 52-82) disturbances over affective ones, a correct diagnosis can frequently not be established, because these patients may not even come into the orbit of the psychiatrist. Certain seemingly neurotic but actually mildly psychotic or prepsychotic (borderline) patients, who do come for psychotherapeutic treatment, may in its course suddenly develop a psychotic episode. Such experiences lend themselves to views which tend to blur the sharp lines of nosological distinction, not only between the two

[1] This is rather ironical, since Jaspers was not only utterly disdainful but also amazingly uninformed about Freud's ideas and their development.

[2] In this connection, it may be noted that in 1949 H. Luxemburger wrote an annex on the causes of mental diseases to Bleuler's *Lehrbuch der Psychiatrie*. Without reference to Freud, Luxemburger applied the concept of the supplementary series of pathogenic factors to the psychoses as well. While emphasizing the constitutional factors, which he carefully distinguishes from the hereditary ones, he makes it very clear that the environmental influences must not be disregarded and that not all people who are constitutionally predisposed to a psychosis develop a psychotic illness.

major groups of psychoses but even between psychotic and neurotic illness.

I

I shall now present some pertinent case material that will permit me to point to certain features which distinguish this schizophrenic-melancholic condition from similar depressive states belonging to the manic-depressive group of disorders. For my purpose, the case of "Janet Q.," a schizophrenic woman in her late forties, seems especially suitable, since I have been able to observe her during her childhood and again from the age of thirty until now, i.e., for a period of about forty years.

There was no evidence of a psychotic heredity in Janet's family. Her father consulted me for the first time when she was seven years old. His wife was a beautiful but very erratic, acting-out, domineering, narcissistic, and infantile woman. From the pathogenic point of view, it was significant that she had already had an affair with Janet's father while she had been married to her first husband, the best friend of her lover's brother. The husband was a highly intellectual man, who made love "according to his theories" and was enslaved to her. When she finally obtained a divorce, he shot himself, with an apology that his suicide might ruin the couple's happiness forever.

Janet's mother certainly never ceased to feel guilty and to take out on this first child her hostility toward Janet's father, who had forced the divorce and later on turned out to be an eternal philanderer. She treated her daughter very cruelly, and never gave her any of the tenderness and affection which she showered on her second child, a son born three years later.

Very early the little girl developed multiple phobic anxieties, especially about insect bites. Her anxiety had a panicky quality that I have hardly ever observed in neurotic children. I saw her tremble with fear when her mother yelled at her like a Prussian sergeant. From Janet's infancy on, her father took over the maternal role. But his behavior toward this lovely girl was and remained extremely seductive. As a result of her mother's cruelty and disciplinary behavior, Janet began to show compulsive traits as early as in the preoedipal period. She became overobedient, dutiful, conscientious, and overconcerned with her possessions. She never played with her dolls and toys lest she ruin them. At the beginning of latency, she developed a compulsive ritual before going to bed, which caused her father to consult me.

Janet had always been a beautiful girl of more than average intelligence, but even as a child she showed a suspicious remoteness, stiffness, emotional emptiness and lifelessness, had a reading and learning block, and complained of continuous "boredom." At that time, the quality of her affective disturbance already made me think of a potential future schizophrenic psychosis. In spite of Janet's conspicuous symptoms, her mother rejected my suggestions for immediate treatment so stubbornly that the father was unable to achieve it. When Janet was fourteen years of age, the family was forced to leave Germany for Belgium. Janet was sent first to Paris, then to a boarding school in England. Her father, who visited her there, took her to the apartment of his mistress in London and, while he made love to his girlfriend, sent Janet alone to a hairdresser. Soon after this incident, which Janet never forgot or forgave, she developed a severe depression.

A psychoanalyst—the late Kate Friedlander—was consulted. She diagnosed Janet's condition as a psychotic depression, possibly a beginning schizophrenia. Janet was taken home to Belgium, where she experienced the German invasion and was hidden away on a farm. In the following years she is said to have gone alternately into melancholic-depressive and manic-excited states, with healthy intervals of up to one year's duration. Because of the cyclic course, Janet was diagnosed as manic-depressive by some Belgian psychiatrists. In those years I did not see her. Her father told me after the war that since the beginning of Janet's illness her mother had become all too closely tied up with her. This seemed only to have increased their mutual hostility, however. I also heard that Janet had been hospitalized twice and had received shock treatments, and that lately she had had longer, more or less healthy intervals between her attacks. When she was not depressed, Janet led a rather promiscuous sexual life and once, with her father's help, had an abortion. He approved of her sexual freedom and told her that "being so sick, she should get whatever pleasure she could out of life." All her affairs ended with her being deserted.

At the age of thirty, a short time after she had lost her father,

Janet came to the United States. This was when I saw her again. She told me that her current lover, a married American man, had promised to obtain a divorce and to marry her. As could be expected, this affair also broke up. Some weeks later, Janet became depressed. She lost weight, suffered from insomnia and anorexia, withdrew from her relatives and friends, developed ideas of unworthiness, and had to give up her work because of her thinking block and severe psychomotor retardation. After several months of depression, Janet suddenly went into a state of severe catatonic excitement with disorientation, confusion, bizarre behavior, and delusional ideas, mainly of poisoning. The whole episode, whose nature left no diagnostic doubts, lasted about a year. She needed several months of hospitalization, and had shock treatments followed by psychotherapy. Although her mother tried repeatedly to interfere, Janet accepted my therapeutic suggestion and tenaciously continued her treatment with the same psychiatrist, Dr. David Milrod, for about fifteen years.[3] She still sees him from time to time, and has never had another episode except for a brief period of depression. He worked with her very patiently and skillfully, and achieved an amazing success. In the course of her treatment Janet managed to obtain a very appropriate job, and during the last years she has made quite a career. Moreover, in her late thirties she married a very suitable partner, to whom she has made a good adjustment. No one can predict whether she will have relapses in the future. While her recovery has been surprisingly good, her compulsiveness and most of her early childhood phobias have hardly subsided.

II

Janet was one of those schizophrenic patients who, because of the cyclic course of her illness, had first been diagnosed manic-depressive (I could not find out what diagnosis had been made in the European hospitals). The depression with which her last episode started certainly resembled very much a simple, not delusional melancholic state. Only a careful psychoanalytic observer would have suspected that this was the beginning phase of a severe schizophrenic episode.

[3] I wish to express my gratitude to Dr. Milrod for discussing this case with me.

Janet's ambivalence conflicts revolved about her father and her previous lovers—evidently father substitutes—who had all first seduced and then abandoned her. Her most profound conflicts, however, arose from her masochistic dependency on her narcissistic, sadistically domineering and interfering mother, and from her futile efforts to liberate herself from this woman. The intensity and quality of her homosexual struggle with her mother, which had always been predominant in her conscious conflicts, made me most suspicious.

There was an additional feature which did not fit in with the picture of a melancholic. Not only in the initial stage but during the whole period of depression, Janet's repetitious "record" of self-accusations would often quite suddenly be interrupted by cold, sharply critical and derogative remarks, especially about her mother, but also about her father, her previous lovers, her relatives and friends. The frozen expression on her face, which never changed in accord with the content of her reproaches or self-reproaches, was likewise conspicuous. Her hostility at that time did not show any delusional paranoid features. However, in her frankly hostile comments she revealed excessively greedy, crude, and rather absurd demands, which she wanted to impose on these persons. Such comments were followed by bitter complaints about her inability to assert herself and attain the fulfillment of her pregenital sadistic wishes.

This leads me to significant features in Janet's disturbances of self-esteem, which differed from what we commonly see in melancholics, including paranoid or agitated depressive types. Her ideas of worthlessness revolved about her inability to work and to make a living—traits characteristic of her mother—or her inability to read and to pursue intellectual and artistic interests—deficiencies for which her mother had always blamed her father. Except for self-reproaches of this kind, Janet expressed hardly any guilt feelings. Even during her depression, she spoke quite matter-of-factly of her previous promiscuous sexual life, of her affairs with married men, and of her past abortion. In other words, Janet did not suffer from feelings of "sinfulness"; nor did she complain about her lack of feelings for others, about her inability to love, as melancholics commonly do. On the contrary, she blamed herself for being unable to make men "spoil" her, to be aggressive and retaliate against her past lovers by getting out of them whatever she wanted, e.g., expensive dresses and the like, and to attain dominance over them, over her mother, and over people in general. Janet's frank demands, her open cold hostility, and her feelings of shame and inferiority about her failure to be a "successful mistress" not only played an outstanding role during her depression, but survived her acute episode for some years.

During that later period it also became clearer that the core of her narcissistic conflicts were actually her identity conflicts. She felt that she would remain a complete "nonentity" unless she could aggressively assert her dominance over others. In contrast to her general integrity, decency, and generosity, and her compulsive concern with her work, these attitudes and ideas made at that time an even more absurd impression. Janet's ambitions to be a "successful mistress" had their origin in her parents' attitudes, especially the seductive behavior of her father who had encouraged her to permit herself complete sexual freedom and to get out of life all she wanted. In her childhood he had already called her his "princess" and promised her a wealthy husband who would give her everything that her loveliness deserved. The father's interest in beautiful women and his loud praise of his daughter's beauty accounted for Janet's unusual vanity and her overconcern with her physical appearance, which during the period of her depression acquired a hypochondriacal quality. For instance, Janet sometimes made quite bizarre remarks about the hair on her body and legs, or about her ugly eyes that looked like "jet buttons." She told me that she did not sweat "from within to without," as ordinary people do, but "from without to within." Evidently, such ideas also expressed her wish to establish an identity of her own.

The strange mixture of Janet's compulsive character traits with impulsive behavior and ambitions to become a successful beautiful mistress reflected her identifications with her immoral father, the successful philanderer, with his values, with his mistresses, and also with her beautiful, vain mother, and was expressive of the confused parental standards and of the contradictory parental attitudes toward her.

Very early Janet had learned about her parents' past. At a children's party, at the age of about eight or earlier, she had overheard some ladies gossip about her mother's affair with her father, the divorce, and the first husband's suicide. Janet had not fully understood the story, but she remembered that at that time she believed that her mother's first husband had actually been her father, and that her mother and the second husband had caused his death. This belief, which not only made her "different from other children" but also served to protect her from guilt feelings about the close incestuous ties between her and her father, developed into a paranoid delusion during one of her excited catatonic episodes. When her father brought her to the hospital, she jumped out of the car and ran away, crying frantically: "You are not my father, you are a murderer! Help, help, he is going to kill me!" (The father was actually held by the police and arrested.) I may add that Janet's panicky and paranoid reactions to her father seemed to screen her underlying fears of her cruel mother and her masochistic surrender to her. The father had in reality tried to protect her from her mother's murderous hostility.

We can now draw an approximate picture of those features in Janet's depressive syndrome which were characteristic of a schizophrenic rather than a melancholic type of depression. Her history reveals the special environmental factors which influenced the vicissitudes of her object relations and identifications. It displays the origins of her instinctual and narcissistic conflicts and their significant role in the development of her psychotic illness.

The mother's complete neglect of her daughter during infancy, her disciplinary, domineering behavior, and later on her narcissistic ties to Janet fixated the child on a sadomasochistic, pregenital, narcissistic-symbiotic level and led first to the early development of severe phobias and later to a compulsion neurosis. They prevented the establishment of a normal sense of identity and of a satisfactory regulation of self-esteem in the little girl.

In addition, her father's overindulgence, his seductiveness, and recurrent abandonments precluded a renunciation of her incestuous desires and the establishment of solid defenses in the ego. These confusing narcissistic parental attitudes, moreover, kept her from building up affectionate stable object relations and successful sublimations.

Feeling neglected, deserted, and deprived of true tenderness by both parents, Janet no doubt already developed depressive states in early childhood, which even then showed schizoid emotional qualities and were expressive of a terrible lonesomeness.

This early history is quite different from what we hear from melancholics, who frequently recall an early phase of parental over-indulgence, followed by experiences of disillusionment and abandonment. In addition to this, Janet was severely traumatized in her beginning latency by overhearing and misunderstanding gossip about her parents' past. I emphasized its effect on her childhood fantasies and on her later paranoid delusions. I also spoke of the traumatic influence of her emigration and the German invasion, and mentioned the event in London that precipitated her first breakdown. I believe that in the history of cyclothymics, such an accumulation of traumatic experiences is not commonly observed.

Of particular interest is the fact that the specific superego and ego pathology also made it appearance during the depressive phase of Janet's episode and was conspicuous enough to permit a correct differential diagnosis at that time. In spite of her severely retarded state, Janet would find a mode of frankly and coldly expressing her hostile attitudes and intentions, although only by virtue of complaining about her inability to gratify her aggressive demands and achieve her ruthless goals. This type of self-reproach pointed to her complete inability to recognize the immorality of these goals. It revealed the defectiveness and deterioration of her superego and the partial retransformation of her intersystemic conflicts between ego and superego demands into an intrasystemic struggle between her sadistic and masochistic strivings (Hartmann, 1950). Hence, what Janet actually complained about during her depression was her masochistic surrender to her mother and to male or female substitute objects—a surrender which had been victorious over her wishes for revengeful, sadistic self-assertion and dominance over these objects.

I may add that the depressive clinging to objects also looked different in Janet from that of melancholics, who usually complain about their helplessness and their dependence on others. Janet simply tried not only to lean on other persons, but to exploit the services of those who attempted to help her. Evidently, she derived some satisfaction from the feeling that at least in this passive-indirect way she could achieve some dominance over them. Later on, when her paranoid delusions developed, she accused the same helpful persons of stealing her most precious possessions and of trying to poison her.

In spite of similarities in the main syndrome, the structure of Janet's depressive conflict is quite different from the superego-ego conflicts in melancholics, whose superego is excessively strict and cruel but not defective and deteriorated. The differences underline not only the failure of neutralization (Hartmann, 1953) and the intensity of the destructive drives, but also the particular vicissitudes they have undergone in the development of schizophrenic-depressive pathology.

III

In cases of psychotic depression which present differential diagnostic problems, a thorough psychoanalytically oriented exploration of the developmental history and past pathology is of greatest value for the establishment of a correct diagnosis. We may need many interviews with members of the patient's family; in these we must make particular efforts to understand the parental attitudes in the past and present, and their effect on the patient's emotional, instinctual, and intellectual development and behavior, and on the building up of his object relations, his identifications, his sublimations.

Furthermore, I tried to show how attempts to reconstruct the patient's history on the basis of such data obtained from the patient and his family may call attention to more or less subtle but significant symptomatic features which reveal the specific structure of the underlying depressive conflicts and thus may permit a correct diagnosis. In Janet's case I emphasized the early onset of conspicuous affective disturbances, her terrors, her emotional emptiness, her stiffness, her boredom, and her severe compulsiveness.

Regarding her current state, I pointed particularly to the content of her ideas of worthlessness, which superficially sounded like the usual "record" of melancholics' self-accusations but actually were of quite a different nature. I discussed the conspicuous lack of feelings of "sinfulness," which are usually so predominant in "acute" depression, and spoke of the frank display of her ambitions to become a rather exploitative mistress, and her feelings of inferiority due to her failure to live up to these glorified ambitions. Finally, from these special disturbances of self-esteem, I drew certain inferences with regard to the structure of this patient's narcissistic conflicts as compared with those of melancholics, and hence with regard to the differences in their superego and ego pathology.

The question arises how far these observations made in Janet's case are characteristic of schizophrenic depressions in general. With regard to the early onset of her affective disturbances, Janet reminded me of another female patient whom I had also seen frequently during her latency years. At the age of twenty-one, this patient developed a severe schizophrenic process that rapidly led to a complete deterioration. As a child she, too, already seemed to have been in a chronic state of depression. The utterly bland quality of her affects, her emptiness and "stupidity," and her inability to relate frequently provoked her playmates and teachers to give her beatings, which she accepted silently, though with signs of terror.

Except for the patients who already show signs of a manifest psychosis in childhood, however, the early onset of such a conspicuous affective disturbance is by no means characteristic of schizophrenics in general; nor is it of those who later on develop severe states of depression. More commonly outspoken emotional pathology develops later, with the onset or in the course of their manifest psychotic disorder, but its forerunners may become apparent in the entire emotional and personality development of these patients.

The absence of feelings of moral worthlessness, which I described in Janet's case, is characteristic of many but by no means all schizophrenic depressives. Among them we also find patients who, at least at certain stages of their illness, suffer from severe guilt feelings or even from delusions of sinfulness. These cases present particularly difficult differential diagnostic problems. In some, the ideas of "sinfulness" may later on give way to feelings of inferiority and of being a "nonentity," such as I discussed above. Sometimes ideas of sinfulness may even combine with complaints about the inability to pursue certain glorified aggressive goals, such as, in Janet's case, the ambition to be a "successful ruthless mistress." These absurd complaints may then be completely split off from concomitant ideas of moral worthlessness.

In my book on *The Self and the Object World* (1964), I briefly discussed the disturbances of ego and superego development and identifications in schizophrenics, and compared them with those in melancholics (pp. 208-210). I also described "the type of schizophrenics in whose states of depression the guilt conflicts may be absent or recede in favor of paranoid fears of exposure, while feelings of shame and inferiority, self consciousness and fears or feelings of loss of identity frequently appear as a characteristic triad of symptoms" (p. 198). In the same chapter, I spoke of "a sadistic-criminal or a glamorous-grandiose pseudo ideal, which . . . certain acting-out paranoid psychotic patients" may develop (p. 210).

Two of my brief case examples in that chapter are pertinent to my current discussion, because these two male schizophrenic patients suffered from intermittent paranoid depressive and agitated states, which in the first case finally led to suicide. These patients did not present differential diagnostic problems. In the present context, however, I want to emphasize that Janet's ambition to be a successful mistress was the counterpart of the sadistic types of gangster ideal which both these male patients had developed. In them, it was likewise maintained during their states of depression, in the form of wishful fantasies and feelings of inferiority about their inability to pursue these aims. In contrast to Janet's symptoms, these manifestations were combined with paranoid fears of exposure or mild delusions of persecution.

The lack of paranoid delusions during the depressive period may, to some extent, account for the diagnostic difficulties in cases like Janet's (see also Chapter 10). I may mention here that in some obsessional-compulsive neurotics, especially those with paranoid trends, we also find such a glorification of complete instinctual freedom and ruthlessness. In these patients such attitudes are expressive of their rebellion against the restrictions imposed on their ego by their compulsiveness; they are not ego syntonic and arouse severe guilt feelings.

IV

Both melancholic and schizophrenic depressives may manifest ideas of reference and persecution and corresponding hallucinations. As Kraepelin (1913) already pointed out, in contrast to paranoid schizophrenics, the cyclothymic paranoid depressives feel they ought to be persecuted. They deserve the persecution because of their "sins." This underscores the lack of conscious guilt feelings which paranoid depressive schizophrenics commonly show, at least at a more advanced stage of their illness. This has not only diagnostic but also important therapeutic implications.

In a paranoid depressive schizophrenic, an untimely hint at the denial of guilt conflicts may arouse a sudden paranoid rage attack. Such a patient, a woman who suffered from circular depressive and hypomanic states, once during a severe depression told me a dream which clearly evidenced her guilt conflict about having neglected her little boy. When I pointed this out to her, she flew into a violent rage, denied having any guilt feelings or any reason for them, and spoke in a grandiose way about her outstandingly high ethical standards and behavior. At the same time she blamed me, her family, and others for our lack of integrity; and she told ugly, distorted stories about her acquaintances. This patient also showed a rather parasitical behavior during her depressions—much more, indeed, than Janet did—and with a grandiose attitude, as though what others did for her were due to her outstanding personality. All these attitudes, which I described above, helped me to solve the differential diagnostic problem posed by this woman, who had likewise been regarded as a manic-depressive with paranoid trends.

Even more grandiose parasitic-psychopathic was the behavior of a schizophrenic young man, whose recurrent attacks of catatonic excitement always started with states of paralyzing depression that frequently made him unable to get out of bed. This patient would then expect to be treated at home without payment by "the best psychiatrists of New York." He lied and cheated to get money and to obtain unbelievable amounts of drugs from many physicians. Exploiting everybody around him, he justified his parasitism by pointing to the severity of his depression. As long as this patient could walk around, he would turn up at any time of the day and want to stay as long as he "needed" it.

This seems to be characteristic of the type of schizophrenic depressives who show frankly grandiose attitudes and behavior even during periods of depression. Because of their psychomotor retardation, melancholics may also have difficulties in keeping appointments, being punctual, and leaving when a session is finished. But I have never seen any melancholics, including paranoid types, impose themselves on their therapist, their friends, or their families as this type of schizophrenic does during periods of severe depression.

A certain group of patients do not show manifestations of a psychotic depression but seek treatment because they suffer from recurring severe depressive states, sometimes alternating with hypomanic conditions. In their case, we may have difficulty in deciding whether they are neurotics or mild psychotics and, if the latter, whether they belong to the cyclothymic or the schizophrenic group of disorders. In impulsive, acting-out patients, who show predominantly hysterical attitudes and behavior, we can usually exclude at least an affective disorder. In manic-depressives, hysterical traits need not be absent, but they are never predominant in the clinical picture. It is frequently more difficult to decide whether such patients are pregenitally fixated, impulse-ridden character disorders or acting-out schizophrenics with hysterical features.

In the first case, they often are accessible and responsive to psychoanalytic treatment conducted in a slow, careful, patient way, whereas this type of schizophrenic is usually unable to tolerate an analytic situation. I may add that in Janet as well as in other schizophrenics, I could sometimes observe pseudo-hysterical behavior, which was actually expressive of the inappropriateness of their affects. In both schizophrenic and melancholic depressives the physical symptoms are mostly psychosomatic rather than hysterical, but in schizophrenics, in whom such symptoms may very rapidly appear and vanish, they combine more frequently with hypochondriacal fears and complaints.

In my experience, certain compulsive depressives present even greater differential diagnostic problems, especially those with paranoid features who show a conspicuous emotional detachment. If they are obsessional-compulsive neurotics, however, their affective disturbances are likely to yield to a consistent analysis of their defenses, especially of their isolation mechanisms. In those who actually suffer from an affective disorder, we observe emotional withdrawal during times of depression, but in spite of their compulsive traits, their capacity for warm affectionate relationships usually returns as soon as the depressive period has ended. This description coincides with earlier observations; e.g., Campbell (1953) quotes Kretschmer as saying, "the average cycloid . . . has a sociable, friendly, realistic and accommodating feel about him. Because his temperament swings with that of the milieu, there is for him . . . no tragically exacerbated conflict, but a life in things themselves, . . . a capacity for living, feeling and suffering with his surroundings" (p. 33).

What characterizes the schizophrenic's compulsiveness is the opposite: a cool formality and politeness, stiffness and affectation, a remoteness and lack of emotional warmth and spontaneity. In Janet's case, these suspicious traits and emotional qualities had already appeared in her childhood. They have markedly improved but are still in evidence.

In manic-depressives, however, I have never found a childhood history of such terrors, of such early and severe compulsive symptoms as in Janet and other schizophrenic cases, although during latency cyclothymics may begin to show compulsive character traits. In the latter there are, furthermore, no such bizarre combinations or rapid alternations between compulsive and impulsive attitudes and behavior (except for the uncontrolled behavior during manic attacks), between sexual promiscuity and puritanism, between decency, altruism, and frank, aggressive selfishness and greed.

In seemingly compulsive, paranoid-depressive patients who are actually mild latent schizophrenics, the basic emotional pathology usually survives the depression and the treatment, although the latter may greatly improve the patient's ability to relate. This is the type of patient who may at first seem to be accessible to analytic therapy, but then in the course of treatment he may suddenly develop a manifest psychotic episode, especially if he is not very cautiously treated, or else not make progress and become ultimately a therapeutic failure. In such cases a thorough study of the patients' psychopathology, particularly their specific superego-ego pathology, the quality of their object relations, and the nature of the instinctual conflicts may offer sufficient criteria for a correct differential diagnosis.

V

I shall once more define the differences between the depressive conflicts of the schizophrenic and the melancholic from the dynamic and structural points of view. I must re-emphasize that my comparison does not extend to schizophrenic and manic-depressive psychoses in general, but is limited to schizophrenic and melancholic depressions.

During the initial stage of a melancholic depression and likewise in the case of a "simple depression," the manic-depressive patient may be very irritable and frankly express his dissatisfaction with himself as well as with his love objects and with the whole world. As his ambivalence conflict increases, however, his destructive drive impulses tend to become completely absorbed by the superego or the critical ego, and then turned against the self—a process which protects the ego from a discharge of hostility onto the external world.

Evidently, the intensity of the destructive forces and the defectiveness and deterioration of the superego and of the defense system prevent even severely depressive schizophrenics from turning their aggression consistently against their own selves (except when they are in a state of catatonic stupor). Despite their psychomotor retardation and their ideas of unworthiness, their hostility thus tends to break through to the surface and to erupt in some form, though devoid of a strong feeling tone and frequently screened by a glorification, rationalization, or idealization of aggressive goals and actions, the true nature of which is denied.[4] This may lend conspicuously absurd qualities to the ideas of unworthiness in such patients.

To put it in structural terms: both the melancholic and the schizophrenic depressive may suffer from intersystemic conflicts—conflicts between superego and ego—as well as from intrasystemic conflicts—conflicts within the ego (Hartmann, 1950). But in the melancholic these conflicts reflect the discrepancy between his overly high ethical, moral, cultural, and intellectual standards and the pathologically distorted, worthless, or even "sinful" image of his own self.

In the schizophrenic depressive the regressive retransformation of the ego ideal into glorified wishful images of a powerful, ruthless, sadistic self permits aggressive fantasies and goals to enter the realm of the ego and to attain consciousness. As a result of these pathological processes, the conflict of the schizophrenic depressive is in part an expression of the discrepancy between such pregenital-sadistic ambitions and the image of his weak, helpless, masochistic self.

[4] Lange (1928) also mentions such sudden, unexpected impulsive actions with inappropriate affect as characteristic of seemingly melancholic schizophrenic depressions (p. 198).

I am aware that for reasons of clarification, my description of the structural differences between the melancholic and the schizophrenic depressive conflicts oversimplifies matters, and thus does not do justice to the variety and complexity of individual cases or to the different stages of illness. What I wished to underscore is the fact that schizophrenics tend to discharge their instinctual drive impulses, and especially their destructive ones, simultaneously or in rapid alternation on external objects and on the self. This tendency finds a symptomatic expression even during states of severe depression. It helps us to understand that schizophrenics, unless they are in a paralyzing depression, may easily alternate between suicidal and homicidal impulses and actions.

These dynamic and structural differences reflect the differences in the object relations and in the psychotic identifications of melancholic and schizophrenic depressives which I discussed in Chapter 10. In schizophrenic depressives, we may find a deficiency of object and self constancy and a tendency to fusions between self and object images—trends that result in a complete mixture of early types of projective and introjective identifications or a rapid vacillation between them. The patient's opposing sadistic and masochistic strivings may be split up and projectively attached to different object images, and then, by virtue of introjective processes, set up in the patient's opposing images of his own self. As paranoid trends color or change the depressive picture or gain the upper hand, the "ruthless"-sadistic self images are likely to become reprojected and reattached to external objects, which then turn into threatening, hateful, persecutory figures—such as in the one episode in which Janet's real father turned into the "murderer." At that stage, the deterioration of the ego and the process of deneutralization (Hartmann, 1953) may advance to the point where the ego is overwhelmed by destructive forces, and the patient, going from a depressive into an excited catatonic state, becomes manifestly homicidal or suicidal, or both.

A clearer clinical and theoretical understanding of the different psychopathology, the different conflicts and mechanisms involved in these two groups of disorders is exceedingly helpful in the treatment of mild or latent psychotic or borderline cases as well as in the case of patients who suffer from florid psychotic episodes. Whatever treatment method we choose in the individual case, the results will not be satisfactory unless we recognize the nature of the illness and understand the specific id, ego, and superego pathology with which we are dealing.

This becomes particularly evident in the rare type of psychotic patient who recovers from a schizophrenic episode with his ego sufficiently intact to permit him to undergo a more or less modified analytic treatment. In such cases the emotional responses and the therapeutic effect of correct interpretations are sometimes amazing, and may enable the patient to conclude his treatment successfully after several years.

Usually, psychotic patients, including latent psychotic or borderline cases, do best in a consistent treatment of very long duration, such as in Janet's case. (Periods of interruption are sometimes advisable, and may at times be necessitated by temporary hospitalizations.)

This seems to be especially valid in the case of manic-depressives and of schizophrenics who suffer from recurring severe states of depression. Those who at the end of a depressive period go into hypomanic states tend to stop treatment at that time, but promptly return when another depression sets in. Manic-depressives, including paranoid types, usually want to stay with the same therapist and should do so, since they are apt to develop an ambivalent, but intense personal attachment to him. Schizophrenics, whose object relations are on a more regressive level, commonly show in rapid vacillation clinging, remote, and hostile attitudes toward their therapist. For this reason, and because of their severe superego and ego pathology and their lack of object and self constancy, they may stop treatment even during a period of depression, or run to another therapist when a new depression sets in. The tendency to change therapists or even to see two therapists seems to be especially characteristic of paranoid depressive schizophrenics. In some such patients, a change of therapist may be advisable. (This issue will be discussed in Chapter 13.)

The differences in the transference of melancholic and schizophrenic depressives point to the different kinds of counterattitudes that the therapist must develop in these two groups of disorders. Because of their libidinal impoverishment, all psychotics and especially those who are in a state of depression need some degree of emotional warmth on the part of the therapist, but above all they need a great deal of patience. Whereas melancholics require mainly gentleness, respect, and encouragement, even with severely depressive and anxious schizophrenics we must sometimes be very firm, or even strict, e.g., when they suddenly want to stop treatment, or behave in an excessively parasitical manner. Setting limits to such attitudes in the patient actually means lending him our ego and superego. Thus, such strictness does not imply that the therapist may not temporarily permit such patients to lean on his ego and "borrow" its strength.

Discussions and interpretations of these attitudes do not in general become meaningful or effective before recovery from the depression or the whole psychotic episode. In suitable cases it may lead to a search for the infantile origin of the patient's instinctual and narcissistic conflicts, and of the past maldevelopment of his object relations and identifications. These patients need a long time before they can admit and understand the defects and contradictions in their value systems, and the corresponding pathological ego attitudes. I mentioned above the paranoid rage which a female paranoid depressive-schizophrenic patient developed when I made an untimely remark about her guilt conflicts. On the other hand, we must very cautiously wait before we can directly approach the melancholic's hostility conflicts.

My brief comments on the different problems arising in the treatment of melancholic and schizophrenic depressive patients were intended to underscore our need for a better understanding of the differences in their psychopathology, differences which determine the correct method of approaching them therapeutically.

12

Transference Problems in the Psychoanalytic Treatment of Severely Depressive Patients

This chapter is devoted specifically to transference problems in severely depressive patients who are in psychoanalytic treatment. The patients to whom I shall refer had several features in common: their entire life problems hinged upon their predisposition to severe depressive conditions; they sought treatment because of such states; and they were accessible to psychoanalytic treatment. Otherwise they presented widely differing syndromes: chronic depressives, patients with irregular mood vacillations, depressives with severe anxiety states, patients with hypochondriacal and paranoid forms of depression, schizoid types of depression, and patients with severe reactive depressive states. In other words, most of these patients were borderline cases, ranging from borderline to both manic-depressive and schizophrenic psychosis.

In all these cases the infantile history had a rather characteristic pathogenic pattern and played a decisive role in the illness, although

---

This chapter is based on two previously published papers. The first one was prepared as a contribution to the symposium on "The Widening Scope of Indications for Psychoanalysis," held at the Arden House Conference of the New York Psychoanalytic Society, May, 1954. It was published in the *Journal of the American Psychoanalytic Association,* 2:595-606, 1954. The second paper, entitled "Interaction between Psychotic Partners: I. Manic-Depressive Partners," was published in *Neurotic Interaction in Marriage,* edited by V. W. Eisenstein. New York: Basic Books, 1956, pp. 125-134.

the influence of hereditary factors was rather evident. This tends to confirm that the depressive constitution is much farther spread out than the clinical disorder as such. But the weight of their heredity and the severe pathology in such patients justify the question—even if they are accessible to analysis—how far we can accomplish the real goal of analytic treatment: structural change, resulting not only in a symptomatic but a causal cure. In other words, is it possible to bring about a change in their predisposition to severe depressive states or breakdowns?

Certain clinical experiences help to relieve such doubts. A woman now forty-seven years old had suffered from the age of sixteen to twenty-eight from typical depressive phases for which she had been regularly hospitalized, though without ever getting psychotherapeutic treatment. When she was twenty-eight her father died. Half a year later she began her first love affair, and after two years without relapse into illness she married. Despite tragic experiences, such as the suicides of her mother and her only girlfriend, she has never again had a real breakdown. But she still shows conspicuous mood vacillations and suffers from mild depressive states. Such cases are not so rare. If life can achieve so much, analysis should be able to do even more.

With this optimistic attitude let me turn to the discussion of problems arising in the analytic treatment of such patients.

The indistinct but convenient term "borderline" epitomizes certain common features in the personality structure and the devices used by such patients in conflict solutions (Kernberg, 1967). These patients show ego distortions and superego defects, disturbances in their object relations, and a pathology of affects beyond what we find in ordinary neurotics. For this reason they usually need many years of analysis with slow, patient, consistent work in the area of ego and superego functioning, with great attention to their particular methods of defense and to the affective responses in which these defenses find special expression. This work is so difficult because such patients call into play auxiliary defense and restitution mechanisms which impair their reality testing to a greater or lesser extent, engaging at the same time the outside world, and in particular the significant objects, for the purpose of their pathological conflict solutions. This can be clearly observed in the analysis of psychotic, especially schizophrenic, patients during periods when they do not show manifest psychotic symptoms. I have dealt with this issue in great detail in my Freud Anniversary Lecture on *Psychotic Conflict and Reality* (1967), which in many respects complements the points made in this chapter.

For the reasons outlined above, severely depressive cases require modifications of the usual technique, which neurotic patients do not need. To be more specific: depressives try to recover their lost ability to love and to function by dint of excessive magic love from their love object. As a melancholic patient once put it: "Love is oxygen to me." For this purpose, they use varying defensive devices. Failing to get such help from without, they may retreat from their love object or even from the object world and continue the struggle within themselves.

In the course of analysis, the analyst inevitably becomes the *central love object* and the center of the depressive conflict. With advancing analysis, the patient may therefore develop even more serious depressive states, and in general, for long periods of time, go into states of ego and id regression deeper than ever before. In other words, we may be confronted with a special variety of what we call negative therapeutic reactions.

Of course, this state of affairs causes great technical difficulties, especially with regard to the handling of the transference. How are we to cope with them? How far and in which way is the analyst supposed to deviate from the usual procedures and respond to the pathological, defensive needs of the patient for active emotional or even practical help from without? Is it dangerous to let his sadomasochistic fantasies, his profoundly ambivalent impulses toward the analyst come to the fore?

I may introduce the discussion of these problems with some more general remarks. Manic-depressive patients do not seek treatment when they are hypomanic or manic because in such states they lack insight. But even though the analytic process advances best during so-called healthy intervals once the patients are in analysis, they usually do not come for treatment during such periods. One patient, whose third depressive phase had suddenly subsided after he had managed to break his leg, decided to do something drastic for himself. But he soon changed his mind; he now felt "too well," after all. Evidently, the restitution processes in such patients work too well; i.e., the denial mechanisms involved constitute strong resistances to treatment.

Depressive patients regularly *begin treatment in a depressed state.* The prerequisite for any sort of psychotherapy with depressives is, of course, a sufficient transference basis. In my experience with such patients, this can often be evaluated during the very first interview. Questions regarding the patient's feeling about the mutual rapport are indicated and usually elicit a frank, simple response. It is mostly yes or no. Depressives tend to establish either an immediate, intense rapport, or none. This makes it very hard and risky, for instance, to refer them to another therapist, who may immediately become the "second best."

In the case of typical, periodic depression, the treatment starts off best in the beginning or end stage of depression, i.e., in the stages where the withdrawal is not yet or no longer at its peak. The therapeutic approach to depressive patients depends, of course, on the individual case and the special type of depression. But in some respects the course of analysis shows common, characteristic features in all such cases.

This I would like to sketch out by briefly describing a rather typical development of transference manifestations and corresponding symptomatic reactions during the analysis of a depressive borderline patient. In so doing I shall neglect many individual details in order to show what I consider the characteristic treatment phases: the initial, spurious transference success; the ensuing period of hidden, negative transference with corresponding negative therapeutic reactions, i.e., waxing and more severe states of depression; the stage of dangerous, introjective defenses and narcissistic retreat; and the end phase of gradual, constructive conflict solution. The case tends to confirm my impression that analytic work is most successful with patients who, when not depressed, show a mixture of mildly hypomanic and compulsive attitudes.

I

Mr. R., a brilliant scientist in his forties, suffered since childhood from irregular states of depression, severe anxieties, and functional intestinal symptoms. When depressed he struggled against the threat of passivity and retardation by starting hectic sexual and professional activities. He was thus often simultaneously depressed, severely anxious, excited, and obsessionally overactive rather than retarded. His personality reflected his conflicting strivings. He was a warm, appealing, lovable human being, eager to please, but proud of being a fighter and of owing his remarkable career to nobody but himself.

The patient had lost his severely depressive mother in early childhood by an accident. After her death, his father developed a chronic depressive state, gave up home and work, and placed his children with foster parents who brought them up in an indifferent emotional atmosphere. The patient's conflicts revolved around his disappointing marital relationship and his unsettled status on the staff of his university. Before consulting me he had been in psychotherapy, with little improvement.

He selected me from among other analysts whom he had met socially because I seemed to be not only competent but "so warm, so motherly, and unaggressive." He had felt in immediate rapport with me. Thus the patient started his treatment with a suspiciously strong enthusiasm for the analyst and for his future analytic work. His transference fantasies reflected his idealization of and closeness to the analyst, who had become the most valued part of himself. In the starlight of this initial positive transference the patient's condition improved rapidly. He was feeling better, that is, more hopeful, than in years. His work seemed easier; he felt closer to his wife, who now appeared to be much more acceptable. Despite continued mood vacillations and anxieties, the patient went on feeling subjectively markedly improved for at least a year. The analysis developed seemingly well, with dramatic revivals of certain traumatic childhood events, in a general atmosphere of optimism and of admiring, affectionate gratitude to the analyst who was giving so much.

So far, the course of events and the transference success would not differ much from what we may see in any case of hysteria, were it not for the highly illusory, magic quality of the patient's transference feelings. There was an exaggerated idealization and obstinate denial of possible or visible shortcomings of the analyst. An important element was the patient's refusal to see that despite his subjective feelings of improvement, no drastic objective results had as yet been achieved. He just felt ever so much more hopeful. He knew that his analysis was but a promise, that it would take a very long time, but he believed in ultimate success, though in the distant future. This attitude, the neglect of the present situation, is very characteristic. Instead of realizing and accepting the past in their present life, depressives live on hope for or fear of the future.

After about a year, the situation began to change as Mr. R. entered a stage of insidiously growing disappointment. The beginning menopause of his wife precipitated severe depressive reactions in him. For the first time there emerged fantasies and doubts about the advanced age of the analyst, her fading charms, her dwindling sexual and mental functions, her ability to give. Such signals of irresistible disillusionment entered consciousness only sporadically, to be followed by immediate attempts to retransform the analyst into a good, ideal, loving image. At that time feelings of hopelessness and doubts about his own advanced age, the biological impairment of his sexual and intellectual abilities, and the like, increased. His emotional state and the transference manifestations indicated that the ambivalence conflict began to assume dangerous proportions and was becoming focused on the analyst. But the patient still used his wife as a scapegoat for his hostility. He now felt sexually and emotionally repelled by her and withdrew from her, feeling a mixture of anger at her demands for love and sex and intense guilt. He was frankly resentful that he could no longer find comfort in sexual escapades, as in previous years. His social relations also deteriorated. He suspected correctly that his intense absorption in the analysis might account for his loss of interest in other persons and matters. While he persisted in blaming his wife for his worsened condition, he became even more closely tied up with the analyst than he had previously been.

There followed a long, typical period during which the patient lived only in the aura of the analyst and withdrew from other personal relations to a dangerous extent. The transference was characterized by very dependent, masochistic attitudes toward the analyst, but also by growing demands that I display self-sacrificing devotion in return. Feelings of rejection by the analyst provoked brief outbursts of defiance, the slogan being: "I don't need you." His transference fantasies assumed an increasingly ambivalent, sadomasochistic coloring, with corresponding fantasy and childhood material coming to the fore. In rapidly changing moods, the patient accused the analyst alternately of being too seductive, or of being herself frustrated and sexually needy, or of being cold and rejecting. To any professional failure or success, as to any "harmful" or "helpful" interpretation, he now reacted with depression and anxiety.

In some cases this period is especially critical because of the patients' exhausting, sadomasochistic provocations. They may unconsciously blackmail the analyst by playing on his guilt feelings, hoping in this way to get the longed-for response. Failing to do so, they may try to elicit from the analyst a show of power, strictness, punitive anger, serving the alternate purpose of getting support for or relief from the relentless superego pressure.

In the case of Mr. R., my taking a spring vacation opened up a new and even worse phase. The patient felt abandoned by me, as he had been by his mother, whom he had lost in the spring at the age of seven. He was thrown into a severe depression. Suspecting correctly that I "left" him to present a paper at a meeting, he decided defiantly, as in his childhood, to make himself independent. He began to write a scientific book which would outdo the one I was allegedly writing. From then on his book became a devouring, obsessional interest: on the one hand, it was the great ideal goal in his life; on the other, it was a monster which tortured him day and night with depression and anxieties. What he expected and was supposed to write was the best work ever done on the subject. Whatever he had written prior to that time appeared to be completely worthless. The book period represented a definite, narcissistic withdrawal from me and the world in general. He had indeed tried to replace me with a book of which in fantasy he had robbed me.

His severe intestinal symptoms, with pain radiating into leg and genital, and the correlated analytic material at this time indicated the underlying incorporation and ejection fantasies. He equated what he called the frightening, painful "lump in his stomach" with the analyst, with his mother, and with the book whose subject related directly to his mother's violent death. At the same time, this "introject," the lump, represented a "baby-penis" of which his penis was, in his fantasy, an outside extension. He wanted to throw up and deposit (ejaculate) the lump on the analyst's lap, but was afraid of dying in this act. Whenever he felt freer of pain and anxiety, he was afraid to lose the lump and be "empty." He was equally frightened of ever terminating the analysis or finishing the book. The final success would be the end of him. At this point the analyst's deliberate, supportive counterattitude helped him over the most critical stage. I showed a very active interest in his book, as far as my vague familiarity with the subject permitted. In other words, I shared the book with him and won him back by allowing a temporary situation of participation.

A phase of persistent transference interpretation, along with the analysis of deep homosexual and preoedipal fantasy material, opened up. The tide turned at last when the primal scene material and his sadomasochistic identifications with both parents could be worked through in the transference. At this point I may stop the case report. Much credit must be given to this patient for his unusual insight and his ceaseless cooperation. He has become a respected member of his professional group and is identified with it. But his marital relationship did not improve at all, even though his sexual life became very satisfactory. In fact, his wife had a psychotic break which made their marital life very difficult but prevented the patient from divorcing her. Whenever he felt unable to cope with this situation, he returned for some weeks or months of treatment.

II

In this section I shall examine the object choices and personal relationships of borderline or psychotic depressive patients, with particular emphasis on the pathological interplay between manic-depressives and their partners. This material demonstrates the degree to which the partner influences the patient's state of mind and therefore the treatment situation, the nature of what is ransferred to the analyst, and the implicit danger to the patient's therapeutic progress when the analyst is cast in the role of the partner.

The personal and marital relationships of depressives often appear to be very good and affectionate. As long as they are not ill, manic-depressives can be delightful companions, since they may show emotional warmth, sexual responsiveness, a capacity for rich sublimations—in short, features which greatly attract their partners. If we examine the marital relations in such cases more closely, however, we can detect the pathological elements which harbor the germ of future breakdowns of the depressive. We find that the seemingly overclose, overwarm marital relationship has actually symbiotic features. The partners greatly depend and lean on each other. They cling too much to each other.

The most favorable constellation seems to be in couples where this mutual dependence has a sound basis either in practical collaboration, as, for instance, in professional work, or in a sharing of interests and hobbies. But in many cases the apparent overcloseness and mutual overdependence of the couple are combined with a striking lack of common interests. The partners are in great need of each other, but have nothing to say to each other, even though each may have a rich, resourceful ego and actually have a great deal to talk about. This situation promotes a type of marital conflict that is bound to precipitate depressive periods in the manic-depressive partner.

When we have the opportunity to investigate the personality structure of either partner more thoroughly from the psychoanalytic point of view, we find that both, as a rule, are preoedipally fixated character types, though often of quite different varieties. Such couples may develop a sort of "oral" interplay which may increasingly build up mutual demands to the point of inevitable disappointment and breakdown in one or the other partner. Sometimes both are manic-depressives who may have to be hospitalized alternately. In other cases one partner stands up amazingly well during the depressive period of the other, but immediately becomes depressed when the other recovers.

Many depressives are very masochistic in their choice of partners. As long as they are not ill, they tend to ward off their own infantile oral demands by playing the active, self-sacrificing, but also domineering mother. In return for their practical support they expect the emotional support they need so badly for maintaining their self-esteem. In other words, to the manic-depressive partner the love object represents above all a superego figure. He needs a highly overvalued love object in which all his love is invested, for which he is ready to sacrifice everything in the hope of getting love and praise.

Indeed, the partner is to the manic-depressive the medium through which he lives and which he needs for his mental balance. Frequently, however, we see that the so-called healthy partner is actually the more passive, more selfish, more frankly demanding character type. He is glad to repay the services rendered him by expressing his deep gratitude and praising his partner. But his attitude is often not backed up by his practical behavior.

Of course, there may be all kinds of combinations in the division of the mother and child roles, such as one partner supplying money and material goods, the other intellectual and spiritual nutrition, and the like. This precarious balance is naturally apt to be easily upset. Frequently the neurotic partner, having tired of his own role in this barter agreement, takes more and more advantage of the other's masochistic attitudes and becomes increasingly dependent and demanding. This is what appears to precipitate the depressive conflict in the other. Thus, in cases where both partners can be studied, it is not surprising to learn that the patient's complaints about the love object, which underlie the depressive self-accusations, hit precisely at the core of the marital problem.

For example, a manic-depressive social worker, Mrs. S., blamed her husband for being childish, selfish in a primitive way, although he pretended to be an idealist and to share her political and social beliefs. It was her opinion that her husband clung to her merely because he was weak and passive; that he had chosen her only because he admired her higher social background, her better education, and her earning capacity. She felt sure that now that he had obtained a well-paying job himself, he would like to get rid of her so that he could marry some simple, stupid girl who would constantly wait on him and cook for him. The husband denied all this. He made a great showing of concern for her, but in fact failed completely when it came to bolstering her during her depressive periods.

The woman suffered a relapse at a time when I was unable to take care of her. Transferred to another psychiatrist, she was given shock treatment, and a week after being discharged from the hospital she committed suicide. The husband immediately went into a brief hypomanic state. After he had sobered up, he came to consult me about some sexual difficulties. It was at this time that he confessed he had never really cared for his wife. He admitted having chosen her because she was superior to him. While admiring her genuinely, he felt unable to love her and to live up to her high standards. Rather brazenly, he stated that he was glad to be rid of her. Immediately after her death he moved to the city, boarded their child with some friends, and took to consorting with prostitutes. After calming down, he became acquainted with a simple girl who was a homebody with no intellectual interests. She would take care of him, and this was what he needed. He did marry this girl, and they got along well.

The case of Mrs. T. is similar to that of Mrs. S. In Europe, many years ago, I had treated a young woman for a severe depression. At that time she, too, had complained that her husband did not really love her, as he would flirt with any pretty girl who happened to be around; that he was weak, inconsiderate, and tactless; that he was superficial, did not care for their baby, was immature, did not want to assume the role of a father, and so forth. Subsequently, during another depression, this girl committed suicide, as had her father and grandfather. Twenty years later, the husband came to see me in New York. He confirmed every one of the patient's accusations. He had married her mainly for her money, had felt tied down and burdened by his early marriage and fatherhood, had wanted to be free and to continue his bachelor life. His affection for his wife had faded from the moment she became pregnant. Unlike Mr. S. in the first case, whose second choice was much sounder, years later this man married a woman who promptly also developed depressive periods after the wedding. The same pattern repeated itself a third time with a girlfriend.

In still another case, Mr. U., the husband of a depressive patient went into analysis during the final stage of her treatment. His analyst, unaware of the wife's complaints which had become conscious during her treatment with me, gave me a gloomy picture of the man's infantile selfishness, of his demanding possessiveness toward her, coupled with his feeling of being entitled to cheat her as much as he desired. All these features corresponded precisely with my patient's descriptions of him.

In all of the foregoing cases, the deceptive overdependence of the husbands on their wives made it difficult for an outsider to believe the patients. In the last-mentioned instance, an amazingly successful treatment of the husband has achieved excellent and lasting results. The consequent improvement of this marital relationship has prevented my patient from having any further relapses.

Thus my experience has shown that however exaggerated the patient's hurt, disappointment, and hostile derogation of their partners may be, their complaints are usually more justified than may appear on the surface.

As to the marital situation as it may develop during the manic-depressive partner's periods of illness, in many cases a rebellious stage precedes the depression proper. During this period the patient often frankly disowns the role of the active, supportive mother or father toward the partner. Several patients have voiced the same typical remarks: "He is such a baby, so selfish, but what about me? I cannot always mother him. I need a mother myself." Thus we may say that the patient's depression aims at forcing the partner to take over the maternal role.

The retardation, the helplessness, the exhibition of self-derogation play on the partner's pity, his sympathy, his guilt feelings. Of course, we are all familiar with the special quality of the hidden sadism in the melancholic, which everyone finds so hard to tolerate. Even in cases where the aforementioned rebellion and complaint about the partner do not become manifest, the latter invariably senses the reproaches and the hostile appeal underneath the melancholic's self-punitive attitude.

In other words, the depressive never fails to make his partner, often his whole environment, and especially his children feel terribly guilty, pulling them down into a more and more depressed state as well. This explains why the supposedly healthy partner, in defense, so often becomes amazingly aggressive and even cruel toward the patient, and may hurt him precisely where he is most vulnerable.

If the depression lasts long enough and the patient is not removed from the family, the healthy partner slowly succumbs to his spouse's severe hidden hostility and tries to ward off his own depressive reaction by aggressive counteraccusations which intensify the patient's pathological feelings of worthlessness. In this way a vicious cycle is set in motion.

When the partner tries to escape from the patient's depressing company by looking for comfort on the outside, either in work or in social activities or in a sexual affair, the patient's feeling of being unloved is bound to increase. If the depression of the patient lasts long enough, the other members of the family will nearly always become infected, as it were, and eventually go into a depression themselves.

As to the hypomanic states of these patients, in one case I saw a husband, who had been relieved of the terrible strain of his wife's depression, go into a mildly elated state during which he constantly called me up to assure me how wonderfully everything was working out.

In other cases the partner finds the patient's hypomanic state even less tolerable than the depressive state, especially if the patient is aggressive—a constant nuisance, as it were—without awareness of his aggression and in general without insight. Where the hypomanic or manic state leads to sexual escapades or to a careless spending of money, the partner may react with shock, disgust, or frank fear, and finally may himself go into a depression. Such responses may lead to an ultimate disintegration of the marital relationship, which the depressive phase had not precipitated.

It should be emphasized that the partly justified negative reactions of husband or wife to the depressive partner's acute phase of illness inevitably increase the latter's conflict. In this case a vicious cycle arises in the pathological interplay of such couples, frequently involving their children and other members of the family as well. Thus a generally pathological family situation may persist and develop to the point where the patient withdraws completely from the whole family. This is one of the reasons why clinicians have recommended hospitalization or removal of the patient from the family environment and only rare visits by the family, at least during the severest stage of psychotic depression.

Certain patients, however, react very badly to hospitalization, and make a much better recovery when brought home. This may be particularly true of patients who struggle very hard not to withdraw their libido from their love objects completely, and who therefore feel that the very presence of the partner helps to maintain the link, however ambivalent it may be.

Finally, I should like to comment on the "contrast" marriages, i.e., between manic-depressive and schizophrenic partners. In the few cases I remember, I have never seen a marriage between a manic-depressive and a schizoid type work out. The manic-depressive inevitably broke down because what he really needed was warmth and affection.

On the basis of their individual emotional needs, it is difficult to see why a manic-depressive would want to marry a schizophrenic. In one such case, the husband was a manic-depressive who usually showed a mixture of compulsive and mildly hypomanic attitudes. In this state he was often very active, very loving, very much out to serve and give love to his wife. Some of these types may perhaps attract schizoid persons whom they "warm up." However, I have never seen a stable equilibrium between such contrasting psychotic types.

I insert a few remarks on the marriages of schizophrenics. I have observed three characteristic types of object choice in such patients. Those who are able to have some sort of personal relations beyond temporary sexual affairs tend to integrate at a lower level by choosing partners who are socially and intellectually inferior to them. Others marry schizophrenics or psychopaths with whom they live in a commonly shared unrealistic world.

A third category are schizophrenics who attach themselves to rigid, compulsive partners. The compulsive reaction formations of the latter seem to serve the special function of strengthening their own compulsive defenses against the threat of a breakdown. Yet in some of these cases I have seen the very compulsiveness of the partner precipitate an episode in the other because he could not longer tolerate it.

Since the pathology of their partners exercises such a profound influence upon the patients' depressive conditions, as well as on their transference situation, it is often necessary for both partners to be treated. In several instances I succeeded in inducing my patients' partners to seek psychotherapy or analysis with remarkably good results.

III

I turn now to some practical considerations of handling the technical difficulties created by the special transference problems of severely depressed patients.

One of the most crucial issues is: how do we let the intensely ambivalent transference of such patients develop sufficiently to permit its analysis, and yet prevent the patient from ending his treatment in resistance, i.e., either after emerging from a depression with a spurious transference success or with a negative therapeutic result, that is, with a severe depression and retreat from the analyst? Can we avoid or do we promote such results by gratifying the patients' need, first for stimulation of their vanishing libidinal resources, then again for an either punitive or forgiving superego figure?

I do not think that I am able to give satisfactory answers to these questions. Generally speaking, I may express the belief that we are at present better equipped for the analysis of such patients by our increased insight into the ego, its infantile developmental stages, and its complex methods of defense. Regarding modifications in the technical approach, the recent developments in ego psychology have enabled us to base such modifications on analytic understanding rather than merely on intuition.

In the early years of psychoanalysis few analysts dared to treat severely depressive and manic-depressive patients. Those who did, e.g., Abraham (1911, 1924), emphasized these patients' oral overdemandingness, but did not yet consider the disturbances of orality in terms of the ego's defensive needs. Later on, when the analysis of the ego's functioning became as important as the reconstruction of libidinal phase development, it became possible to treat many more depressive patients. This new focus of attention induced some analysts to discount the predominant role of orality in depression (e.g., Bibring, whose views I discussed in Chapter 6). I believe this to be correct only in the case of neurotic or normal persons who suffer from a depression, but it does not apply to borderline and psychotic patients, who generally show profound regressions.

With regard to the frequency of sessions, the prevailing attitude among analysts has been to give severely depressed patients daily sessions. My experience has taught me differently. I believe that the emotional quality of the analyst's responses is more important than the quantity of sessions. In fact, many depressives tolerate four or even three sessions weekly much better than six or seven. Giving these patients the opportunity to put some distance (in terms of both time and space) between themselves and the analyst tends to reduce their ambivalence rather than increase it. Daily sessions may be experienced as seductive promises too great to be fulfilled, and then again as intolerable obligations which promote the masochistic submission. If patients during a depressive period are very much retarded, we may have to prolong and, in times of suicidal danger, to increase the number of sessions, but this too should be done with caution. I remember a very retarded, paranoid depressive patient who frequently needed ten minutes to leave the couch; later on she blamed me resentfully for having stimulated her demands by the sixty-minute sessions.

As long as patients are severely retarded and inhibited in their feeling and thinking, they can neither associate freely nor digest interpretations. Even if they are able to establish and maintain contact, they may be so absorbed by anxieties, guilty fears, and compulsive brooding that they may need the therapist mainly as a patient listener to whom they are allowed to address their repetitious record of complaints. For weeks or months the only profit such patients derive from the treatment may be no more than support from a durable transference, which may carry them through the depression.

Abraham stressed that in manic-depressives, analysis proper is usually restricted to the free intervals. But in some cases the analytic process may proceed during the depressive periods even when there is marked retardation, provided the analyst has sufficient patience and empathy to adjust to the slowed-up emotional and thought processes of such patients. This adjustment to their pathological rhythm is especially difficult in treating patients with strong and rapid mood vacillations. One such patient would accuse me correctly of either being too quick and impulsive or being too slow and torpid in my responses and interpretations. In this respect I have learned much from trial and error. There must be a continuous, subtle, empathic tie between the analyst and his depressive patients; we must be very careful not to let empty silences grow or not to talk too long, too rapidly, and too emphatically; that is, never to give too much or too little.

In any event, what those patients need is not so much more frequent and longer sessions as a sufficient amount of spontaneity and flexible adjustment to their mood level, warm understanding, and especially unwavering respect—attitudes which must not be confused with overkindness, sympathy, reassurance. In periods of threatening narcissistic withdrawal, we may have to show a very active interest and participation in their daily activities and especially in their sublimations. I have observed that analysts who are rather detached by nature experience difficulties in the treatment of depressives. Beyond this warm, flexible emotional atmosphere, without which these patients cannot work, supportive counterattitudes and interventions may occasionally be necessary, but they are only a lesser evil for which we have to pay. With these patients, we are always between the devil and the deep blue sea; this cannot be avoided.

Despite the greatest caution, during certain analytic stages depressive patients will alternately experience the analyst's attitude and interpretations as seductive promises, severe rejection, lack of understanding, or sadistic punishments, all of which may increase the insatiable demands, the frustration, the ambivalence, and ultimately the depression. The most precarious point is the patient's temporary need for the analyst's show of power. My experiments in this respect have not always been fortunate, but at critical moments, the analyst must be prepared to respond either with a spontaneous gesture of kindness or even with a brief expression of anger, which may carry the patient over especially dangerous depressive phases. Since these patients are frequently very provocative and exasperating, such a deliberate show of emotional response naturally presupposes the most careful self-scrutiny and self-control in the analyst. What I wish to stress, however, is less the necessity for or the danger of such supportive counterattitudes, than the way in which they can and must be utilized for the analysis.

It seems advisable to begin early during the period of positive transference to connect interpretations of the illusory nature of the transference expectations with warnings for the future. Whenever critical transference situations arise that require special emotional counterattitudes, we must keep them carefully in mind, refer back to them later on, and explain the motivations of our behavior in terms of the patient's defensive needs and methods. In paranoid schizophrenic cases I have learned to avoid such interpretations carefully during periods when the patient accuses the analyst of having wrong emotional attitudes. At such times any explanation is misused to blame the analyst even more for what appears defensive behavior on his part.

Finally, some words about the question whether it is indicated to carry the analysis of such patients to the point where their preoedipal fantasies and impulses are produced and interpreted. It appears that with some depressive patients this is simply not possible. In such cases we must limit ourselves to interpretations in the area of ego-superego and transference conflicts, i.e., point to the introjective and projective mechanisms rather than to the underlying incorporation and ejection fantasies. But my experiences suggest that the most thorough and lasting therapeutic results were achieved in cases where this deep fantasy material could be fully revived, understood, and worked through. In this connection I refer to Gero's (1936) excellent paper which shows how the analysis of pregenital fixations brings the castration fears into focus and promotes progress to the genital level. (My case report of Mr. R. showed that decisive dynamic changes occur when such patients become aware of their unconscious equation of their genital with the incorporated "bad object").

When patients are carefully prepared for this material by the slow and precise analysis of their ego-superego and transference conflicts, they can tolerate it and work it through successfully. When such deep preoedipal fantasies come to the surface, the patients may go through transitory, very disturbed, or even slightly confused emotional states, often with violent psychosomatic (respiratory, circulatory, intestinal) reactions of a kind they had not previously experienced. But apart from the recurrence of depressive periods during the treatment, in true manic-depressives I have never had the experience of a patient going into a psychotic state provoked by the breaking through of deep id material. (The patient whose case I reported in Chapter 8 is the only exception.)

What seems to me important in all borderline and prepsychotic cases is to discourage and discard premature, isolated, fragmented productions of such deep material which may be brought up very early, without adequate affects, in a peculiar, easy manner, reminiscent of but quite different from the detached, rationalized id interpretations which obsessional-compulsive neurotics are inclined to give. In the type of cases to which I refer here, such productions have the true, uncanny coloring of the id. But they are and must be interpreted as defensive, regressive escapes, until years later they turn up again, and can then be understood in the infantile frame of reference and related to what is going on or what has been interpreted for years in the area of the ego and its defenses. The therapeutic success with depressives can best be gauged by their ability to remodel an unfortunate life situation which prior to analysis was bound to precipitate depressive states.

13

Acting Out and the Urge to Betray in Paranoid Patients

In the large group of acting-out patients, we find certain individuals whose behavior is characterized by a tendency to betray either people they had formerly loved and admired, or ideals, causes, and convictions to which they had previously fervently adhered. In my experience, these patients are always persons who suffer from conspicuous paranoid trends. In fact, all of my patients showing a paranoid personality structure and symptom formation developed problems in this area or even committed acts of betrayal which played a predominant part in their conflict situation. Usually, these tendencies were combined with flagrant identity conflicts, which found expression in their inability to commit themselves enduringly to one person, or one opinion, cause, or vocation. While some patients temporarily showed a suspicious overloyalty and devotion to certain ideals or ideas or activities, and corresponding representative persons or groups, they developed after some time an increasingly paranoid hostility toward them. At this point, a characteristic kind of acting out would set in. Trying desperately to hold on to their pursuits, they would feel an irresistible urge to look for another group with different or opposite opinions, and to complain to these people about their supposedly bad experiences in the past. They

This chapter is based on a paper which was first presented in a somewhat different form as a Fenichel-Simmel Memorial Lecture to the Los Angeles Psychoanalytic Society, 1965. It has not previously been published.

tended to involve them in their struggle against their former friends and the ideas they represented, and would finally abandon the latter and join this group.

It is not accidental that in the two cases which had originally called my attention to this problem, the patients' acting out had occurred in a historical stage setting. Although it is by no means limited to the field of politics, the latter seems to lend itself to this kind of acting out which may in certain cases remind us rather painfully of Judas, the hateful and pitiful betrayer of Christ.

The character of this Biblical figure has been the subject of two very interesting studies by Tarachow (1960) and Reider (1960). While Judas apparently was not a historical figure, persons whose role was quite similar to that of Judas frequently appeared on the political scene during certain historical periods. Such persons are at first fanatical followers of a political or ideological "cause," which they later abandon for another cause or group with different convictions. Such individuals may become habitual renegades. Some of them turn into real traitors of their former friends and allies, and may even accept the role of informer.

It is self-evident that I cannot present material from patients who had been active in politics, but I want to make a few remarks about one of them because his pathology epitomizes what I wish to stress.

This patient, who came to see me in a severe paranoid depression, had spent his life in several countries. He had worked under different names for different ideological groups, to each of which he had quite fanatically adhered for some years. Then a paranoid conflict situation would develop; each time he broke away, left the group and the country, only to join a new group which profited from his knowledge and past experiences. By now he was profoundly disappointed in all his former ideals and activities. His current illness had been precipitated by another attempt to erase his past life by means of creating a new identity, i.e., by establishing himself in a new country, with a new name, a new marriage, and a new ordinary vocation. After some years of treatment, this patient finally seemed to settle down in a rather satisfactory type of work and could be discharged. Fifteen years later, however, I saw him again in a very disturbed state. Once again he had given up his position and divorced his last wife. He did not come for treatment.

He wanted to let me know that he was still grateful to me, although he no longer believed in "Freudian analysis" and attacked it furiously. He had become a mystic and a passionate follower of Jung.

I shall now present some clinical material that will permit me to explore this kind of problem more thoroughly. It will of course be readily understood that I have had to omit many relevant facts in order to disguise the identity of the patients.

I

Mr. V. was a rather extraordinary, but severely paranoid man in his thirties, who suffered from alternating states of hyperactivity and paralyzing depression. When he was in high spirits and in a somewhat grandiose state of mind, this patient would be flooded by numerous new and interesting ideas. He would then start a series of promising enterprises. For such purposes he would establish suitable associations and look for collaborators whom he regarded as "good tools for the execution of my plans." But it was not long before he developed paranoid conflicts with these collaborators. As soon as they failed to live up to his expectations and demands or objected to his provocative behavior, he felt hurt, let down, exploited, and, finally, cheated and persecuted. Sometimes he made sufficient concessions to terminate his project successfully. Under less favorable circumstances, he became so frustrated and enraged at his supposed adversaries that he relinquished the whole project and immediately concentrated on another enterprise in an entirely different field. If problems of a similar nature developed in this project, too, Mr. V. became profoundly depressed and retreated completely from all work. Weeks or months later, as he emerged from his depression, new ideas began to spring up in his fertile mind. Then he would embark once more on new daring enterprises, again in different settings. Despite his illness, Mr. V.'s achievements in several fields of work had actually been so outstanding that he had already attained prominence and the reputation of being an erratic but exceptionally brilliant man.

It was characteristic of this patient that he had always been unable to commit himself to one specific place, type and line of work, and even to one specific vocation. His continuous fear of a collapse of his work always compelled him to leave another road open for a potential escape. He himself found both his mood fluctuations and the vacillations between different interests and pursuits inevitable, but quite intolerable. He complained about his lack of belonging, continuity, and direction. Although he had increasingly become aware of the paranoid nature of his conflicts, he was unable to avoid them or to cope with them.

The difficulties which I described had played an important role, years ago, in his transference situation with a former therapist. Dissatisfied with the latter's treatment methods, Mr. V. had tried to impose on him his own ideas concerning the therapy he needed. When the psychiatrist refused to accept his directions, the patient found another therapist who did. But instead of giving up the first therapist, he then continued treatment with both, seeing them alternately for some time and complaining to one about the other. The outcome of this experiment was that Mr. V., in a severe state of depression, finally left both psychiatrists.

During his treatment with me, the patient repeated his acting out not in the transference, but with another person, and in a way that illuminated the unconscious motivations of his behavior and the infantile origins of his underlying conflicts. These actions involved the career of an old friend, Max, who had exerted a decisive influence on the patient's personal and intellectual life during his late adolescence. On occasion Mr. V. still corresponded with this old friend. This time Max wrote to him because he urgently needed Mr. V.'s support to obtain a very important executive position in a firm whose president had been a close friend of Mr. V.'s father. Years ago, these two older men had been the main targets of Max's and the patient's criticism for their ultraconservative views and their sharp business policies and practices. As Max knew, Mr. V. was now rather closely associated with the firm and its president. The patient promised to help his friend and immediately saw this man. But instead of giving the required recommendation, he provided him with the most unfavorable information about his old friend, whom he described as a "likable fellow" but a "dangerously liberal person" who would ruin the firm. Thereupon, Mr. V. and the president agreed upon the following conspiratorial plan: Mr. V. would write to his old friend that he had highly recommended him. Max would be rejected by the firm, but for reasons that would preclude any suspicions about Mr. V.'s role in this rejection.

This plan was successfully carried out and actually ruined Max's career. After the completion of his secret act of betrayal, in which even the Judas kiss—in the form of a very friendly letter—was not omitted, Mr. V. went into a profound, almost suicidal depression. He totally denied the immorality of his action and its relation to his depressed state. He insisted that he did not feel any hostility toward Max and therefore did not feel guilty. His foremost duty in this case had been to the president and to the firm, which would have been seriously harmed by his friend.

Some data concerning this patient's infantile and adolescent history will help to give insight into his act of betrayal and his paranoid acting out in general. He was the oldest child of a very cold, narcissistic, and rather stupid mother, and of a brilliant, tyrannical father who had led a promiscuous sexual life and warned his son never to get closely attached to anyone, especially not to any woman. The parents hated and continuously fought each other, without concern for their children. Both of them completely rejected their eldest son who was a very bright, but frail, and rather unattractive boy. Although the younger siblings had evidently been preferred, the parents' hatred and contempt for each other had created a sadomasochistic atmosphere that survived in all the children, especially in their relations to each other.

During his early childhood the patient had made great efforts to gain his parents' love and praise, but to no avail. Intimidated by the mother's cold neglect and the father's disciplinary, critical, authoritarian behavior, he became an extremely submissive child, who silently accepted their hostile attitudes, and never dared frankly to rebel against either of his parents. But his hostility found an outlet in sadistic behavior toward the younger siblings and, besides, in an acting out with his parents which I shall describe below.

In late adolescence the boy finally attempted to detach himself from his family and especially from his tyrannical, ultraconservative father, to whom he had been very masochistically attached. In order to liberate himself he formed a close, homosexually tinged relationship with Max. A study of this friendship revealed that the patient had become a follower of Max for the very purpose of using his friend as a shield and weapon against his father and similar authoritative figures. During that period he greatly admired and tried to emulate his friend who, unlike himself, dared to stand up for his convictions and fearlessly expressed his rather progressive ideas. When in his relationship with this friend the patient became once more the meek, passive-submissive follower, he made a successful attempt to detach himself from Max, too. This was facilitated by the fact that his friend, the potential genius, failed to make a striking career.

It is significant that after rupturing his close bonds to Max, the patient changed his ideas again quite radically. He developed a strange and contradictory mixture of liberal and ultraconservative views and attitudes. At that time, he made great efforts to assert himself in an independent and dominant position. He married and began a prolonged period of training in several fields. Since the patient had never been able to identify enduringly with either of his parents, however, he could not commit himself to one particular type of work. It turned out that in his mind, any attachment or commitment to one special object—be it a person, a field of work, or a work project—involved the threat of the kind of attachment he had had to his father: the threat of a profound passive-masochistic enslavement that might captivate, engulf, and destroy him unless he could gain complete dominance over it.

Mr. V.'s conflicts and fears found expression in his behavior, in which he alternated between masochistic and overdemanding-tyrannical attitudes. This aroused the hostility of his collaborators to such an extent that each time he actually managed to get again into a helpless, frustrating situation with the persons and organizations on whose help he most greatly depended. Afraid of either yielding to his sadistic, destructive impulses or becoming the victim of his masochistic, self-destructive trends, the patient would at this stage engage in an acting out that was essentially of the same kind as his behavior in the case of Max and the company president. Playing off and using one person, one group, one project as a weapon against another, he would secretly complain to one about the other, trying to arouse their hostility and to solicit their support in his struggle with the others; on other occasions he would attempt to use such persons as "informers" on each other. As a result of this conspiratorial game, he developed paranoid ideas that centered on his fear that the whole group would finally join forces against him, and expose and ruin him by destroying his work. This was indeed quite frequently the effect of his behavior. I believe that this type of acting out is characteristic of paronoid patients.

In Mr. V.'s case, the deeper meaning of his acting out became clear when he mentioned a gangster who had made the headlines because he was probably responsible for a series of recent murders. The patient felt that this man's crimes would never be proven because he had been shrewd enough never to do the killing himself, but to employ others "for the execution" of the murders. We recall that Mr. V. had used this term when he described looking for organizations and collaborators that might be suitable, "for the execution of my plans." This term had, indeed, a literal meaning for him. As in the situation with Max and the president or father, the patient's acting out in his work was designed to make the other persons "execute" each other. Turning them into projective representations of his own sadistic and masochistic self, he managed to induce them to take on the parts that he himself wanted but did not dare to assume: the roles both of the destroyers and of their victims.

This device could be traced back to his childhood. I have emphasized his submissive attitudes as a child toward his parents, and his inability ever frankly to rebel against them. But his submissiveness covered a tremendous hostility which had found an indirect outlet in his secret vacillations between the fighting partners. Alternately siding with one against the other, complaining about the one to the other and informing each partner about the other's bad behavior, he left it to them to destroy each other. This attitude was clearly reflected in the patient's primal scene fantasies, in which he played the role of a passive observer who gleefully watched his parents make murderous sexual assaults on each other. In these sadomasochistic fantasies he was clearly identified with both parents and participated in both roles: that of the murderous sexual aggressor and that of the victim. The boy's fantasies certainly foreshadowed and became the model of his future acting out.

It is significant that by virtue of his elaborate manipulations he could use external objects both as a gratification of his destructive and self-destructive wishes, and as a defense against those impulses with which his own defective ego was unable to cope. The failure of this attempt led to paranoid symptom formation. The patient's betrayal of Max threw light onto another aspect of his acting out. We recall that in this situation Mr. V. had assumed the role of the secret adviser and rescuer of the firm and its president, i.e., of the father figure who had previously been the target of his and his friend's hostility.

It was no accident that this act of betrayal, which ruined his friend, occurred after the death of the patient's father, toward whom he had felt intense death wishes. It turned out that his acting out not only was intended to gratify and protect him from his destructive and self-destructive drives, but served at the same time an ideal purpose: that of rescuing the victim, the destroyed object, as well as his own self which in his fantasy was equated with the victim. It is interesting that in the patient's acting out destructive and restitutive strivings were always intermingled, and that his rather grandiose rescue fantasies effectively screened his own hostility. By preserving for himself the role of the rescuer, he became able completely to deny his own guilt feelings. Since his acting out so frequently ruined his work, however, it could not protect him from the severe states of depression and paranoid symptom formation.

I must finally emphasize two important differences between the patient's behavior and position in childhood and as an adult. Mr. V. was no longer the helpless child who had meekly and masochistically surrendered to his parents. In fact, it was his postadolescent rejection of that intolerable position, his rebellious effort to become a powerful, dominant person, which actually precipitated his paranoid homosexual conflicts and an acting out in which manipulations, planning, plotting, and acts of betrayal played such a prominent part. Furthermore, the persons about whom his infantile conflicts had revolved had been his parents, i.e., two persons of different sex. Later on, his vacillations, his betrayal, and the resulting paranoid conflicts usually involved a group or groups of men.

II

Before drawing any inferences from the case of this patient with regard to paranoid development and symptom formation in general, I should like to present another brief vignette that will permit a comparative study of the paranoid conflict situation and the role of betrayal in it.

The patient, Mr. W., was a lawyer in his thirties. I reported his case in my Freud Anniversary Lecture (1967), but from a different perspective. In that lecture I focused on the tendency of prepsychotic or latent or ambulatory psychotic patients to cling to reality and to external objects, and to use them in their attempts to solve their psychotic conflicts. Only if these attempts fail, do such patients withdraw from the external world to which they have previously clung. It is then that their psychotic condition becomes manifest. I believe that these observations were also confirmed by the acting out and symptomatology of Mr. V.

Very much like Mr. V., Mr. W. continually changed his friends, his place of residence, and his vocation; he had formerly worked in the political field. During a previous treatment in a city on the West Coast, he had lost both parents within a short time and soon thereafter developed a manifest psychotic state with delusions of persecution. They revolved around the belief that his superiors and the whole group with which he worked had designed a plot intended to expose him as a homosexual, to throw him out, and to ruin or even kill him. He had barricaded his room and kept a gun ready to shoot his persecutors, in case they should invade his home. The patient needed several months of hospitalization and then recovered under further psychotherapy with his first psychiatrist. He then stopped regular treatment, moved to the East Coast, and became a criminal lawyer in a suburb of New York. At times, however, he would fly back to his former therapist, who finally suggested further treatment in New York, preferably with a female psychiatrist. The patient followed this advice, but requested that I permit him occasionally to see his former therapist while working with me. I decided not to raise immediate objections. As he began to understand his acting-out problems, he himself gave up his visits with the other therapist. Interestingly, the relative intactness of his ego enabled Mr. W. to undergo a successful, regular analytic treatment without a real psychotic relapse.

From time to time however, he would get into paranoid conflict situations, occasionally with certain clients, but especially with a psychopathic young boyfriend, who for some years lived in his apartment under his care. In such situations he developed brief paranoid attacks with delusional ideas, which he quickly overcame and corrected. These paranoid conflict situations had a long history. As in the case of Mr. V., they had started when he had made himself financially and personally independent of his family. Mr. W., a highly intelligent man, had had various jobs. Usually, he had found good, rational reasons for his change of work, but in fact he had each time felt compelled to give up his positions after a paranoid conflict situation with his superiors and coworkers had developed. It turned out that Mr. W., too, always tried to get "control" of the organization in which he worked in order to improve the standards of the work or the administration. In a manner similar to Mr. V.'s, he tried to gain support for his plans from other workers. For this purpose he aroused their anger at the authorities and other opponents and also played them off against each other. As was the case with Mr. V., Mr. W.'s ideas always were quite constructive and his work satisfactory until these paranoid conflicts interfered. His manipulations then made his position untenable. He would end up in a paranoid depressed state and, after recovery, he would start another type of work.

Mr. W.'s childhood history was even more troubled than that of Mr. V. His mother was a prepsychotic woman, who gradually deteriorated. She was completely disorganized and a spendthrift. His father was an irresponsible paranoid psychopath. The parents constantly moved from one house, one town, one state to another, supposedly because of their debts. The patient was the oldest child who mothered, fathered, and later on supported the younger siblings, but sometimes also played sadistic games with them. In his case, too, the parents hated and constantly fought with each other. His mother had done her best to turn him into a girl. She expressed her disgust at his genital organ and told him that men were "wild animals." Moreover, she tried to make him depend on her and promised to live with him when he was grown up, provided he remained a good, soft child. The father attempted to turn him into a real boy, but began to treat him very cruelly as he grew up, and from puberty on forced him for some years to sleep in one bed with him.

Under these circumstances, Mr. W. became as submissive a child as Mr. V. had been. However, after having witnessed a rather violent sexual scene between his parents at the age of fifteen, he frankly expressed his disapproval of both parents and began to rebel especially against his father. Refusing to sleep in one bed with him, he developed a friendship with a younger boy. When his father accused him of having a homosexual affair with this boy, the patient spitefully started homosexual play with the latter; and after finding out that his father had stolen money from his savings account, he went on stealing adventures with his friend.

Then he decided to liberate himself from his family and also from this boy on whom he had become very dependent. He moved away and, similarly to Mr. V., now made definite efforts to assert himself in a dominant, independent position. He went to college and law school, supporting himself completely. He planned to devote himself entirely to his work and lead an ascetic, puritanical life. Since these goals were based mainly on reactive counteridentifications with his parents, he never quite succeeded. He went through a very brief marriage and had a few homosexual affairs, in which he always assumed the role of the aggressor.

As soon as the patient made money, his parents began to appeal to him for practical and financial support. Despite his resentment, he felt compelled by his conscience to engage in repetitive rescue actions, especially with regard to the younger siblings. He finally refused to help his parents at a time when his father as well as his superior, who supposedly resembled his father, had actually interfered with his work in a rather hostile manner. Soon thereafter his parents died. The patient reacted to their deaths with intense guilt feelings and the magic idea that his behavior had actually killed them. At this time a paranoid conflict situation with his superior developed. The ensuing psychotic episode induced him to seek treatment.

I have already described the patient's acting-out behavior in his former political jobs. In his current work as a criminal lawyer, i.e., after his psychotic episode, his paranoid acting out was less conspicuous. It turned out, however, that in his mind he equated his clients, who for the most part were delinquent adolescents, with the boy who had lived in his home for some years. Although he had once seduced this boy, he had then abstained from any sexual relations with him and made as great efforts to rescue him as in the case of his young clients. He wanted to cure the boy of his alcoholism and homosexuality, and even sent him for treatment.

In fact, however, Mr. W. constantly offered drinks to the boy and directly encouraged his homosexual activities. Moreover, while arousing the boy's hostility against his disciplinary parents, he repeatedly telephoned the parents as well as the boy's therapist in order to "inform" them about the boy's destructive and self-destructive behavior. Naturally, he also complained about him to me and expected me to suggest that he take constructive punitive measures. He had great difficulty in admitting that in reality he himself sometimes drank quite heavily and occasionally had brief, mostly unpleasurable, homosexual affairs. It turned out that his encouragement of the boy's bad behavior was intended to help Mr. W. lead the ascetic life he wanted; he could achieve this only by secretly participating in this boy's bad conduct. He could then betray him, inform on him, and let the boy's parents, therapist, and superiors blame and punish him for it.

Unconsciously, the boy represented a variety of people: himself in the past, his younger siblings, and both parents, especially in their irresponsible, infantile traits. He certainly mothered and fathered this boy in the way he had treated his siblings and had wished to be taken care of himself. But with regard to his betrayal conflict, the most significant fact was his equation of the boy with his sister, Louise, who was two and a half years his junior.

From early childhood on, the patient, who had been unable openly to rebel against his parents, had tried to arouse Louise's anger at her mother's strictness and to induce her to do all the "bad things" that he did not dare do. As soon as he saw her doing something bad and forbidden, he ran to his mother and denounced Louise, i.e., assumed the role of the informer. His betrayal regularly had the same effect: Louise was severely punished, and he would watch these punishments with pleasure, participating in all roles: in that of the sinful rebel, the sadistic, punitive mother, and the masochistic part of the victim.

Later on he repeated this acting out with his parents by complaining to one about the other and then witnessing their violent fights. He, too, of course, produced primal scene fantasies similar to those of Mr. V.; but, in contrast to the latter, Mr. W. as an adult never deliberately or consciously assumed the role of an informer or traitor, either professionally or in his personal life. Only when he became aware of his urge to pit people against each other did he remember his acting out with his sister and, later on, with his parents.

During his psychotic episode Mr. W. had suffered from delusions of persecutions, but with regard to his boyfriend he experienced brief attacks of paranoid jealousy when he suspected him of homosexual activities with an effeminate older man (a "bitch"). He became aware that he could not tolerate his equation of these persons with his own effeminate self, i.e., with his passive, homosexual, anal desires and his wishes to merge and be devoured by the aggressor. He was indeed jealous of both, his friend and the latter's supposed partner.

III

The two cases I presented here have many features in common: the paranoid conflict situations, the acting out, the fantasies, the defensive and restitutional efforts. Genetically, we found in both cases a childhood history not only of maltreatment, neglect, and cruelty, but also of severe hostility and fights between the parents. In both cases, the fathers had affairs with other women. Another feature that these patients conspicuously had in common was their early development of submissive, masochistic attitudes toward the parents, while their underlying severe hostility found expression only in the cruelties they inflicted upon their younger siblings and in their attempts to pit the other members of the family against each other and let them fight it out. In both cases, the parents' mutual hostility and behavior facilitated this acting out. This was the forerunner of the acts or fantasies of betrayal which subsequently played such a significant role in the paranoid conflict situations of these patients. It was characteristic that they did not dare openly to rebel against their parents until late adolescence, and that their efforts to assume and maintain an aggressive, dominant position led to the development of conspicuous paranoid trends. It is of special interest that both patients were highly gifted and able to work. Their ego functions broke down only during periods of acting out, which preceded the paranoid episodes.

The question arises how far my observations on these patients, and in particular on the role that their betrayal conflicts played in their paranoid pathology, are generally valid and may contribute to our understanding of the paranoid personality and symptom formation.

To begin with the childhood history, we frequently hear similar reports about the parental relationship from paranoid patients, but by no means in all cases. In my experience, however, there is usually a history of early emotional or even physical cruelties inflicted upon the child. I generally had the impression of an intensely sadomasochistic family atmosphere, created by at least one of the parents—either the father or, it seems, more often the mother—who has assumed the role of a constant aggressor. In such cases the main complaints about the "good" parent usually refer to his "weakness," which means his inability or unwillingness to protect the child from the other parent's sadistic behavior and, as a consequence, from his own sadomasochistic responses to this behavior. Not one of these patients, strangely enough, ever complained about having felt "betrayed" by his parents; but some of them mentioned contemptuously that the parents, despite their mutual hostility, had had sexual relations with each other.

I emphasized above that during the childhood of both Mr. V. and Mr. W., the acting out in the family group involved members of both sexes, whereas later on their paranoid conflicts revolved essentially about male figures. This leads us to the problem of homosexuality in paranoid patients.

We are familiar with the link between paranoia and homosexuality and the denial and projection mechanisms from Freud's classic papers (1911, 1922). While Knight (1940) stressed that in his paranoid patients the homosexual strivings served as a defense against the tremendous aggression, Bak (1946), following Nunberg's (1936) line of approach, put the emphasis on the role of masochism in paranoia. In addition, Bak tried to answer the question why the persecutors usually are a "group," which Cameron (1959) described as a "pseudo community."

Bak regards the "regression from sublimated homosexuality to masochism" as "the *first* defensive action of the ego," the "withdrawal of love" as "the *second* step in the defense," and the "increase of the hostility, hatred of the love object, and the appearance of sadistic fantasies" as "the *third* step" (p. 296). Concerning the role of the "group" in paranoia, Bak assumes that the "infantile prototype of this cohesive, hostile group may be traced in the fused image of the parents, their 'common front', representing the image of the phallic mother. This concept is later widened and includes the group of siblings" (p. 297).

All the paranoid cases I was able to study confirm Bak's observations and statements. Nor do they conflict with those of Knight, which actually supplement Bak's findings. But I would stress a number of additional findings in my own cases.

The first relates to the fact that some of my paranoid patients were not only homosexual but actually bisexual. I made such observations in the case of Mr. W. as well as in two other patients. One of them, Mr. X., was a paranoid schizophrenic who suffered from ideas of persecution and paranoid jealousy attacks. While he had many affairs with women, he frankly admitted that he also had to adhere to his homosexual relationships because they protected him from developing paranoid ideas of being cheated, robbed, or persecuted. He was truly bisexual, using the comparatively harmless reality of his homosexual acting out as a defense against his underlying, severely destructive, sadomasochistic strivings.

Secondly, all my paranoid patients developed conspicuous paranoid trends only after they had tried in late adolescence to assert themselves in an aggressively dominant position. This has not been stressed by other authors, although it is implied in Bak's observations and assumptions.

The third finding concerns the role of betrayal in paranoid acting out. The material I presented certainly underscores these patients' involvement, scheming, and manipulations with a group; i.e., with two or more people who are first used as secret weapons against each other, then are suspected of joining forces against the patient, and finally turn into persecutors. I have not had much experience with heterosexual patients suffering from delusions of jealousy, but, judging from the cases I have seen, I would infer that in paranoid jealousy, too, a group is involved, i.e., images of the heterosexual as well as the homosexual partner, as are wishes to betray them. Mr. W., for example, felt cheated by both his boyfriend and the latter's supposed effeminate partner, the "bitch." Mr. X., the paranoid schizophrenic briefly mentioned above, lent his apartment to both his boyfriend and a girlfriend, with both of whom he had previously had sexual affairs. When they promptly started a sexual affair with each other, he became violently jealous and almost killed his boyfriend. In such delusions of jealousy, the role of hostility and sadomasochism should also be stressed because these strivings turn the cheating partners into phallic sadistic figures and their victims.

In general, I feel that the study of the urge to betray in paranoid patients is important for our understanding not only of the role that the group plays in their paranoid ideas, but in particular of the acting-out behavior that precedes the fully developed paranoid state. This has not been sufficiently explored and described. In this connection it is significant, however, that Cameron (1959) mentions his paranoid patient's "restless, roving existence, his frequent unexplained changes of employer, and his endless shifting from his own headquarters" and "that he never succeeded in identifying with any of the concerns for whom he worked [or] in developing any lasting loyalties" (p. 522f.).

In my case reports I emphasized that the tendency of paranoid patients to betray those to whom they had formerly masochistically submitted and adhered is particularly significant from the therapeutic point of view because this tendency is invariably acted out in the transference. Mr. V. and Mr. W. are not the only paranoid patients who tried to change psychiatrists or be in treatment with two psychotherapists, alternately or even simultaneously. Sometimes a friend or a marital partner may become involved in this kind of acting out. A paranoid schizophrenic patient was referred to me for consultation because, according to the case report, he "pits his wife against his psychotherapist, abdicates himself, and lets them fight it out." Another paranoid schizophrenic patient succeeded in simultaneously seeing a large number of psychiatrists and in obtaining enormous amounts of drugs from each; none of the psychiatrists knew anything about the patient's contacts with the others. In fact, there is hardly a paranoid patient who does not run from one psychiatrist to another and complain to each about the others.

Interestingly enough, some therapists utilize this tendency for therapeutic purposes. Flescher (1966), for instance, has experimented with what he calls "dual therapy" not only in the case of such patients, but also in other types of cases. Others "structure" the therapy of paranoid schizophrenics along this line, primarily in order to divert the patient's aggression to another person. Such a dual therapy may be of value if the two therapists collaborate closely, if they know what they are doing, and if they have a similar approach. Otherwise, it may merely lend itself to an acting out which, as in Mr. V.'s case, cannot be handled and leads to a negative therapeutic result.

IV

In conclusion, I should like to return to my initial reference to the figure of Judas and make some remarks about the relationship between the paranoid "Judas conflict" and the Christ identification, so frequently seen in schizophrenic patients. In some of these cases I observed that the Christ fantasies were interwoven with problems of betrayal or, more frequently, developed later on. Judas was, after all, Christ's follower and thus identified with him: with his rebellion and struggle against the authorities, and with his suffering which the new religious ideals and ideology inflicted on the believers. Whereas Christ was ready to save the sinful world by dying for it, Judas reversed this position. His betrayal, though bringing about Christ's crucifixion, also led to his own ignominious suicide; while Christ's death on the cross, making him the savior of the world, led to grandeur and glory: to resurrection and mystical union with God. Thus we may say that in contrast to the role of Judas, the Christ identifications, which imply an acceptance of the masochistic surrender to God, the Father, succeed in the restitution of the object and of a grandiose self.

Appendix

In this Appendix I should like briefly to discuss the value of follow-up studies of depressive patients, and, in particular, of maintaining a positive transference with those who are psychotic.

The case material presented in this book makes it evident that I regard such studies as very significant from the diagnostic, prognostic, and therapeutic points of view. The first long-time observation of a case, which came about almost accidentally, impressed me so much that I decided to continue with such studies. The patient had been the first case of a severe recurring reactive depression that I had attempted to analyze. She suffered from intense guilt conflicts and complaints about her lack of feelings and her inability to grieve. Her current depression had been precipitated by the death of her aunt, a mother substitute. In spite of the severity and nature of her depressive illness, the patient was accessible to analysis and, after several years of treatment, showed definite improvement. But her transference problems could not be properly worked out because the political situation in Berlin suddenly forced me to give up my practice and to leave Germany. Since the patient was unable to find another analyst in the city to which she had moved, she began to write to me whenever she felt she could not cope with her problems. The ensuing correspondence, interrupted only by the war years, continued for thirty-five years. In 1951 and 1970, on visits with friends in Germany, I saw her again. In the meantime I had discovered that this infrequent but long-lasting correspondence was not only very helpful to her, but interesting and useful to me.

The patient still suffered from recurring but mild depressive states, during which she would write to me asking for moral support. But of particular importance was the fact that her masochistic attitudes had completely changed. She was able to build up an excellent home for defective children, to make a professional career and become a prominent person in her field. Although her religious preoccupations played a very important role in her life, she definitely was not schizophrenic and did not ever develop a schizophrenic condition.

Thus the follow-up study showed that in this case the diagnosis had been correct, the prognosis better than I had anticipated, and the therapeutic effect satisfactory and lasting. In the course of these years she developed only one severe depression—during the Nuremberg trials—even though she had been anti-Nazi and had helped members of resistance movements. The patient is now an old, bedridden woman suffering from a severe heart condition. In spite of this, she is still very active in giving advice and support to the current leader of the home.

In Chapter 8 I presented an extensive report of the case of Peggy M., another patient with recurring depressive states. Maintaining some follow-up contacts with her for many years, I learned at least that she was definitely not schizophrenic, that she remained clinically healthy over the next twenty-five years, that she was happily married, and was successful in her work.

In the case of Janet Q., special circumstances (that I mentioned in Chapter 11) permitted me to follow up this schizophrenic patient almost throughout her life, although she had never been in treatment with me. Of great significance was the fact that the consistent treatment after her last episode appeared to have been of eminent therapeutic value because the positive transference was maintained for a prolonged period. From my experience I believe this to be generally valid in schizophrenic patients, in contrast to neurotic cases.

The beneficial effects of maintaining a positive relationship with psychotic patients are illustrated by the following example: thirty years ago a paranoid schizophrenic patient, a physicist, whom I had treated in Berlin, called me up in New York a few minutes after he had arrived here and wanted to see me "immediately." He told me that he had searched for me in Sweden and England and was happy to have found me at last in this country. He could not come back for treatment with me because he had found a job in another city. But he wanted me to refer him to another psychoanalyst since he could not consider being treated by anyone whom I did not "know." Because of his paranoid conflicts the patient had to change his job several times. Each time he wrote to me telling me what had happened to him and asking to be referred. After his death from a coronary attack, his son called me up and came to see me. He too suffered from a mild schizophrenic condition and wanted me to refer him to another psychiatrist since I could not accept him for treatment. In this case the son had taken over the father's transference to me.

The same occurred in the case of a man whom I had analyzed in his latency years. This patient's parents, with whom I had a friendly personal relationship, brought the eight-year-old boy to me for analytic treatment. He had developed a depressed state and anxieties after the loss of his nurse-governess, a very maternal person who had brought him up and to whom he had been devoted. He had several years of successful analytic treatment, and thereafter maintained a positive attachment to me throughout the many years he lived in France. When he came to New York, he consulted me occasionally because of problems in his work and with his father. When he became engaged, he visited me with his fiancée because he wanted to know whether I approved of his choice. As he had anticipated, his parents did not find her quite acceptable—for social and intellectual reasons. Since the patient moved away from New York, I received news about him only from his parents, who said he was happily married and had made a career.

I saw him again when he was in his forties. He had heard about my arrival in his city in the South and immediately invited me, with the special purpose of consulting me about one of his adolescent sons. To my surprise, he told the boy, who had recently broken off his psychotherapeutic treatment, what a wonderful time he had had with me while he was in analysis and that he had learned from me how to shoot with an air gun. His boy promptly responded by asking the father whether I could not move to their town. He was eager to be in treatment with me. Evidently the father's transference feelings had been revived by my visit and then had been adopted by the son.

At this point I should like to make some more remarks on follow-up studies of patients whom I had treated as children. In five such cases I was able to find out how the patients developed after their psychoanalytic treatment had been terminated. I discovered that their further development had been much better than I had anticipated. Only one of them, a borderline case, required treatment as an adult.

One case was of special interest. The treatment of this very disturbed eleven-year-old boy was abruptly interrupted when Hitler came to power in Germany. As a gentile he had been utterly confused by the anti-Semitic atmosphere and did not know who was "bad," Hitler or his Jewish analyst. After the World War his mother wrote to me that her son was in a Russian war prisoner camp and had asked for me because he was severely depressed and needed my help.

In his first letter he told me that he had soon found out that not I but Hitler was bad. In other words, he remembered the insoluble conflict which had led to an interruption of his treatment, and his positive memories survived thirteen years of separation. We began a correspondence which was amazingly helpful to him and which continued for years, since he had no money for psychotherapeutic treatment. In 1951, on a visit to Germany I met him and discussed his personal and professional problems with him. From then on I heard only occasionally from him and about him. He, too, succeeded in gradually resolving his problems. After completing his studies, he maintained a good job, was happily married, and adopted two children.

The child cases show the great value of follow-up studies of patients who were in treatment as children, especially with respect to the prognostic aspects, and, in this last case, also from the therapeutic point of view.

I return to my adult case material. I have spoken above of the paranoid schizophrenic patient who constantly changed jobs and each time wanted me to refer him to a psychiatrist in the city where he lived. In general, schizophrenic patients, in particular paranoid ones, frequently tend to move around and change their jobs and the place where they live. But those whom I treated always managed to keep in touch with me, to maintain an occasional correspondence or even to visit me in New York in order to get advice.

This was true in the case of Mrs. P. whom I described in Chapter

10. Of special interest is the fact that this patient, who suffers from schizophrenic episodes and now lives in California, calls me up whenever she feels that she is on the verge of a breakdown. Each time she tells me that somebody else—her boyfriend or her boss—is likely to have a breakdown, whereupon I tell her that she is projecting again and advise her to go immediately into a hospital. She always follows my advice.

Some of these patients express their gratitude for the help they get and are getting, e.g., for the advice to resume treatment.

Another patient who also lives on the West Coast is worth mentioning because I had treated her for what I then regarded as a compulsion neurosis with depressive states. I met her occasionally after the termination of her analysis and she seemed to be well. But after about twenty-five years, she suddenly appeared in New York for a consultation. She had developed involutional depressions. She first refused to see another psychoanalyst, but finally accepted my suggestion to begin treatment at the place where she lives. Recently she wrote me that her therapist had greatly helped her, especially in a complex marital problem, and that she was in pretty good shape again.

It has been much easier to follow the severely depressive analytic patients who live in or near New York because after some years they often need re-analysis. As new problems arise, they may react with renewed depressions. They may also come again for occasional discussions or for longer periods of treatment of one or two sessions a week. Interestingly enough, even these patients want to lie down on the couch and continue to work analytically. They refer to their old memory material and to the interpretations made in the past and behave as though they had never interrupted their treatment. This was especially interesting in the case of a patient who had terminated his analysis over twenty years ago, had never consulted me since that time, and now had to resume treatment because he had undergone some very traumatic life experiences.

From the therapeutic point of view, the follow-up studies of my severely depressive patients showed that in the chronic depressive patients the treatment had been least successful. The results were not very satisfactory either in those who already in their childhood had suffered from depressive states with suicidal ideas.

I hope that the cases to which I referred in this Appendix, including those which I presented in this book, demonstrate the value of such follow-up studies. They may confirm or change the original diagnosis and prognosis, give evidence of the long-term therapeutic results, and often serve therapeutic purposes.

Bibliography

Abraham, K. (1911), Notes on the Psycho-Analytical Investigation and Treatment of Manic-Depressive Insanity and Allied Conditions. *Selected Papers on Psycho-Analysis.* London: Hogarth Press, 1927, pp. 137-156.

——— (1924), A Short Study of the Development of the Libido, Viewed in the Light of Mental Disorders. *Selected Papers on Psycho-Analysis.* London: Hogarth Press, 1927, pp. 418-501.

——— (1927), *Selected Papers on Psycho-Analysis.* London: Hogarth Press.

Angel [Katan] A. (1934), Einige Bemerkungen über den Optimismus. *Int. Z. Psychoanal.,* 20:191-199.

Arieti, S. (1959), The Manic-Depressive Psychosis. In: *The American Handbook of Psychiatry,* ed. S. Arieti, 1:419-454. New York: Basic Books.

Arlow, J. A. (1959), The Structure of the *Déjà Vu* Experience. *J. Amer. Psychoanal. Assn.,* 7:611-631.

——— & Brenner, C. (1964), *Psychoanalytic Concepts and the Structural Theory.* New York: International Universities Press.

Asch, S. S. (1966), Depression: Three Clinical Variations. *The Psychoanalytic Study of the Child,* 21:150-171.

Atkins, N. B. (1967), Comments on Severe and Psychotic Regressions in Analysis. *J. Amer. Psychoanal. Assn.,* 15:584-605.

Bak, R. C. (1939), Regression of Ego-Orientation and Libido in Schizophrenia. *Int. J. Psycho-Anal.,* 20:64-71.

——— (1943), Dissolution of Ego, Mannerism, and Delusion of Grandeur. *J. Nerv. Ment. Dis.,* 98:457-468.

——— (1946), Masochism in Paranoia. *Psychoanal. Quart.,* 15:285-301.

——— (1954), The Schizophrenic Defence against Aggression. *Int. J. Psycho-Anal.,* 35:129-134.

Bellak, L. (1952), *Manic-Depressive Psychosis and Allied Conditions.* New York: Grune & Stratton.

——— (1958), The Schizophrenic Syndrome: A Further Elaboration of the Unified Theory of Schizophrenia. In: *Schizophrenia: A Review of the Syndrome,* ed. L. Bellak. New York: Logos Press, pp. 3-63.

Beres, D. (1966), Superego and Depression. In: *Psychoanalysis—A General Psychology,* ed. R. M. Loewenstein, L. M. Newman, M. Schur, & A. J. Solnit. New York: International Universities Press, pp. 479-498.

——— & Obers, S. J. (1950), The Effects of Extreme Deprivation in Infancy on Psychic Structure in Adolescence. *The Psychoanalytic Study of the Child,* 5:212-235.

Bergler, E. (1950), Further Studies on Depersonalization. *Psychiat. Quart.,* 24:268-277.

——— & Eidelberg, L. (1935), Der Mechanismus der Depersonalisation. *Int. Z. Psychoanal.,* 21:258-285.

Bergson, H. L. (1911), *Laughter: An Essay on the Meaning of the Comic.* New York: Macmillan.

Bibring, E. (1953), The Mechanism of Depression. In: *Affective Disorders,* ed. P. Greenacre. New York: International Universities Press, pp. 13-48.

Bird, B. (1958), Depersonalization. *Arch. Neurol. Psychiat.,* 80:467-476.

Blank, H. R. (1954), Depression, Hypomania and Depersonalization. *Psychoanal. Quart.,* 23:20-37.

Blatz, W. E., Allin, K. D., & Millichamp, D. A. (1936), A Study of Laughter in the Nursery School Child. *Univ. Toronto Studies, Child Develpm. Series,* 7.

Bleuler, E. (1911), *Dementia Praecox or the Group of Schizophrenias.* New York: International Universities Press, 1950.

——— (1949), *Lehrbuch der Psychiatrie,* 8th ed., ed. M. Bleuler. Berlin: Springer.

Bonaparte, M. (1928), L'identification d'une fille à sa mère morte. *Rev. Franç. Psychanal.,* 2:541-565.

Bowlby, J. (1960), Grief and Mourning in Infancy and Early Childhood. *The Psychoanalytic Study of the Child,* 15:9-52.

——— (1961), Processes of Mourning. *Int. J. Psycho-Anal.,* 42:317-340.

——— (1963), Pathological Mourning and Childhood Mourning. *J. Amer. Psychoanal. Assn.,* 11:500-541.

Brackett, C. W. (1933), Laughing and Crying of Pre-School Children. *J. Exper. Educ.,* 2:119-126.

Brenner, C. (1966), The Mechanism of Repression. In: *Psychoanalysis—A General Psychology,* ed. R. M. Loewenstein, L. M. Newman, M. Schur, & A. J. Solnit. New York: International Universities Press, pp. 390-399.

Brierley, M. (1937), Affects in Theory and Practice. *Int. J. Psycho-Anal.,* 18:256-268.

Bühler, C. (1930), *The First Year of Life.* New York: John Day.

Cameron, N. (1959), Paranoid Conditions and Paranoia. In: *The American Handbook of Psychiatry,* ed. S. Arieti, 1:508-539. New York: Basic Books.

Campbell, J. D. (1953), *Manic-Depressive Disease.* Philadelphia: Lippincott.

Cobb, S. (1950), *Emotions and Clinical Medicine.* New York: Norton.

Dearborn, G. V. N. (1900), The Nature of the Smile and Laugh. *Science,* 2:851-855.

Despert, J. L. (1940), A Comparative Study of Thinking in Schizophrenic Children and in Children of Preschool Age. *Amer. J. Psychiat.,* 97:189-213.

Deutsch, H. (1927), Über Zufriedenheit, Glück und Ekstase. *Int. Z. Psychoanal.,* 13:410-419.

——— (1933), The Psychology of Manic-Depressive States, with Particular Reference to Chronic Hypomania. *Neuroses and Character Types*. New York: International Universities Press, 1965, pp. 203-217.

——— (1942), Some Forms of Emotional Disturbance and Their Relationship to Schizophrenia. *Psychoanal. Quart.*, 11:301-321.

Dickes, R. (1967), Severe Regressive Disruptions of the Therapeutic Alliance. *J. Amer. Psychoanal. Assn.*, 15:508-533.

Eissler, K. R. (1953), Notes upon the Emotionality of a Schizophrenic Patient and Its Relation to Problems of Technique. *The Psychoanalytic Study of the Child*, 8:199-251.

——— (1955), An Unusual Function of an Amnesia. *The Psychoanalytic Study of the Child*, 10:75-82.

——— (1959), On Isolation. *The Psychoanalytic Study of the Child*, 14:29-60.

Enders, A. C. (1927), Laughter of the Pre-School Child. *Papers of the Michigan Academy of Science, Arts and Letters*, 8:341-356.

Fairbairn, W. R. D. (1954), *An Object-Relations Theory of Personality*. New York: Basic Books.

Federn, P. (1926), Some Variations in Ego Feeling. *Int. J. Psycho-Anal.*, 7:434-444.

——— (1929), The Ego as Subject and Object in Narcissism. *Ego Psychology and the Psychoses*. New York: Basic Books, 1952, pp. 283-322.

——— (1936), On the Distinction between Healthy and Pathological Narcissism. *Ego Psychology and the Psychoses*. New York: Basic Books, 1952, pp. 323-364.

——— (1952), *Ego Psychology and the Psychoses*. New York: Basic Books.

Fenichel, O. (1926), Identification. *The Collected Papers of Otto Fenichel*, 1:97-112. New York: Norton, 1953.

——— (1932), *Outline of Clinical Psychoanalysis*. New York: Norton, 1934.

——— (1939), Trophy and Triumph. *The Collected Papers of Otto Fenichel*, 2:141-162. New York: Norton, 1954.

——— (1941), The Ego and the Affects. *The Collected Papers of Otto Fenichel*, 2:215-227. New York: Norton, 1954.

——— (1945) *The Psychoanalytic Theory of Neurosis*. New York: Norton.

Fisher, C. (1954), Dreams and Perception: The Role of Preconscious and Primary Modes of Perception in Dream Formation. *J. Amer. Psychoanal. Assn.*, 2:389-445.

——— (1956), Dreams, Images and Perception: A Study of Unconscious-Preconscious Relationships. *J. Amer. Psychoanal. Assn.*, 4:5-48.

——— & Joseph, E. D. (1949), Fugue with Awareness of Loss of Personal Identity. *Psychoanal. Quart.*, 18:480-493.

Fleming, J. & Altschul, S. (1963), Activation of Mourning and Growth by Psycho-Analysis. *Int. J. Psycho-Anal.*, 44:419-431.

Flescher, J. (1966), *Dual Therapy: Triadic Principle of Genetic Psychoanalysis*. New York: D. T. R. B. Editions.

Frank, J. (1959), Treatment Approach to Acting-out Character Disorders. *J. Hillside Hosp.*, 8:42-53.

Freud, A. (1936), *The Ego and the Mechanisms of Defense*. New York: International Universities Press, 1946.

——— (1952), Studies in Passivity: Part II. Notes on a Connection between the States of Negativism and of Emotional Surrender (*Hörigkeit*). *The Writings of Anna Freud,* 4:256-259. New York: International Universities Press, 1968.

——— (1960), Discussion of Dr. John Bowlby's Paper. *The Psychoanalytic Study of the Child,* 15:53-62.

——— & Burlingham, D. (1944), *Infants Without Families.* New York: International Universities Press.

Freud, S. (1900), The Interpretation of Dreams. *Standard Edition,* 4 & 5. London: Hogarth Press, 1953.

——— (1905a), Three Essays on the Theory of Sexuality. *Standard Edition,* 7:125-243. London: Hogarth Press, 1953.

——— (1905b), Jokes and Their Relation to the Unconscious. *Standard Edition,* 8. London: Hogarth Press, 1960.

——— (1911), Psycho-Analytic Notes on an Autobiographical Account of a Case of Paranoia (Dementia Paranoides). *Standard Edition,* 12:3-82. London: Hogarth Press, 1958.

——— (1914), On Narcissism: An Introduction. *Standard Edition,* 14:67-102. London: Hogarth Press, 1957.

——— (1915a), Repression. *Standard Edition,* 14:141-158. London: Hogarth Press, 1957.

——— (1915b), The Unconscious. *Standard Edition,* 14:159-215. London: Hogarth Press, 1957.

——— (1916), Some Character-Types Met with in Psycho-Analytic Work. *Standard Edition,* 14:309-333. London: Hogarth Press, 1957.

——— (1916-1917), Introductory Lectures on Psycho-Analysis. *Standard Edition,* 15 & 16. London: Hogarth Press, 1963.

——— (1917), Mourning and Melancholia. *Standard Edition,* 14:237-258. London: Hogarth Press, 1957.

——— (1920), Beyond the Pleasure Principle. *Standard Edition,* 18:3-64. London: Hogarth Press, 1955.

——— (1921), Group Psychology and the Analysis of the Ego. *Standard Edition,* 18:67-143. London: Hogarth Press, 1955.

——— (1922), Some Neurotic Mechanisms in Jealousy, Paranoia and Homosexuality. *Standard Edition,* 18:221-232. London: Hogarth Press, 1955.

——— (1923), The Ego and the Id. *Standard Edition,* 19:3-66. London: Hogarth Press, 1961.

——— (1924a), Neurosis and Psychosis. *Standard Edition,* 19:149-153. London: Hogarth Press, 1961.

——— (1924b), The Economic Problem of Masochism. *Standard Edition,* 19:157-170. London: Hogarth Press, 1961.

——— (1924c), The Loss of Reality in Neurosis and Psychosis. *Standard Edition,* 19:183-187. London: Hogarth Press, 1961.

——— (1925), A Note upon the 'Mystic Writing-Pad.' *Standard Edition,* 19:227-232. London: Hogarth Press, 1961.

——— (1926), Inhibitions, Symptoms and Anxiety. *Standard Edition,* 20:77-175. London: Hogarth Press, 1959.

——— (1927a), Fetishism. *Standard Edition,* 21:149-157. London: Hogarth Press, 1961.

——— (1927b), Humour. *Standard Edition,* 21:159-166. London: Hogarth Press, 1961.
——— (1931), Female Sexuality. *Standard Edition,* 21:223-243. London: Hogarth Press, 1961.
——— (1940a), An Outline of Psycho-Analysis. *Standard Edition,* 23:141-207. London: Hogarth Press, 1964.
——— (1940b), Splitting of the Ego in the Process of Defence. *Standard Edition,* 23:271-278. London: Hogorth Press, 1964.
Frosch, J. (1967a), Delusional Fixity, Sense of Conviction, and the Psychotic Conflict. *Int. J. Psycho-Anal.,* 48:475-495.
——— (1967b), Severe Regressive States during Analysis: Introduction and Summary. *J. Amer. Psychoanal. Assn.,* 15:491-507, 606-625.
Furman, R. A. (1964a), Death and the Young Child. *The Psychoanalytic Study of the Child,* 19:321-333.
——— (1964b), Death of a Six-year-old's Mother during His Analysis. *The Psychoanalytic Study of the Child,* 19:377-397.

Gaddini, E. (1969), On Imitation. *Int. J. Psycho-Anal.,* 50:475-484.
Garma, A. (1932), Die Realität und das Es in der Schizophrenie. *Int. Z. Psychoanal.,* 18:183-200.
Gehl, R. H. (1964), Depression and Claustrophobia. *Int. J. Psycho-Anal.,* 45:312-323.
Geleerd, E. R. (1965), Two Kinds of Depression. In: *Drives, Affects, Behavior,* Volume 2, ed. M. Schur. New York: International Universities Press, pp. 118-127.
Gero, G. (1936), The Construction of Depression. *Int. J. Psycho-Anal.,* 17:423-461.
——— (1953), An Equivalent of Depression: Anorexia. In: *Affective Disorders,* ed. P. Greenacre. New York: International Universities Press, pp. 117-139.
Gesell, A. L. (1925), *The Mental Growth of the Pre-School Child.* New York: Macmillan.
Gill, M. M. (1963), *Topography and Systems in Psychoanalytic Theory* [*Psychological Issues,* Monogr. 10]. New York: International Universities Press.
Gitelson, M. (1958), On Ego Distortion. *Int. J. Psycho-Anal.,* 29:245-257.
Glover, E. (1939), The Psycho-Analysis of Affects. *Int. J. Psycho-Anal.,* 20:299-307.
——— (1947), Basic Mental Concepts and Their Clinical and Theoretical Value. *Psychoanal. Quart.,* 16:482-506.
——— (1948), *Psycho-Analysis: A Handbook.* London: Staples Press.
Goldstein, K. (1951), On Emotions: Considerations from the Organismic Point of View. *J. Psychol.,* 31:37-49.
Greenacre, P. (1952), *Trauma, Growth, and Personality.* New York: International Universities Press, 1969.
——— (1971), *Emotional Growth.* New York: International Universities Press.
Greene, W. A., Jr., (1958), Role of an Object in the Adaptation to Object Loss. *Psychosom. Med.,* 20:344-350.
Greenson, R. R. (1953), On Boredom. *J. Amer. Psychoanal. Assn.,* 1:7-21.
——— (1962), On Enthusiasm. *J. Amer. Psychoanal. Assn.,* 10:3-21.

——— (1954), The Struggle against Identification. *J. Amer. Psychoanal. Assn.*, 2:200-217.

——— (1959), Phobia, Anxiety and Depression. *J. Amer. Psychoanal. Assn.*, 7:663-674.

Grinker, R. R., Sr., et al. (1961), *The Phenomena of Depressions.* New York: Hoeber.

Hart, H. H. (1947), Problems of Identification. *Psychiat. Quart.*, 21:274-293.

Hartmann, H. (1922), Ein Fall von Depersonalisation. *Z. ges. Neurol. & Psychiat.*, 74:592-601.

——— (1927), *Grundlagen der Psychoanalyse.* Leipzig: Thieme.

——— (1950), Comments on the Psychoanalytic Theory of the Ego. *Essays on Ego Psychology.* New York: International Universities Press, 1964, pp. 113-141.

——— (1953), Contribution to the Metapsychology of Schizophrenia. *Essays on Ego Psychology.* New York: International Universities Press, 1964, pp. 182-206.

——— & Kris, E. (1945), The Genetic Approach in Psychoanalysis. *The Psychoanalytic Study of the Child*, 1:11-30.

——— ——— & Loewenstein, R. M. (1949), Notes on the Theory of Aggression. *The Psychoanalytic Study of the Child*, 3/4:9-36.

Hendrick, I. (1951), Early Development of the Ego. *Psychoanal. Quart.*, 20:44-61.

Hinsie, L. E. & Shatzky, J. (1940), *Psychiatric Dictionary.* New York: Oxford University Press.

Jacobson, E. (1930), Beitrag zur asozialen Charakterbildung. *Int. Z. Psychoanal.*, 16:210-235.

——— (1936), On the Development of the Girl's Wish for a Child. *Psychoanal. Quart.*, 37:523-538, 1968.

——— (1937), Wege der weiblichen Über-Ich-Entwicklung. *Int. Z. Psychoanal.*, 23:402-412.

——— (1949), Observations on the Psychological Effect of Imprisonment on Female Political Prisoners. In: *Searchlights on Delinquency*, ed. K. R. Eissler. New York: International Universities Press, pp. 341-368.

——— (1952), The Speed Pace in Psychic Discharge Processes and Its Influence on the Pleasure-Unpleasure Qualities of Affects. *Bull. Amer. Psychoanal. Assn.*, 8:235-236.

——— (1954), The Self and the Object World: Vicissitudes of Their Infantile Cathexes and Their Influence on Ideational and Affective Development. *The Psychoanalytic Study of the Child*, 9:75-127.

——— (1964), *The Self and the Object World.* New York: International Universities Press.

——— (1967), *Psychotic Conflict and Reality.* New York: International Universities Press.

Jekels, L. & Bergler, E. (1934), Transference and Love. *Psychoanal. Quart.*, 18:325-350, 1949.

Justin, F. (1922), A Genetic Study of Laughter-Provoking Stimuli. *Child Develpm.*, 3:114-136.

Kaila, E. (1935), Die Reaktionen des Säuglings auf das menschliche Gesicht. *Z. Psychol.*, 135:156-163.

Kanzer, M. (1952), Maniac-Depressive Psychoses with Paranoid Trends. *Int. J. Psycho-Anal.*, 33:34-42.

Katan, A., *see* Angel [Katan], A.

Katan, M. (1949), Schreber's Delusion of the End of the World. *Psychoanal. Quart.*, 18:60-66.

——— (1950a), Structural Aspects of a Case of Schizophrenia. *The Psychoanalytic Study of the Child,* 5:175-211.

——— (1950b), Schreber's Hallucinations about the "Little Men." *Int. J. Psycho-Anal.*, 31:32-35.

——— (1952), Further Remarks about Schreber's Hallucinations. *Int. J. Psycho-Anal.*, 33:429-432.

——— (1953a), Mania and the Pleasure Principle: Primary and Secondary Symptoms. In: *Affective Disorders,* ed. P. Greenacre. New York: International Universities Press, pp. 140-208.

——— (1953b), Schreber's Prepsychotic Phase. *Int. J. Psycho-Anal.*, 34:43-51.

——— (1954), The Importance of the Non-Psychotic Part of the Personality in Schizophrenia. *Int. J. Psycho-Anal.*, 35:119-128.

Kaywin, L. (1960), An Epigenetic Approach to the Psychoanalytic Theory of Instincts and Affects. *J. Amer. Psychoanal. Assn.*, 8:613-658.

——— (1966), Notes on the Psychoanalytic Theory of Affects. *Psychoanal. Rev.*, 53:275-282.

Kenderdine, M. (1931), Laughter in the Pre-School Child. *Child Developm.*, 2:228-230.

Kernberg, O. (1967), Borderline Personality Organization. *J. Amer. Psychoanal. Assn.*, 15:641-685.

——— (1968), The Treatment of Patients with Borderline Personality Organization. *Int. J. Psycho-Anal.*, 49:600-619.

Khan, M. M. R. (1960), Clinical Aspects of the Schizoid Personality. *Int. J. Psycho-Anal.*, 41:430-437.

——— (1964), Ego Distortion, Cumulative Trauma, and the Role of Reconstruction in the Analytic Situation. *Int. J. Psycho-Anal.*, 45:272-279.

Klein, M. (1935), A Contribution to the Psychogenesis of Manic-Depressive States. *Contributions to Psycho-Analysis.* London: Hogarth Press, 1948, pp. 282-310.

——— (1940), Mourning and Its Relation to Manic-Depressive States. *Contributions to Psycho-Analysis.* London: Hogarth Press, 1948, pp. 311-338.

——— (1948), *Contributions to Psycho-Analysis, 1921-1945.* London: Hogarth Press.

Knapp, P. H. (1957), Conscious and Unconscious Affects: A Preliminary Approach to Concepts and Methods of Study. *Psychiat. Res. Rep.*, 8:55-74.

Knight, R. P. (1939), Psychotherapy in Acute Paranoic Schizophrenia with Successful Outcome: A Case Report. *Bull. Menninger Clinic,* 3:97-105.

——— (1940), The Relationship of Latent Homosexuality to the Mechanism of Paranoid Delusions. *Bull. Menninger Clin.*, 4:149-159.

——— (1953), Management and Psychotherapy of the Borderline Schizophrenic Patient. *Bull. Menninger Clin.*, 17:139-150.

Kohut, H. (1966), Forms and Transformations of Narcissism. *J. Amer. Psychoanal. Assn.*, 14:243-272.

——— & Levarie, S. (1950), On the Enjoyment of Listening to Music. *Psychoanal. Quart.*, 19:64-87.

Kraepelin, E. (1913), *Ein Lehrbuch für Studierende und Ärzte* (Band III, *Klinische Psychiatrie,* 2. Teil), 8th ed. Leipzig: Barth.

Kris, E. (1934), The Psychology of Caricature. *Int. J. Psycho-Anal.*, 17:285-303, 1936.

——— (1938), Ego Development and the Comic. *Int. J. Psycho-Anal.*, 19:77-90.

——— (1939), Laughter as an Expressive Process: Contributions to the Psycho-Analysis of Expressive Behaviour. *Int. J. Psycho-Anal.*, 21:314-341, 1940.

———(1950), On Preconscious Mental Processes. *Psychoanal. Quart.*, 19:540-560.

——— (1952), *Psychoanalytic Explorations in Art.* New York: International Universities Press.

——— (1956), The Recovery of Childhood Memories in Psychoanalysis. *The Psychoanalytic Study of the Child,* 11:54-88.

Kubie, L. S. (1951), The Role of Symbolic Distortion in Neurosis and Psychosis. *Psychoanal. Quart.*, 20:500-501.

Landauer, K. (1938), Affects, Passions and Temperament. *Int. J. Psycho-Anal.*, 19:388-415.

Lange, J. (1928), *Handbuch der Geisteskrankheiten* (Band VI, Spezieller Teil II, pp. 1-231, Die endogenen und reaktiven Gemütskrankheiten und die manisch-depressive Konstitution). Berlin: Springer.

Laufer, M. (1966), Object Loss and Mourning during Adolescence. *The Psychoanalytic Study of the Child,* 21:269-293.

Lehrman, P. R. (1927), The Fantasy of Not Belonging to One's Family. *Arch. Neurol. Psychiat.*, 18:1015-1023.

Levitan, H. L. (1969), The Depersonalizing Process. *Psychoanal. Quart.*, 38:97-109.

——— (1970), The Depersonalization Process. *Psychoanal. Quart.*, 39:449-470.

Lewin, B. D. (1937), A Type of Neurotic Hypomanic Reaction. *Arch. Neurol. Psychiat.*, 37:868-873.

——— (1950), *The Psychoanalysis of Elation.* New York: Norton.

——— (1961), Reflections on Depression. *The Psychoanalytic Study of the Child,* 16:321-331.

——— (1965), Reflections on Affect. In: *Drives, Affects, Behavior, Volume* 2, ed. M. Schur. New York: International Universities Press, pp. 23-37.

Lidz, T., Fleck, S., & Cornelison, A. R. (1966), *Schizophrenia and the Family.* New York: International Universities Press.

Linn, L. (1953), The Role of Perception in the Mechanism of Denial. *J. Amer. Psychoanal. Assn.*, 1:690-705.

Little, M. (1958), On Delusional Transference. *Int. J. Psycho-Anal.*, 29:134-138.

Loewald, H. W. (1958), Transference and the Therapeutic Action of Psycho-Analysis. Abstr. in: *Int. J. Psycho-Anal.*, 39:293.

Loewenstein, R. M. (1957), A Contribution to the Psychoanalytic Theory of Masochism. *J. Amer. Psychoanal. Assn.*, 5:197-234.

MacCurdy, J. T. (1925), *The Psychology of Emotion.* New York: Harçourt, Brace.

Mahler, M. S. (1952), On Child Psychosis and Schizophrenia. *The Psychoanalytic Study of the Child,* 7:286-305.

——— (1966), Notes on the Development of Basic Moods: The Depressive Affect in Psychoanalysis. In: *Psychoanalysis—A General Psychology,* ed. R. M. Loewenstein, L. M. Newman, M. Schur, & A. J. Solnit. New York: International Universities Press, pp. 152-168.

——— & Elkisch, P. (1953), Some Observations on Disturbances of the Ego in a Case of Infantile Psychosis. *The Psychoanalytic Study of the Child,* 8:252-261.

——— Ross, J. R., & De Fries, Z. (1949), Clinical Studies in Benign and Malignant Cases of Childhood Psychosis (Schizophrenia-Like). *Amer. J. Orthopsychiat.,* 19:295-305.

Meiss, M. L. (1952), The Oedipal Problem of a Fatherless Child. *The Psychoanalytic Study of the Child,* 7:216-229.

Mendelson, M. (1960), *Psychoanalytic Concepts of Depression.* Springfield, Ill.: Thomas.

Modell, A. H. (1961), Denial and the Sense of Separateness. *J. Amer. Psychoanal. Assn.,* 9:533-547.

Moore, B. E. & Rubinfine, D. L. (1969), The Mechanism of Denial. *Monograph Series of the Kris Study Group of the New York Psychoanalytic Institute,* 3:3-57. New York: International Universities Press.

Nagera, H. (1970), Children's Reactions to the Death of Important Objects. *The Psychoanalytic Study of the Child,* 25:360-400.

Neubauer, P. B. (1960), The One-Parent Child and His Oedipal Development. *The Psychoanalytic Study of the Child,* 15:286-309.

Novey, S. (1959), A Clinical View of Affect Theory in Psycho-Analysis. *Int. J. Psycho-Anal.,* 40:94-104.

Nunberg, H. (1920), On the Catatonic Attack. *Practice and Theory of Psychoanalysis,* 1:3-23. New York: International Universities Press, 1953.

——— (1932), *Principles of Psychoanalysis: Their Application to the Neuroses.* New York: International Universities Press, 1955.

——— (1936), Homosexuality, Magic and Aggression. *Practice and Theory of Psychoanalysis,* 1:150-164. New York: International Universities Press, 1953.

Oberndorf, C. P. (1933), A Theory of Depersonalization. *Trans. Amer. Neurol. Assn.,* 59:150-151.

——— (1934), Depersonalization in Relation to Erotization of Thought. *Int. J. Psycho-Anal.,* 15:271-295.

——— (1939), On Retaining the Sense of Reality in States of Depersonalization. *Int. J. Psycho-Anal.,* 20:137-147.

——— (1950), The Rôle of Anxiety in Depersonalization. *Int. J. Psycho-Anal.,* 31:1-5.

Ophuijsen, J. H. W. van (1920), On the Origin of the Feeling of Persecution. *Int. J. Psycho-Anal.,* 1:235-239.

Ostow, M. (1970), *The Psychology of Melancholy.* New York: Harper & Row.

Pao, P.-N. (1968a), Depressive Feeling, Depressive Illness, Despair. Presented at the fourteenth annual Chestnut Lodge Symposium.

——— (1968b), On Manic-Depressive Psychosis. *J. Amer. Psychoanal. Assn.*, 16:809-832.

Peto, A. (1967a), On Affect Control. *The Psychoanalytic Study of the Child*, 22:36-51.

——— (1967b), Dedifferentiations and Fragmentations during Analysis. *J. Amer. Psychoanal. Assn.*, 15:534-550.

Pious, W. L. (1949), The Pathogenic Process in Schizophrenia. *Bull. Menninger Clin.*, 13:152-159.

——— (1950), Obsessive-Compulsive Symptoms in an Incipient Schizophrenic. *Psychoanal. Quart.*, 19:327-351.

Pollock, G. H. (1961), Mourning and Adaptation. *Int. J. Psycho-Anal.*, 42:341-361.

Rado, S. (1928), The Problem of Melancholia. *Int. J. Psycho-Anal.*, 9:420-438.

——— (1951), Psychodynamics of Depression from the Etiological Point of View. *Psychosom. Med.*, 13:51-55.

Rangell, L. (1963a), The Scope of Intrapsychic Conflict. *The Psychoanalytic Study of the Child*, 18:75-102.

——— (1963b), Structural Problems in Intrapsychic Conflict. *The Psychoanalytic Study of the Child*, 18:103-138.

——— (1965), Some Comments on Psychoanalytic Nosology: With Recommendations for Improvement. In: *Drives, Affects, Behavior, Volume* 2, ed. M. Schur. New York: International Universities Press, pp. 128-157.

Rapaport, D. (1942), *Emotions and Memory*. New York: International Universities Press, 1950.

——— (1953), On the Psycho-Analytic Theory of Affects. *Int. J. Psycho-Anal.*, 34:177-198.

Reich, A. (1949), The Structure of the Grotesque-Comic Sublimation. *Bull. Menninger Clin.*, 13:160-171.

——— (1953), Narcissistic Object Choice in Women. *J. Amer. Psychoanal. Assn.*, 1:22-44.

Reid, J. R. (1950), Introduction: Semantics and Definitions. In: Cobb, S., *Emotions and Clinical Medicine*. New York: Norton, 1950, pp. 13-34.

Reider, N. (1960), Medieval Oedipal Legends about Judas. *Psychoanal. Quart.*, 29:515-527.

Reik, T. (1913), Psychoanalytische Bemerkungen über den zynischen Witz. *Imago*, 2:573-588.

——— (1929), Zur Psychoanalyse des jüdischen Witzes. *Imago*, 15:63-88.

Reiser, M. F. (1966), Toward an Integrated Psychoanalytic-Physiological Theory of Psychosomatic Disorders. In: *Psychoanalysis—A General Psychology*, ed. R. M. Loewenstein, L. M. Newman, M. Schur, & A. J. Solnit. New York: International Universities Press, pp. 570-582.

Reymert, M. L., ed. (1928), *Feelings and Emotions: The Wittenberg Symposium*. Dorchester, Mass.: Clark University Press.

Rochlin, G. (1965), *Griefs and Discontents*. Boston: Little, Brown.

Root, N. N. (1957), A Neurosis in Adolescence. *The Psychoanalytic Study of the Child*, 12:320-334.

Rosen, V. H. (1955), The Reconstruction of a Traumatic Childhood Event in a Case of Derealization. *J. Amer. Psychoanal. Assn.*, 3:211-221.

Rosenfeld, H. A. (1965), *Psychotic States.* New York: International Universities Press.

Ross, N. (1967), The "As If" Concept. *J. Amer. Psychoanal. Assn.*, 15:59-82.

Rubinfine, D. L. (1968), Notes on a Theory of Depression. *Psychoanal. Quart.*, 37:400-417.

Sachar, E. J. Personal communication.

Sachs, H. (1928), One of the Motive Factors in the Formation of the Super-Ego in Women. *Int. J. Psycho-Anal.*, 10:39-50, 1929.

Sandler, J. & Joffe, W. G. (1965), Notes on Childhood Depression. *Int. J. Psychol-Anal.*, 46:88-96.

——— ——— (1969), Towards a Basic Psychoanalytic Model. *Int. J. Psycho-Anal.*, 50:79-90.

Schafer, R. (1964), The Clinical Analysis of Affects. *J. Amer. Psychoanal. Assn.*, 12:275-299.

——— (1968), *Aspects of Internalization.* New York: International Universities Press.

Scharl, A. E. (1961), Regression and Restitution in Object Loss. *The Psychoanalytic Study of the Child,* 16:471-480.

Schilder, P. (1928), *Introduction to a Psychoanalytic Psychiatry.* New York: International Universities Press, 1951.

——— (1935), *The Image and Appearance of the Human Body.* New York: International Universities Press, 1950.

Schmale, A. H. (1962), Needs, Gratification, and the Vicissitudes of the Self-Representation. *The Psychoanalytic Study of Society,* 2:9-41.

Schur, M. (1960), Phylogenesis and Ontogenesis of Affect- and Structure-Formation and the Phenomenon of Repetition Compulsion. *Int. J. Psycho-Anal.*, 41:275-287.

——— (1966), *The Id and the Regulatory Principles of Mental Functioning.* New York: International Universities Press.

Searles, H. F. (1960), *The Nonhuman Environment in Normal Development and in Schizophrenia.* New York: International Universities Press.

Shambaugh, B. (1961), A Study of Loss Reactions in a Seven-year-old. *The Psychoanalytic Study of the Child,* 16:510-522.

Siegman, A. J. (1967), Denial and Screening of Object Images. *J. Amer. Psychoanal. Assn.*, 15:261-280.

——— (1970), A Note on the Complexity Surrounding a Temporary Use of Denial. *J. Amer. Psychoanal. Assn.*, 18:372-378.

Silbermann, I. Personal communication.

——— (1961), Synthesis and Fragmentation. *The Psychoanalytic Study of the Child,* 16:90-117.

Sperling, O. E. (1948), On the Mechanisms of Spacing and Crowding Emotions. *Int. J. Psycho-Anal.*, 29:232-235.

Spiegel, L. A. (1966), Affects in Relation to Self and Object. *The Psychoanalytic Study of the Child,* 21:69-92.

Spitz, R. A. (1946), Anaclitic Depression. *The Psychoanalytic Study of the Child,* 2:313-342.

——— (1965), *The First Year of Life.* New York: International Universities Press.

——— & Wolf, K. M. (1946), The Smiling Response: A Contribution to the Ontogenesis of Social Relations. *Gen. Psychol. Monogr.*, 34:57-125.

Stärcke, A. (1920), The Reversal of the Libido Sign in Delusions of Persecution. *Int. J. Psychol-Anal.*, 1:231-234.

Sterba, R. F. (1946), Toward the Problem of the Musical Process. *Psychoanal. Rev.*, 33:37-43.

——— (1947), *Introduction to the Psychoanalytic Theory of the Libido.* New York & Washington: Nervous and Mental Disease Monographs, No. 68.

Tarachow, S. (1960), Judas: The Beloved Executioner. *Psychoanal. Quart.*, 29:528-554.

——— & Fink, M. (1958), Absence of a Parent as Specific Factor Determining Choice of Neurosis: Preliminary Study. *J. Hillside Hosp.*, 2:67-71.

Tausk, V. (1919), On the Origin of the "Influencing Machine" in Schizophrenia. *Psychoanal. Quart.*, 2:519-556, 1933.

Thompson, C. (1940), Identification with the Enemy and Loss of the Sense of Self. *Psychoanal. Quart.*, 9:37-50.

Valenstein, A. F. (1962), The Psycho-Analytic Situation. *Int. J. Psycho-Anal.*, 43:315-325.

Waelder, R. (1951), The Structure of Paranoid Ideas: A Critical Survey of Various Theories. *Int. J. Psycho-Anal.*, 32:167-177.

Wallerstein, R. S. (1967), Reconstruction and Mastery in the Transference Psychosis. *J. Amer. Psychoanal. Assn.*, 15:551-583.

Washburn, R. W. (1929), A Study of the Smiling and Laughing of Infants in the First Year of Life. *Gen. Psychol. Monogr.*, 6:397-537.

Weigert-Vowinckel, E. (1936), A Contribution to the Theory of Schizophrenia. *Int. J. Psycho-Anal.*, 17:190-201.

Weiner, H. (1958), Diagnosis and Symptomatology. In: *Schizophrenia: A Review of the Syndrome*, ed. L. Bellak. New York: Logos Press, pp. 107-173.

Weinshel, E. M. (1967), Some Psychoanalytic Considerations on Moods. Abstr. in: Panel report: Psychoanalytic Theory of Affects. *J. Amer. Psychoanal. Assn.*, 16:645-646, 1968.

——— (1970), Some Psychoanalytic Considerations on Moods. *Int. J. Psycho-Anal.*, 51:313-320.

Winnicott, D. W. (1958), *Collected Papers.* New York: Basic Books.

Wisdom, J. L. (1963), Fairbairn's Contribution on Object-Relationship, Splitting and Ego Structure. *Brit. J. Med. Psychol.*, 36:145-159.

Wolfenstein, M. (1966), How Is Mourning Possible? *The Psychoanalytic Study of the Child*, 21:93-123.

Zetzel, E. R. (1953), The Depressive Position. In: *Affective Disorders*, ed. P. Greenacre. New York: International Universities Press, pp. 84-116.

——— (1965), Depression and the Incapacity to Bear It. In: *Drives, Affects, Behavior, Volume 2*, ed. M. Schur. New York: International Universities Press, pp. 243-274.

——— (1966), The Predisposition to Depression. *J. Canad. Psychiat. Assn.*, Suppl., 11: 236-249.

Index